Tarot
DISTINCTIONS

A Comprehensive Exploration Into the
Ancient Wisdom of Tarot

RUANNA MARIE SEGAL

Testimonials

Ruanna's Tarot classes explored all the depths and nuances to be discovered in the pictorial cards. Without her guidance to take a closer look at what appeared before me in a layout, I would not have appreciated the story that was hidden. The Tarot is an incredibly useful tool to remember the multifaceted and not get too serious. We were taught with humor and frank insight, which allowed for learning on many levels.

Sue Caldwell – Feng Shui Consultant

I did the full tarot course with Ruanna many years ago and remember that year with fondness. We become friends over our weekly sessions and it was with fun, humor and her deep insight that I learned the mysteries of each card in the deck. To learn the tarot is to follow its Spiritual path and Ruanna was a wonderful guide. Her teachings were thorough yet very approachable. I always thought I would find another tarot deck to work with, but I quickly grew to love the Rider Waite deck I learned with her – and like old friends, I know all their colors, symbols and layers of meaning. Insights of which I still use and love these many years later.

Margaret Copland
Uncle Festers - Creator of Astrolenergies and Partner in Uncle Festers
a specialty online retail business that has been trading over 20 years

Attending Tarot classes enabled me to develop a comprehensive insight and understanding of each and every card in the deck. I was taught the significance of numerology and shown how to do different spreads so I could offer simple or more complex 'readings'. I found Ruanna very easy to understand, despite her immense experience and she was able to explain at a level that suited each participant. I became more intuitive and confident in my abilities to do readings with all the practice we (participants) did on each other.

Lyn-Marie Richards

I had the wonderful pleasure of meeting Ruanna in 2009. I always wanted to learn Tarot, It was an incredibly detailed course and Ruanna's unique way of teaching enabled me to interpret her words into my own. I loved every minute of it, and couldn't believe how incredibly accurate the cards are and the story that they tell, it's enabled me to utilize the Tarot in my life, such a wonderful tool! Anyone thinking of learning Tarot you cannot go past Ruanna, amazing Teacher in every respect together with personality plus!

Melinda Fitzgerald – Reiki Master

I had the privilege of being one of Ruanna's tarot class students in the mid 90's Ruanna opened up my heart, mind and spirit to the beauty of The Tarot. The significance of the colors, the numbers & the rich symbology. I learned that not everything we think and feel is as it seems on the surface. Every human interaction and event in our lives has a deeper meaning and our task to achieve self actualization is to explore these meanings and how they positively impact on our personal growth. My favorite memory of Ruanna's class is this. It is ideal if a person receiving a tarot reading, leaves the reading with more questions than they arrived with. This is true empowerment. Love it.

Dan Tiomkin

For me, learning to read tarot encompassed a wide range of disciplines and learning. From ancient mythology, symbology, and modern day psychology; tarot has a lot to offer. The skill of drawing meaning from images has provided an ability to see opportunities and options in seemingly impossible situations, options I might not have seen without help from the cards. Better yet, I can use my skill to assist those close to me. Tarot pushes a reader toward personal growth, no matter how skilled, there's always more the cards can teach you.

Ann Cutajar – Artist and Writer

Throughout Ruanna's tarot classes I gained a very concise, deep and respectful understanding of both major and minor arcana cards. She made sense out of the individual cards as well as providing clarity out of card combinations that can be tricky to interpret.

Tarot has been very empowering for me, I have been able to help myself and others by providing accurate readings, which are able to be clarified by certain parts of the tarot spreads, such as past, present and surrounding energies.

Ruanna's knowledge is invaluable and I am honored to have had the experience to participate in her classroom.

Love Natalie Skelly

I studied Tarot with Ruanna Segal back in 2000 learning the Introduction to Tarot. It was a small class, which was very favorable to me.

Being brought up a strict Catholic I was skeptical about Tarot but curious.

The classes started with the basics and from memory we studied two minor cards per week. It was extremely detailed and I came away from that each week feeling that I had learnt so much, however on the other hand realizing how much more, I needed to learn.

Right from the very beginning, Ruanna allowed me to develop a trust in my intuition, which had been shut down for decades. When we arrived at the stage of actually performing readings, I was amazed at the flow that was coming through. I would surprise myself and think where the hell did that come from, was that me?

Ruanna has a sound depth of knowledge, skill and intuitiveness to be a confident teacher. It all happens in a relaxed manner with loads of passion.

I went on and did the Advanced Course and then a refresher some years later.

I have learnt so much from Ruanna teaching me about Tarot, which I realize is all about the Ancient Wisdom.

I must thank Ruanna for giving me the confidence and belief in myself, when I have been receiving these messages all my life but never trusted the message.

Through learning Tarot, Ruanna has inspired me to further my knowledge and continue on a path of studying Complementary Therapies and now I practice Reflexology.

So I thank you for that gift.

Maureen Wilson – Cosmic Cocoon

I completed the tarot course with Ruanna and was blown away by her knowledge. Ruanna gave very detailed information and insights that only a passionate and dedicated educator can. She demystified the Tarot and made the cards intelligible. I highly recommend this course for beginners like myself and for those who want a deeper understanding. I can't thank Ruanna enough for opening my eyes and spiritual knowledge enough.

Andre Conate – Website Angels

I completed the Tarot in action advanced certificate program a number of years ago. Ruanna's passion, experience and knowledge of the cards was apparent and also her quest to understand all things deeply.

Prior to completing the course, I had used cards 'intuitively', however I wanted a foundation to expand my knowledge. Not only did I learn ways of confidently using the cards in a practical way, I also enjoyed learning the history, symbology, mythology colors and energy of the cards. This course surprisingly took me on a journey that offered an insight into myself and others, and firmly placed the responsibility on me to positively change the way that interact with others in the world.

Love Janette Culbert

The following comments are from Pat Grayson the publisher and editor of this book.

For many years I have had tarot readings and therefore have had first-hand experience with them. But yet, I have never really understood them, and so it did not surprise me that the Universe 'sent' me this book to help put life too.

As I was working through the manuscript, I kept questioning; how does the tarot work? For instance, you have a question that is playing on your mind and so you pull a card, and as soon as you see the card you know it is right. Or, you have a reading and as the cards reveal themselves, what was obscure is shown to be obvious, but only made obvious through the cards.

So back to the question; what intelligence allows the cards to reveal the truth as they do? I had been pondering that question for some time, when the penny finally dropped: it is the same Intelligence that governs the mass migration of animals in many parts of the world. It is the same Intelligence that orchestrates the efficient cohesion of the 100 billion cells that make up the human body. That cohesion is what we call biology. It is 'that Intelligence' that created the miracle of life itself. For instance: when one reads about the likelihood of there being life on earth, or rather life developing on earth as it did, it was a one in a million – yet, here we are.

The intelligence that supports all things that are, is just that – it is an Intelligence and it is that intelligence that creates and enlivens all life. We mortals can only marvel at it, but its workings are beyond our comprehension.

Back to the question as to how Tarot works. There are three important components, the first is the intent, that is, your intent to understand things of deeper meaning. Then of course there is the tarot, and lastly the 'The Intelligence'. It is The Intelligence that takes the two ingredients (the cards and your intent), to furnish the truth.

I mention intent, for without it there is no efficacy. The intent that you offer aligns you with the very vibration that created 'all that there is'. So when you pick a card, know it has been kissed by that Intelligence, or as Ruanna calls it in the book, Spirit.

Part of my questioning was also; how on earth did those first people who created the cards manage to imbue so many meanings or nuances within the cards? As you read through the cards you will see that there are literally hundreds of permutations and each one, when needed, is a truth. The meaning in each card is perhaps akin to the wonder of the biology that I mentioned above in as much as that infinite wisdom that is reflected in the cards is truly breath taking. Each card is like looking into a hologram where there are layers upon layers of genius that would seem to be beyond any mortal to create, but mortals did.

So certainly with the design and creation of the cards; it was that same Intelligence that gave the creators the inspiration, where by, the creators merely fed what they had received into the tarot cards.

Tarot Distinctions

"Discover the hidden keys in the tarot and experience profound personal growth.**"**

by Ruanna Marie Segal

Dedication

To my folks Raffaela and Matteo D'Antuono.

For having the courage and trust to go on their own Hero's Journey to the other side of the world and begin a new life in a new country.

Published by

Heart Space Publications
PO Box 1085
Daylesford
Victoria
3460
Australia
Tel +61 450260348
www.heartspacebooks.com
pat@heartspacebooks.com

Book layout done by April Basubas
E-mail at apleshap888@gmail.com

Copyright © 2018 **Ruanna Marie Segal**

All rights reserved under international copyright conventions. No part of this book may be reproduced, stored in a retrieval system, or transmitted in any form or by any means electronic, mechanical, photocopying, recorded or otherwise without written permission from Heartspace Publications.

Whilst every care has been taken to check the accuracy of the information in this book, the publisher cannot be held responsible for any errors, omissions or originality.

ISBN: 978-0-9944028-2-0
To learn more about Ruanna Marie Segal work, go to:
www.tarotinaction.com.au
www.facebook.com/tarotinaction

Prologue ☺

There are many reasons why I wanted to write this book. The first reason is because I always wanted to write a book, who doesn't? I also wanted to do something special to commemorate my twenty years of teaching tarot professionally, and throughout the years many of my students would also ask for me to comprise my tarot classes in a book form, so here it is.

I wanted to create a fabulous teach yourself manual that was as comprehensive as it could be, one that was fun to read. It may be the only book I ever write, so I wanted it to be in color and overall a beautiful book as well as a great resource – at your fingertips.

I also wanted to show how much involved tarot really is, how much it encompasses other modalities and how they all intertwine with tarot, from astrology through to kabbalah, all the associated knowledge of history and counselling skills that are needed as well. And how much time it takes to digest all these learnings for you to become a good tarot reader. So if you are on the path, keep going and all the opportunities will present themselves to you along the way, right on time.

Not only do you have to know the information, you also have to be passionate about it. People do get attracted to positive and exciting energy, they intuitively know. I was so passionate about tarot and still love all the exploring. Since 1990 everyone kept asking me to teach them tarot and astrology and today I have a successful 'Tarot in Action' business. Crazy world, who plans to be a tarot teacher? Well, maybe on some level I wanted to.

To write a book, all the pieces have to come together. I started gathering the notes and writing as much as I could here and there whenever I had the time and inclination. I didn't know how and where to start in writing a book, but I just kept at it, collecting ideas and placing them all in a folder. Things like the name of the book, I actually had the name of the book three years ago! I had dreams of how the cover of the book would look; even the subtitle of the book came to me in a dream. I included everything; like artist contacts in case I needed some artwork done, I just kept compiling all these ideas into the folder till that one day I knew would eventually arrive and materialize in 3D.

I have been looking for a publisher for years. Many of my friends have written books, I checked out their publishers, researched their work and what their processors were. Then I met Pat my Publisher in 2013 through a mutual friend, in Adelaide when I was doing tarot readings at the Mind Body Spirit Festival. He explained his process and I felt he was on the right path for me, that he would be able to understand me and the tarot book that I wanted to create. We exchanged contact details and then three years later, after many emails and meetings we have produced the book.

I love how the right pieces have all come together, just like magic and I have believed in magic from when I was young. For me this journey started when I was ten years old. Back then we played a simple game, where we plaited and tied colorful bracelets around our wrists made out of wool. I remember this particular game because I wanted a record player so bad that I would do anything to get one. So I tied seven knots and made my wish, after seven days I had to get the boy I liked (at that time) to break off the bracelet and my wish would come true. It was a Saturday morning and I saw him enter my folks Milk Bar, I thought that was great because it was all working to plan, so I asked him to break off the bracelet. By 2pm that Saturday afternoon a friend of the family came over with a portable mini record player and two records especially for me. No one knew I wanted a record player, I had not even mentioned it to my folks. I was dumb founded, and I have believed in magic ever since.

To this day I feel the magic is always working for me. I committed to work for the highest good, supporting others, making that little difference wherever I could, through my work, my activities and my projects. I said to myself, if I worked for the higher purpose I would somehow be supported, and by Joe (whoever he is) I have seen the support, the wins, the remarkable outcomes and results over and over again.

The main purpose of this book is to provoke or encourage something or someone into action. This is what the mission is behind my business name, 'Tarot in Action.' It is great to know all the information, but making it real in the world is what it is all about – getting into, 'action.' As the classic saying goes, "Action speaks louder than words". By my writing this book, you may be inspired to move towards something you love to do. So when you get to the Homework section in the book, please take the time to pick a tarot card per day and to then activate it in the real world, you will gain a wonderful experience about the card and also about yourself.

There may be a lot of fear to act; what would others think, and so on. But as many of you already know, these are all excuses to stop yourself from doing something. Face the fear, face your failures, face your inner critic, muster all the courage within and do it anyway. Courage equals fear plus commitment plus action. I discuss more about this throughout the book, as to how the ego always wants to be in control and is in fear of losing you over to your spiritual side. The ego will do whatever it has to do, carry on like an uncooperative three-year-old to keep the control if it has too.

I remember seeing Oprah where she mentioned "failure is that 'thing' that gets you back on track". Basically suggesting that there is no such thing as failure. Another quote by Elon Musk was "if things aren't failing, you are not innovating enough". Here again suggesting to get in motion and it is by our mistakes and failures that we learn and grow.

So it is in the trial and error that we learn to fly, like that little bird that took its first step out of the nest, it fell and tumbled and fell some more until it started to flap its wings and finally take off.

Another thing that keeps us in action is the 'goal.' Is your goal big enough? If it is, you will do whatever you have to do to get it. You will feel inspired and your actions will inspire others. Goals are very important and I learned this early on through my studies. Many clients I have seen over the years, do not have goals. But you need that focus on that bull's eye to keep you in the groove towards the end result. Many people that don't have plans get caught up in wasting their time and energy on drama.

By having a goal, you create plans and achievable steps to reach them, you can gauge and track how you are going. Every successful person and every successful business in the world has plans, projections, do surveys, attend workshops, train staff, do whatever it takes to attain the goals. A top CEO today reads a book per week per minimum to keep abreast of the latest trends. Basically, if you do not plan to succeed, you plan to fail.

This is how I have fashioned my life. Every project I get involved in has to have a goal and it has to benefit the community in some way, it has to make a difference. From my Lunabears group that I started in 2008 where all the funds go towards sponsoring the Bear Sanctuary in Laos through the *Free The Bears organization,* to end the horrendous bear bile farming. The martial arts club where I taught for twelve years teaching juniors about respect, self defense and raising their self esteem, through to all the work I did with charity organizations that benefited children, such as *Rotary, Lions Club* and *Before It's Too Late*. Today, I support the environment through the *GENI Foundation to which I have been a Trustee of since 1990*. I also tithe to various animal charities.

And so it is with this book. If I can create a book that is going to make someone's life better, then I have accomplished my mission. Not only satisfying my own needs by doing what is of value to me, but also giving you, the reader of this book, value in your world, awakening or inspiring you to create a better world for yourself, by heeding the taps along the way, to learn what you need to learn quicker and let go of what you need to let go of and achieve your goals faster. By empowering yourself you can discover your truth and do what is right for you. And along the way, you are also demonstrating to those around you how they can achieve their goals so they too can discover their own truth for themselves.

One of my favorite mentors is Dr. R. Buckminster Fuller. Fuller was asked once "what was his most important discovery?" he answered, "the importance of truth". We have to tell the truth, not just to others but to ourselves. Only then will all of us on the planet create the world we all want to live in and all live in peace.

This is what the last two Major Arcana cards, Judgement and the World, are all about. Once you have awakened and dealt with all your ego issues, understand them and take personal responsibility for them, only then are you ready for that something extra — hear the calling and that is when you step up, make a stand for what you believe in, your truth. This is what the tarot teaches us, to believe in yourself, that each of us has the power to change ourselves and in turn change the world for the betterment of all.

I hope you use and re-use this book over and over again, apply the lessons and share the information with others. Remember it is just another step in your journey, and I am glad that we have shared this short time together.

Heaps of Specialness
Ruanna

Contents

SECTION 1 — SET UP

Chapter 1

Introduction	Page 2
What to Get Out of this Book	Page 2
Earning the Right	Page 2
How to Read This Book	Page 5
Tarot Deck	Page 6
Dictionary	Page 6
Questions	Page 7
Why the Tarot in Action Program in Book Form	Page 7

Chapter 2

Background and Set Up	Page 8
Physical and Metaphysical Game	Page 8
Listening to the Taps	Page 12
When to use Tarot Cards	Page 15
Tools of the Trade	Page 16
Divination	Page 17
Golden Dawn Group	Page 18
Archetypes	Page 20
Free Will	Page 23
Choice Game	Page 25
Construction of Deck	Page 26
Attachments	Page 27
How to Store the Cards	Page 33
No Ego Please	Page 34
Masculine or Feminine	Page 35
Roman Numerals	Page 36

SECTION 2 — THE MAJOR ARCANA

Chapter 3	The Hero's Journey	Page 39
Chapter 4	0 The Fool	Page 53
Chapter 5	I The Magician	Page 63

Chapter 6	II The High Priestess	Page 73
Chapter 7	III The Empress	Page 81
Chapter 8	IV The Emperor	Page 89
Chapter 9	V The Hierophant	Page 97
Chapter 10	VI The Lovers	Page 106
Chapter 11	VII The Chariot	Page 114
Chapter 12	VIII Strength	Page 122
Chapter 13	IX The Hermit	Page 130
Chapter 14	X Wheel of Fortune	Page 137
Chapter 15	XI Justice	Page 146
Chapter 16	XII The Hanged Man	Page 153
Chapter 17	XIII Death	Page 161
Chapter 18	XIV Temperance	Page 168
Chapter 19	XV Devil	Page 175
Chapter 20	XVI Tower	Page 183
Chapter 21	XVII The Star	Page 191
Chapter 22	XVIII The Moon	Page 197
Chapter 23	XIX The Sun	Page 207
Chapter 24	XX Judgement	Page 214
Chapter 25	XXI The World	Page 223

SECTION 3 — THE MINOR ARCANA

Chapter 26	The Four Elements	Page 230
Chapter 27	No 2 – Choice and Balance	Page 241
Chapter 28	No 3 – Growth and Expansion	Page 251
Chapter 29	No 4 – Foundation and Stability	Page 263
Chapter 30	No 5 – Change	Page 271
Chapter 31	No 6 – Harmony	Page 280
Chapter 32	No 7 – Reassessment	Page 292
Chapter 33	No 8 – Power	Page 302
Chapter 34	No 9 – Completion	Page 312
Chapter 35	No 10 – Beginning a New Cycle	Page 322
Chapter 36	Aces – Cards of Triumphant	Page 332
Chapter 37	Court Cards – Summary	Page 340
Chapter 38	Court Cards – Overview	Page 349
Chapter 39	Pages – Beginning Stage	Page 356
Chapter 40	Knights – Action Stage	Page 368
Chapter 41	Queens – Reflection Stage	Page 381
Chapter 42	Kings – Mastery Stage	Page 395

SECTION 4 — ATTACHMENTS

Attachment 1	Recommended Book List	Page 410
Attachment 2	Psychology	Page 412
Attachment 3	Astrology	Page 414
Attachment 4	Colors	Page 416
Attachment 5	Numerology	Page 418
Attachment 6	Symbology	Page 420
Attachment 7	Tarot Activation and Homework	Page 428
Attachment 8	The Hero's Journey	Page 430
Attachment 9	Questions and Answers	Page 431
Attachment 10	Acknowledgement and Sources	Page 444
Attachment 11	Bibliography	Page 450
Attachment 12	Index	Page 456

Section 1 - Set Up

Chapter 1

Introduction

> "If the doors of perception were cleansed we could see to infinity."
> - William Blake

The band *The Doors* took their name from Blake's quote. It also suits the world of tarot. Through the use of the tarot (pronounced taro) cards and spreads, we can see to infinity and beyond. Tarot cards are about the exploration of issues and of the self.

What to Get Out of this Book

- Discover the keys in each tarot card.
- Uncover and experience profound personal growth through the use of the cards.
- Getting balance in one's life and reaching interdependence.
- Connect with your unconscious world and become conscious about what is going on in your inner self.
- Cover topics such as numerology, astrology, mythology, symbolism, colors, key words, shadow words and actions to assist you to activate the energy of each tarot card.
- A lot of examples using my true life experiences to explain the energy that you can easily connect with and recognize where and how it is playing out.
- Understanding the milestones that we all experience through our journey in life.
- Over twenty years of my professional tarot experience.
- Learn to understand the archetypal energies that are ever present today.
- Guidance and understand projection.
- A deeper understanding of human beings.
- Opening up to spirituality and your truth.
- A hands on reference manual.

Earning the Right

What is it in me that has the right to say what I'm saying to you?

Since 1990, I have been professionally dealing with tarot and it is only natural that an overdue book manifested in the physical sense. I first had to get the website right with an online shop so I can sell all my products. I then had to create the products to sell. It has been a natural progression of one thing leading on to the next.

Some of my products/channels are:
- *Tarot in Action* website and online shop.
- Blog and multimedia.
- 12 zodiac astrology stickers.
- 6 month tarot beginner's program.
- 12 week advanced tarot program.
- 6 month astrology program.
- 1 day numerology class.
- 10 week spiritual, shamanic and sorcery class.
- 22 tarot video lessons.
- And now this book, e-book and audio tarot book.

As far back as I can remember I have always been involved in multiple businesses. Even though I was too young to understand or know how to run a business, I always had fun doing them. I was passionate about what I did, hence I learned quickly. I believe this is because my folks had a deli shop and we lived out the back. I grew up with the knowledge of running a deli shop, and learned to deal with customers early on, understanding how to give great service.

Let us start when I started work in 1982 as a bar person, in an excellent hotel called *The Prospect Hill Hotel* where I saw two bands play per night and met some wonderful people. I worked there for five years and worked my way up to managing the hotel during the day. It was a very exciting time for me, I was only twenty-two years of age and I had a lot of fun there.

During the time at the hotel, I married and decided to get myself a better job. I was fortunate enough to be accepted into *Telecom*, which at the time was Australia's largest company. Today it is known as *Telstra*. Back then, *Telecom* employed 95,000 Australians. I was there for seven years, and once again, worked my way to the top to become an administration manager, then personal assistant to a branch manager.

In 1990, my life totally turned around. I retired from *Telecom* to focus on the IVF procedures that we were trying to start a family with. After so many attempts we were still unsuccessful, this is when we decided to sell up and move to Kyneton, central Victoria. It was during this time that I started my tarot and astrology journey.

By 1996, I was working one day a week doing tarot readings in a fairy shop. This then turned into two days per week. Along with my new business partners, we created tarot t-shirts and started to sell them in other shops. We also had stalls at various alternative healing markets around Melbourne where we also sold other various tarot and astrology products.

During this time, my fascination with tarot and astrology definitely emerged; I absorbed and devoured as many books as I still do today. I enrolled into as many workshops as I could afford to do on tarot, astrology, kabbalah, numerology, and counseling subjects through RMIT or anywhere else that held certificate courses. I even did art classes to see and paint the world from the invisible.

I became passionate about my new found love of the metaphysical world. It was then that people started to ask me to teach them, so I found myself teaching classes and sharing my new found knowledge of tarot and astrology – hence my journey with *Tarot in Action* truly began.

I attended the newly formed Tarot Guild of Australia meetings every month. This allowed my business partner and I set up our little stall to sell our various tarot products, and to mingle with like-minded people.

I then completed the professional transition process and became a Member of the Tarot Guild of Australia in 1995, followed by a Professional Member with the Australian Psychic Association in 1998.

During this time, I also worked on various tarot phone lines when they first began, even before counseling and other various help lines started. At first I wondered how I could do tarot work over the phone line. Then I realized that a phone cord was not going to hold back Universal energy.

The long nights can really be a lonely time for some and I learned how many lonely people there were out there. But after three years of working on these tarot phone lines, I could not do it anymore. I was surprised I had lasted that long. I did have an amazing experience whilst working on the tarot phone lines and I would encourage you to experience it as well; to learn how many people are in need and to appreciate how tarot can really assist. Additionally, it was great to discuss issues with people and teach them about how tarot could give them guidance and choice. This is lovely way to help those in need and of using the tarot.

I would like to share one particular phone call I had with you that has remained with me. I use this example in my classes today.

One afternoon I received a call from a lady. I will keep the long story short, but she noticed that I picked up on the fact that she was not being truthful with me, so she opened up and told me the truth. In actual fact, she was a reporter for the *John Laws Radio Show* investigating tarot phone lines. I specifically asked her to mention in her report how helpful the tarot lines can truly be for people in need, and gave an example of a particular girl who lived in the St Kilda area of Melbourne. Let's call her Sarah.

Sarah was a young girl and had a baby. Her question to me was whether it was ok for her to become a prostitute? Sarah believed she could make more money than she currently was. This was so as to look after herself and her baby. Sarah told me that she had friends who were prostitutes and they made a lot of money from it.

We opened it up for discussion and looked at the difference between Sarah and her friends, why was it ok for them to do it, and why was Sarah having a discussion with someone on the tarot line about whether it was a good idea for her to do it? We looked at it in every way possible. I do not know to this day whether Sarah went on to become a prostitute or not, but she sure had a good mind to ask questions, even if it was to a tarot reader through a hot line.

All of a sudden the reporter said, "Oh My God! This is my exact story, I lived in the St Kilda area, I too had a young baby, and I too was thinking of becoming a prostitute to make ends meet". I will never forget those words. Of all the examples I could have used, I had tapped right into her story, which blew us both away. The reporter told me that she decided not to follow through with becoming a prostitute, and I congratulated and acknowledged her for being strong enough to stand up for herself. I said to her, "Let's hope that the young girl Sarah was strong enough to stand up by herself as well."

Spirit works in wonderful ways. Maybe Sarah's story was so the reporter had a personal connection and realization? Who knows? But I do hope that the reporter gave us tarot readers a good wrap that day when she gave her report on that Radio Show.

How to Read this Book

As I explain to my students, the best way to learn and understand tarot is by layering – a slow buildup of information and a slow uncovering of hidden meanings and secrets, thus discovering the keys to every tarot card. This is the process I have used throughout this book.

By sharing your real life experiences, you will gain further understanding and insight into the tarot. This helps you to make connections or associations with the cards. It will also assist you in understanding how the tarot manifests or plays out in your life. As we go through each tarot card, where possible, I share my stories as examples. There are also exercises for you to do, to assist you in making these connections with the tarot cards.

Getting to know the terminology I use throughout this book is important. For example, I use the word 'Spirit' wherever possible instead of 'God,' 'Angels' or 'Spirit Guides.' Yet you may use whichever feels right for you, but Spirit encompasses both energy and meaning for me.

I use Psychology a lot throughout this book. I like to say I teach Psychology Tarot as well as Psychology Astrology in my classes. I love to learn and understand the being of human beings.

In my book club that I ran for a few years, we studied all of Robert A. Johnson's books, starting with *Owning Your Own Shadow*, and we went from there. He basically has rewritten Carl Jung's work in a way that we can understand and absorb the information in layman's terms. It was a fabulous journey. At the end of the all the books we emailed him through his counterpart Jerry M. Ruhl, and asked if we could kindly receive a Certificate of Completion from studying his work. We did receive a prompt reply to which we were very excited. It said, *"We are humbled that you committed yourselves to this study and for making contact with us. Unfortunately, we are unable to forward a certificate as such, but definitely send you our blessing".* We were chuffed to receive this reply.

My purpose of this book is for you to discover your truth. To think for yourself, to believe in yourself and to trust in your way of doing it. Not to give your authority away to someone else. To be confident in yourself so you feel that strength and power within, whereby you can make a difference in the world through your own demonstrations. This is what I believe the tarot is teaching us and this is the message of the Judgement and the World Major Arcana cards. When we can get to the point of putting our ego in its proper perspective only then can we hear the call (trumpet in Judgement), rise to our potential and truly make a difference in making the world a better place for everybody.

Tarot Deck

I have used the *Standard Rider Waite* Tarot Deck by Edward Arthur Waite and Pamela Colman Smith throughout this book because I believe they have the best symbolism and the best colors. This deck is also the most popular and most recognized tarot card deck in the world today.

Dictionary

The dictionary I use throughout this book is *The Australian Macquarie Concise Dictionary*.

Understanding a new word, especially in relation to the tarot is important as they are tools. Words are tools, and knowledge is power. Once you understand what the word means, it will open you up to new understandings and how to make those distinctions.

For more detailed information on anything in this book, I encourage you to do your own research. Google or Wikipedia is a great tool used to uncover what you are looking for, I have used them greatly, assisting me with the process of creating this book.

Questions

Hopefully, I will answer many questions for you along the way. However, at the back of the book is a Q and A section. As you read this book, your questions will be answered. But with the tarot, there are always more questions. I have often said it is almost sad to answer questions for your clients because it stops them from the thinking process and realizing things for themselves.

I feel I have written enough in this book to illustrate my way of teaching and how to understand tarot cards. Hmmm! However, after writing this, my first book, there could be a second book to cover all the points missed or new points that will evolve from this first book.

Why is the Tarot in Action Program in Book Form?

We are all different and we all prefer to learn in different ways: by watching DVDs, listening to CD's or by reading books. This book was a natural progression for me, especially after completing my twenty-two *Tarot in Action* video lessons (http://www.tarotinaction.com.au/tarot/tarot-online-packages). This book is an accompaniment to these video lessons. Books hold a lot more detail, it can also be used as a quick and easy reference guide.

If you decide to purchase the *Tarot in Action* video lessons, you will see that it was filmed over a six month period in 2012, working with one particular tarot class. Of course I received permission from the students to film this class. You cannot see the students in the picture, but you can hear the many questions that they ask throughout the class; as if you are in the class asking these questions yourself. We cover intense discussions each week, and you will also notice how we all grow and learn through the particular situations and evolve over this six month period.

I have noticed that since my humble beginnings of teaching tarot, there are a particular set of questions about the cards or about the spreads, dealing with clients, etc. that come up in every class. The questions that were raised throughout the videos are typical of these questions.

Being in a class with others is the best way to learn tarot because everyone learns from each other's experience. It is an organic way of learning and dealing with the tarot in the ever-present mode.

Chapter 2

Background and Set Up

"All the world's a stage, and all men and women are merely players."
- William Shakespeare

We will now go back in time and start with tarot in the early 1900's and bring it into our present day.

Physical and Metaphysical Game

First, let us start with a game that I call the physical metaphysical game. I believe that using your physical body and your personal experience is the best way to connect with the tarot. You ground it when you understand it on that inner physical level or when you see it in yourself. After all, we are all projections for each other.

In Diagram 1 below, you will notice I have listed a graph showing two columns. On the top of one column is the heading 'Physical,' and on the other is the heading 'Metaphysical.'

The *Australian Macquarie Concise Dictionary* describes the words Physical and Metaphysical as:

Physical: *1. Pertaining to the body; bodily; physical exercise. 2. Pertaining to material nature; material. 3. Denoting or pertaining to the properties of matter and energy other than those that are chemical or peculiar to living matter; pertaining to physics. 4. Denoting or pertaining to the properties of matter and energy other than those peculiar to living matter; pertaining to physical science.*

For me, the word physical refers to something I can touch, see, is tangible, made of substance and has physical mass.

Metaphysical: *1. Philos. Concerned with abstract thought or subjects; as existence, causality, or abstruse.*

Therefore, the word metaphysical simply means something I cannot touch, or see, but it too has metaphysical mass.

For this particular exercise and using your body as the sample, you will see listed in the columns below everything that is physical about you. I listed many things that your body possesses, from the inner and the outer sides. Please feel free to add your own words to this list. I am sure there are many more items that can be listed as this was a quick brain-storm.

When you cannot think of any more words to write in the physical list, notice the words listed in the metaphysical column. These are many things your body possess but you cannot see or know where they reside in the body, because it is in the metaphysical. Once again, please feel free to add your own words to this list.

When you have finished, you will notice that the metaphysical list is twice as long as the physical list, if not longer.

Diagram 1

Physical	Metaphysical
Hair	Supernatural
Skin	Emotions
Bones	Fears
Skeleton	Anger
Blood	Love
Water	Feelings
Nails	Passion
Veins	Moods
Heart	Thoughts
Stomach	Ideas
Brain	Culture
Eyes	Attitude
Sexual Organs	Values
Lips	Beliefs
Face	Vitality
Lungs	Energy

Section 1

Physical	Metaphysical
Kidneys	Happiness
Liver	Strength
Muscle	Ethics
Cells	Morals
Teeth	Sadness
Tissue	Talents
Spleen	Anxiety
Fat	Confidence
DNA	Personality
Plasma	Conscious
Atoms	Unconscious
Adrenalin	Jealousy
Hormones	Memory
Nerves	Ego
Matter	Impeccability
92 Elements, e.g.:	Gift
• Iron	Psyche
• Magnesium	Kindness
• Zinc	Understanding
• etc.	Stress
	Religion
	Empathy
	Sympathy
	Mind
	Vibrations
	Déjà vu
	Butterflies in tummy
	Passed Lives
	Imagination
	All your experiences from the moment of conception
	Metaphysical mass
	Persona
	Mask
	Perception

Physical	Metaphysical
	Inner Wisdom
	Integrity
	Dreams
	Visions
	Gut feelings
	Insight
	Intuition
	Senses
	Psychic
	Sight
	Kind Hearted
	Aura
	Chakra
	Knowledge
	Intelligence
	Spirituality
	Soul
	Spirit
	Passion

It is often said that 99% of the universe is invisible, that we only see 1% of what is really there. You can see from Diagram 1 that the list is longer, we are made up more of the metaphysical mass than the physical mass.

And the universe is the same, as it is made up of more metaphysical mass than physical mass.

> "99% of the Universe is invisible."
> - Dr. R. Buckminster Fuller

Dr. R. Buckminster Fuller believed that the brain deals with tangible physical things and the mind deals with the invisible metaphysical things. The brain sees the objects and the mind sees the relationship between the objects, it tries to bridge the gaps.

Another example I like to use is how your left brain connects to the logic side, where it needs to know the title and specifics of everything you do, so it knows what box to put it in, to understand it on that practical level. It wants to know the start date and the end date, etc.

Whereas the right brain connects to the receptive side, understanding that there is no beginning and no end, knowing the universe is infinite.

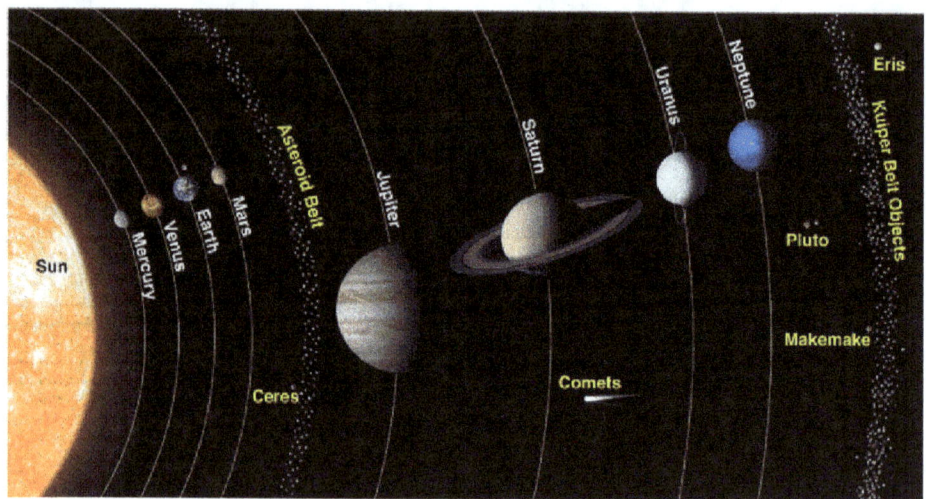

Our Solar System – we are only seeing 1% of Universe.

Listening to the Taps

Spirit is tapping us all the time. It is always trying to tell us something, or assist us, to wake us up, to help us reach our goal, so we become conscious about an issue. Basically, Spirit wants us to become aware of our spiritual side. Spirit will never judge us but only gives us the opportunity to get in balance, to learn and to be open.

But our ego does not want us to wake up to the spiritual side. The ego wants to be in charge because it has been for a long time. The ego will always throw doubt onto our sensibility, to the point where it can render us motionless. So we end up ignoring all the taps, but when we hit that wall we say to ourselves, "Why didn't I listen to myself? I knew I should have gone the other way, why didn't I stop, turn around, and go the other way?"

To give an example, let us say we are heading down the road of life and we get our first tap that we may be heading in the wrong direction. I believe Spirit taps us first in the intuitive area. This is where we first sense things, but we shrug it off and dismiss it because we do not think it is important or trust ourselves enough.

If we are still not listening, Spirit will tap us next in the feeling area. This is where you may start to feel sick or guilty, feeling heavy and emotional, but you still think you are being silly, so you keep heading down the path you are on.

If you still choose to ignore these feelings, Spirit will tap you next in the thinking area. This is our third tap, and here we may say to ourselves, "Well this is the third time now, maybe I should do some research about going the other way. Maybe I should start saving more money, and create a plan B just in case I decide to go the other way". But you probably will keep heading down the old path.

If we continue to travel along this pathway, Spirit taps us once again, but this time in the physical area. This is where we may get sacked from work, break a leg, fall sick with a cold, and so we are laid up in bed. Once this happens we have nothing else to do but review where we have been heading, and realize we were going down the wrong path.

Another example is the husband that comes home drunk. The wife says to him "If you come home drunk tomorrow night, you are on the couch". The first tap!

So what do you think he does? That's right he comes home drunk, and the wife says to him, "If you come home drunk tomorrow night, I'm locking you outside." The second tap!

So what do you think he does? Yes, right again, he comes home drunk so the wife does what she told him she would do and locks him outside. Again, she says. "If you come home drunk again tomorrow night, that's it, I am divorcing you." The fourth tap!

So what do you think he does? That is right he comes home drunk again!

Then when the husband is divorced and alone, that is when he says to himself, "Why am I in this position? Why didn't I listen to her? Why didn't I stop? Why could I not stop? She was telling me all along, why couldn't I change my path?"

We all have these experiences, and I am sure you have a few stories to share yourself.

Note, that men have a stronger ego than women, therefore some men may hit the wall or that Mack Truck as it is often called, before they will change their path.

No matter what the client's story or what the reading is about, the client has been tapped along the way, they already know the truth inside.

Note, that the taps are always subtle, but they are there. Yet, for those people who do not heed the finer taps, a louder version may be necessary – some people need to be hit on the head harder than others to wake up.

With the learning of tarot, you are likely to hear the taps in the intuitive, feeling or even thinking areas, and turn onto the correct path way before you hit the physical wall or the physical world hits you back!

If you refer to Diagram 2 below, you will notice three columns:

The first column is the Carl Jung Psychology Type, the four basic types he associated with the elements. In the second column are the Elements, and in the third column are the tarot suits they all connect with.

Under the Elements column, I have also listed the Astrology Zodiac signs that relate to the four Fire, Earth, Air and Water Elements. Also note that the masculine zodiac signs of Fire and Air connect, as does the feminine zodiac signs of Water and Earth.

Diagram 2

No.	Carl Jung Psychology Type	Element	Tarot Suit
1.	**Intuitive**	**Fire (Masculine)**	**Wands**
	Knew something was not right, did not listen to the first taps.	• Aries • Leo • Sagittarius	Remember that wood burns.
2.	**Feeling**	**Water (Feminine)**	**Cups**
	Feeling yucky and uncomfortable, feeling emotional.	• Cancer • Scorpio • Pisces	Cups hold water.
3.	**Thinking**	**Air (Masculine)**	**Swords**
	Thinking of ways to get out of the situation through asking questions, making a plan B.	• Gemini • Libra • Aquarius	Swords can cut through the confusion
4.	**Physical**	**Earth (Feminine)**	**Pentacles**
	You get sacked, car accident, break a leg, you get sick and are laid up in bed.	• Taurus • Virgo • Capricorn	Pentacles look like gold money or seeds you can plant in the soil.

This is Spirit's role and purpose – to get you back on track to what you agreed to do in this lifetime. Your inner spirit knows this and will always do what it has to do to wake you to your consciousness for you to become enlightened and get back on the right path, whether it is through your dreams, particular clues and signs for you to connect with, through to people you meet in your daily life, through your life's lessons, or a need to learn the tarot or some other spiritual discipline and/or personal development work.

As you develop through your spiritual work, you will vibrate higher and you will understand things from another level. You may find yourself drawn to taking meditation classes or even becoming a vegetarian. You may even join a worthy cause organization and start helping others or the environment in some way.

All of a sudden you will notice that you are not getting those parking tickets like you used to get because you are now giving back to the Universe. You will know when to leave an argument or how to settle one, you are doing the job you love to do and you believe you have reached inner contentment. This realization will hit you, you will feel like you are traveling on the right path, and everything around you will be supporting you.

I would also like to bring your attention to the masculine and feminine connections. Fire and air elements are masculine, and the earth and water elements are feminine.

All the fire zodiac signs would get on best with the air zodiac signs because they share that basic commonality of the masculine's direct and active energy. Also remember that fire needs air to fan it to set it alight, and together they make hot winds. These guys would jump in with no hesitation, and if it does not work out, oh well, they will quickly change to the next new adventure.

Earth and Water are feminine, more passive and indirect energy. Together they make mud and stick well together. They would take their time with projects and put in all the effort towards planning and preparing everything, making sure they have covered all the bases.

Have a look at your family members and friends around you to see what their zodiac signs are and to see if their elements match.

I think it is important to know your client's zodiac sign when doing a reading for them, it will give you so much more information about whether they are proactive and jump into it masculine energy or a more reactive and take their time with the situation feminine energy.

When to Use Tarot Cards

I have always understood that a tarot reading is a psychological map (or a snapshot) of a moment in time. For example, when you do a few readings one after another, the same cards may show up, the same theme or story may repeat itself. But when you do a tarot reading the next day, the cards or the story may have changed or shifted positions, which shows you have changed your mind or you have opened up to another level of understanding.

I look upon a tarot reading the same way as when you consult a street directory or Google Maps nowadays, just before you set out on a journey. Today we have GPS to show us the shortest and most direct route to our destination, but it is still a travel directory that we consult.

I often get asked, "When is the best time to have a tarot reading?" I reply that "It is most beneficial when you are at that cross road. When you have a plan A and are thinking of a plan B and you are feeling confused which way is the best way to go".

Sometimes the ego may be involved or you are too emotional and the urge is to go in the direction of plan A, when deep down, you know the correct path is plan B. This is when a tarot reading can bring clarity to your dilemma or assist you in looking at it from a different perspective. Therefore, you become more conscious of what is going on, then make the correct decision and feel more in charge.

Also, talking to an independent person like a tarot reader and consulting with the tarot brings a fresh point of view and new insights as to which way is the best direction for you to go at this particular moment in time. Sometimes people prefer to speak to someone who is objective about their personal issues, like a tarot reader rather than a friend, to get an impersonal point of view.

Tools of the Trade

The tarot cards do have spiritual power. They are an amazing intuitive tool and they belong to the line of the Goddess. They hold her feminine energy and through this passive insightful tool, we can access the unconscious world and catch a glimpse behind the veil.

The church during the Burning Times, or the Holocaust of Women as it is also known, reconfirms that tarot cards belonged to the line of the Goddess when over three million women were insanely tortured and killed; even men were burnt at the stake or drowned for their work of alternative healing methods; for being a so called 'Witch'.

Tarot cards are tools of the trade; they are like a hammer to a carpenter. A healer today uses many tools to assist them with their work, from crystals, runes and sage to perform clearings through to playing particular meditation music or burning different colored candles to assist them or the client in concentrating their focus on the issues at hand.

Today, many people have and use tarot cards in their professional work: psychologists, counselors and other alternative healers use tarot cards as a way to assist their clients to open up and simply begin the conversation.

We have the Gypsies to thank for spreading tarot card readings around the world. They made a lot of money from it and hid a lot of the information. Gypsies also spread their wild dancing around the world. Look at Tarantella in Italy, belly dancing in Turkey and the Greek handkerchief dance – the origins are all the same.

Gypsies with Indian origins worshipped the Goddess Kaali, one of the great Goddesses. In the Western world, the Goddess Kaali is known for her destructive side, whereas in India she is well known and accepted for her destructive side just as much as her abundant creative side. The Goddess Kaali connects us to the Virgin, Mother and the Crone, our wise women, the feminine Goddess.

Because of the Gypsies influence, people today still refer to tarot readers as foretellers. A tarot reader today does not necessarily wear a scarf around her head, hoop ear-rings and sits behind a crystal ball. Yet people still ask if I can read a crystal ball or read their palms. They do not have any understanding of the fine psychological tool that tarot has turned into.

Divination

Tarot cards are a divination tool. Let us first understand what the word divination means. Divination is a derivative of the word divine. In the *Australian Macquarie Concise Dictionary,* the word divine means: *1. of or pertaining to a God, the Supreme Being, appropriated to God; religious; sacred. 2. The discovering of what is obscure or the foretelling of future events, as by supernatural means, augury, a prophecy, instinctive prevision.*

Therefore, the use of tarot cards is a real divining tool, not only in a spiritual sense but a tool to use when searching or looking for a deeper meaning, through to understanding what is really going on deep down inside and finding the answers that you seek.

Many people are open to using Oracle cards, or Angel cards as they seem less threatening. Oracle cards are different to tarot cards, although you can still use Oracle cards to do a tarot spread. There may not be seventy-eight Oracle cards in the deck. The meaning of the Oracle card is written on each card and there is usually a book that accompanies the cards. Then there are those who want to know more, that is when they are ready to explore the tarot cards.

St Augustine (13 November 354 – 28 August 430 AD) was a scholar, a Latin philosopher and theologian from Roman Africa, generally considered as one of the greatest Christian thinkers of all times. His writings were influential in the development of Western Christianity.

According to his contemporary, Jerome, Augustine 'established a new and ancient faith.' After his conversion to Christianity and baptism in AD 387, Augustine developed his own approach to philosophy and theology, accommodating a variety of methods and different perspectives. He believed that the grace of Christ was indispensable to human freedom, and he framed the concepts of original sin and just war.

He taught his students in various ways. He would open the Bible and would ask his students to choose a reading or a word for the day. He would then ask them to look deeper into the meaning, look behind the veil and the many hidden layers to describe or communicate the meaning through the use of alternative means, such as playing charades, drawings, creative art, acting, etc.

What a wonderful opportunity for these students to tap into the many symbolisms and what a way to bring them up to the surface so they become conscious of what it is telling us. To crack the code, find the key meaning to the hidden messages in the bible.

Mythology

Throughout the book we will explore mythology, which goes back 3,000 years. We will travel through Greek, Roman and Egyptian stories and see their similarities and differences, and how they connect with the Tarot. Other connections may be Jewish, as well as some old English connections.

I truly fell in love with the mythological stories associated with the tarot and somehow wish these stories were taught in schools today.

It is beneficial to understand the mythology of tarot. You will have a deeper understanding and connection to the tarot card and see the relevancy of how they play out in your lives today. These mythological stories are grand stories that have survived over the centuries and given us wonderful information and symbolism, which connects us to our dreams and our sub-conscious mind, just like the tarot does.

Tarot introduced me to the grandfather of mythology, Joseph Campbell, who was a true master of spinning stories, connecting stories from different cultures and breaking them all down to understand how every culture developed the same underlying meanings.

Mythology has its place in our world even today. We lose a lot of the deeper meanings of our cultures when we let go of our rituals. Rituals and mythology have their place in our world. When we let go of the rituals; mayhem and chaos reigns.

The Golden Dawn Group

In 1910, a group formed, calling themselves *The Hermetic Order of Golden Dawn Group*. In this group there was Arthur Edward Waite and Pamela Colman Smith who together created the Rider Waite Tarot Deck.

On every tarot card of the Rider Waite Tarot Card you can see Pamela Colman Smith's signature. If only she knew what a wonderful legacy she left behind, or maybe she does know!

Pamela Coleman Smith and Edward Arthur Waite.

It is absolutely fascinating as to how Waite and Smith gained the inspiration for each card and their given meaning. They must have been totally open to source/spirit for the information to come through. How they put these cards together with so much meaning and understanding? Perhaps it is a bit like looking at Shakespeare and marveling at the philosophical and spiritual beauty of the wisdom that he offers, but it is not just the wisdom of one story here, and one page there. As you know Shakespeare's work is massive and for the wisdom, philosophy and spirituality to encompass such a wide body of work is truly breathtaking. I see the cards as the same.

Wikipedia mentions on Smith and Waite, that when the Golden Dawn splintered due to personality conflicts, Smith moved with Waite to the Independent and Rectified Rite of the Golden Dawn (or Holy Order of the Golden Dawn). In 1909, Waite commissioned Smith to produce a tarot deck with appeal to the world of art, and the result was the unique Waite-Smith tarot deck. Published by William Rider & Sons of London, it has endured as the world's most popular 78-card tarot deck. The innovative cards depict full scenes with figures and symbols on all of the cards, including the pips, and Smith's distinctive drawings have become the basis for the design of many subsequent packs.

I especially like how there is always an extra tarot card in every Rider Waite deck you purchase that has a picture of Pamela and her life's history. I also like how they have finally honored and acknowledged Pamela (or "Pixie" as she was affectionately known) creative tarot work with the addition of the 'Commemorative Tarot Set' and the 'Smith-Waite Centennial Tarot Deck.'

There were other well-known people in the *Golden* Dawn group such as Bram Stoker from the Dracula movies, Paul Foster Case, Dion Fortune and William Yeats the poet, in fact, Pamela Colman Smith worked for Yeats and was introduced to the Golden Group through him. Rudolf Steiner as you may know wrote many books and many of you may know of the Rudolf Steiner schools that are around today. Eden Grey was also part of this group; Grey wrote many books on Tarot and passed away recently in 1999. There was also Madame Helena Lablansky and Bailey who went on to start the Theosophical Society.

I have heard many conflicting stories about Aliester Crowley. Some stories say he was a part of the Golden Dawn group and other stories say that they would not let him be involved because he used the power for personal reasons. Aliester Crowley was greatly responsible for the 1960's revolution; the new belief system that came about from this time, that we have adapted in our culture today.

This Golden Dawn group reminds me of the movie *The Dead Poet's Society*. In the movie, students used to meet at night in secret, exploring and reaching new heights and insights. Robin Williams stared in this movie, where he said the famous quote, 'Seize the Day.'

Can you imagine what a group of artists, creative persons, psychics and Kabbalists; all open to exploration and interested in deeper esoteric studies all meeting in the early 1900's achieved? Back in the early 1900's, they still would have been burned at the stake as witches and trouble makers.

At this stage, I would like to encourage you to start collecting various books especially from secondhand dealers or purchase them secondhand online. Many of the classic tarot books are not printed any more. Secondhand books are much cheaper and are a great resource.

I have attached a great recommended book list for you in the attachment section in Section 4 to help you get started.

Recommended Book List

Attachment 1, page 410

Archetypes

The archetypes in the tarot are the twenty-two Major Arcana. Understanding archetypes is a big part of understanding the tarot.

Let us break the word archetype down. 'Arch' means archaic; of something ancient. 'Type' means a model or a pattern. Therefore, archetype refers to a standard, a blueprint, an original pattern, a model, a mold or a central theme.

For example, the Empress card represents mother. We all have a basic understanding of what a mother is; she is nurturing, unconditional and abundant – this would be the standard. Yet some mothers are smothering mothers, and others do not care about their offspring.

The Word Arcana Means Profound Secret

The archetypes live in our Collective Unconscious. What does Collective Unconscious mean?

Collective refers to absolutely everybody on planet earth. The word unconscious means we do not even know that we know, we are totally unaware. Unaware of what you may ask? Let me go on.

> Carl Jung called the Collective Unconscious
> a source of wisdom that has purpose and meaning

The language of the subconscious mind and dreams are symbols. We dream in pictures, pictures are representative of symbols, and it is because of this that connects us with the tarot. Everything on the tarot card is symbolic.

A Picture Says A Thousand Words

In times past we all agreed to certain symbols, for example; snakes, the image of water, etc. to mean certain things, and on some level we all apply and agree on these same understandings. We all share in this agreement. It is in our collective and we are unconscious of it. This is real primitive programming.

Archetype Game

Here is another game I would like to share with you so you can have an experiential experience about archetypes. I ask my students to give me five words to describe the following words.

The three words are: **sun, snake, and a cup of tea.**

Write your five words here and compare them with my list below:

Sun	Snake	Cup of Tea
_____	_____	_____
_____	_____	_____
_____	_____	_____
_____	_____	_____
_____	_____	_____

Here are my words, see how many words you got the same as me or very close to it:

Sun	Snake	Cup of Tea
Bright	Wisdom	Warmth
Hot	Slimy	Soothing
Yellow/Gold	Power	Healing
Fiery	Long & Thin	Goodness
Energy	Venomous	Flavor

I bet the majority of you had scary words for snake. Isn't this interesting how the poor snake gets a pretty bad wrap all the time? Where does all this fear come from?

If we use the eighty twenty rule (which I use a lot throughout this book) to illustrate my point – eighty percent of people are coming from the Collective Unconscious and believe that snakes are evil – this is what they have learned and now believe. Unless you educate yourself and learn otherwise, right?

In fact, in the world of tarot or symbolism, the snake represents sexuality, wisdom and transformation. It was a snake that awoke Adam and Eve from their blissful state in the Garden of Eden. When you have dreams of a snake or critters biting you, it is something from deep down in your psyche or your inner spirit that is trying to wake you up to some higher form of consciousness.

I grew up with a fear of spiders and mice because my mother was scared of them and of course, I learned from her. When I lived in the country, I learned to live with many Huntsman spiders and plenty of mice. This is when I discovered that I had a choice. I could continue to be afraid like I was taught to be, or I could choose to see it in another complete way. Luckily I chose the latter.

Free Will

If we are all automatically coming from the collective unconscious, when do we use our free will? Where does our free will fit in? What is our free will? It is important to be aware of our free will.

In my classes, we would spend a good amount of time discussing what free will means. Everyone has a different point of view on this matter. This is the purpose of the discussion, to share each other's perspectives and try to understand what Free Will is all about, and to open up to remembering that you always have choice, to open up, to remember that you always have free will. Some people do not think they have choice, even today!

For example, a lot of people when they come for a tarot reading want you to make the decision for them. They are basically asking you for the permission to leave their partners, or their work place, whatever the situation may be.

Some of my student's viewpoints of Free Will are:

- Allowing yourself to enjoy and take advantage of things that bring you joy.
- Free to make your own choice.
- Your willpower to make the choice and then follow through with, like giving up smoking; making the decision first, and then having the willpower to step up and make it happen.

As much as I really wanted to open it up for discussion and really get into it, after a few ideas were brought up everyone would always go quiet. It shows me how much we really misunderstand what free will really means. We have a vague idea but we are not really sure.

It is very important to make sure you always bring up in the reading that we always have free will and put the responsibility right back on to them to make the right decisions for themselves. Even if the tarot reading suggests a good outcome, the client always has Free Will to change that outcome.

People also forget to use their free will so they automatically tap into and work from their subconscious or collective unconscious.

If we use the eighty twenty per cent rule, I would say eighty per cent of people are driving on the roads unconsciously and I find it surprising sometimes that there are not more car accidents. It takes a lot of work to stay present.

> "If you are not on the edge, you are taking up too much space."
> - Anon

We humans are a lazy bunch. If the situation we find ourselves in is not a serious situation, we will always fall back into and operate from the collective unconscious. One of my favorite sayings is "If you are not on the edge, you are taking up too much space". Meaning it is when you are in the midst of a difficult situation, you really feel alive; like you are on the edge and the pressure is on and you really have to think about things, maybe for the first time ever.

When you are not on the edge of the cliff, you are directing your vehicle on the freeway of life, it all seems really easy to do but you are driving in the world of the collective unconscious.

Free will for me is one of my main reasons for learning Taekwondo and entering all those state and national competitions. It was a way I could mentally prepare for the real world. I knew that when I put myself under such immense pressure, learning to fight and defend myself, to be aware and alert of my peripheral vision, I could get myself out of any prickly situation and hopefully never have to fight.

> "Do what's difficult when it's easy."
> \- Lao Tzu

I would also share what Tony Robbins says, 'When you are under the most pressure, when things are going the worst in life, that's when you get the most excited because that's when you are going to work the hardest.'

This is what Dr. Bruce H. Lipton says about free will. 'We can actively *choose* how to respond to most environmental signals and whether we even want to respond at all. The conscious mind's capacity to override the subconscious mind's programmed behaviors is the foundation of free will.'

For me, when someone uses their Free Will, it means they are truly present. They have the power to choose. How does one learn to be present? There are many various ways – meditation, education and reading, yoga or having a tarot reading or doing a tarot course and learning to listen to the taps.

Some people know how to be present, to manipulate other people to do their own bidding. These people know how unconscious some people really are and how to take advantage of them and the situation. For instance, like a good chess player, they can foresee the outcomes and can position their queens, kings and knights to check mate and win the game.

This is one of those subjects that I would encourage you to further research – read books on free will or even Google it.

Choice Game

To make the point of using your free will clearer, I have this choice game for you.

Please choose one: strawberries or chocolate? Write down your answer below:

_____

_____

_____

_____

Now write down why you chose strawberries or chocolate:

_____

_____

_____

_____

_____

If you were to ask me which one I would choose, I would say strawberries. If I was to tell you why I chose strawberries, my answer would be…because, I *chose* strawberries!

Now, what is the difference between what you said and what I said? I did not justify to you why I picked my answer. I just *chose* strawberries.

What does all this mean?
It means that YOU do not have to justify yourself to ANYBODY!!

Why do we feel we have to justify ourselves? We do not have to justify ourselves to anybody at all.

There are some people who will give you ten reasons why they are doing something. Is this a way of drawing attention to themselves? Wanting to be heard? Wanting to seem more important? Maybe it is their ego? Or maybe they are just trying to talk themselves into it?

We tell our boss if we need a day off work, but we do not have to tell everybody else in the office. Justifying is an easy escape for us today, or maybe it is just a habit?

The other thing we hide behind is what is called laying blame. Laying blame is when we point the finger at everyone else, for example…he made me do it, or it has always been done that way, or that is what was written, I am only doing what I was told to do, etc.

Responsibility

———————————

Lay Blame

Justify

Above the line we have the word responsibility – the ability to respond to any situation. Below the line we have the words justify and lay blame. Basically, this means it is easier to lay blame or justify, rather than take responsibility for our actions.

It takes a lot of courage to be responsible for yourself; it is much easier to point the finger at someone else and blame them, rather than looking at yourself. The ego never wants to admit that it is at fault, never wants to see the blame within, and will justify itself out of any predicament.

Where do you sit? What do you understand this to mean for you? Write down your thoughts here:

_____

_____

_____

_____

_____

Construction of the Deck

There are twenty-two Major Arcana, which represent the physical and spiritual archetypes of our unconscious cycle or our lessons along our pathway. The twenty-two Major Arcana represent our journey of life, though not necessarily in order.

There are fifty-six Minor Arcana cards. These are made of four suits: Wands, Pentacles, Swords and Cups. Each suit has fourteen cards each – the ten numbered cards, also known as PIP cards in the old text books. Then there are four Court cards, Pages, Knights, Queen and Kings, which represent the people cards.

There Are Seventy Eight Tarot Cards in Total

With normal playing cards, there are fifty-six cards, plus two jokers, totaling fifty-eight cards.

The Major Arcana tells us about our deep unconscious energies or our archetypes. The Minor Arcana tells us what departments or areas of our life that we are using those energies in, and the court cards are the energies that make it all happen. They carry the energy, the internal energies that get things done. Sometimes other people have that energy around you and they project the energy back to you.

Tarot is similar to astrology in that the planets tell us about the deeper unconscious energy or the archetypal energies. The zodiac signs that the planets are in tells us how the energies will play out, and the house tells us what department or area of life it will play out in.

Attachments

All the attachments are in Section 4 at the back of the book. You can refer to all the references as you work through the tarot cards and for your readings. They will assist you in bringing the cards to life.

Psychology

Attachment 2, page 412

Carl Jung created many words like unconscious, the shadow and individuation. Individuation is what Carl Jung says we are all striving for.

We now use these words in our everyday life, but when they were first devised it was during extraordinary times and they may have been seen as hocus pocus.

The unconscious mind acts as a balance to our conscious mind, this is a compensatory fact. The unconscious image of whatever mood we are in can be extracted, looked at and used for you to counterbalance the energies. By doing this you can empower yourself because you can use it.

The unconscious may also be seen as a spiritual or soul mirror from which we can study ourselves and correct the imbalance.

People find it easier to talk about their dreams rather than discuss tarot readings. For me, interpreting a tarot card is like interpreting a dream.

When you have a recurring dream, it is your unconscious trying to wake you up to something so you can heal it and clear it away. Dreams will also bring in the balance. A simple example is if you think of yourself as high and mighty, you will dream of being a drunk in the gutter. And if you are feeling low, you will dream of flying high in the sky to lift your spirits back up again.

There are many layers to the unconscious, and as an example – the often used classic analogy of an onion; the deeper you go the more layers there are. As we keep peeling back the layers, we keep discovering ourselves and learn more about our inner world.

Astrology

Attachment 3, page 414

In this attachment, I have covered all the basic ingredients of astrology, such as the dates for the zodiac signs that you need to know and can assist you with a tarot reading.

Every tarot card has either a planet or a zodiac sign that connects with it. I will also highlight the astrology associations as we work through the cards in this book.

The best place to start from with astrology are the elements – fire, earth, air and water. This is the base of both astrology and tarot. There are twelve zodiac signs in astrology and twelve houses.

When I do readings for people, I always like to ask what their zodiac sign is. This adds valuable information to the reading. For example, a fire person will be more pro-active and make things happen, whereas an earth person may be too cautious or not trust themselves to move forward.

Colors

Attachment 4, page 416

Colors convey an emotion to us. There is a reason why we lean towards a particular color. As we grow and evolve, these colors may change for us.

There are primary colors and secondary colors and all the colors of the rainbow in between. We all have favorite colors. For example, we may use our favorite power colors

Numerology

Attachment 5, Page 418

Every tarot card has its particular number or purpose. Numbers give an overall tone of the life span or life path. For example, there is no mistake that the Wheel of Fortune is number ten, the number one and zero representing things turning onto a new level, and Death is number thirteen, one plus three equals four, meaning the end of an old and transformation of a new order.

Everyone has their favorite number. For example, your birth date may be your favorite number and you use it whenever you play the Tattersalls or need to pick a box.

Whenever I do tarot readings, I personally have to know the clients' numbers. By doing this simple and basic numerology spread you may find out their power numbers (what best numbers work for them), thereby giving them a more detailed reading.

There are many ways of working out numbers. Diagram 3 below is my simple way of working out birth date numbers. Keep it simple and you will always remember it.

For numerology I like to use long division. Many books and numerologists suggest using the formula of adding up along the line.

Diagram 3

Day	11
Month	03
Year	1960
Total	1974

External Personality

Birth date day number is 11, 1+1=2. **This position is the External Personality or Out number.**

Note: The number eleven is also a master number. More about master numbers below. No need to worry about the month or the year numbers either, as this will be tallied towards the total.

This 'External Personality,' or I also like to call it the 'Out there number,' is how you are seen out there in the world and how you would like to be seen. This out number is your mask. We all wear masks. The mask acts like a scout, it goes out there first to make sure everything is ok before you allow your true self to come out. This is what the External Personality does; it portrays your mask to the outer world. We use our mask when we enter a room, a party, a project, or commence a relationship.

As an astrologer, I often get asked, "Guess what my star sign is?" People do not realize that I would be guessing their mask sign that they are hiding behind. I need to get to know the client first to see what their sun sign is.

Master Numbers

The number eleven is also a master number. I look at both the master number and the single digit number. Yes, I always like to bring it down to a single digit. Some numerologists leave it as the double number. Master numbers are all double numbers such as eleven, twenty-two, thirty-three, forty-four, etc.

Master number people are here to master something. They all do what I call special work – helping others or the environment in some way. This may be through vocational and higher purpose work; the person is here to somehow be a leader in the community.

Master numbers may show up anywhere, even as the month date. Where ever they may show up, this person holds the master number energy. Even if the person does not yet connect with it, I always say that they will eventually fall into the bucket.

Some master number people end up on drugs or become alcoholics as a way of numbing themselves to their calling. Maybe their up-bringing did not support them emotionally and they have ended up using these toxic devices to cover up their pain. But they can turn it around and become great supporters of others.

Natural Talent

Back to our example in Diagram 3. The total is 1974. **1+9+7+4= 21. 2+1=3. This position is the Natural Talent or the 'in-number'.** When you add up all the numbers together, you will get your natural talent number. This is also known as your Life Path number.

This is what is natural for you to tap into, what you can easily access. The in-number in the example above is the number three.

Power Numbers

In this example, this person is seen in the outer world as a number two and they have easy access to their number three – natural inner energy. The number two and the number three for this person are their 'Power numbers.' You may also connect these numbers to the tarot cards. For example, number two connects us to the High Priestess energy and number three to the Empress.

Remember every number has a positive and negative aspect. For some people it may be a real challenge for them to be number two energy and the number three energy naturally. This may be their lesson in life, to learn how to balance these energies, to make the most out them and use them creatively and constructively, this is when the person is most happy.

> "There is a balance; I see it every time I swing past."
> - Ruanna

If they do tap into their External Personality number positively, it will also enhance their Natural Talent number. Therefore, enhancing their Outer energy which will enhance their Inner energy once again, and on it goes.

I also like to mention that sometimes the pendulum swings the other way and everything the person does just does not work; they are operating out of the negative side. But the challenge here is to get the pendulum to swing back and operate from the positive, creative and constructive side. Remember the pendulum swings both ways.

Sometimes the 'out number' is the same number as their 'in number'. In this case, I always tell this person, what you see is what you get. The person does not have a mask and are showing their natural being state, it is easy for them to be themselves.

If the client has a combination of a number one and number nine, no matter where it shows up, whether it is in the External Personality or the Natural Talent, this is what I call the 'Millionaire's Hook'. They have the ability to begin something and take it right through to the end, through to manifestation. Some people know how to beginning things and then they stop, and beginning something new again. Others are very good at completing things but have no sense of how to begin something. When the one and nine show up, this person knows how to make it work and accomplishes much.

Another way I like to use numerology is when I do small spreads of up to seven cards. I will add up all the card numbers together and get the one root number. I connect this root number to the Major Arcana to get more answers or insights.

Symbology

Attachment 6, Page 420

Symbols are the language of dreams. We dream every night but many people say they do not remember their dreams. We interpret a dream like we would interpret a tarot card.

For example, a boat may symbolize a process of growth, of course travel or an emotional journey, or movement in the environment.

Dreams belong to the unconscious world. By understanding the symbols, you will understand the scared knowledge that the unconscious mind is using in trying to wake you up to some level of consciousness.

Dreams, as do tarot, convey messages for us, and our job is to interpret the message as clearly as possible, understanding what the symbols mean in the cards or in the dream can gives us the answers we seek. Just like a corporate logo, mission statement of a business or an objective of a project, the message should be that clear.

Symbology may mean different things to many people. By writing your dreams down or writing what you see in the tarot card, you may discover what that particular symbol means for you.

I have listed a few items on the symbology attachment, use it as reference and after a while you will see that symbology is quite easy to work with. Sometimes we may overthink the symbolism and it just does not feel right, and usually the first thought you had was the right one.

Tarot Activation and Homework

Attachment 7, Page 428

The homework is easy, but it is the doing of it that may be the tricky bit. You really need to commit to doing your homework every day as it is the most important part of learning the tarot.

Remember that your ego does not want you to wake up to your spiritual side, so you may want to put off the homework or have doubts that you are not connecting with the cards but if you put in the effort you will definitely be rewarded when it comes time to doing the tarot reading.

All you have to do is *pick one tarot card* per day and then activate the energy of the card by using your lively imagination. Start your personal journal and write down whatever comes up for you at that particular moment. You may want to return to your journal again and again.

You may choose the same card two days in a row, but the thoughts, ideas or actions you write down may be different from one day to the next. By doing this, you gain the experience with the tarot cards, more interpretations and a deeper understanding, there are many levels in the tarot, just like when you do a tarot reading for someone that knows a little about tarot, the reading is just that much deeper and on another level.

Now, the most important part of this exercise is to actually activate the card. By activating it I mean you actually need to do something about it, actively act it out. Your inner self is forever trying to tell you something and by connecting with your tarot card you may understand what your inner spirit is trying to tell you. You will make it conscious. For example, if you see flowers on the tarot card, one idea is that you may wear a shirt that has flowers on it. Another idea is to wear a flower in your hair, or spend some time in your flower garden, or even purchase flowers for yourself or for your mum.

The real magic happens when you make the connections and become conscious about the messages that are revealed. Maybe you have wanted flowers for your kitchen all week, this could be why you noticed the flowers in the tarot card. By cutting or purchasing the flowers, you will complete this process and you will feel content and happy that you have finally put yourself first and done something for yourself. This will raise your energy and make you happy.

How to Store the Tarot Cards

Many people use different methods and that is fine, whatever works for you works well. I do recommend silk scarves, silk bags, and wooden boxes, preferably something that is breathable. By doing so, your cards will hold your energy and will come alive for you.

I recommend using a silk scarf to wrap up the tarot cards. The scarf will keep them bundled together after you have completed your reading. Also the scarf helps to keep your tarot cards clean when doing the reading because they will not touch the surface of the table.

For me, I learned that every time I wrap up my cards in the scarf, a type of protection is formed, not only for the cards but also for myself. I learned how to shut down and close myself off and how to protect myself from other people's pain or issues.

To clean the tarot cards, if they are plastic, you can wipe them down with a damp cloth. I always like to keep a crystal in the pouch along with the cards, which keeps them clean, sharp and protected. I like the clear quartz crystal, but you can use which ever crystal connects with you.

Some people knock or tap the cards three times before putting them away or in between each reading if they are doing a lot. This will tap out any unwanted energy or stuck energy.

Some people do not like other people to touch their cards; this is your personal preference. For me it depends on the environment. For example, when I do tarot readings at a Hens party, I only have five minutes to spend with each person; they really do not have time to shuffle the cards. I will shuffle and cut the cards into three stacks and ask them to choose a stack and I go from there. Also the girls are probably holding a glass of wine and eating finger food, so in this case, I prefer to handle the cards myself.

A fun activity I get my students to do is to actually sleep with their tarot cards. Make sure they are all wrapped up in their scarf and in the pillow case so they do not go everywhere. This will really connect you with your tarot cards and put your energy into them. Notice if your dreams are enhanced.

A couple of examples: one student wanted a relationship and slept with the two of cups card under her pillow. Another student was planning a world trip and you guessed it, she slept with The World card underneath her pillow. This is also another creative way of using the tarot. Both students successfully attained their goals. I don't know if the first student's relationship is still going today, but at the time she did attract someone in her life to date. The second student did achieve her goal of travelling to America.

If you put your energy into the cards, they will become your friends. So why not take them with you everywhere you go. Be creative with them. There are smaller pocket sized cards that you can purchase that can make life easier.

Also, when you shuffle another person's tarot cards, you should be able to feel how different their cards feel to your deck. Some cards feel lighter, others feel thicker, etc.

No Ego Please!

The last thing I would like to mention before we get started with the tarot card meanings is that the tarot will always present you with the truth. They will connect with your inner most motivations because they are pure, not your ego motivations. Tarot cards will always cut through any ego; I always tell my students to trust their cards!

A great example I can give you is a reading for a girl who could not decide between a photography course and an acting course. The outcome of the reading told her to go traveling, that she needed to go away somewhere and really think about what was really important at that moment in her life. Obviously she was not content with her reading. Which leads me to some important points to remember when doing tarot readings.

For the client to not be happy with their reading means they were expecting a different answer. You did not specifically say what they wanted to hear, or they had no idea how a good tarot reading or an effective tarot reading works.

People do put high expectations on the tarot cards. Remember, client's always have free will and they need to take responsibility for their life's direction, and as a good tarot reader you can point this out for them.

The unfortunate thing is that these people will then say you were not a good tarot reader. Please do not be offended by this. Stick to what the cards say to you during the reading, it is just what the client needs to hear at that time, trust that.

Trust your Cards!

To build your confidence with doing tarot readings just takes practice. Practice in this case really does make perfect.

Also, when you first start doing readings, I recommend doing an exchange with your client. They pay for the reading by offering you a cup of coffee. Start there until you feel you can charge twenty dollars, then fifty dollars, etc.

By having an exchange, the client feels they are receiving something of value; they will listen more attentively and respect the reading more. This also says you are offering a service that is of value and you value what you are doing.

Also, do not think after the reading, "I should have said this" or "I wish I mentioned that". Whatever you said at that time was perfect and that is all they needed to hear, that is all they could understand at the time.

Sometimes the tarot reader just does not connect with the tarot card spread. Do not be tempted to do another spread, challenge yourself to work through this initial spread. Work backwards, start with the outcome and work towards the present cards. There is always another way to work around the spread. Try this first before turning over other cards on top as this should be your last resort.

And if you do not connect with your client, it is ok to say to them that you cannot read for them, that you are finding it hard to read them, and get yourself out of the situation. The reading will deteriorate because your confidence is shot.

Some people are closed off or defensive, wanting to just test you. I wonder sometimes why these people want to waste their time and money in having a reading in the first place when they are so skeptical, or is this Spirit's way of testing you?

It is also wise not to do a reading if you are not feeling one hundred percent or if you have had a couple of drinks.

Masculine or Feminine

I always review this exercise with my students before we start with the tarot cards because times have changed and you have to remember that when these tarot cards were created it was a different era – people thought differently back then. Sometimes I think we still think like this today!

This is a good fun exercise to do, many emotional discussions have been had in my classes and it is great to see how far our thinking has progressed.

Many people are often surprised with the outcomes but they do understand the thinking at the time. It is also another chart for reference purposes. You can also add to this list.

Masculine	Feminine
Positive	Negative
Yang	Yin
White	Black
Animus	Anima
Seen	Unseen
Conscious	Unconscious
Right	Left
Active	Passive
Sun	Moon
Outer	Inner
Spirit	Soul
Order	Chaos
Extrovert	Introvert
Superior	Inferior
Day	Night
Summer	Winter
Ego	Shadow
Logic	Receptive
Conditional	Unconditional
Hot	Cold
Material	Spiritual
Good	Evil
Heaven	Hell
Physical	Metaphysical
Magical	Mysterious
Head	Tail

Roman Numerals

Another exercise I like to do with my students is to list the roman numerals that associate with each card.

Many people do not actually know them so it is important to review them because the Rider Waite tarot cards do use this numbering system.

Once you get the pattern it is easy to remember. This is also another good reference.

Number	Roman	Number	Roman
1	I	11	XI
2	II	12	XII
3	III	13	XIII
4	IV	14	XIV
5	V	15	XV
6	VI	16	XVI
7	VII	17	XVII
8	VIII	18	XVIII
9	IX	19	XIX
10	X	20	XX
		21	XXI

Section 2 - Major Arcana

Chapter 3

The Hero's Journey

"We shall not cease from exploration, and the end of all our exploring, will be to arrive where we started, and know the place for the first time."
- T.S. Elliot

Tarot represents life as a full circle following the journey and the experiences of the Spirit (The Fool).

It begins with the Fool meeting his divine parents to learn intuition and the power of manifestation (The High Priestess and The Magician). He then incarnates and meets his mortal parents where he is nurtured and given guidance (The Empress and The Emperor).

Through his childhood, he faces society's expectations (The Hierophant) about his place in the world. He will learn about many loves and conflicts (The Lovers and The Chariot).

As an adult he encounters the trials of his world (Justice), how to balance this with his inner world (Temperance), learn about his own inner power (Strength) and his wisdom (The Hermit).

Halfway through his journey the Fool experiences change (Wheel of Fortune). He undergoes some sort of loss, crisis and healing (The Hanged Man, Death and Temperance), where his journey leads him into the underworld in order to discover what is responsible for his crisis (The Devil and Tower).

After his struggles, he goes on to encounter the celestial bodies, peace and harmony (The Star), nature's dark side (The Moon) rebirth and transformation (The Sun), resulting in triumph over darkness (Judgement) and victory (The World), which leads him back to the beginning where he is prepared to recommence a new journey all over again but on another level.

The Hero's Journey

Attachment 8, page 430

If you look at how the Major Arcana are laid out in their numbered order, you will see three rows with The Fool on the left, on his own in the left hand side column. He represents our Spirit and the Hero's Journey.

First Row

We all have to go through this first row. We will all experience birth and grow to adolescence. This row represents the mind. It is a personal experience meaning it is personal to me. Notice how they all wear crowns, except for the Lovers where they are naked.

Second Row

This adulthood row is where we learn to take responsibility for ourselves and for our actions. This row represents the body. It is an interpersonal experience, meaning it is about me and my immediate family, and those close to me.

Third Row

Not everyone wants to travel along this last row. This is the wisdom gaining row where we are searching for that something more in life. It is our great journey. This row represents the spirit. It is a transpersonal experience meaning it effects not only me and my family but the extended community and environment around me. Also notice how everyone are naked in the cards, except for the Lovers in the Tower card.

Other Connections

Another interesting phenomena is that if you add up the Magician card number one from the first row and add it to the Devil card number fifteen from the third row, they add up to sixteen. When you divide the number sixteen by two, it equals eight. That connects to the strength card number eight from the second row.

If you add up the Magician card number one from the first row, and add it to the World card number twenty-one from the third row, they add up to twenty-two. Divide twenty-two by two equals eleven, which connects to the Justice card number eleven, again from the second row.

Then if you add up the Chariot card number seven from the first row, and add it to the Devil card number fifteen from the third row; they also add up to twenty-two. Dividing twenty-two by two equals eleven, which connects to the Justice card number eleven, again from the second row. This makes the Justice card the middle card or halfway mark of the Major Arcana journey.

Basically the middle row, the adulthood line, is the halfway mark between the first row above and the third row below. You can tap into the middle row of adulthood energy and take it either; up to the first row and experience the understanding that comes from these Major Arcana or archetypal energies, or take the energy down to the third row and learn about the experience in a totally different and responsible way. Maybe it was a karmic experience you needed to learn from or maybe it took this life's journey to fully understand and complete the process once and for all.

In many tarot card games, The Fool tarot card number zero, actually becomes card number twenty-two.

Different Faiths

Another interesting fact about the tarot cards is that you can see all the various religions displayed together.

For instance; The High Priestess holding the Tora, the Tora is also in the Wheel of Fortune, both bringing in the Jewish Faith.

The Lovers' card clearly displays the Christian Myth of Adam and Eve in the Garden of Eden.

There are also the four Archangels; Raphael (The Lovers), Michael (Temperance), Gabriel (Judgement) and Lucifer (The Devil) connecting us to the Christian Faith.

The Tower of Babel (Tower) built by the Babylonians.

The Death card is quite Gothic looking and the St George's cross of the Judgement card connects us to the Church of England faith.

We have the sphinx in the Chariot and in the Wheel of Fortune connecting us to Egyptian mythology.

There is no discrimination here; tarot has no religion and is available for everyone.

I will now take you through The Fool's Journey, also known as the Hero's Journey. The Fool, our spirit will encounter all the various archetypes in their numbered order. As previously mentioned, this is the layering effect method that I like to use, and another way of getting to know, meet and greet or connect with each of the Major Arcana archetypal energies.

Once we have completed working our way through all the Major Arcana, we will begin again with the Fool and get to know them on a much deeper level. I will then introduce all the other connections – such as the astrology, whether it is a planet or zodiac sign, mythology, numerology and any other connection associated with the card. All these various modalities give you a deeper meaning when you are doing a reading; they show you how the energy of the card actually plays out in real life. I will also give key and shadow words and then some actions that you can do to physically activate the energy of the card.

This Fool's Journey is the same journey for all of us. The tarot is showing us one uniform. For instance, as Joseph Campbell likened this same journey that we will all experience to *Star Wars* and Luke Skywalker's journey. Briefly, and to give you the idea, we have Luke Skywalker (The Fool) meeting Obi Kenobi (The Magician). Then Luke Skywalker meets the wise one Yoda (The Hermit), followed by meeting his father Darth Vader, where he has to face his dark side (The Devil), work through all his challenges before he can create his new life (The World).

The first row represents our birth through to adolescences, we will all experience this.

0 THE FOOL

The image of the Fool starts off the major arcana sequence. The energy of the Fool is trust and innocence. I like to think that trust is his middle name.

The Fool is us at the moment of conception. He is the new beginning, the seed. He is the creation of energy and that eternal flame of renewal.

Our soul begins the grand journey, just like a baby. He is not prejudiced, but he is filled with faith and enthusiasm for the journey he is about to undertake. Our soul chooses a particular life path in each life time.

The card is numbered zero and can mean all or nothing, which connects well with the Fool having no karma and no preconceived ideas.

The Fool is not foolish; he is just ready and open to receive anything that the cosmos offers.

The Fool represents excitement and a carefree attitude. He takes his knocks from life but does not lose sight of his ideals. He takes more chances, breaks conventions, trusts his intuition and takes that leap of faith.

I THE MAGICIAN

The Magician represents our willpower. He represents the 'I am' principle. He is the Animus, masculine passive energy and our inner spirit.

His energy is formed in the womb. For example, the first thing new born babies do is cry. This cry has power in its essence without using words and it demands what it needs.

The Magician is the first person the Fool encounters on his grand journey. The Magician is the card of inspiration and manifestation.

With one arm raised and the other pointing downwards, he can blend the spiritual and the practical, through his mastery of the four elements: fire, earth, air and water.

The Magician is confident, articulate, and manipulative; he has will-power and charm with good communication skills. He can put his ideas into practice.

When you tap into your Magician's energy, you have a feeling of great power with the possibility to manifest your desires or even attract a powerful individual into your own life.

II THE HIGH PRIESTESS

The High Priestess represents dreams and intuition. She is the Anima, feminine passive energy, and the inner soul. Her energy is also formed in the womb, meaning we are all powerful intuitive and psychic individuals. The High Priestess wants to be unknown and wants to be left alone.

The High Priestess holds all our memories of our past lives. Because of her passive energy she communicates to you via your gut feelings and your dreams. I like to call her our emotional guidance system, as it is through your feelings that maneuver you one way or the other.

The Fool now turns his attention towards spiritual matters. The High Priestess understands her potential; she is the symbol of eternal wisdom and inspiration. She makes us see the good in all that surrounds us and is the figure of serenity and knowledge.

The High Priestess represents guidance, wisdom, intuition of the spiritual realms. She is the passive aspect of the feminine principle and widely known as the Virginal Moon Goddess.

The Magician and the High Priestesses' energies are both formed within the womb; these energies operate on the inner side; meaning we are all born with these powerful energies. We all have access to them, we all understand these energies on some level. It is up to us to evolve this energy.

The Magician and the High Priestess represent our celestial parents, our divine parents or as I like to call them our God Parents, or Adam and Eve.

III THE EMPRESS

The Empress is our mother; she is the creation principle and the pleasure principle. The Empresses' energy represents the feminine active aspects. She is all nurturing love energy, demonstrates unconditional love and she wants to be with others.

The Empress is the Fool's mother; she gives birth to the Fool, and it is through the mother that the baby has its needs met. She is frequently shown as being pregnant to denote her fertility, which symbolizes growth and the need to nurture and to be nurtured.

She is the emblem of fertility and abundance and also symbolizes the natural cycles of the year with a time for seed, blossom, fruit and decay.

The Empress indicates a pleasant, welcoming environment, a comfortable home, love, sex, marriage, childbirth and motherhood, generosity and willingness to help others.

IV THE EMPEROR

The Emperor is the Fool's father. He is the active masculine energy and represents the authority figure in our world. The Emperor's role is to show conditional love, he is the one that sets the limits and boundaries in our life.

It is our father who is the first to discipline us, to take us out in the world and the first one to say "no", to teach us material success through structure, stability, order and control.

Our life's desires have to be aligned and the Emperor, our Father, is the one that helps us to create structure in our life, establish new foundations, set boundaries, teach us strategies and enforce us to work within the rules and laws of society.

The Emperor instructs the Fool on matters of authority and administration as well as giving guidelines on moral and ethical behavior. He is the male symbol of law and order with organizational abilities, enabling opportunities for promotion and success.

The Empress and the Emperor represent our Earthly parents, our Mum and Dad in the real world.

V THE HIEORPHANT

It is time for the Fool to get to know the Hierophant. The Hierophant represents society and dogma, our inner moral policeman and represents the urge to find out about inner wisdom.

At around age five, the Fool goes to school to learn about the rules, whether they are the laws of the inner spiritual world, about religions and their spiritual leaders, discovering your wiser self, your own inner teacher and about healing energy. As well as laws of the outer world, we learn about policeman, government and society's rules and regulations.

The Fool explores his inner and outer worlds; he receives religious guidance through a high priest, a Pope, or one that brings faith and hope. In the outer sense, he may receive assistance from a wise or helpful person, such as a doctor, teacher or a solicitor.

The Hierophant is the symbol of earthly rituals, a ruler in our society, either a spiritual or a professional advisor. The Fool must integrate the advice of both worlds and move forward with his own integrity. Discovering his own beliefs, then creating and practicing his own traditions.

VI THE LOVERS

The Fool now starts to question the standards of society. The card of the Lovers represents a matter of choice, rather than love – an emotional choice that deserves careful consideration, our first conscious choices and decisions.

The Lovers is about our first relationships, choosing the partner you want, creating your own families, your own groups and the urge to merge with another, but now it is on your terms.

It is now time for the Fool to stand at the first trial of his youth, namely love and puberty blues. The Fool must learn that love is not a simple matter decided by physical attraction and that affairs of the heart are neither easy nor straightforward.

The Lovers indicate a trial or choice. Standing at the crossroads, being drawn in different directions all at once, be it affairs of the heart, moving house or career matters, whatever the situation a decision may need to be made.

VII THE CHARIOT

The Chariot represents the developing ego, adolescence, the beginning of independence and controlling your external world.

The Fool, having struggled with love's complexities, is now ready to encounter war, the next trial of youth. The Chariot is the card of true power, will, and mastery in the plain of reality.

Here the Fool learns to deal with the environment; sometimes we learn the hard way, e.g. car crashes. The ego of a young man feels indestructible. The male ego is stronger than the female ego.

The Fool still has to control himself, control his virility, manly, strength and force. He has the wish to go forward and the simultaneous wish to stay secure in the tried and tested. A combination of self-control, equilibrium and emotional discipline is needed to overcome problems and difficulties.

Because The Chariot is the last card on the first row, a lot of people may get stuck in the energy of this card. For instance, when you hear someone say "It is not my fault that I lost my job," or "You made me angry, etc". This is just the ego not wanting to admit fault and responsibility and it will always want to blame someone else.

The Fool learns from the Chariot the quality of energy needed to strive for a desired goal. It shows a struggle or conflict of interests, and can even mean a fight for self-assertion. Success is assured as it triumphs over difficulties and obstacles.

Now we move onto the second row of Adulthood. Learning about responsibility and having the courage to transform ourselves.

VIII STRENGTH

The Fool now asks himself "Who Am I" on the inside. "Who am I" is a Buddhist concept, which is nearly 2,700 years old. This is a time to understand oneself fully, only then will you get to know your inner strength, and confront your inner lion.

It takes a lot of courage to confront one's own fears. When you do you find your own strength, become braver and then you want to go after more knowledge.

The Fool has gained experience in thought and feeling; now he needs to develop the capacity to control, discipline and weigh up these elements within himself; creating balance within and controlling his interior world. It is you controlling your fears and not allowing your fears to control you.

The Strength Tarot card represents powerful emotions that when channeled properly in a balanced way and with the love from the Divine, become a source of strength, the strength that comes from within, from having respect for one's self and loving one's self.

IX HERMIT

The Hermit is about the inner journey, an inner quest to understand your own wisdom.

The Fool now arrives upon the stillness of the Hermit. He lives inside us and is our guide. He offers us higher understanding, one of wisdom and knowledge, to seek a new direction without interference from others.

This card indicates that the time is ripe for withdrawal from the busy outside world in order to enter the quiet inner one, one of solitude. The Hermit stands on the pinnacle and holds the lamp waiting for you to come up, always willing to show you the way, but only if you look.

The Hermit represents a time for soul-searching and meditation, the need for patience and a time to work things out quietly. You need to look inward to see the light and the answer has to come from within. For example, through meditation you may receive your answer.

The Fool has become wiser and older and is now ready to guide other people.

X WHEEL OF FORTUNE

The Wheel of Fortune is a symbol of stability and change. Choice verses Fate. Now the Fool is at the point where he realizes that there is more to life and him than the external world.

Fate is the moving circumference of the Wheel, while the true self is the center. The hub enables the rim to turn and is thus responsible for all that comes its way. It was meant to be the turn of the wheel, all for a reason.

Time to look at yourself, going down into the internal unconscious. When you come back up, you will change. A great question to ask yourself is, "When I am on the downside, what am I to learn?" When you have learnt something about yourself, this is the luck and fortune associated with this card.

The Fool learns the workings of fate and is a warning to be prepared to adapt to new circumstances.

The Wheel of Fortune signifies a new chapter is starting, a new run of luck is commencing. Awareness is your own power over your destiny.

XI JUSTICE

The Fool is now at a halfway mark in his life and has the opportunity to discover his own truth. Justice teaches the Fool to discriminate, to make dispassionate evaluations and impersonal decisions.

He must learn to solve his problems impartially, to weigh up, to balance and then to make rational judgements. To take responsibility for the self. This is the turning point, the point of adulthood when we stop blaming our parents and others.

Justice stands for the need to weigh things up, to find fair and rational solutions, for reason and thought to over-ride emotion.

It is not about active energy as yet; it is about weighing things up in the mind, the mental shift, and is about accepting the consequences of our actions.

XII THE HANGED MAN

The Fool starts his descent into the underworld to explore the realms of his subconscious. This card represents the turning point in psychological development where the individual must come to grips with unconscious forces within him.

He needs to sacrifice control of his conscious ego by surrendering to the unknown territory of his inner world. This can only be done by conscious choice.

The Hanged Man indicates a time of greater understanding. It also indicates that a sacrifice may have to be made to gain something of greater value.

This stage is about surrender and acceptance. The Fool must surrender blame and acknowledge all aspects. He does not want to hang in suspension, contemplation or limbo any more. He will remain stagnate until he cannot stand it anymore, until the penny drops, then things will turn around for him.

XIII DEATH

Now the Fool must die. Within death, there is always the seed of life for without death there can be no new life. Death is the end of something unproductive and self-destructive.

A transformation, regeneration and resurrection will take place. A letting go of old patterns, habits and attitudes that do not work for you anymore.

An analogy I like to use is that of an old tree. We need to prune the tree during winter, which is symbolic of letting go of dead wood and leaves and allowing for the new sprouts. It is the natural development both physically and psychologically in the life of man.

This card is connected with transformation, transition and change, rather than death of the body. Death represents letting go of something that has outlived its purpose.

The pain that is suffered under the effect of Death is related to the willingness or unwillingness to surrender to the inevitability of change.

XIV TEMPERANCE

The Fool has learned the value of a balanced mind in Justice, which he now needs to compliment with a balanced heart in Temperance.

Temperance offers the quality of compassion and forgiveness. Taking into account the feeling in the situation, rather than just the factual circumstances and time should be taken to weigh up the best course of action here. A wait and see attitude.

Temperance stands for cooperation, the successful blending of opposites and signifies compromise. Having a mature and balanced personality, able to deal with the situation with tact and efficiency and acting with a sense of calm and serenity.

The Fool has the opportunity to keep the old values and take in new perspectives, then blend, mix and harmonize to create balanced emotions. This balances the male and female energies, to rehabilitate, integrate and allow for all to settle down within.

This is the last card of the second row and The Fool may be feeling blissful. Temperance brings a sense of creating a comfort zone, restoring the equilibrium effect.

Now we commence the third row. You will notice that most of the figures on the third row are naked, thereby displaying their vulnerability.

XV THE DEVIL

The Devil teaches the Fool to recognize and accept all aspects of his nature, both dark and light. It is time to face the shadow.

As the first card on the third row, we meet the Devil who stands at the Gates of the Unconscious. Before you truly know yourself, you have to know the shadow self to be whole. You can own or disown the shadow.

The Devil represents the blockage of repressed fears and feelings. Once removed, they can release a great deal of positive energy. 'Out of apparent evil, much good can come.'

It may be an unpleasant and uncomfortable experience that we place ourselves in. It makes us feel trapped and restricted. Now the Fool explores the possible solutions available.

XVI THE TOWER

This card can represent a sudden blow or an unexpected event to our ego and pride, which can be a blessing in disguise to learn a lesson in life. It may be an experience that is necessary, like a catalyst for enlightenment.

At this point the Fool must sort out for himself which way is right for him. He must abandon whatever is not truly his own. For years we live as we have been taught. There comes a time when our needs, thoughts and ideas need to be tested, evaluated and lived by.

Accept the blow as a gift of divine intervention – an explosion of the unconscious to the conscious that is so strong that it blows up and out.

It can be seen as a breaking down of the ego or a shattering of control. It may be an internal lesson or a rude awakening in the real world. They say the truth shall set you free.

XVII THE STAR

The Star has always been an emblem of hope and promise; a light to steer by. The shining promise of the Star refreshes and renews the Fool's drooping spirits, bringing inner calm and peace, especially after the storm of the Tower.

We all need faith, and the belief that our hopes and wishes will be fulfilled, that our dreams will come true. The Star is symbolic of faith and hope, meditation and replenishment, a change and healing that comes from within.

The Star is that emblem of the inner light to guide us. A bright light, it suggests inspiration, a sense of purpose and the renewal of life's forces and energy.

There is a stage during midlife when we gain peace. You see yourself as you are, and you like yourself, warts and all. We become open to life; this is symbolic of the figure shown as naked, a back to basic nature, showing your natural and vulnerable state.

XVIII THE MOON

The Fool now realizes there is still much to learn and here is an opportunity to open up to the deeper unconscious.

The Moon symbolizes feelings and emotions which are by nature volatile, nebulous and uncertain; the unconscious in its unpredictable and uncontrolled aspects. These aspects need to be transformed into wisdom to be able to work together harmoniously to form a well-integrated personality.

The Moon represents a feeling of confusion, brooding in the past, depression and deception. Not a good time to trust the emotions. Self-delusion, believing in half-truths, or you may slip back into old ways and patterning.

There actually may be a lot of fear associated with this card. For example, the time just before labor and giving birth. Or like when one loses a lot of weight – they do not know themselves and get scared, because all of a sudden they are getting attention, so they put all the weight back on. You are fearful of letting go of everything you used to be.

It can suggest that solutions to problems can be found through dreams and intuitions, rather than logic and reason.

The crustacean lives on the bottom of the sea and acts like a psychic vacuum cleaner. Here is an opportunity to clean up all the rubbish and debris from the past once and for all.

XIX THE SUN

Here the Fool feels the Sun's cheerful and welcome image after the misty uncertainty of the Moon. The Fool now walks from the night of the Moon into the daylight of the Sun and is reborn.

The Sun is positive; the Fool will not get caught up in the same old stuff anymore. No more hang ups and no more urges – life begins again for him. A rebirth.

The Sun indicates joy, success and personal achievement, optimism, giving energy to pursue personal ambition and desires. It is not only success but also fun and excitement in the process of reaching the goal.

The card represents energy and a source of strength. It stands for success, prosperity, happiness and true friends. It seems to brighten all the other cards, adding a sense of optimism and good cheer.

XX JUDGEMENT

Judgement is the penultimate stage of the Fool's journey. As its image suggests, Judgement is a card of summing-up, of balancing accounts; through this card the Fool's progress is evaluated and assessed.

The card of Judgement means an inner calling; a higher calling to rise to a more meaningful existence. A push from within to recognize a need for change.

The card signifies the final settlement of a matter, the 'cleaning of the slate.' Paying off old debts and a preparedness for the resurrection of a new beginning.

It means to reach beyond petty concerns of others and stand there as a role model for truth and justice. A calling to your responsibilities and a rising of the consciousness of people and the planet by teaching others through your own demonstrations.

A universal feeling, a doing for others, this card is often seen as the Karma Card. It indicates that things that have lain fallow will come to life, and reward for past effort will finally be forthcoming. It is a time for rejoicing and renewal.

XXI THE WORLD

The World is the last card of the third row. The Fool now returns back to the zero as in the Fool card and completes a full cycle, a wholeness and completion energy. Balancing the male and female energies within.

It involves the supreme integration of self and the cosmos with a sense of unity, harmony and balance, individuation (the word Carl Jung termed and suggests we are all striving towards).

The Fool is now at one with nature and the world; there is a sense of satisfaction and achievement at finding one's rightful place in the world, being who you are in the world and doing it well.

This card represents the completion of one phase or stage of life; a sense of fulfillment and elation by knowing that the Fool has 'made it' spiritually, emotionally and on a material level.

Once this cycle is completed, you begin again but on a new level.

The Fool, the Magician and the High Priestess energies are the most important of all the Major Arcana's, they live on our inner side; we are born with these energies, we do not use these energies as much as we should in the world today because they are just not in our reality.

As we go through each tarot card you will see these three energies repeated throughout all the cards in one form or another.

From reading this Tarot Distinctions book, you will begin to open up to these energies and your intuition much more, picking up the taps quicker and correcting your course of action faster, therefore achieving your goals quicker.

Chapter 4

...Tarot represents life as a full circle, following the Journey of the Spirit...

0 THE FOOL

SUMMARY

The Fool is the principle of creation. He is the breath of life, the spark of being, and full of energy, spirited and young at heart.

The Fool aligns to the spirit of man. He is the life force that keeps going, the eternal flame, the flame that keeps burning, youthful energy, rather than aging. It is this flame that goes out when one commits suicide.

Usually when one draws the picture of the sun, the color is normally yellow but here the sun is white, which is another clue that the energy of the Fool is pure and comes from the source of creation, spirit and God's energy. He is the human soul.

NUMEROLOGY

The number zero has no beginning or end. It means all or nothing. It has a deeper meaning, deeper knowledge and deeper understanding. An infinity symbol that goes round and round – the circle of life and the seed.

The zero is The Ohm, the primordial sound is a powerful sound. Once again it is cyclic because when you start you take in a breath and when you make the sound, it peaks and then as you lose the breath, you have to take in another breath and round you go again.

It is interesting that Arthur Waite called the Fool 'the Fool' and not the Hero. The Major Arcana begins with the Fool, the Journey of the Fool. The word Fool has two zeros in it.

When he reaches his destination, he will become something.

In many tarot games the Fool is the most valuable card and it takes on the number twenty-two. Known as the highest Wild Card or Trump card, for example the Joker is wild.

ASTROLOGY

The planet that connects well with this card is Jupiter. Jupiter is all about expansion, trust, faith, higher beliefs, higher learning and higher knowledge.

Jupiter rules Sagittarius – the ninth house of the zodiac. It is a fire element; this always attracts them to the exciting and the new. Sagittarians are interested in law, religion and mysticism, hence their belief system is a big issue as is the outdoor life.

Sagittarians love to exaggerate. They cannot help themselves – it is the fire in them. They get excited, they are exciting to be around and this attracts people to them.

Sagittarius also loves to travel, to explore and experience the totality of the place. But a true Sagittarian does not like to fly; they need to keep their four legs on the ground, suggesting they may travel by car, train or via a book. You can see that the Fool looks like a traveler with his kit bag over his shoulder.

Quite often Sagittarians are known as the eternal bachelor. They want to always be free. There is a song that goes 'Wherever I Lay My Hat (That's My Home)' by Paul Young.

The best thing for Sagittarius is to commit to doing something – whether it is commitment to a relationship, buying a house or starting a business. It is the commitment that will truly make them feel free. They need a base that they can always return back too, otherwise they will be lost wandering around.

MYTHOLOGY

In Mythology, the god Dionysus connects well with the Fool energy. Dionysus is always portrayed as being 'off his tree,' he seems to have two left feet. Dionysus is known as the God of wine and the God of ecstasy. He is about no inner bitterness. He is about letting yourself go, having fun and pleasure.

When one has a glass of wine you do let go, but when you have too much wine you are not in control anymore, but the fool is. When someone has had a few too many drinks you often hear people say, "They are making a fool of themselves" or "What a drunken fool". You can actually see the retard come out.

The Fool refers to 'Il Matto' in most Italian tarot decks translating as 'The Madman' or a 'Vagabond.' He usually is depicted as someone poor with no shoes and carrying all his worldly possessions in his kit bag over his shoulder.

When I was teaching the Fool tarot card one night in class, the very next day I saw an article that read:

One drink's good, two is bad: get drinking for the good of your health – just not too much or you'll undo all the benefits. Canadian scientists have found a glass of alcohol once a day is good for your heart and blood vessels, but a second erases the positive effects. After a drink, volunteers' blood vessels were more dilated, which reduced the work for the heart. But after two drinks, the heart rate, amount of blood pumped and the action of the nervous system all increased.

Every time we explored a tarot card, everyone in the class (including myself), would connect to something throughout the week that would connect us to the card's energy. Even reading this book is enough to invoke the Fool's energy within yourself. So throughout the day make a mental note about your connections or write these experiences in your journal as you explore each card.

SYMBOLOGY

This symbology section is a huge section. We will cover many areas; some will be intricate stories and others will be intriguing. All this goes towards your deeper understanding of the tarot and how we can connect the metaphysical tarot to our physical outer world.

Remember that symbology should be easy because it is happening around us all the time, for example; we all dream. The Tarot just makes you become more aware or conscious of what is unconscious.

Gold Background Color

Let's begin with looking at the background color of the Fool tarot card. Is it a yellow background? No, it is a gold background. Compare the background color of the Fool card with the background color of the Magician card. The Fool tarot card is the only card with a gold background color.

How strange is this? First we have a sun that should be yellow but is white and now we have the only gold background of all the cards. What does the gold color mean? Gold connects us to the divine, the force, God energy, higher awareness and knowledge, our higher self, our superconscious and the energy that is above our normal level – the force that is stronger than you alone.

This gold color alone is telling us that the Fool card is very special, that we have all come from the source. We often call our Sun the source; we come from oneness and we are born into duality.

Yellow Hair

The yellow hair symbolizes that the Fool contains all possibilities to create whatever he wants.

Yellow connects us to the mind and ideas, the intellect, knowledge and expansion, having a great imagination and great vision.

Red Feather

The Red Feather in his cap suggests he is confident and sure of himself. You often hear one say when someone has done a good job "That's another feather in your cap". It means you have done well, achieved something and that you are agile and assertive.

The feather also corresponds to birds and angels; birds connect us with Spirit, a spiritual messenger coming from above.

The color red suggests a passion for life, our desires, action, energy and courage.

This feather in the cap always reminds me of the actor Errol Flynn playing the character *Robin Hood*. Swinging through the trees and standing on a branch high up in the trees, it is a classical Fool pose. Robin Hood also wore a short skirt, tights, boots and a feather in his cap. He was cocky and always surrounded by his merry men. He robbed from the rich and gave to the poor whilst having fun with his merry men.

White Dog

Animals in the tarot correspond to our primal animal instincts. They represent the five senses and our individual nature desires.

Here we have a white dog on the left side of the Fool. The color white suggests purity and being on the left side connects us to the unconscious feminine side.

Dogs are usually tame and loyal companions to their owners. They are known as man's best friend. This suggests that your primal instincts are loyal to you and only you. Allow your animal instincts to lead you, trust your loyal companion to move you forward.

I have always found it interesting that we have a dog here and not a wolf. The Fool is still in spiritual form — he is not born yet. Why not the wolf where the energy is still untamed, natural and wild? Having the dog suggests that the spirit is tamed or controlled in some way. Maybe it suggests it is already conscious.

The other interesting point I would like to make about the dog is that it has its paw across the Fool's foot, as if it is holding his foot back from stepping forward. The Fool looks up and trusts his mate the dog to steer him so that he does not stumble and fall off the edge.

White Rose

The white flower the Fool holds in his left side suggests purity. It is the only white rose you will see in this whole tarot deck.

The rose connects us to his purity, innocence of heart and his appreciation of beauty and his pure essence. You can see the freedom in his pose because of this essence.

The Fool's Dress

Straight away the white undergarment suggests he has inner purity. When a baby is born, we first dress them in a white singlet, put white nighties on them and use white sheets. Basically everything is white.

His colorful dress brings forth all the colors of the universe. His big sleeves look like wings, suggesting he has flare and that he is open to all possibilities. You can see the orange on the inner sleeve suggesting he has courage and that it does or does not take a lot of courage to be open.

The belt he wears has seven visible ornaments. The number seven is attributed to having certain magical properties. Seven is a number of great powers, a lucky number of secrecy and the search for inner truth. I like to call the number seven God's number because on the seventh day he rested and reflected on what he did. There are seven days of the week that we received through the Sumerians and their twenty eight day cycle of the moon. There are seven colors in the rainbow, seven musical notes and seven chakras to name but a few.

There are also ten wheels on his outfit representing the ten planets and the zodiac. This shows me that the Fool knows the answers to life, universe and to everything. These ten wheels also connect me to the Ten Commandments and the Ten Hermetic Principles.

Wand

The wand the Fool holds over his right shoulder is a measuring tool and the symbol of his will. His will power connects us to the flame of eternal life.

Travelers are always seen with this type of wand and their kit bag over their shoulder suggesting that a journey or a voyage is underway. Wanderers and hermits hold a lot of wisdom from all their traveling. The Fool, our spirit, is traveling through the universe and bringing wisdom with him into our world.

This wand over his right shoulder on the conscious side represents our will power. This is a stark contrast to where he standing – on the edge of a precipice, the unknown or the unconscious.

Wallet

The wallet at the end of the wand has a flap sewn with ten stitches on it. Once again the ten stitches correspond to the ten planets, the ten Hermetic Principles and the Ten Commandments.

I looked up the word hermetic and it means "of alchemy or magic". Alchemy was founded by Hermes. Hermes was a great magician who we will explore more in the Magician tarot card. Alchemy is known as a medieval chemistry attempting to turn base metals into gold to find the elixir of life. I wonder if this is where Fool's Gold comes from. And we still have alchemists with us today, better known as chemists.

Hermetic also connects us to the Hermit and one that lives alone. Just like the Fool traveling through his journey alone. Also, we are born by ourselves and we will eventually all die by ourselves.

The wallet has a lock on it. When you lock your wallet, you protect all your personal valuables, your worldly possessions and the untapped collective knowledge. The wallet may hold your past experiences or secrets, your essence of your memories and all your personal previous lifetimes.

On the wallet you can see a picture of an eagle's head, which connects us to the zodiac sign of Scorpio. Scorpio rules or represents our sexuality and through sexuality we create new life and new Fools. It could also represent your inner eye through which we can tap into the secrets.

We do have access to the contents of the wallet. I believe through tarot or past life regressions and other such like modalities, we can tap into the secrets of the wallet.

All the experiences of our past life we bring with us. This also lends itself to reincarnation and being reborn again and again through many lifetimes and each time we are reborn, we bring all our past experiences and knowledge with us. I am sure you have heard the saying 'We are all born with baggage.'

The Wand and Wallet together represents our will power and essence of our past experiences.

Icy Mountain Peaks

In the background you can see white icy peaks representing cold abstract principles held in high esteem.

The Fool ignores that they are there but they are there to remind us of the polarities; that nature can be both warm and cruel. They remind us of our life's journey, our troughs and peaks or simply our ups and downs in life.

The blue connects us with our emotions and our deeper unconscious issues.

A Leap of Faith

IN A READING

When the Fool tarot card comes up in a reading, it suggests that the client is going through a state of life power just before the beginning of a new cycle of self-expression. The Spirit is in search of experience.

The Fool is about inexperience, spontaneity, impulsiveness, having no judgements and depicting folly. The energy of the fool knows nothing as is and contains all possibilities to create whatever he wants. He is a dreamer. He is foolhardy and lives in a fool's paradise. He does not have a care in the world. He is resilient.

Spontaneous to all the possibilities of life, he is a dreamer; he is courageous and full of optimism. Totally trusting, Trust is his middle name. Innocence and naivety like a child. One of my favorite sayings is, 'Dare to be Naïve.'

His stance is always looking off towards tomorrow; therefore, he is always able to have faith. Tomorrow will always be better than today. The Fool's energy is about recreation, restlessness and therefore the urge to create.

Your client may be actually experiencing flutterings of anticipation, butterflies in their tummy or (as they say) ants in their pants as if they intuitively know that something is about to happen. This person wants a new life adventure. It is hard for them to be held back; they do not want to stay in their current position.

They feel alive, they can feel their inner life energy, they want to create something new and they will take the risk, or the 'Leap of Faith' to do it. Sometimes they have no choice; they have to jump into it. They have itchy feet or sitting on the edge of their seat.

They want to reinvent themselves; they feel energized with nervous creation energy. Something is about to burst out of them; they will throw caution to the wind.

This card may indicate that a significant change is about to happen.

Total trust and no fear, even if they can't see where they are going. Like the analogy of parachuting, you don't know if the chute is going to open but you will jump. You do not know where you will land either but you will land somewhere.

The courage to take fresh steps in unknown circumstances. Confronting your fears and taking risks. At times, this can be a cliff hanging experience.

The Fool is pumped and he can feel the adrenaline pumping through the course of his veins. Overall, the Fool has enthusiasm to follow his dreams. When you do you may hear other people say "What a Fool," but the Fool is saying "I am not a Fool. You are the fool for not following your dreams". This is one of the keys to this card.

I am Not the Fool

The Fool also connects us with the Joker in the normal playing deck of cards. He is also known as the Jester. The Jester is like a clown: jovial and he makes people laugh. I think this is the hardest act to do. Anyone can make people cry but to make people really laugh is an art.

Jesters in the court days of kings and queens had special privileges in the castle. They would wander around and be the eyes and ears of the King. Then through song, poetry or merriment, the Jester would report back to the king of what was happening under their roof.

Shamanic healers and medicine men of tribes would also have special privileges and were often excused for their somewhat strange behaviors.

The following shadow words may also be used for reversed card meanings.

Note that the tarot cards do not have to be reversed for it to have a negative meaning. All the cards hold a positive and negative energy. It depends on the question, what

position the card is in, what it is next too. It may also depend on the client if they are a doer or a reactor. There are many interpretations and many levels to the cards, explore them all and give your client the best possibilities and scenarios for them to consider the best course of action.

SHADOWS	KEYS
Irresponsibility	Versatile
Out of control	Novice
Unrealistic	Innovative
Lack of focus	Eagerness
Recklessness	Fresh ideas
Eccentric	Enthusiastic
Erratic	Cheerfulness
Elusive	Young at heart
Stupid	Element of chance
Rebellious	Extrovert
Foolish	Daring
Rebellious	Keen
Thoughtless	Passionate
Lawless	Beginner's luck
Madness	Carefree
Immature	Innocence
Impulsive	Joy
Daring	Trust
Risking	Faith
Beggar	Taking a risk
Tricky	Fearless
Crazy	Travel
	Adventure
	Pollyanna
	Jovial
	Mystical cleverness
	Laughter
	Lightness
	Spontaneous

To evoke the energy of each tarot card, I have created action steps. You may like to try some of the following suggestions:

Tarot in Action

Be spontaneous, allow yourself to be a little foolish and carefree.
Plan a travel trip.
Create a new routine.
Lighten up.
Be a little foolish.
Follow your dreams.
Have one drink.
Play with your dog.
Laugh and the world laughs with you.
Draw a caricature of yourself and ask others what they think.
Eat something different. Wear something different.
You are a genius.

Quotes

Einstein's definition of insanity: 'A Fool is someone that does the same thing over and over, expecting a different result.'

'The glass is half full attitude.'

'Today is the first day of the rest of my life.'

'Fools rush in where Angels fear to tread.'

'Don't suffer fools lightly.'

'Beginner's Luck.'

'Tripping the Lights Fantastic.'

'Laugh and the world laughs with you.'

Books to Read

Magical Child by Joseph Chilton Pearce.
Journey to Lxtlan by Carlos Castenada.

Chapter 5

...The journey begins with The Fool meeting his divine parents. First he meets The Magician and learns about the power of manifestation...

I THE MAGICIAN

SUMMARY

This card is passive masculine indirect energy. The Magician is our animus and he is about our willpower. He could also be a renegade.

The Magician has to do with the intellect, your intelligence and the mind. It is our mind that separates us from animals. We humans use the frontal lobe and animals operate instinctively, in this way we are superior to nature. The frontal lobe is substantially more developed in humans and this area of the human brain is associated with intelligence.

The Magician is a juggler, an occultist, a practitioner and an artist. He presents the opportunity to tap into the divine motive of man. Scholarly and spiritual knowledge.

NUMEROLOGY

The number one is about power, independence and control. It has leadership and pioneering qualities. It is connected to the Spirit of Air. It is about the self and our ego, can also be self-indulgent.

Sometimes number one people can really feel alone but they are not lonely because they have so much to do. As they say, "It's lonely at the top". They understand this yet they are active people with lots of irons in different fires.

Number one energy is unique. It has originality and is strong willed.

ASTROLOGY

There are two planets that connect well with this card.

The first planet is Mercury. Mercury is the Roman name for Messenger of the Gods. Hermes is the Greek name. Mercury connects us with the air element, to the mind, thoughts, ideas and is all about communication.

Mercury rules two zodiac signs, Gemini and Virgo. Mercury plays out differently in both signs but ultimately it has to do with the mind. Perhaps that is why many Gemini and Virgo people come together because they connect on that mind level.

The Magician wears a red robe and this brings in the energy of Mars. We know the planet Mars as a little red hot angry masculine planet. It is the color red because it actually is rusted.

Mars is the Roman name and Aries is the Greek name, also known as Ares. The God Mars is known as the God of War – he was a courageous God. Mars is known for his distrust and vengeful side, as well as his determined and assertive side. The color red is about action and desire.

MYTHOLOGY

Hermes from the Greeks was said to be a great magician, a master magician, a magic man, and a healer. He had the wand of miracles and one story goes that he would wave his wand and people would fall asleep. He was a great communicator, charismatic and known as a messenger of the Gods.

Hermes founded alchemy and the Hermetic Principles. He was also associated with movement, action, the wind, profit (both lawful and unlawful) and games of chance. Hermes was called upon in matters of knowledge, commerce, healing and magic.

He was also the messenger of the Gods, a task which he carried out with great diplomacy and tact. Later he became an Emissary to God Hades, the patron of travelers both in this world and the next, where he was a conductor of souls.

People that come to my mind with this amazing ability of great communication are people like, John F. Kennedy. His words still make my hairs stand on end. 'Don't ask what your country can do for you, but what you can do for your country.' Another is Martin Luther King when he said, 'I have a dream.' What about Hitler? He too was an amazing communicator that turned a whole nation around. The nation was very hungry and poor in the 1920's and 30's, and so when someone comes along with a powerful vision, it is enthralling, enrapturing an entire nation.

I think the best example of all is Jesus. Jesus is always portrayed as wearing red and white robes just like in The Magician card. Jesus was a fine orator that attracted many. He too performed miracles and was a healer.

In old decks The Magician is known as the Magnus, and often seen as juggling balls and cups.

The Magician also connects with the Egyptian God Thoth, a God of the Moon, knowledge, writing and magic.

SYMBOLOGY

Yellow Background

You can see the yellow background in the Magician card is distinctive compared to the gold background of the Fool card.

The color yellow connects to the air element. Connects to communication, the creative mind, the intellect and all possibilities. It is a bright happy color, just like sitting outside in the sunshine, it makes us feel warm and friendly, happy to chat the day away.

The Word Magic

Magic connects us to ancient name for science, a Hermetic name for science. In the old way it was spelt Magik, Magick, Magickal and Magickian.

What we are really talking about here is the magic power of the mind. Positive thinking, affirmations and mind over matter. It is about setting intentions, willing something to happen mantras, incantations and meditations.

When you invoke an intention, providence steps in and manifests it. When we say Amen or Blessed Be we are sealing the end results. This is the power of magic – you will it to happen. Humans can create our destiny.

Everything originates and is created first in the mind. Without the idea first how can you create it? How do you know what steps and what direction to take? How do you know what to work on? How can you create something if you have no idea?

The Red Robe

The color red brings in the desires, our desirous nature, our actions and fiery qualities. It connects us with that masculine energy from Mars, the active conscious, ambitious and assertive energy.

White Undergarments

These connect us to our purity, our naiveté and innocence, our inner purity and our pure will. Having pure intentions and a pure heart.

Red and White Robes together

The meaning of these two items coming together represents the magic of the power of positive thinking.

Our pure will and desires are associated with action, choice and force. Therefore, through our pure desires we manifest our reality.

Ouroboros Belt

The Magician wears the ouroboros as his belt. The ouroboros is a dragon or serpent biting his own tail. It demonstrates joining the two ends together to create balance; joining heaven and earth, desires with reality, metaphysical with the physical, the beginning with the end, now with eternity and so on.

The serpent is a symbol of great wisdom. Therefore, the ouroboros represents cycles, transformation, eternal wisdom forever turning, forever moving, learning and growing.

In the dictionary it is defined as: (Classical Myth & Legend) an ancient mythical serpent used to symbolize perpetuity.

Lemniscate

The figure eight above the Magician's head is representative of the infinity symbol, known as the Lemniscate.

It is an auspicious symbol of infinity and dualism and is just like the symbolism of the snake shedding its skin. It represents cycles and transformation.

In the dictionary it is defined as: (Mathematics) a closed plane curve consisting of two symmetrical loops meeting at a node. Equation: $(x^2 + y^2)2 = a2(x^2 - y^2)$, where a is the greatest distance from the curve to the origin. The symbol for infinity (∞) is an example.

Roses on the Top

First of all, the roses are red, which connects us to our will and to our desires. It symbolizes that you do have the power to create whatever you want in your life. The question you have to ask yourself is how much do I really want it?

Remember everything in life is motivated one way or other, so why not ask for what it is you really want. Remember the new born baby when it screams for what it desires. We all have the power to demand what we want.

Green Leaves

The green leaves represent a lush environment, a lot of creativity, flexibility and adaptability. It is a fresh and living fertile color and is the potential of growth of his desires.

Black Hair

The Magician has black hair and this is interesting because the color black signifies ignorance, un-manifested light and represents the unknown.

I love the fact the Magician understands that he does not know everything and he cannot really believe that he knows everything either. This leaves it open for him to learn more. Maybe we are not meant to know everything and that all of our life is spent learning.

Sometimes I feel that the more I learn, the less I know. You can say that the only thing the Magician really knows is nothing.

White Band around his Head

This is also interesting because having this restraint around the brain symbolizes a form of restriction. Maybe in his ignorance he knows everything then knows nothing.

It also connects well with his black hair and the lemniscate above his head. It makes me think about how our left brain and right brain work. The left brain just knows things; it is logical and wants to know the beginning and the ending, what name to call things and what box to put it in. The right brain understands that the universe is forever and ever, and accepts it as it is with no question. This is the constant battle we are dealing with every day.

Uplifted Right Hand

He points to the Red Roses above his head. He is pointing to his desires, points to the source, like tapping into the cosmos. Pointing to the mental power and drawing it down from above. The right hand is active, conscious, masculine energy. He is conscious that he is drawing his desires down and into reality and the material plain. He has the ability to bridge the gap between Heaven and Earth.

White Wand

The white wand looks like a phallic symbol; it also looks like an aerial, holding it out into the universe, tapping into all that universal energy.

It also connects to the Fool's wand. This time the wand is burning at both ends.

Left Hand Pointing Down

He is directing his power down, drawing his desires down on to the material plain. The power can be manifested into the physical reality. They say God plants the seed from the source and man grows it.

As Above so Below

I would say the key to this card is 'as above so below' or 'as within so without'. Tap into it above and ground it below. The lesson from one realm is then to master another lesson in the next realm. The Magician can transcend duality.

One needs to watch what they are really asking for, because you might just get it and it may not be what you thought it would be.

The Table

On the table, the Magician's field of attention, are the four suits that signify the elements of our natural life and our world. There are also magical symbols around the edges around the table.

The Magician's ability can arrange his life in proper order. He can organize himself. He has all the tools he needs, he has the tools of trade and they are our resources. He has learned the fundamental elements of the universe.

The four implements on the table correspond to the four ancient esoteric principles: To Will (Wand), To Know (Cup), To Dare (Sword) and Silent to keep hidden (Pentacle).

They could also correspond to the four Noble Truths: Life is suffering (Wand), Cause of Suffering (Cup), Learn new ways (Sword) and Cure it (Pentacle).

The Magician's Garden

The Magician's garden is opposite to the Fool's open spaces. The Magician's garden is fertile. This garden connects us to the subconscious mind and how fertile our mind really is; hence we have to watch what we tell ourselves. The garden shows us that we can cultivate and manifest our desires. Once again it connects us with our willpower and how to create in the conscious world. We all want to create that something special in the world.

There are red roses and white lilies in this cultured garden. The red roses symbolize our desires and what we are passionate about and all our loves. What you really want. All desires are related to our senses and there are five roses that connect to our five senses.

The white lilies connect us to our abstract thoughts, our ideals and our inner purity. These two flowers in this garden show us that we do get what we truly desire but we also get what we need.

Just like that *Rolling Stone* song, "You can't always get what you want, but you get what you need". An example I can give you is; one day I wanted to purchase a particular pair of red shoes and when I finally went to the shop to buy them, they did not have my size. So I resigned myself to the black pair. Two weeks later I remember thinking how pleased I was that I did purchase the black pair because I have more wear from them.

The red and white robes of the Magician also connect us to the red roses and white lilies.

The Magician Has the Ability to Arrange his Life in Proper Order

IN A READING

When The Magician's card shows up in a reading, it may be time for people to be aware of their own power or maybe they are already feeling powerful and confident. The message is to tap into one's potential rather than holding oneself back.

All magic is in the will, the willpower. The willpower is connected to the true source. It is about pure intentions, not egotistical intentions to make things happen in the world. There are choices and directions to take.

You will succeed because you are coming from your true self, your integrity. It is the true self that is connected to the source. Therefore, the power of your will is always directed with success.

The mind is your magic wand. Words are tools and once you know and understand the meaning of the word, you have power. Knowledge is power. They also say the pen is mightier than the sword. According to Dr. R. Buckminster Fuller, words are man's best ever invention.

Getting clarity, gaining understanding, it is a good time to set your intention, standing tall in your power and cutting through communication issues. Great ideas may come through when we have clarity of mind.

With clear communication, it is a good time to write a letter, this card suggests it should be easier for you to access your thoughts and write your new ideas down on paper in the real world.

A great time for meetings, a brain storming session, going for interviews or having people over for a dinner party.

In the negative sense, you may confront a witty person, someone that is clever or playing mind games with you. He may not have your best interests in mind. You may be also confronting your own ego and intoxication of that willpower.

My father always told me that if you do not use your mind you will use your hands. Remember what you think you ultimately will become, so careful what you ask for.

SHADOWS	KEYS
Too intellectual	Discrimination
Skeptical	Dexterity
Con man	Writer
False façade	Self-determined
Trickster	Thoughtful
Able to justify anything	Concentration
Acting all the time	Affirmation
Cunning / Sly	Full exchange of belief & ideas
Coaxing	Research
Indecision	Language
Abuse of power	Good PR
Shifty	Author

SHADOWS	KEYS
Confusion	Linguistic
Manipulating	Diligent
Petty criminal	Vigilant
Car salesman	Confident
Tyrant	Public speaker
Stalker	Actor
Monkey mind	Multitasking
Bully	Intelligent
Secretive	Engage
Illusions	Multi-lingual
Lost	Magic
Clever mind games	Charming
Impractical	Willpower
Stagnation	Communicator
Chaos	As above so below
Lies	Action
	Consciousness
	Personal power
	Practicality
	Energy
	Creativity
	Movement
	Precision
	Conviction
	Self-confident
	Being objective
	Focused
	Determination
	Courageous
	Clarity
	Soul wisdom

Tarot in Action

Have a magical day or week.
Set goals, set intentions.
Explore the unseen.
Question things.
Think before you speak, think before you act.
Discuss things that need to be discussed.
Write affirmations.
Put your thoughts into action.
Do something alchemical e.g. bake a cake.
Create a vision board or vision album.
The use of mind over matter.
Focus your attention.
Going in the right direction.
Start a blog.
Write a book, write poetry.
Thoughts into action.
Capable of performing miracles.

Quotes

'There are no such things as pure men; just pure intentions.' – Kevin Costner in Robin Hood.

'A good wizard is never a minute late or a minute early, he arrives precisely when he means to.' – Gandalf, Lord of the Rings.

'Today knowledge is your greatest asset.' – Ruanna.

Books to Read

The Alchemist by Paolo Coello.
The Magician's Way by William Whitecloud.

Movies to Watch

Aladdin.
Harry Potter.
Lord of the Rings.
The Magician.

Chapter 6

*...The Fool now meets his divine mother
The High Priestess and learns about his intuition...*

II THE HIGH PRIESTESS

SUMMARY

The High Priestess represents dualism. If the Magician is Adam, then the High Priestess is Eve. They are our celestial parents, our godparents.

The High Priestess is the anima; feminine energy, passive, receptive and indirect. She does not talk to you in the normal way. She speaks to you through your dreams and via your intuition so you can sense things. The High Priestess represents your perception and intuition.

NUMEROLOGY

The number two is all about the creation of balance. This is the power and the realms of the feminine. She is the middle pillar. The feminine is equal to two. It is the woman that carries the child whether that child is male or female.

We see this instantly with the black and white pillars shown on the card. The white pillar connects us to the Magician – the masculine energy of mind, active and conscious. The black pillar connects us to the High Priestesses' energy – our unconscious, inactive and feminine energy.

The High Priestess does not lean towards one side or the other; she stands in her own energy; she is the middle pillar. This is another reason why she has an almost blank look on her face. She is not too happy or too sad; she just understands that not too far in the future things will turn around again.

In the diagram the black pillar with the triangle pointing down represents feminine and the white pillar with the triangle pointing up represents masculine and the middle pillar is the union of both.

ASTROLOGY

The moon is the astrological ruler of this card. The High Priestess is referred to as the Moon Goddess. The moon rules our emotions, our feelings and the feminine intuition. The moon connects us to the water element.

We also refer to the moon as Mother Moon. The moon rules the zodiac sign of Cancer. Cancer rules the home, family, our heritage and our roots. Our relationship with mother, how we perceived mothering to be.

There are various rituals in many cultures held around the time of the full moon when the energy is at its peak.

The moon rules the feminine cycles, although not so much nowadays. During the full moon is when the gravity is at its strongest and we all notice there is more emotional activity during this time. I always say to be aware of the full moon time. It is an irrational time and a time not to make any major decisions, but it is a good time to reflect as the moon reflects the sun light. You can see the moonlight is shining on her clothes.

MYTHOLOGY

The great story of Persephone connects with this card. Persephone became the Queen of the underworld and our inner world. The story goes that the God Hades fell deeply in love with her and he talked his brother Zeus in assisting him to abduct her and take her down to the underworld.

When Persephone was in the underworld, Hades offered her a pomegranate to eat. She did not want it at first, but then she realized that she could not be her mothers' daughter forever so she ate three granules of the pomegranate. You can see the pomegranates on the veil behind her.

When Persephone's mother Demeter, Queen of Agriculture found out what happened to her daughter, she made everything die. So a deal was struck between God Hades, God Zeus, Persephone and Goddess Demeter. Persephone was to come to the surface for six months of the year to be with her mother. This is when we have spring and summer and all is in full bloom. Then when it is time for Persephone to leave and go back down to the underworld, we have autumn and winter because Demeter is sad once again without her daughter. This is the mythology as to how the seasons came about.

Other mythological stories that entail single ladies are stories like the Vestal Virgins and the Delphic Oracle and the Great Goddesses like Kaali, Lilith and the Morrigan. We also have Medusa, Mary Magdalene and the Lady of the Lake. In other tarot cards she is also known as 'La Papessa'.

The High Priestess connects very well with the Virgin Mary; you can see she wears the colors blue and white and wears the cross, the symbol of Christianity, unity and duality. The Virgin Mary represents the symbol of virginity. Nuns also wear the veil, maybe not so much now-a-days though.

The High Priestess is known as the ice maiden. The energy of the High Priestess is meant to be frigid, pure and untouched.

She is the sacred feminine and represents secret women's business. When a woman has had her time with having babies and being a mother she can return to the pure energy of the High Priestess and she is then referred to as the Crone, Granny's wisdom, the Chief female elder and the Wise Woman.

The High Priestess Talks To You Through Your Intuition And Dreams

The story of Lilith also connects to the High Priestess card. Lilith known as the Feared and the Fearless. Basically, Lilith was the first wife of Adam, I was never taught anything about her at primary school and felt annoyed that she was never mentioned. Today, I understand they probably did not know anything about her energy or just did not acknowledge her existence. I can totally relate to her today.

SYMBOLOGY

The Veil

You can see the veil is hanging like a curtain between the two pillars behind the High Priestess. The veil is hanging in front of the horizon of the sea and this symbolizes that we are cut off from the Sea of Knowledge, the Sea of Wisdom, the Sea of Unconscious and our inner knowledge. We are cut off from the greater mysteries and she guards these mysteries of the deep.

The veil represents the hymen and virginity. The veil is intact and still holds the virginal energy. Just like a wedding veil or Holy Communion veil, we still play out these rituals of wearing the veil today.

Behind the veil you can see pomegranates symbolizing fertility and abundance. The pomegranates represent the feminine fertility, also known as the fruit of love or the forbidden fruit. It represents the reproductive system and the undeveloped creative potential.

The palms and green ferns are phallic looking and represent male fertility. Once again, these images are showing us the dual aspects of the High Priestesses' energy.

The Color Blue

Blue is the color of feelings and emotions. The blue water connects us with the receptive nature of the ocean. Water is life and retains memory.

This is her energy. She is the sea of power. Her energy rules telepathy, prophecy, psychic ability and intuitive powers. She rules all these realms.

Her blue robes demonstrate a coldness. Her clothes also look like water; you can see how her skirt flows into the water behind her. This water will flow into the Empress card, the Emperor card and throughout other tarot cards.

Her Crown

Her crown looks like two quarter moons on both sides and the full moon in the center. The moon rules the cycles of life and corresponds to our feelings and intuition. You can see three faces of the moon like the Trinity. Some say that she wears the pearl as her crown.

There is also a crest moon at her feet. This controls the tides, the orb and tides, the ebb and flow of our lives. Our stream of consciousness.

The moon shades over things. Sometimes we are in the dark; the moon does cloud over things, sometimes we know and sometimes we are unknowing.

Scroll

The scroll has TORA written on it. It connects us back to the Jewish book of knowledge. The Old Testament also known as the Five Books of Moses.

The Two Pillars

Connects us with the Temples of ISIS and Solomon's Temple. These two pillars were bronze with images of ferns and pomegranates (masculine and feminine) around the top and the interior of the temple had black and white checkered floors.

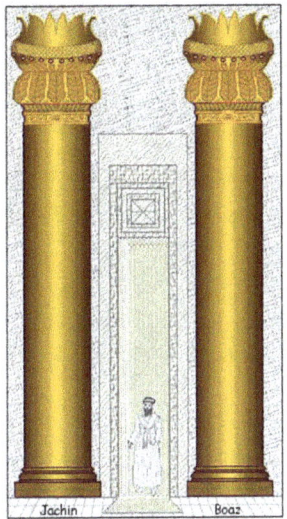

The bronze pillars before the porch of Solomon's Temple. On the right was Jachin; on the left Boaz – *I Kings 7:21*

The two pillars, one black and one white, represents the darkness, mystery of the unconscious mind and intuition in contrast with the conscious mind. The Balancing of yes/no, light/dark, positive/negative, etc.

The B on the black pillar stands for Boaz or Boas. Boas was the great grandfather of David. Jesus was born in the House of David. The David we are referring to was the same David that fought the giant. He later became King David. King David was also the father of King Solomon.

J on the whiter pillar stands for Jachin, Yakin or Joaquin. Joaquin was the name of the father of the Virgin Mary. Yakin also means surety, certainty and stability.

Yakin and Boaz were said to also be mystics in the Temple of Solomon.

The High Priestess Is Your Inner Knowing

IN A READING

The High Priestess does not have human emotions. She is the queen of universal love not human love. It is like how God loves us love, how the Virgin Mary loves us, this is Divine Love.

She represents things that are hidden from us, dark and mysterious things. The veil is up. We need to see through the veil. Something will be revealed or you are holding onto the truth – read between the lines. She is the secret keeper.

The High Priestess connects us to the subconscious role of woman. Women are supposed to know things and hold powerful feminine influences. This is above human frailty. Remember this energy is formed in the womb, therefore we are all born psychic. When I get a call from a client wanting to book a reading, I often get asked, "Are you psychic?" My reply always is, "We are all psychic". "How often does your phone ring and you know exactly who it is?"

The card suggests all has not been revealed. Like the processes of menstrual cycle, we do not really know when a woman has her period. This card represents the hidden internal, and the women's reproductive system is all on the inside. Sure, some women that have done a lot of work on themselves may understand their bodies more than others, have learned to read the signs and can pin-point the exact arrival time.

We only see one face of the moon. Our emotions are controlled by the moon. The High Priestess reflects this glory. A long time ago in our evolution, the women's cycle was in sync with the full moon. There are many various cultures that have all had moon tents, stationed outside the community and down wind, where the woman and her family would be looked after by their mothers or daughters.

When the High Priestess shows up in your spread she is saying to trust your initiative and your feelings, you will get your answers from within. When the Magician shows up he says to go for it logically.

The High Priestess may represent a perfect woman in a man's life, or an independent woman, perhaps a solo woman without a man.

SHADOWS	KEYS
Superstitious	Premonition
Nostalgic	Deja Vu
Lack of maternal instinct	Reminder
Uncontrollable fantasies	Clairvoyance – clear seeing
Emotional insecurity	Clairaudience – clear hearing
Hidden opponents	Claircognizance – clear knowing
Hidden obstacles	Clairalience – clear smelling
Unconscious desires	Clairambience – clear tasting
Feminism	Psychometry – reads jewelry
Feelings are blocked	Mediums
Not wanting to be known	Telepathic
Mystery	Impressions
Puritan	Empathic
Cloister - nun like	Insight
Sexual manipulation	Knowingness
Frigid	Receiving
Hallucinations	Sanctuary
Prudish	Impregnation
Dementia	Fluids
Psychotic	Gut Feelings
Bi-polar	Channeling

SHADOWS	KEYS
Fantasies	Visions
Schizophrenia	Reiki
Secretive	Seichim
	Dreams
	Pendulums
	Astral traveling
	Intuitive
	Inner Wisdom
	Neuro Linguistic Programs
	Understanding
	Independence
	Dreams
	Feminine Intuition
	Astral traveling
	Understanding
	Mystery
	Divine Love
	Sound Judgement
	Receptiveness
	Mystical visions
	Introspective
	Otherworldliness
	Spiritual love

Tarot in Action

Sense who is calling you on the phone.
Sense who knocks on the door.
Meditate.
Start a dream journal.
Flips cards over to see if you pick up what it is.
Read about astral traveling.
Practice Psychometry. Hold in your a piece of jewelry and see if you can sense something, and image or a color.
Empty your mind and see what feelings and images come to your mind.
Your ability to relate to women.

Quotes

'Behind every good man is a good woman.' – Anon.

'The power of intuitive understanding will protect you from harm until the end of your days.' – Lao Tzu.

'The channels of intuitive knowledge are opened according to the intensity of individual need.' – Jane Roberts.

Book to read

Women that Run with the Wolves by Clarissa Pinkola Estes.

These first three Major Arcana are the main energies. The Fool, The Magician and The High Priestess are the most powerful archetypes. We inherent these three energies before we are born. As we go through the rest of the Major Arcana cards, they will appear throughout the deck in different forms.

The Fool connects us to our Soul/Anima, Spirit/Animus, and Superconscious.

The Magician connects us to the masculine energy, intellect, self-conscious and rational mind.

The High Priestess connects us with the feminine energy of receptivity, subconscious and the feeling energy.

Chapter 7

...It is time for The Fool to incarnate through his mortal parents. The Empress gives birth to The Fool she nurtures him and loves him...

III THE EMPRESS

SUMMARY

The Empress is about human love and the human heart's capability of loving. She is all about the love in your life.

She is the principle of pleasure and the principle of creation. The Fool is born through the Empress or the Empress gives birth to the Fool.

The Empress represents the creator of life, romance, art and women's business.

NUMEROLOGY

The number three is all about the concept of creation. When we add the Magician card number one and the High Priestess card number two together, they add up to three and the Empress energy. 1 + 2 = 3.

The number three represents fertility and fecundity. When two people come together they create a third.

It is also the function of creativity. Joining the creative mind of the High Priestess and the rational mind of the Magician creates opportunity and possibility on a mental level before manifestation. It is about giving birth to something on the mental level and then into the physical plain.

ASTROLOGY

Venus is the astrological ruler of this card. You can see the symbol of Venus on the card. I like the way the center is colored in with green. Green is Venus's color. It also connects to the green heart chakra.

We know her as the Goddess of love, beauty and what we need to nourish ourselves, just like a mother loves her baby. This is also the symbol for woman.

Venus rules two zodiac signs, Taurus, an earth element, and Libra, an air element. Venus connects well with both these zodiac signs in different ways.

Taurus is all about security and self-worth. They love material possessions and are usually beautifully presented or the best they can afford. Taurus also loves food. Food is a form of nourishment and nurturing.

Libra wants harmony in her world and so does Venus; Venus and Libra play out more on a mental, rational and logical air level, rather than on the physical earthy level like in Taurus.

MYTHOLOGY

All the Goddesses are mothers that connect with the Empresses' energy like Aphrodite (Greek) and Venus (Roman). Venus and Ares had a son and they called him Eros, the God of Love.

Demeter – the mother of Persephone, Cleopatra, Goddess Isis and the Goddess Hera. They are all representatives of earth mothers. The feminine active intuitive energy, hence she is the principle of creation.

Gaia is the name we give to our living, breathing planet Earth.

The Empress is usually portrayed as pregnant, or pregnant with something. I like to think she is in gestation mode and just like that gestation period, it will take up to nine months to give birth to your baby or your project, your idea or your new endeavor.

The Venus symbol on the rock is colored green in the center. Green is Venus's color – it is the color of creativity, growth, and it is a living fertile color. Green also connects to the heart chakra and the symbol of love. The heart heals through love.

The Empress is the Principle of Creation

SYMBOLOGY

Pomegranates

The pomegranates are now on her gown. With the High Priestess, the pomegranates were hanging behind her on the veil. They were not a part of her.

With the Empress they are now a part of her, therefore she represents the embodiment of love, she is the fruit of love. It is the women that bear the fruit.

Red Shoes

The Empress sits with her legs open exuding sexuality. She also wears the red shoes depicting her sexual desires, hidden underneath. Today, wearing red shoes does not matter so much but in the early 1900's women who wore red shoes were considered ladies of the night or loose.

The shadow side of the Empress, if she truly is obsessed in a relationship, her energy can become possessive, jealous and vindictive.

Yellow Background

The yellow background connects us with the Magician card, to the mind and intellectual energy, in what you think you ultimately create. The yellow symbolizes the hopes and ideas of the mind.

Remember, you first have to have the thought before you can manifest it in reality. The Magician's intellect comes through on the subconscious level and is depicted through the background in this card.

The green environment of the Empress also connects us to the lush Magician's garden, representative of our subconscious fertile mind.

Cypress Trees

The trees in the background are cypresses. They are tenacious trees, hard to kill off and evergreen. The evergreen trees belong to the Goddess Venus. The energy connects us to Roman villas where the hillsides are lined with rows of cypress trees.

There is a main tree that is in the front of the cypress. I like to think of this special tree as a Silver Birch. This tree connects us to the Venus energy, beauty, harmony, the moon, fertility, protection, renewal and growth according to old Wales's folklore. Apparently wreaths made from the leaves of the Silver Birch were worn as love tokens.

The water that is flowing behind the Empress and through the trees is carried over from the High Priestess. All that greenery needs water to keep it growing, like the blood flowing through all living things. You can see everything is actively manifesting and the water is cascading in her Garden of Eden.

Jewelry

The Empress wears nine pearls as her necklace; these nine pearls connect us to the planets in our universe. Her crown has twelve stars that connect us with the twelve zodiac signs. The Empress wears the universe as her jewelry; she is the Queen of Heaven.

The scepter she holds is a symbol of sovereignty and her power over life. She has authority in her area, and rules women's business. The Empress holds the scepter in her right hand, she is conscious that she has this authority and she knows how to use it and protect it.

The Grey Platform

There is a grey platform underneath her seat and her feet, and also colorful fluffy cushions. There is focus on red and orange cushions connecting us to passion, desires and the courage to pursue them.

Grey is the color of wisdom, detachment, analysis and aloofness. She may come across as a push over but I would not bet on that.

Corn

The corn out the front of the card is symbolic of fertility. Connects to the Goddess Demeter, the Queen of Corn and the ruler of agriculture. She is the Queen of Nature and our Earth mother in the material and physical world, her dominion over life and growing things.

The Empress energy represents the life system, which exists on Planet Earth, or Gaia. And at the moment we are waking up to the Empresses' energy through all the environment issues that are going on.

The Empress Love Energy is Abundant and Unconditional

IN A READING

The Empress provides love as she stands for abundant and unconditional love. The question you have to ask yourself is how do I love? How passionate about life am I really?

The Empress represents human motherly love, all the nourishment and nurturing that a mother can provide to her baby. She represents fertility, that nine month gestation period, all the feminine sexuality and women's issues.

This card also represents all the ideas and hopes in the mind before manifestation, the creative energy in the mind as well as in the real world. How creative are you? How fertile is your mind?

The Empress is the concept of growth and productivity. It connects to bringing home the harvest, the corn. The Empress is like a cornucopia shell – forever spewing out magnificent abundant fruit.

Positive

The positive side of this card is being able to nurture yourself and others on a feeling level, able to provide sustenance for both.

Her energies are beneficial. She gives life and loves to celebrate life.

Negative

On a negative side we have that devouring, overprotective, possessive and smothering mother that does not know when to stop and start looking after herself. There comes a point in your life when you have to let go of mothering because you need to provide for yourself again.

Her negative energy can take away or challenge you, which can offend you, hurt you or break your heart. These challenges may let you to rise above the situation and satisfy your own needs, essentially to grow stronger.

Another negative could be withholding the love and nurturing energy because of the anger, fury and grief a woman may feel. For example, just like when Demeter made everything die when she found out her daughter was kidnapped and only when Persephone returns does she make things grow again.

Maiden

When you are doing a reading for someone who may be in their early twenties, note that they are at the beginning of a cycle. Therefore, we are looking at new mothering issues, beginning of relationships, marriage and feminine issues.

Mature Woman

When you are doing a reading for someone in their later years, get them to ask the question; do I still need to nourish my children or do I need to let go and start nourishing myself?

For a mature woman, she could have health problems, menstrual cycle issues, menopause and all the issues at the end of her cycle.

Also today, grandparents are looking after their grandchildren and so is there relevance in this situation.

For a Man

We are looking at their feminine energy and their needs for nourishment and nurturing. Man's role in society today is different to yesteryear. Look at man's role reversal as a stay at home father looking after the children.

The Empress may represent a strong woman's presence in his life.

There could be mother and daughter issues going on here. We are always looking for the love and approval of parents or a loved one.

Ultimately, this card is about how we give and receive love. If one cannot give and receive love, there may be some form of eating disorder. Food is a form of nourishment and if there is a disorder we could be looking at bulimia, anorexia or even obesity.

The fundamental and base meaning of this card is all about the love energy in your life and the concept of creativity:

Love Energy

Love energy is an abundance of unconditional love. The Empress loves to surround herself in beauty, she wants to be beautiful. Beautiful clothes, beautiful music, chocolate, champagne, luxury darlings! Venus loves beauty, she wants to be gorgeous, she is luxurious, she feels sexy, she feels rich.

Concept of Creativity

The creative energy is just like a door to a room; The Empress is the doorway to creation, with no closed doors, therefore no limits, somewhat like Roman times with no walls and doors. Creating a space.

Always look at the beginning and the end of the cycle. It may represent hysterectomy, when a woman is at the end of her cycle, maybe menopause, grieving for loss of a child. This card is every part a woman.

SHADOWS	KEYS
Too protective	Empathy
Plastic surgery	Tactful
Buying love	Beauty within
Dependency	Self-worth
Too Sweet	Mid-life
Careless and unprotected sex	Gracious
Relying on one's looks	Kisses, hugs and cuddles
Timid	Family
Fear of getting old	Charming
Dislike being alone	Companion
Women's magazines that reinforce stereotypes	Giving birth
Vanity	Community
Domestic upheaval	Maternal
Emotional blackmail	Motherly
Overprotective	Artistic ambition
Poverty	Prosperity
Infertile	Making love
Unwanted pregnancy	Motherhood
Suppression	Harmony
	Nature
	Love and joy
	Being magnetic and attractive
	Tantric sex
	Pregnancy
	Nurturing others
	Creativity
	Abundance
	Fertility
	Abundance
	Material prosperity
	Pleasure
	Comfort
	Nature, natural
	Delightful

SHADOWS	KEYS
	Physical attraction
	Sensuality
	Satisfaction
	Harvest

Tarot in Action

Create something. Bring out your creative side, paint, sew, bake a cake.
Entertain, invite others over for dinner.
Go out for dinner, or have high tea at the Windsor Hotel.
Go to a music or art show.
Spend time with your mother.
Spend time with your children, hug them.
Wear something green.
Wear a dress and jewelry.
Buy flowers for yourself or for others.
Pamper yourself, have a massage.
Bubble bath, with chocolates, champagne, music.
Spend time in the garden.
Plant a veggie garden.
Look after the environmental issues.
Love of pleasure and beautiful things.

Quotes

'In the end, these things matter most:
- How well did you love?
- How well did you live?
- How deeply did you learn to let go?' - Buddha.

Books to read

Return to Love by Marianne Williamson.
Eat Pray Love by Elizabeth Gilbert.

Chapter 8

...The Emperor teaches The Fool structure and how to align his goals in the outer world...

IV THE EMPEROR

SUMMARY

If the Empress is all about unconditional love, the Emperor is about conditional love.

He is the partner of the Empress. He is the one that sets the limits and is the one to say "Everything in moderation".

A question I often ask my students is to look at their own life and ask, "Who was the conditional parent and who was the unconditional parent role in their upbringing?" There is always a mix of responses. It is not necessarily the father who was the traditional conditional parent, sometimes the mother was the conditional parent, or vice versa. Sometimes both parents were conditional or both unconditional.

We need the discipline of the Emperor energy so we can create strategies to achieve our goals.

Another example I often share is to imagine children in a bath tub. The Empress energy would want to put the whole bottle of bubble bath in the tub, whereas the Emperor energy would say, "No not the whole bottle, just a cap full is enough".

NUMEROLOGY

The number four has to do with order and being in control. It is the square and it has four sides. The square is the container and represents boundaries.

It is the Emperor's material universe and he sets it in order. He is the ultimate store man and packer. If you let him loose in your pantry, everything will be arranged alphabetically, in order of size and color coded.

Number four has to do with responsibility, stability and foundations. When there are steady foundations there is a sense of security and organization. You can build as high as you want on a solid platform and base.

ASTROLOGY

There are two planets that connect with the Emperor, the first planet is Mars. You can see the Emperor wears a lot of red; this red color also comes from the Magician card.

The planet Mars rules the zodiac sign of Aries and is a fire element. Mars and Aries connect us with the masculine that is courageous, feisty, determined and forceful action energy. This is also the symbol for man.

The other planet associated with the Emperor is Saturn. Saturn rules the zodiac sign of Capricorn and is an earth element. Saturn rules all the foundational structures, such as your bones, which is the base structure or foundations for your body.

You can see the ram heads and the goat heads on the Emperor's throne. Notice the platform or stable base under the throne. The goat is a wonderful image of Capricorn – goats can climb the mountain and have the ability to stand on tippy toes on the top of the mountain.

MYTHOLOGY

In mythology we have Zeus the God that rules the heavens and Mars the courageous God, also known as the God of War. Both are strong rulers and leaders.

The Emperor is the Principle of Divine Reason. He is the intellect of the Magician with added humanity. It is his task to reason and to set things in order.

I remember long ago that I did not really like the Emperor's energy, but I realized soon enough that if I wanted order in my life, whether it was work, organizing an event, winning in sports or having a successful relationship, I needed his energy.

The Emperor is the archetypal father and represents the archetypically conditional love. To the Emperor it is simply a mathematical structure.

I remember watching a movie called *The Emperor and the Assassin*. It was about the first Emperor of China, Emperor Qin (pronounced Chi), 221 BC. He was the first Emperor to start building the Great Wall of China. This Emperor was benevolent; he loved his people and the land so much that he wanted to protect them all by building the wall.

If the Emperor is our logic energy coming from the left brain, then the Empress is our creative and receptive energy coming from the right brain.

The Emperor is the Principle of Divine Reason

SYMBOLOGY

Red Clothes

The Emperor's top and bottom clothes are red; this comes from the Magician. Red is the color for passion, action, power, energy and desires.

Red rules the planet Mars and connects us with the courageous, determined and forceful energy of the God Mars.

Golden Mountains

Mountains represent our aspirations. People always want to climb their own mountain, aspiring to reach the top. It is challenging, it is about conquering, like the goat climbing and standing on the top of the mountain.

They are golden and orange, which connects us to the Superconscious energy, our higher intellect, the exaltation of the Sun in Aries. The color orange symbolizes confidence, vitality and strength.

The mountains also look like igneous volcanic rock. They actually look like the fiery quality of the planet Mars. They look forbidding and barren; men are barren and they symbolize his energy. He is cut and dry, strong and authentic.

His power is absolute and unyielding, the ultimate male ego and the ruler of the world.

Steel Armor

The symbol of courage and valor. Knights wore armor, and this shows the Emperor is a soldier, a straight up and down type of guy. This armor also protects his softer self and helps protect the human side.

The silver color of the amour shows he has magical, mystical powers and that he has cool emotions. Do not underestimate him; he knows how to protect himself. He is vigilant and made of steel.

Venus Scepter

The Venus scepter, which also looks like an Egyptian Ankh, the symbol of life. It is held in his right hand, symbolizes he is consciously using love in his decision making and creations; that he is benevolent, kind and charitable, like King Solomon was said to be.

He knows that the Empress provides the love. You can see the blue sleeve showing on his right arm. His energy is to set things in order, to prioritize things, therefore he expects the Empress to provide the love – that is why he holds the Venus scepter.

It also shows he gives discipline with love. This is the female energy within the male. In the background you can also see water running along the bottom of the mountains. This little bit of blue water connects us to our emotions; this water is carried over from the Empress.

Globe

In his left hand he holds a globe or an orb, which also represents a dominion symbol. It is symbolic of the Emperor's worldly success and holding the whole world in his hand. He has power. He rules the world.

The White Beard

The Emperor is the grand old architect of the universe. This is God and the Father Saturn – the father of the universe. Saturn is also known as Father Time.

Another name I like to call him is the wise old goat. Look at the long white goatee he wears.

The Crown

Is a very traditional and conventional looking crown. It demonstrates power, ego and authority, that he likes his routines, traditions and rituals.

Grey Throne

The throne is also traditional looking. This grand heavy throne demonstrates his steady, authoritive and authentic energy.

The platform also shows us how stable he really is. His legacy is built on strong principles.

The color grey is all about wisdom. It denotes fearlessness, detachment and aloofness. A true leader shows these qualities, you cannot make proper decisions from the emotions. He truly is the wise old goat.

The Emperor Represents the Archetypical Conditional Love

IN A READING

When the Emperor shows up in a reading we are looking at the authority figure. This may be yourself, as in you have finally stepped up into your own authority or there may be someone around you exerting their authority over you.

You are in control or you realize that some things are uncontrollable.

The Emperor card may be asking you to look at who the authoritative figures are in your world. We have husbands, fathers, bosses, societies law's that keeps us all aligned, policemen, judges, teachers, counselors, doctors and politicians to name a few. You may have some interaction with one of these authority figures.

This card may also suggest a promotion in the workplace to a position of authority.

It could also represents a decision maker in the material world, a responsible person. They have charisma, they are leaders. Someone that uses their power of the analytical mind in a logical practical manner.

Having stability and order in your life. There are people that know how to strategize and get things done.

The Empress needs the Emperor as a container for her emotions. Men usually have much more physical strength.

Positive

A positive example may be a little girl crying and her father sweeps her up in his arms. You need the energy of your father to contain you and put you back in some order.

Negative

A negative aspect would be if you are too hard on yourself, for example, you do not allow yourself to deserve things. You check the price tags and then you deny yourself – that patriarchal voice in your head is too loud and restricts you. This is when you have too much Emperor energy in you.

If the Empress is the feeler and dreamer, the Emperor is the thinker and doer.

SHADOWS	KEYS
Harsh	Direct
Too combative	Muscular system
No second chance	Dare-devil
Mercenary	Vigilant
Too impatient	Hero
Too domineering	Pioneer
Dictatorial	Brave
Rigid	Reliable
Fear of losing control	Self-assertion
Ruthlessness	Sport
Judgmental	Rules of the game
Righteous	Fairness
Boring	Respected
Square	Hierarchy
Rash	Achievement
Weakness	Authority
Immaturity	Protection
Failed ambitions	Support
Status driven	Trustworthy
Tyrannical	Discipline
Over bearing nature	Provider
Aggression	Consolidation
Unstable	Reason
Status Quo	Willpower
Egocentrism	Priorities

SHADOWS	KEYS
Inflexible	Systems
Stagnation	Research
Personal Entitlement	Headstrong
Corruption	Management
Dictator	Building
	Structuring
	Responsibility
	Order
	Fathering
	Strategies
	Stability
	Powerful
	In control
	Commanding
	Common sense
	Tradition
	Leadership
	Organization
	Determination

Tarot in Action

Put a system in place: if there are no systems, then people create their own systems, and when things go wrong, people blame other people.
Do your taxes.
Buy a filing cabinet and file things away.
Organize and priorities.
Cross your T's and dot your I's.
Read the small print.
Read the instructions.
Study if you have to.
Be prepared; such as a first aid course.
Do you have you a fire plan ready?
Establish strong groundwork.
Relating to men.
Not a dreamer, a doer.

Quotes

'A stitch in time saves nine.'

'Measure twice, cut once.'

'Prevention is often better than the cure.'

'The wisdom of this world is foolishness with God'. – Ester Williams, Swimming Film Star.

Books to Read

Midas Touch by Donald Trump and Robert Kiyosaki.
The E Myth by Michael E. Gerber. *7 Habits for Highly Effective People* by Steven Covey.

Chapter 9

...The Fool starts to mature and it is time to face society's expectations, the Hierophant teaches inner guidance...

V THE HIEROPHANT

SUMMARY

In other tarot decks this card is called the Pope or the High Priest. I like that he is called the Hierophant as it gives this card an old world feel. I often visualize the Hierophant as a tall Egyptian High Priest in long robes walking into the temple.

The Hierophant is our link to God, to the supreme Spirit. He speaks to spirit, he is a spiritual leader or a spiritual guide, therefore this is the spiritual healing card. He is the teacher of wisdom and prepares us for life.

The Hierophant represents society and dogma. Society's rules do impact our lives. The Hierophant assists us to understand the boundaries of self and the community and this helps us to construct our very own identity.

The Fool, the Magician and the High Priestess are integrated in the Hierophant card. Therefore, the Hierophant is the revealer of scared things. Through the Hierophant we can access the Fool, Magician and High Priestess energy.

NUMEROLOGY

The number five basically means 'quintessence,' a Latin word combining the number five and nature. It also means change, movement, freedom and travel, for example, even the church changes with the times.

We are a five figured human. We have a head, two arms and two legs, five fingers and five toes. We also have five senses, i.e. taste, touch, smell, hear and sight.

Leonardo Di Vinci's Vitruvian man comes to mind, a worldwide symbol of health and healing.

Another five pointed symbol is the Pentacle, which is also an auspicious symbol. Once again it represents man spread eagled and the circle symbolizes the universe surrounding the five points. The Pentacle is widely recognized in the Wiccan and Pagan world as a protection symbol.

And another five pointed symbol is the Pentagon in America, which is a powerful symbol for the United States, just like the Hierophant symbolizes sitting upon his throne ruling the world of the senses and authority in the community, so do all the chiefs at the Pentagon.

ASTROLOGY

This is the first card that is represented by a zodiac sign, the sign of Taurus. Taurus corresponds to the throat, ears and nose area. The neck area is what I call the psychic center for the body. This is where you take your pulse, where you find the pituitary gland, thyroid gland, voice box, parotid glands, tonsils, Adam's apple, larynx, aorta, jugular and lymph nodes to name just a few things.

There is a lot of attention around the neck area, such as the blue scarf around his neck and the yellow and white floppy things along his ears. The color blue connects to the throat chakra, our inner emotions and to the blue of the High Priestess card.

The neck is the link between head and the body. The function of this card has to do with the listening function, like how you listen to a tuning fork, you strain till you hear the last pitch. Priests listen to confessions; they read between the lines and then give penance.

I always remember the scene in the movie *My Big Fat Greek Wedding* when the mother says to the bride, 'The man may think he is the head of the family, but it is the neck that makes the head turn.'

MYTHOLOGY

The myth of Chiron the Wounded Healer connects beautifully with this card.

The story goes that one day a scuffle broke out and Chiron was accidentally hit in the leg by one of Hercules' poisonous arrows. It was unintentional. Chiron was the son of Zeus and therefore he was a demigod and so he could not die nor heal his wound.

But because of his wounded leg he turned to learning about herbs and natural alternative healing modalities to heal it. But everything he tried could not heal the wound so he learnt to live with the pain. Chiron became a herbalist, a healer, a high priest, a high teacher. He also played the flute and is known as the wounded healer.

In 1977 the planetoid Chiron was discovered. Too big to be called an asteroid and too small to be called a planet, it is called a planetoid. Since this time we have become more open to other natural healing modalities in the Western World, such as chiropractic, reiki, acupuncture and other hands on healing practices. We say in astrology that when we all vibrate and understand at a certain level, the planet appears.

Also during this time, Elizabeth Kubler-Ross wrote her book *Death and Dying*, and the five stages we all go through to acceptance. The five main stages are:
1. Denial.
2. Anger.
3. Bargaining.
4. Depression – this is the Hanged Man stage; being stuck and stuffing it back down.
5. Acceptance – once we accept, everything else is easier to move through.

When we arrive at fifty years of age, we go through our first Chiron Return. Here we have the opportunity to heal the wounds that we were born with, or our wound of our animal side, or in our unconscious. It may be a family matter that we can finally resolve and lay to rest, tie up a loose end and finally let it go. It is also a powerful time for spiritual awakening. You may find a lot of people around fifty years of age start to travel and have an urge to reconnect back with the old country or they may take up painting or even learn a new language.

The Function of the Hierophant is to Listen

SYMBOLOGY

The Neck

The blue around the neck really draws your attention to the throat chakra. It also connects us to The High Priestess energy because his undergarment is blue.

The yellow floppy things around his ears are also drawing your attention to the listening and hearing function, allowing us the opportunity to speak our truth.

The neck is the link between the head and the body. The Hierophant is the bridge maker between the source and the Fool, between the thinker and the feeler, the inner and outer worlds, the Magician and the High Priestess, between the Empress and the Emperor.

The name Pontiff comes from the Latin ponte, literally meaning bridge. Therefore, the Pope means bridge-maker and is our direct link to God, meaning to link back.

The Grey Pillars

There are two grey pillars carried over from the High Priestess and now they are both grey in color. In the High Priestess card, the pillars are still black and white.

The pillars are a male phallic symbol. The drawings on the top of the pillars are meant to be ovaries and link us to the feminine. Together they represent the union of masculine and feminine energy.

The throne and the base of the card are all grey in color depicting wisdom and power.

Also note that there are two checkered black and white strips both traveling from the Hierophant to each priest.

Red Gown

The red and white gown the Hierophant wears connects us to the red and white outfit of the Magician. This suggests our outer world. Underneath he wears the blue undergarment that connects us to the High Priestess energy, suggesting the inner world.

The white sleeves symbolizes inner purity, as do his white shoes poking out underneath his outfit.

You can see the little crosses on both his garment and on his shoes connecting us again to the union of masculine and feminine and to the Magician and the High Priestess.

Gold Crown

The color gold connects us to the source. The W on top stands for God's name Yahweh.

The triple tiara or Visica Pisces looks like the Pope's hat. The tripled tiered golden staff he holds connects us to the trinity, the three levels of Father, Son and Holy Spirit, mother, father and child, mind, body and spirit, life, death and rebirth, etc.

The Golden Staff in his left hand is also a symbol of dominion, sovereignty and the power of rule, meaning he has power over the unconscious world and the spiritual world.

Two Fingers

The two fingers he holds up are a symbol of a blessing, a benediction also called a genuflection. It is the right hand representing the conscious masculine side.

He is actively directing his energy, just like the Magician holds up his right hand to the roses above his head. This is another symbol of forming a link with heaven.

The Keys

Once again the keys are making a symbol of a cross meaning the union between the OUT-er and IN-ner way. As within, so without. Solar and Lunar. The Emperor and the Empress, the Magician and the High Priestess.

Keys are symbolic of unlocking a mystery, suggesting he can unlock the mystery of the Tora. Keys also lock things suggesting something is under lock and key.

These keys are possibly referring to the Keys of Heaven, to the Gates of Heaven, the Pearly Gates. In some decks the keys may be gold and silver. The gold refers us to the rational mind, The Magician, Heaven and the outer world. Whereas, the silver color refers us to the subconscious, The High Priestess, hell and the Inner world.

Also known as the Vatican Arms. The symbol for the Vatican.

The Two Priests

One priest wears white lilies, connecting us to thought, reason, the ideals and the mind. The other priest wears the red roses, symbolizing desires, passions, the heart, and our feeling function. We first see these flowers in the Magician card.

The yellow "Y" shaped stripes that the priests both wear on their garments are solid and quite obvious, suggesting they have consulted both their left logical side as well as right receptive ways. The Hierophant also wears a white "Y" stripe bringing the union of both sides together as well.

It is as if the two priests cannot get it together to work something out, so they have gone to an authority, to consult with them to get an answer. The Hierophant gives them the answer, which is, you are both right! The Hierophant is the middle road, the junction of both, the middle pillar, just like the crosses he wears, the union of both sides.

Outer Way versus Inner Way

Our inner tuition; our intuition corresponds to the Hierophant. This card represents the union of all opposites The Magician and the High Priestess, Sun and Moon, etc. On the card you will notice there are many unions: the two priests, two pillars and the two keys.

Many would say he is an androgynous figure, once again symbolizing the union of both the masculine and feminine. Remember the blue connects us to the High Priestess and the red connects us to the Magician.

The Pope stands for the outer way, dogma, church, law and society's rules and expectations. Dogma means a body of opinions. The inner way is what we are doing here exploring the world of the tarot, discovering our spirituality and tuning in to our inner voice.

I love how the Hierophant follows the Emperor tarot card. What this says to me is, after you have listened to the practical and logical world of society, you have to also listen to our intuition and what our inner world is saying as well.

Note that our intuition is not called into action until we have exhausted the practical world. You will keep doing this until you tick all the boxes. This is the time when we start asking ourselves, what do we really want?

Let us now look at some outer ways and inner ways — listening to our inner voice versus listening to the outer voice:

Inner way

Connects to our own inner wise priest, your Inner teacher, your moral codes and principles, your values, your gut feelings, this is tapping into your spirituality. Our intuition, our inner voice, our beliefs, our hunches and our integrity.

The acting principle of what the High Priestess represents, all her knowledge is found in Hierophant. Through meditation and connecting to your inner sanctuary, you can tap into your inner wisdom, to what the High Priestess is trying to tell you.

Outer Way

Represents society's law, the rules and regulations, family traditions, conditions set from birth. People see gurus to connect through to our inner voice. Guru stands for Gee You Are You.

Marriage is a rule of society. It is an outer world union. Traditional medicines and education is an outer world tuition.

Chanting is an outer form of meditation, same as playing the drums.

The Hierophant Represents The Link Between Our Inner and Outer Worlds

IN A READING

When the Hierophant shows up in a spread he is asking you to integrate your inner and outer worlds. The Hierophant integrates the Magician and the High Priestess energies. For example, a doctor becomes a doctor and uses both traditional medicine and his intuition to get to a result and a diagnosis, he knows to integrate the two methods.

I know of many stories of engineers, scientists, inventors all using this inner voice that wakes them up from a deep sleep. They then run to the laboratory to give their hunch a try and this missing part is what ties the whole project together and they succeed.

The Hierophant is about healing without or within, listening to the without and the within, teaching without and within, the union of the without and within. He is our inner guide, our wise self and teacher, our spiritual self and conscience, our higher self, our Guardian Angel.

The union of friendships, alliances and even marriage.

You may need to consult with an authority, someone who is respected and represents a 'Pillar of Society' before making a decision. This could be consulting a spiritual healer, or a shaman for a healing. A teacher of ideas, principals and morals, someone who understands and respects history and traditions.

Perhaps consider going back to some form of traditional education.

There is a question that I always ask my clients who draw this card, and undoubtedly whenever I ask this question, my clients get what it is that is the source of their problem. "Are you doing what you want to do or are you doing what society expects of you?"

Straight away my clients know that they are making everyone else right and that is why they feel so wrong. Doing what others expect of us just puts extra pressure on ourselves. We will never make others happy. But in our society we are expected to step up to some extent. This is where the Hierophant assists us because he says to both, "Do what is expected of you to a point that is right for you".

Another question I may ask is, "Are you bucking the system?" Society has created rules so we all have some sense of order, otherwise there will be chaos. Bucking the system is totally going against society's rules. For example, the punks, when they first appeared in the UK they rebelled against authority, against the establishment and created anarchy. They then created their own uniforms and their own systems.

The idea with the Hierophant is to be who you truly are or who you want to be but working within the system, using the system that has been created for you already. It is about 'you and me,' not 'you or me.' Abraham Lincoln put it succinctly, "United we stand, divided we fall".

There are simple exercises you can do or suggest to clients to bring your two hemispheres together to get to your right answers. Simply create a pro and con list. Brain storm and write every idea down. Create a vision board or work through a mind map.

SHADOWS	KEYS
Dogmatic	Dream interpretation
Autocratic	Vocation
Too many charities	Community
Celibacy	Fraternity
Orthodoxy	Magi
Put on a pedestal	Revelation
Politics	Mantras
Patriarchal	Communion
Social position	Ethics
Hypocrisy	Integrity
Fundamentalists	Tradition
Matriarchal	Integrate
Misinformation	Wise counsel
Lack of Faith	Spiritual consultation
Deviousness	Knowledge
Bad Advice	Identification
Confusion	Faith
Disorderly conduct	Prayer
Status quo	Meditation
Institution	Self-belief
Deception	Union
Lies	Learning
Opposition	Teaching
False	Education
Flawed	Leadership
Radicals	Discipline
Rebels	Maturity

SHADOWS	KEYS
Heretics	Formality
Corrupt	Respect
Rebellion	Duality
	Social convention
	Belief system
	Maintains
	Protects
	Influence
	Enlightened
	Inspiring

Tarot in Action

Meditate, pray, go to a temple or go to church.
Do some research and link things.
Write down your values in your journal.
Get a massage or have an alternative healing.
Build a bridge.
Be a good listener.
Listen to your friends – that is healing.
Work within social structures and hierarchies.
Listening and speaking.
Understanding the system.
Receiving professional advice.
Open your ears to the master inside.

Quotes

'And above all else to thy own self be true.' – Shakespeare, Hamlet.

'There's more to life than just heaven and earth Horatio.' – Shakespeare, Hamlet.

Books to Read

God is Not Great by Christopher Hitchens.
Holy Blood Holy Grail by Baigent, Leigh and Lincoln.

Chapter 10

...The Fool now learns about his place in the world and begins to fall in love...

VI THE LOVERS

SUMMARY

There are three figures in this card. The man represents the conscious, the female represents the unconscious and the Angel represents the Superconscious.

Here with the Lover's card we start to question the standards of society. We decide accordingly with this card, we make our first choices, our first decisions and the urge to merge with another but on our own terms. We want to be open in a relationship; this is why they are shown as naked on the card.

Temptation of the heart. Something may need to be sacrificed, for example, letting go of being a bachelor and gaining a relationship.

The Hierophant is about linking on the inner side, where as the Lovers is about linking with the outer world, in the physical world.

NUMEROLOGY

The number six is all about harmony and balance. Especially after the change we want to restore the calm, the peacemaker energy. Number six is to do with family, there is a fine line between love and hate. Number six people bring peace and harmony to the family or to their group of friends.

This number is also associated with vulnerability and the protection of it. Number six people love to surround themselves with beauty, appreciating things of beauty. All this has to do with creating peace and harmony, whether in the family, group of friends or in the work environment.

ASTROLOGY

Gemini is the ruler of this card and here we are looking at the twins. Gemini is ruled by Mercury, indicating that this card has something to do with the mind, ideas and thoughts. Remember Mercury was the Messenger of the Gods and he ruled communication.

Once again it suggests that we need to use the mind here, a decision has to be made and Gemini and Mercury are great signs and planets to aid us in making that clear and well thought out decision.

MYTHOLOGY

With the Lovers' card, we are looking at the classic Christian story of Adam and Eve in the Garden of Eden. You can see the snake in the tree behind the female figure.

A situation may occur to tempt you out of the garden, into the real world and into adulthood. Once you have stepped out there is no going back. The Lovers' card has a connection to the Devil card who may well be the source of the temptation.

In Greek mythology we have the story of Paris. He was a beautiful human, the three top Goddesses were all in love with him. We have Hera the first lady and wife of Zeus – she wanted to offer him the world. Aphrodite wanted to offer him passion and love, and Goddess Athena wanted to offer him strategy. Out of all these three Goddesses he chose Aphrodite who gave him Helen of Troy and look what happened next, the fall of Troy.

This story is told again and again with Tristan and Iseult, Cleopatra and Mark Antony and the classic story of Camelot with King Arthur, Guinevere and the first knight Sir Lancelot. These myths are still told and retold. I have seen so many clients experience these passionate associations and probably that is why they consult the tarot cards to assist them in making the right choice.

Look at what happens when one follows their desires only; disaster happens and everyone loses. Everyone knew not to touch the forbidden fruit but they had no self-control and so they got caught out, just like Adam and Even in the Garden of Eden. God told them they can have everything in their sight but not to touch that one forbidden fruit. Of course they did and so were cast out of Eden.

The energy that the Lovers are depicting is a human quality; we are looking at power and Eros. Eros is intense sexual passions and we will all feel this at some point in our lives. We cannot deny our human qualities and nor should we. Some people have killed for love, sometimes passion overrides all sensibility. Also when couples argue, they usually follow up with make-up sex. There is a fine line between passion and pain, or so the song goes.

But this is what this card is suggesting we do; to make the right decision in our world; that we have choice in the matter. This card is about being conscious of your decisions.

By using the reasoning and intellectual aspect of the card, which is represented by the male figure, applying it to the feeling and intuitive side, as represented by the female figure, we can strive towards the higher self, the higher purpose or the higher ideal for all involved or which is represented by the angel. The decision should be the best case scenario for everyone.

The balance between reasoning and feeling, which are the qualities of the Emperor and the Empress energies. If the Emperor is the erotic energy then the Empress is the exotic energy.

If the Hierophant joins the energy of the Magician and the High Priestess through an inner way, then the Lovers join the Emperor and the Empress on the outer way or a more human physical way. They do say that two heads are better than one.

The Lovers Represent The Urge To Merge With Another But On Your Own Terms

SYMBOLOGY

The Lovers

The two figures are displayed naked; this is very interesting because all the other cards around them are dressed and wearing crowns symbol of status. The lovers are not afraid to show their vulnerability, they are liberated, open and free.

You can see the man looks towards the woman and the woman looks towards the angel, who is representative of the source. Angels are God's messengers. The woman is the center piece of this triangle.

The two figures represent duality of life and the angel is the mediating force, the higher force, the higher purpose, just like the Hierophant is the mediator. Whatever decisions we need to make we need to make them through love, because man looks to woman. Even the Emperor looks to the Empress and makes his decisions through love. Remember that the feminine is our creative side and the masculine is our action side that puts it out in the world.

To make a correct choice we need to know who we are and what we want, which are the qualities of the Empress and the Emperor. Therefore, the ideal choice or decision we make should be the balance between these two sides of ourselves.

A great example I like to use in my tarot classes is *Star Trek*. Yes, I love *Star Trek* and have been watching the series and movies for years. In the original series we have Captain Kirk, and on his right conscious side he has Mr Spock, who is totally logical and rational. On his left side, the unconscious side, he has Doctor McCoy who is more emotional and sensitive to what is going on and often asks the Captain to have a checkup because he can see he is overworked or stressed. Captain Kirk consults with both sides and ultimately he decides what direction to steer the starship or the situation. This is symbolic of how we operate in the universe, consulting both the logical and intuitive sides and moving forward with the balance of both.

By using our sixth sense we can make the right choice. Discernment is the feminine Yin energy, it draws distinctions and is discrete. This also suggests freedom to act upon one's pleasures. Although discrimination is masculine Yang energy, it has good taste and judgement.

Note that when a person is confronted with choice they may feel they are going to lose and most people feel that they cannot have both, or deserve any at all. For some it takes a great risk, so they remain in their current unforgiving and unproductive circumstances because they truly believe in the saying 'better stay with the Devil you know than the Devil you don't know.'

There is a fundamental belief in our society that there is not enough to go around, so people horde and stock up. What they are really doing is stopping the abundant flow. Some may think for someone to win someone has to loose. They do not understand the win/win concept at all.

Archangel Raphael

The angel in this card is one of the Archangels. Archangel Raphael is a healing angel and a messenger of the Gods. He connects well with the planet of Mercury, the ruler of communication, messenger of the Gods and rules the zodiac sign of Gemini.

The angel is coming down from the clouds. The grey of the cloud represents spiritual wisdom. There is a touch of pink here and there, bringing in the unconditional love.

Archangel Raphael wears violet, the color of spirituality. His red wings are the fiery quality of desire and the fire of choice. There is a connection to the Fool card because the Fool wears the red feather in his cap as well.

Mountain

The mountain is a phallic looking symbol. It points towards the mediating force of the angel. It also looks like a volcano ready to blow – this could be our energy when we are so overwhelmed with passions.

Mountains represent aspirations, something we want to climb and conquer. We all want to aspire to climb our mountain.

This mountain suggests aspirations of God or connecting to the source, may also represent the House of God.

Man's Tree

Represents the Tree of Life. There are twelve fires burning on this tree. Fire is the symbol of renewal. The twelve fires connect us to the twelve zodiac symbols. This tree also connects to the story of the burning bush.

Woman's Tree

Represents the Tree of Knowledge. There are meant to be five fruits representing our five senses, again suggesting the feminine intuition.

In this tree you can see the snake representing wisdom, transformation and sexuality. The snake connects us to the story of Adam and Eve in the Garden of Eden and the forbidden fruit. Prior to eating the pomegranate, Adam and Eve were in total bliss, they did not even know they were male and female; they were totally living in the unconscious world.

When they ate of the pomegranate they woke up, they became conscious and covered themselves with the grape vine leaves. They realized they were naked and different. The snake is the symbol of wisdom and knowledge and he offered them awareness and consciousness.

It is at this very moment of eating the pomegranate that we chose a life of duality.

When we dream of snakes, it is so symbolic of us being awakened to some form of higher consciousness. We usually remember these dreams of snakes or creepy crawlies biting us, once again demonstrating to us that we are becoming aware.

Green Grass

You can see where the man is standing that the ground is firm and solid looking, suggesting that he stands stable and strong. Compared to the where the women is standing, it looks uneven, suggesting she is not standing steady. This is also true of the feminine side being the creative and emotional side and the masculine being the stronger side and usually a container for her emotions.

On a Psychological Level

The relationship between the Lovers is and should be intimate. This is another reason why they are displayed nude, both showing their vulnerability, and there should be no secrets between them.

In the relationship there is always a constant strive for balance. Often couples do not talk. It is like a see-saw effect or a dance between the Emperor energy leading, or the Empress energy leading.

On a personal level, sometimes we are emotional and sometimes we are rational and in charge.

The Lovers Is The Balance Between Who We Are And What We Need

IN A READING

To get balance, we really have to be clear in the mind and have to know what we want. We can talk to the experts, or we can do some research and write our own pros and cons lists, we can do vision boards and mind maps to aid us in getting clear in the mind and focused. Through meditation and tapping into the Hierophant energy, we can find what we need.

When you fall in love, you try to get the balance through the other person. It is a compensatory relationship; it is about making allowances, but not to the point that you lose your own identity. Ideally, we want resolution between both parties and not to compromise ourselves, because when we compromise ourselves too much it does not work out anyway.

The urge with the Lovers is to unite with others but the difference now is that it is on your terms. You join with others that are into the same things you are into. You align to the same goals, you are on the same page and there has to be alignment, otherwise it just will not work out. Sabotage will show up.

It may also be time to look at another's garden if the one you are in is not growing for you any more or it is not your style.

The Lovers tells us that you do have the power to choose what is right for you. You can choose your responses and realize your habits. You have the power to choose your friends and remember you do not have to justify yourself.

Section 2

The Lovers remind us that we do need other people in our world: lovers, friends, partners, family members. Each one teaches and stretches us into being better human beings.

There is an impulse that will drive you away from home, away from your comfort zone. Obey this impulse but also be aware of the situations around you – you have choices to make and directions to take.

Equality for both and win/win solution for all parties involved.

SHADOWS	KEYS
Flings	Considerate
Promiscuity	Companion
Too flirty	Emotionally secure
Emotional dependency	Friendship
Secret lover	Good rapport
"love is Blind' attitude	Closeness
Reading too many romance novels - Mills & Boon	Faithfulness Relating
Seeking only pleasure	Togetherness
No trust	Same goals
Lack of commitment	Mutual exchanges
Unrealistic pleasure	Global cooperation
Insecurity	Equality
Lust	Mandala
Moral laps	Relationships
Temptations	Physical attraction
Indecisions	Love
Separation	Sexual commitment
Failed love affair	Passion
Emotional loss of control	Commitment
Doubt	Vulnerability
Dilemma	Choice
Temptation	Values
	Union
	Sexuality
	Pleasure
	Desire

SHADOWS	KEYS
	Closeness
	Connecting
	Affinity
	Bonding
	Romance
	Heart
	Support

Tarot in Action

Talk and share with friends.
Invite friends over for a dinner party.
Have a romantic getaway.
Trust yourself.
Show affection and respect.
Love both sides of yourself.
Create a mind map.
Listen and trust yourself.
Making decisions and being responsible.
Making choices in relationships.
Be willing to negotiate.
Love yourself first then others will love you.
Team work.
Make a decision through love.
Loving relationships.
Personal beliefs.

Quote

'The love for one another exceeds the need for one another.' – Dalai Lama.

Books to Read

Men are from Mars and Women are from Venus by Dr John Gray.
Venus and Mars in the Bedroom by Dr John Gray.

Chapter 11

...The Fool quickly learns about conflicts and his ego when he encounters The Chariot...

VII THE CHARIOT

SUMMARY

The Chariot is the card of victory. You can see the wreath around his helmet symbolizing success. There are battles ahead and they are achievable if you have the willpower.

The two Sphinxes, once again demonstrate our two sides; the black inner way and the white outer way. The Magician and High Priestess, the Empress and Emperor energies. Through balance and plain hard work they can be managed and steered in the right direction to achieve your goals.

The hero now leaves the Garden of Eden to make a life for himself out in the world.

NUMEROLOGY

Number seven is a powerful number meaning reassessment; it is a very spiritual number and one of faith. Analytical and evaluating everything, meditation sits well with this number. I like to think of number seven as God's number on the seventh day he rested and he reflected on what he did. It is an internal assessment energy, it has power, analyzing and evaluating everything.

Once you reassess the situation, you will have a need to let go of some things, a trimming of your life in some way.

The Charioteer may represent traveling through the mysteries of the universe. He also may represent the seven gates of hell that Inanna passed through.

ASTROLOGY

Cancer is the astrological ruler of this card. You can see the hard shell of the crab in the armor the Charioteer is wearing, symbolic of the mask that we hide behind.

Cancer is ruled by the Moon and it is a water element – therefore emotional, sensitive and a feeler. We have to contain our emotions, protecting our softer inner side, just like the masculine protects the feminine side.

MYTHOLOGY

Apollo the Sun God connects well with this card. Apollo wore his golden armor and rode his golden chariot (the Sun) through the sky during the day bringing light to the Earth. The danger may be flying too high when unprepared.

Apollo had a twin sister – the Goddess Diana, she was the huntress of the night. Diana was born first; she grew quickly and helped her mother give birth to Apollo. Diana drove her silver chariot (the Moon) through the sky at night.

The Ego is the hard shell that we wear, our outer personality, our persona. This is the vehicle we use to move forward with, our vehicle that we use through life, like a mask that we hide behind. Our personality is our vehicle we use through life.

I see the ego working like a scout. The scout goes out ahead to make sure it is safe for you, for your true self to come out. Another way I like to see the ego is like a three year old. If it does not get what it wants, it will carry on like a three year old child.

One thing I have learned about the ego is that we have to develop our ego first before we can put it in its proper place. Ego is not a dirty word. The world today has changed and we need a strong ego to move forward with. It is healthy to develop a strong ego that you can use and make work for you.

Then there is the Id. The Id is a very different story, but it does explain a lot. It does explain why we can love and kill the one person you love, and all the time protecting the self.

Another famous Chariot driver was the God Krishna, who in the Bhagavad Gita drove King Arjuna's Chariot and gave him illumination as an example for us all.

The Ego Is Our Vehicle In Life

SYMBOLOGY

The Chariot

The chariot these days is the modern car. We choose our car to fit our image, our ego. We express our personality through the car we drive, the clothes we wear, the music we listen too, where we shop, our hairstyle, our pursuits, our career, our house and which suburb we live in, where we eat, even the friends we have, etc.

He also looks like he is cemented in the chariot. The grey block shows he has strength, courage and wisdom. It shows he is strong, in control, solid and stable.

The starry canopy above him shows the celestial faces or the metaphysical faces shining down on him and protecting him on all sides. He has shelter.

His Legacy

In the front of the chariot, you can see the blue wings that connect us to the sign of the Scorpio and the Phoenix. Also to the Egyptian sun dial and the winged God 'Horus' the symbol for high intellectual pursuits.

In this gorgeous picture we have the blue wings of Horus, the sun dial above the birds' head. Horus is usually portrayed as an eye. The eye of Horus.

The red thing on the plaque represents the Hindu symbol of the lingam and yoni, the union of the masculine and feminine. This is his ideal emblem that he stands behind, showing his two sides, the joining of our two forces.

All this reminds me of the Lovers card, the bringing together of the feminine and masculine and striving for the highest perfection, the angel.

He is balanced to make it out there on his own. He is balanced so he can make proper decisions then he can move forward successfully.

The Charioteer

The charioteer behind all that armor is the human soul, connecting us to the Fool. You can see he has the yellow hair.

He holds the wand that belongs to the Fool and the Magician in his right hand showing that he has power and is powerful.

The breast plate symbolizes the hard shell of the crab. In the center of his breast plate there is a white square. When we see a square it represents the masculine. This square is pure white and it symbolizes his inner purity, pure heart and shining light from within.

His gold belt has magical symbols on it as does the apron he wears. These magical symbols mean he has power.

He holds no reigns, this is strange but he does not need any because he has power and control over the two sphinxes sitting in the front. They are settled, calm and sitting together.

The Crown

There is an eight pointed star on his crown that corresponds to the star card, which symbolizes our growth and potential. It also connects to the following card of strength, which is the number eight. There is also the victory wreath showing he is winning, that he is a winner.

The Two Moons

The two faces on his shoulders represent comedy masks. One is known as severity, the black mask and feminine energy. The other is known as mercy, the white mask and masculine energy.

These two faces also connects us to Urim and Thummim, translated as Light and Truth. They were seen as divinatory tools and oracle instruments of the High Priests of ancient Israel.

Emperor's City

In the background is a city of the Emperor. The charioteer leaves the father behind and the developing ego strides out to make it on his own. What we have here is the beginning of independence. You can see the chariot is parked on the grass; he has crossed the moat and is resting on this other side.

The Fool leaves home. He leaves the protectiveness of the city and the family home. When we first leave home we can experience what I call "the elastic band effect". This is also known as the Boomerang kid, who is a child that lives outside of the home for a while and then returns home.

We need to protect ourselves so that we can stand out in the world on our own; we have to protect our very own ideas and identity.

What we have here is victory in the plain of reality. Being able to control our environment, our outer world through the force and use of our inner willpower. Being assertive and not aggressive.

This card is always the card of victory. You may never feel that you are winning but you are.

The Charioteer is the energy of the Fool; the chariot is the mask or our ego, our human personality. The base of the chariot is our base we have to stand on, it has to be on solid and stable ground.

The Chariot can Control Himself in the Environment

IN A READING

The most basic way of looking at this card is that you have a battle on your hands, a war, a struggle, obstacles to get over or dealing with a battle within.

The two sides are represented by one black sphinx expressing the feminine and emotional side. The other is white, masculine and representing the reality side.

The upside of this card is that you have the two sphinxes running smoothly together, you are in control of the reigns and steering in the right direction of your life. Remember he does not have reigns, this shows there is something magical going on here.

The downside of this card is that the two sphinxes want to run in opposite directions, you are struggling to keep them both together.

The ideal scenario or challenge is that you have the two horses running together in tandem, perfect balance and running the same direction.

Note that seventy percent of people out there in society are struggling. There is a need to keep whatever the two things that are important to you running smoothly in perfect balance.

Confidence and control is needed to face the opposing emotions and circumstances. This card shows that you also have the motivation to move through a stagnant situation.

Interesting how he is shown as totally armored but also shows him as cut off and fighting alone. This suggests he has the conviction to push through the charge but also it shows a diehard and ruthless energy to win at whatever cost. Be mindful to use your energy appropriately, to save and use your energy to fight the right battles.

Also note that you can run out of energy trying to hold the reigns of the two horses running smoothly together. For example, you have to go to a funeral and you are ill, you are trying to keep in control in an emotional and taxing situation.

How many times do we try to please others and ourselves at the same time, and why do we put ourselves in this position? I know this is a loaded question and there are many reasons that quickly spring to mind to illustrate the point. The first answer that everyone says is that we want people to like us. We do it for recognition. It could be the ego just keeping the peace – it feels good to help, sometimes we have an agenda, acceptance, approval and if I do this for them they will do the other for me. Another main example is trying to work and keep a family at the same time.

It takes a lot of self-discipline to be able to control yourself in your environment. Through the use of your willpower you can take charge, but this is not sustainable forever. It is not that the energy leaves you. You just have to find another way to control yourself and the circumstances you find yourself in. There may be a smarter or easier way and this brings us back to reassessing your life and trimming your life in some way.

When this card comes up acknowledge, acknowledge, acknowledge the querant. Acknowledge their emotions, their achievements and their efforts. Remember it is a struggle for them to maintain the two horses running steady. Even though this card is a victory card sometimes people can be running on adrenaline. Like a mother demonstrating superhuman strength that can lift a car off their baby.

The Chariot may represent a man or a youth in a car. Or it may be you will encounter someone in a new or fancy car. I often ask the question, "do you need a new car?"

Today's youth seem to learn the hard way through car crashes. This is the ego of youth - feeling indestructible. Yes the male's ego is stronger than the female's ego.

Also, in our western society we do not have rituals for our youth to find their purpose, like the Native Americans do. Native Americans have their vision quests. Here in Australia our Aborigines go on walkabout when the time comes for them to leave and explore. Indians have pilgrimages as rituals and rites of passage in their culture.

You are being called to walk your own path on a calling, an exile or a random journey. The danger is that you are called to the wrong journey, become overwhelmed and not know how to get back. He may be warning to you to be aware of forces that are calling you that you may not understand, therefore to protect yourself like the armor he wears.

Another thing to note with this card, because it is the card of ego, a lot of people get stuck in this energy. When you hear someone say, "It's not my fault I lost my job," or "You made me angry," you can be sure it is the ego talking.

SHADOWS	KEYS
Overprotective	Guarding
Invading	Cherish
Closed	Purposeful
Scattered in all directions	Bodyguard
Feeling under threat	Selective
Being Pulled	Knowing what one wants
Lack of personal barriers	Triumph
Moody	Tenacity
Distracted	Exploring
Disempowered	Setting intentions
Over-inflated ego	Insulation
Arrogance	Aims
Delays	Goals
Frustration	Visions
Rage	Purpose
Tyranny	Mission statement
Sexually inactive	Strategy
Aggression	Movement
Anxiety	Change
Egocentrism	Vigilant
Hard control	Self-belief
Inflexible	Assertive
	Good news
	Moving
	Travel
	Ambition
	Determination

SHADOWS	KEYS
	Honor
	Conquest
	Victory
	Energy
	Confidence
	Conviction
	Assertion
	Discipline
	Bravery
	Commanding

Tarot in Action

Insulate the house.
List your goals daily, weekly.
Assert yourself.
Drive somewhere different.
Buy the car you really want.
A project taking off victoriously.
Write your accomplishments list.
Write your purpose and mission statement.
Learning to protect oneself.
Taking care of yourself and others.
Proving yourself out in the world.

Quotes

'Every man must know his limitations.' – Clint Eastwood, *Dirty Harry*.

Books to Read

The New Earth by Eckhart Tolle.
Losing My Virginity by Richard Branson.

Chapter 12

...The Fool learns all about his inner power, his courage and strengths...

VIII STRENGTH

SUMMARY

Now we start to wonder and take control with what is going on the inner side. We start the death of the ego after we just built it up in the Chariot card. It is like saying to yourself "Why am I doing this?" and "Who am I?"

It is also interesting to note that in the old way the strength tarot card was traditionally number eleven, and the justice card was in this number eight position. Arthur Edward Waite turned this around to have Strength in this number eight position and Justice in position number eleven. In many new decks, some people have reverted back to the old traditional placement. Nonetheless, they both have something to do with balance.

Personally, I prefer Strength as number eight, primarily because Strength is ruled by Leo, and Leo naturally follows Cancer astrologically and Cancer ruled the Chariot card. I also feel you have to know who you are on the inner side before you can make clear decisions out there in the world which connects us to the Justice card, but more about Justice later.

NUMEROLOGY

The number eight is all about power and control, but true power and true control. Eight is also about wealth, whether its material wealth or personal values they are both of value. To me, true prosperity comes from when you believe in yourself.

The word courage comes from the French 'le coeur' meaning the heart. This is your inner strength, your true strength, your true wealth and your true power.

ASTROLOGY

Leo is the astrological essence of this card. The Sun rules Leo and is the fifth house of the zodiac. Leo is all about self-expression, tapping into your inner child and your creativity. Leo's are fiery, they are the most optimistic of all the zodiac signs and the most generous, this comes from within.

Leo's are here to learn affairs of the heart and may suffer much heartache. The challenge for them is to give their heart, to love whole heartedly as they expect to, but also to keep their heart intact for themselves.

MYTHOLOGY

Here we have Earth Mother shown as Venus; she is the lady part of the card. The old Earth Mother was seen as taming the lion, the wild beasts.

The lion from the *Wizard of Oz* connects well with this card; he was looking for his courage along the yellow brick road, where he discovered he had it all the time.

There are three Biblical connections:

1. We have the story of Daniel and the lion where Daniel removed the splinter from the lion's paw.
2. Samson fought the lion in another story.
3. A passage in St John's Revelations where he wrote, "The lion shall lay down with the Lamb".

We have the movie *The Lion King*, and we have Aslan, the lion from the famous C. C. Lewis book *The Lion the Witch and the Wardrobe*. By the way, the name Aslan is Turkish for lion.

Hercules had to endure twelve challenges before he became immortal, and these twelve challenges also correspond to the twelve signs of the Zodiac. In his fifth challenge, Hercules was to fight the lion in the den, which is the fifth house of Leo in the zodiac.

So Strength connects us to our inner power, and empowerment happens when you get to know your true self.

Strength Comes From Your Heart

SYMBOLOGY

The Lady

Once again the tarot cards are showing us our two sides of ourselves. We have the woman wearing white, signifying purity connecting us to the Empress. Now the flowers are around the waist, not on the gown, like in the Empress card.

When we are being the lady, we are keeping the peace, being polite and smiling, being nice and nurturing. This is the side of ourselves that we always want to show in public.

For me, the word NICE means Nothing Inside Cares Enough to tell you the truth, to tell you what I really am feeling inside. It is almost a dismissive word, it does not mean anything, "Oh yes she is nice."

The Lion

The Lion represents our inner desires, our animal instincts and our inner hunger.

The lion shows us that we may be neglecting this energy. What happens next is that when the lion's roar gets fiercer and louder, it is trying to get our attention. Just like when you are hungry and your tummy growls. We have to listen to this side of ourselves; if we do not listen the power will scream out of us through our anger, our fear or our sexuality.

If you do not acknowledge this part of you, resentment may set in or even disease.

We need to look at what we desire in life and acknowledge it. Ideally we can harness the energy of the lion force and use it to propel us to what we want, where we want to go and how we want to be.

Magician and Empress Garden

The woman is wearing her white pure robes just like the High Priestesses' dress. The garland around her waist connects us to the Magician and Empress's lush garden. This Strength card is asking us to look at the balance between these two points.

The Strength tarot card suggests that is has the reverse meaning of the Magician card. With the Magician he can tap into the cosmos with his magic wand and transmit his desires down onto the physical plain and into his garden. With the Strength card it, is about tapping within and transmitting it up and out onto the physical plain.

Kundalini

The lion is gold in color or orange, signifying our life force, our vitality, our Kundalini energy. Aliester Crowley calls this card Lust, in his Thoth Tarot deck.

My dictionary says the Kundalini is energy that lies dormant at the base of the spine until it is activated, as by the practice of yoga, and channeled upward through the chakras in the process of spiritual perfection.

It may represent our sexuality is blocked. In some cases the lady can be a submissive woman and the lion may be seen as sin. We have been taught by society not to respect or love this side of ourselves. For example, the Church teaches us that sex is bad. But this is a human quality – how can we suppress it?

Therefore, the energy has to explode up and out, or we get sick and depressed. Remember Leo is all about expressing yourself, your self-expression, your human self.

This card shows us that we need to love ourselves before we can love others.

The lion is tamed; you can see his tail between his legs; her hand is in the lion's mouth and the lion is licking her hand. She acknowledges her inner needs.

Movie and Song Analogies

A few movies that demonstrate the Strength energy are *Born Free* with Joy Adams and *Elsa the lion*. Joy Adams was a powerful woman for her time; she was friends with Amelia Earhart who was the first woman to fly a plane. Joy Adams was also an artist and when she was in South Africa she drew national flowers and these prints are still hanging in the museum today.

There is also the story of *Beauty and the Beast*. It is a very popular theatre show and an interesting story line because here we have ourselves falling for the beast, loving the beast within, totally seeing right through the mask.

Another classic animated movie popular today is *Shrek*. In this movie the princess falls in love with the Ogre, the monster and she opts to become an Ogre herself. For me, this movie shows that society has evolved into one where we are accepting our animal side, our ugly ogre nature.

Another classic Shakespeare story is *The Taming of the Shrew*. Here we have the energy totally on the lion side. The first time I saw this movie was in black and white with Elizabeth Taylor and Richard Burton. He finds her and she is totally outraged and wild, and he locks her up in the barn and slowly he tames her, bringing the lady side out and the balance is restored.

Today, we have this same story line being played out with *My Fair Lady* and *Pretty Woman* and Jodie Foster's *Nell* movie. All these movies show the wildcat side of this card, which can be tamed and restore the balance.

There are also a couple of classic songs I would like to highlight. Helen Reddy's classic *I am a woman, hear me roar* and Katy Perry's latest song called *Roar*. Interesting that this song of Katy Perry's is a world number one, her first hit just soon after her divorce, showing that she is back and she is standing strong.

Love Your Inner Lion

The meaning of this card is that we need to love and respect that part of ourselves that is the lion, for that is our true strength and our true power. You have a responsibility to yourself. You also have to trust that the lion will not bite you back.

There could be a lot of fear to love that part of ourselves, and society may want you to quash this side. You may hear "how can you be so selfish," but by allowing yourself to love this side of yourself, then you also allow others. Also, you may find that people live their life through you. They will say, if you can do it so can they.

Remember Leo is your self-expression; it is all about the self. How can you close it off?

Lemniscate

The infinity symbol above the woman's head signifies that we must get the balance, to get the balance between ourselves and within ourselves. This is the card of balance.

Blue Mountains

You can see a blue mountain on her right side. To me it looks like a volcano ready to erupt. Mountains represent our aspirations, they are there for us to surmount and conquer and claim our prize.

The color blue connects us with our throat chakra. Blue also connects with our emotions and feelings and our intuition. It is about speaking our truth before it erupts and we lose our control.

This mountain also connects to the mountain in the Lovers card. Also remember that people climb their mountain at their own pace.

People are trying to maintain the energy of the Chariot, totally in charge and looking like they know where they are going, and in the meantime the energy builds up like the roar of the lion. People should look at their lion energy, if not the rage will scream it out. For example, in the work place, you may have been overlooked and you may not be acknowledged, but you do not say anything, in fact your loved ones usually cop the rage at home. Then one day it will come screaming out of you and this is probably the day you will lose your job.

You Have the Courage to Face Your Challenges

IN A READING

The more you express yourself, the more your true self will come out or like a pressure cooker, it could explode, like that volcano ready to erupt at any time.

The lion is your vitality and this card speaks about controlling your inner self for that is your true power. It is not just controlling your exterior world, which is what the Chariot is about.

When you are embracing the lady energy, you do not want to hurt anyone. You want to keep the peace, you are making others happy, but what about yourself? If you do not have the balance this is when the rage and anger starts to build and probably explode.

Patience and calm is required to face the situation. No matter how fierce the situation can be, a soft hand can tame the wild beast as the imagery suggests. There is a battle going on outside, for example in a relationship, but there may be more going on in the inner side.

Let this card remind you that more is achieved with patience and kindness. Your true strength is when you show your vulnerable side. Do not be tempted by impulses and desires.

This card speaks about honesty. You have to put it out there, because if you do not, you deny them and deny yourself to correct it. One of my rules is to tell the truth with compassion. When you do, people get what you are saying, they will get where you are coming from. Also as Dr Phil says, "You cannot change what you do not acknowledge".

If you do not acknowledge your inner desires, you become subservient to them because they end up in the shadow. The Devil card sits underneath the Strength card. The shadow can eat you up to the point that you become the animal. Pride and ego can over take you.

This card shows courage, determination and self-awareness. Potential integration and individuality is achieved by releasing all negative feelings, thereby encouraging only the positive.

This card is saying that you do have the courage to follow through and face your challenges and your true desires.

Another saying I have is that there first has to be an emergency before people emerge. It takes courageous people to step up. Also say what you have to say before it gets to that emergency situation.

SHADOWS	KEYS
Lazy	Vigilance
Aggressive	Courage
Vanity	Loyalty
Interfering	Merciful
Uncontrolled sensuality	Generosity
Too hot blooded	Sovereign
Pompous	Proud
Lust	Pride
Body building	Challenges
Flashy	Warmth
Lustre	Hot
Pretentious	Royalty
Snob	Regal
Arrogant	Respect
Overcompensation	Willpower
Fear	Compassion
Sexual harassment	Patience
Show off	Appropriateness
Inertia	Triumph
Defeated	Fortitude
Loss of opportunity	Desire for creativity
Ego	Self-control
	Moral strength
	Integrity
	Composure
	Kindness
	Serenity

SHADOWS	KEYS
	Discipline
	Moderation
	Passion

Tarot in Action

Face the fear and do it anyway.
Have to courage to do it.
Self-respect.
Stand in your power and let others know where you stand.
Connect with your wild side or your cat.
Wear the badge, no more Mr Nice Guy!
Express sex positively.
Speak your truth.
It is OK to say no.
A challenge calling for great strength and endurance.
Strong passions and desires.
Heart aches.
Learning lessons of the heart.
To follow your hearts deepest yearnings.

Movies to Watch

The Lion King.
Shrek.
Born Free with Elsa the Lion and Joy Adams.
Beauty and the Beast.

Quotes

'I am woman, hear me roar.' – Helen Reddy.

'Hell has no fury like the woman scorned.' – William Congreve (1670-1729, English poet and playwright).

FEAR stands for False Evidence Appearing Real.

Book to Read

Breaking the Habit of Being Yourself by Dr Joe Dispenza.

Chapter 13

...The Fool learns about wisdom when he meets the wise man, the Hermit...

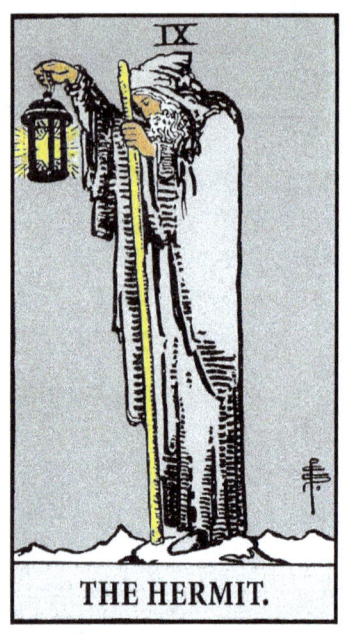

IX THE HERMIT

SUMMARY

The Hermit is about Universal love and higher spiritual knowledge. He is the healer and a great teacher, the wise man.

He represents a great inner journey and gaining of wisdom. Being the wise man and showing others the way. The wise man understands responsibility and demonstrates it.

NUMEROLOGY

The number nine has to do with attainment, completion and endings. When we complete something properly we can heal and finally let it go.

We also learn wisdom and knowledge from coming to the end of a journey. We understand responsibility and that we always have to clean up after ourselves.

The number nine is a magical number. No matter how you multiply the number nine, it always ends up adding up to nine. For example, 9 x 9 = 81, 8+1 = 9. 5 x 9 = 45, 4+5 = 9.

There are also 108 Rama beads.

ASTROLOGY

Virgo is the ruler of this card. Virgo is an earth element.

Virgo rules the sixth sign of the zodiac and is to do with health. Virgo governs our digestion system, and it has to do with analyzing and serving, this is how the Hermit serves us. The Hermit is the inner digestion of our knowledge; he is the processor of what we eat.

MYTHOLOGY

The God Hermes, who conducts souls to their resting place, connects well with this card. Long ago many cultures used to be buried in tombs and caves.

All stories that associate with hermits tell of wilderness, caves, wombs, anything to do with isolation. Even Jesus spent forty days and nights alone. Moses also spent forty nights alone on Mount Sinai before receiving the Ten Commandments.

When this card comes up, I ask my client what the Hermit means to them. The first thing most says is that Hermit is a recluse, someone that lives alone. I reply that this is true, and I also add to this by saying he actually lives between two worlds, like the ferry man. He can be with others when he has to be and is also happy to be by himself. They agree with this and can see themselves going through a hermit stage.

The Hermit is a guide, a guru, and a saint like St Francis of Assisi. Also, he connects to Gandalf from *Lord of the Rings*, Yoda from *Star Wars* or Merlin from *Camelot*. He has power and is more human.

In many grail legends we have stories of hermits as guides, where they blessed travelers. In Indian culture, pilgrims go on their pilgrimages, and Native Americans have their vision quests.

It is about a journey to a place of solitude. Something you do on your own.

Zarathustra was a German philosopher that lived circa 1800's. He lived in the mountains as a hermit. He walked around in the snowcapped mountains with his staff and he questioned absolutely everything. Some of his famous sayings were, "Everyman should be a God unto himself," "I have come back to myself. Now I can go forth," and, "The will to power".

Jung said without stimulation the unconscious does not activate.

A Journey to a Place of Solitude

SYMBOLOGY

Grey Outfit

An interesting phenomenon is that many Virgo women always wear black and white. More black than white, very classic styles, very Chanel. I have had many Virgo women in my tarot classes over the years that have proved this to me. If they do wear patterns, this is very rare. These are just like the Hermit's outfit; he wears a simple grey dress, grey is the combination of black and white.

White Beard

The white beard also denotes a wise man. White connects us with purity. Reminds me of Pei Mei in the movie *Kill Bill 2*. Grey is the blending of positive and negative energies.

Gold Wand

In his left hand he holds a gold wand. This wand connects us to the Fools and Magician wand, but now it is gold in color. Gold stands for universal wisdom, an internal wisdom. This is also his support mechanism.

It is in his left hand because he has arrived, he knows this energy intuitively. The left hand is the passive and unconscious side.

Lantern

In his right hand he holds the light of wisdom. The right side usually means active conscious energy.

The Hermit holds the light for us to follow. He sees the light and leads the way. You can see he stands on the snowcapped mountain looking down, waiting for us to look up and see the light.

Six Pointed Star

In the lantern you will notice a six pointed star. This connects us with the zodiac sign of Virgo and the sixth house.

 The point going up connects to the masculine energy of fire and air.

 The point going down connects to the feminine energy of earth and water.

 Together they make a six pointed star, meaning the union of the masculine and feminine energy.

The Hermit is Your Own Inner Counsellor

IN A READING

If you have ever owned a copy of Led Zeppelin's *Volume 4*, you will see this image of the Hermit on the top of *the Stairway to Heaven*.

When this card shows up in the reading, there may be a need to be alone, to spend time with the self, timeout. They like it, they want to be alone. They are alone but not lonely.

This card suggests the journey of discovery of the self. It is not an active 'out there' time, but one of an inner journey. And yes of course, for some this can be a lonely one.

It is a time of reflection, a reviewing time and maybe a time of going on a retreat. I was fortunate enough to do the ten day Vipassana mediation. I did not speak or look at anyone for ten days. It was one of the best experiences I have had in regards to getting to really know who 'I Am.' I can recommend this experience to any who is ready to live like a nun for a period and learn what meditation is really all about.

This is a great card to follow the Strength card when we are just starting to question who we truly are inside, now with the Hermit we can get some answers.

People do not understand you all that well while you are going within. That is why the Hermit holds the light for you to see. The light reminds me of my bedside light; it is comforting and makes me feel like all is well in the world. I am warm, cozy and ready for sleep.

People will climb their own mountain at their own pace. For example, we are all like eggs in an incubator and we will all hatch when we are ready. Interesting fact is; if you crack the egg for the chick while it is hatching through, the chick will die. The chick needs to make its own way out, fight through the outer shell to gain the strength it needs to survive in the world.

Or as the saying goes, 'when the pupil is ready the teacher appears' to teach you whatever that lesson may well be. People you do not like in life may be your guides. And what do guides do? Guides are there to show you the way to your own inner Hermit, to your own inner knowledge.

We all have the Hermit living inside of us. The Hermit resides inside the Fool's bag at the end of the staff.

No one teaches you anything new, you already have the knowledge inside you. Guides or people just help you bring it out. They help you to access your voice. Help you set your boundaries. You did not even know you did not like it until your guide brought it to your attention.

We have to unlearn what we have been taught so we can access our inner genius. I have heard wise men say many times, "Empty your cup, so I can fill it up".

Leonard Cohen said, "There is a crack in everything and that is when the light gets in". Which makes me think, the bigger the crack the more light gets in.

In this part of the journey we take all we have been taught and it is time to take it internally to process it. To digest it or discard what we do not like. It is crunch time. It is time to give yourself counsel; acting as your own counselor. This is when you use more than intuition; you use both intuition and your rational mind.

The Hermit asks you to be aware of your pace, to know thyself. For example, do not make agreements you know you cannot keep. In the Kabbalah we say, 'To think before you speak and think before you act.' The Hermit is the pause before the action. To allow yourself time.

To be integrated. Integrity is the filter. Dr Phil says, 'Integrity is what you do when you do not have to do it, and integrity is what you do when no one is watching.'

It is time to lead by example, to be the example. Demonstrate your stuff. Walk your talk. Practice what you preach. Talks cheap, etc.

Remember the number nine is about responsibility and wisdom. A feeling of trusting yourself and the ability to know.

SHADOWS	KEYS
Being in the dark	Appraisal
Coldness	Meditation
Narrow mindedness	Fasting
Seclusion	Writer
Worrier	Spiritual journey
Unsociable	Alternative medicine
Manipulating	Modest

SHADOWS	KEYS
Shy	Retreat
Perfectionist	Thinker
Unable to relate to people	Meticulous
Alienation	Prayer
Obstinacy	Quest
Suspicious	Healing
Fear	Humble
Impatience	Author
Ignorance	Zen
Arrogance	Integrity
Folly	Introspection
	Solitude
	Guidance
	Advice
	Patience
	Solitude
	Perfecting
	Seeking
	Seer
	Sage
	Wisdom
	Knowledge
	Independence
	Inner search
	Contemplation
	Self sufficiency
	Maturity

Tarot in Action

Be inaccessible.
Meditate, have time out alone.
Go camping, hiking or bushwalking.
Read a book.
Write in your journal.
Write poetry.

Lunch alone in the park.
Go to the movies alone.
Zen the room.
Study quietly.
Go on a vision quest.

Quotes

'We make rules for others and exceptions for ourselves.' – Ruanna.

'When you look out there you're dreaming, when you look inside you awaken.' – Carl Jung.

'If you don't go within, you go without.' – Ruanna.

'Everyman should be a God unto himself.' – Zarathrustra.

'I have lots of company when I'm alone.' – Ralph Waldo Emerson.

Books to Read

Conversations with God I, II and III by Donald Neale Walsch.

Chapter 14

*...Halfway through his journey it is time for The Fool
to experience life's changes with the turning of the Wheel...*

X THE WHEEL OF FORTUNE

SUMMARY

This card is representative of the wheel of life and life keeps turning. This wheel turns anti-clockwise. There is a time for every purpose, just like the four seasons. There is a time for summer and winter, a time to be happy, and a time to be sad, etc.

There is value at being on bottom of the wheel, just as much as there is value at being on top of the Wheel. You can say the Hermit lives at the bottom of the wheel. When you are on the bottom of the wheel, you are visiting your inner Hermit. Being on the bottom is when you turn inwards and you have to withdraw from the outer world to learn and understand the inner lessons.

Justice lives on the top of the wheel. You can see the sphinx holding the sword that also connects us with the sword in the Justice card.

Note that society places more value on being out there; on top of the wheel, but it is more important when you go within.

NUMEROLOGY

The number ten suggests a new beginning but on the next level. The number one connects us with the Magician and all the new energy and the zero connects us with the Fool, coming full circle and the continual movement.

The number ten is about coming full circle, cycles and regeneration, turning forever inwardly and forever outwardly. Evolution and Revolution, like the fractals.

The wheel is forever turning just like your birthday comes around every twelve months and every time your birthday comes around, you are another year older, damn it!

ASTROLOGY

Jupiter rules the Wheel of Fortune. Jupiter is the planet of growth and expansion, travel and your belief systems. Remember Jupiter rules the Fool card and he is also known as the traveler, ready to extend himself on a new level, always searching for the truth.

When we begin something new on a new level, it says you are ready to expand and gain further knowledge, higher knowledge. Circumstances may be making you stretch.

MYTHOLOGY

In the old pagan days, they would build a huge wooden wheel known as the Wheel of Time. It would be set alight and rolled down the hill. This was a ceremonious occasion to celebrate the harvest Imbolc, and to ensure that the seasons keep turning. Today this may not be such a good idea so we have bonfire nights around the Solstices, but bonfires today may also be a threat and an environmental hazard.

The first of May is spring time in the Northern Hemisphere, which was celebrated with merriment and song; known as May Day with dancing around the May Pole.

Other symbols of wheels in our everyday life are: tattersalls, roulette wheels, spinning wheels, medicine wheels, merry-go-rounds, the zodiac, bicycles, steering wheels, Ferris wheels, water wheels, clocks, balls, planets, and man's first major invention was the wheel.

The gorgeous fairytale of *Sleeping Beauty* connects well with this card. How she pricks her finger on the spinning wheel and falls asleep for a thousand years before her Prince Charming finds her and awakens her.

The Wheel suggests reincarnation and the law of cycles.

Another mythological story is *The Three Fates* or *Crones*; one Fate spins the wheel, one weaves and the other cuts the thread.

Goddess Fortuna also connects well with this card. She says there is fortune, whichever way the wheel turns for you.

And of course there are the fortune cookies.

The Wheel of Fortune Always Brings Fortune No Matter Which Way the Wheel Turns

SYMBOLOGY

Sphinx

Sphinxes appear throughout history and in many cultures are representative of guardians, our guides and a symbol of protection. We have the classical sphinx in front of the pyramids in Egypt. Today, we can have lions at the entrance of our front gates or sometimes we see eagles.

The sphinx in the Wheel of Fortune card holds the sword of discrimination and detachment. Discrimination because it can cut through all the confusion and doubt, detachment because it can sever what is of no longer use.

The sphinx does not use the sword to stop the wheel, nor hurry it up. It is watching the flow or going with the flow. The sphinx may be our true self and is observing the turn of the wheel, watching to see how our life is turning out, how our life is unfolding.

The Four Figures

The four figures correspond to the four fixed signs of the zodiac:
- The Bull, the fixed sign of Taurus and the Earth element.
- The Lion, the fixed sign of Leo and the Fire element.
- The Eagle, the fixed sign of Scorpio and the Water element.
- The Angel, the fixed sign of Aquarius and the Air element.

They all have many things in common. They are all sitting in a grey cloud, which symbolizes wisdom. They are all gold in color, wearing wings, suggesting they come from a higher consciousness, connected to the source, and are spiritual messages.

There is a Bible connection here to Matthew, Mark, Luke and John. All reading from the book of life or they may be writing their gospels, writing the scriptures. In Revelation 4.7 it speaks about the Wheel of Ezekiel.

Fixed

In astrology, Fixed refers to the middle of the season when we are in the midst of summer, winter or fall. People born during these fixed terms can be quite static and unbending in their decisions making processes.

In this tarot card, fixed, basically suggests that certain things in life stay fixed. For example, if we die tomorrow, everything else will still be turning. Our little cog does not affect the other cogs.

Snake and Jackal

You can see the snake is heading towards the bottom of the Wheel. The snake represents wisdom and rebirth. The snake is that part of us that can shed the old skin, accept the rational and intellectual from visiting the Hermit at the bottom of the Wheel.

One major thing I have learned from working with tarots is that when we are on the bottom of the Wheel we are deep in our emotions. This is not a good place to make any decisions from.

The snake then turns into the Jackal, coming back up the Wheel. The Jackal represents the head and our intellect. It suggests we need to use the rational intellect to get back on top. We can make clear decisive decisions from there.

The Jackal connects with the Egyptian God Anubis. Anubis is the Egyptian God of the dead. It also connects to the Greek God Hermes. He represents consciousness from lower to higher form.

Letters and Symbols

You can see there are letters around the Wheel.

There are English letters that make up distinctive words such as:
- TORA, connecting us to the Hebrew book of knowledge that the High Priestess holds
- TROA, is a Hebrew word for gate, suggesting this card is a gateway
- ROTA, meaning rotate, Latin for wheel, such as the wheel is turning
- ORAT, Latin for orate, to speak, argue or entreat
- ATOR, known as Athor or Hathor, Latin form for Earth Mother, or Egyptian Goddess of Joy
- TAOR, also known as the Egyptian Goddess of Darkness
- TARO, a particular food root readily available from Polynesian Islands
- TAROT, maybe this is where the name tarot comes from?

Then there are Hebrew letters. These Hebrew letters means God. God of the Self. They are:
- 2 HEM, letters that connect us to conditions, order, the Emperor and the Aries zodiac.
- RESH, connects us to rebirth and the energy of the Sun.
- YOD, connects with going within, the zodiac of Virgo and the Hermit inner journey energy.

The Yod also means blessings in disguise, gifts from the Universe or pleasant surprises.

In the inner circle there are also alchemical symbols suggesting evolution and involution:
- Next to the T there is symbol of Mercury and connects to the Air element.
- Next to the A there is the symbol of Salt and connects to the Earth element.
- Next to the R there is the symbol of Water and connects to the Water element.
- Next to the O there is the symbol of Sulphur and connects to the Fire element.

It is suggested that these were the first four main elements discovered. There are 92 natural elements, the rest are all man made. Last time I checked there were 116 known elements.

Salt is a fascinating element. It is made up of sodium and chloride together. What happens when these two elements are pulled apart? They are two highly volatile elements. Together they create synergy, and we need salt in our system.

Salt was and still is a valuable resource. In times past, we used to get paid with salt, this is where the word salary comes from and the saying "the salt of the earth," meaning that it is good. I also learned that lithium is a type of salt, and those suffering from bi-polar episodes are tested for their lithium levels.

In the middle of the Wheel we have the hub. The internal constant. I see the hub of the Wheel as the bull's eye, our goals and aims. We need goals to move towards, otherwise we just go round and round on the Wheel of life.

I do not think it is too good to have both feet in the hub of the Wheel. Likewise having both feet on the outer rim of the Wheel. When you are on the top everything is great, and when you hit bottom everything is disastrous.

I like to think, having one foot in the middle of the Wheel and staying focused on what you are aiming at and having the other foot on the outer Wheel aware and alert that life will keep throwing challenges at us is a proper balance to have, so we can move out of the way.

Our outer lives turn and turn in all of life's drama. It is the inner self that needs to change and is all the more important.

The Wheel of Fortune Teaches Us to Be in the Flow

IN A READING

The Wheel of Fortune means the end of a chapter, therefore the beginning of a new chapter. Turning over a new leaf, or a new page. When we first set off on a journey, this card tells us to be aware that there may be random change along the path, which can either help or hinder the journey.

We have the choice to either write our new chapter, like the four figures who are writing their destiny, or we can get out of the way. Life will still work out for us. You may choose to just sit there and breathe and life will still unfold. Or in the work place, you know your work is coming to the end of term, do you start looking for another job immediately or eventually get sacked before you start looking for another job?

There are some people who will search for a new position, maybe have a week off in between the two jobs. And there are others that want a longer period off and may have the whole year off and start looking for a new position in the new year.

Destiny versus Fate

They seem to have a similar meaning yet different. For me, destiny has happier connotation and fate more of bad luck energy.

Destiny: one's lot of fortune; predetermined cause of events; designed; intended; certain distinction. Fate: destiny; a divine decree; inevitable destined doomed; a prophetic declaration of what must be.

Remember the sphinx is just sitting there, she stays out of the way. It will all happen in its own time, do not use the sword. There is always a cause and consequence.

But successful people do not just sit back and wait for things to happen. They choose to wait, but they also know when to act. They trust themselves; they are tactful, appropriate and purposeful. They do not make decisions from their emotions. When they go for it, the sphinx watches everything turn in their favor.

This always reminds me of the TV show called *The Apprentice* when Mark Bouris says to the contestants, "Do not take this personally. Its business, you're fired".

This card suggests that you are about to change your position on the wheel of life; that it is turning in your favor whether you are on the top of the Wheel of on the bottom. So this card says be aware of the turn of the wheel, there is a change a-coming!

There are two distinct views. An internal change followed by the external change in your environment – this is seen as proactive. Or an external change of your environment followed by an internal change, which is more a reactive. If our inner energy changes our outer exterior changes.

A few of my favorite sayings are: "For things to change first I must change", "If it's to be it's up to me." And at times it is important to just "Go with the flow."

This is one of those cards that I like to ask my client the question, "Look at your life and where you are going, where do you see yourself on the wheel?" Some may say on the top, and others may say on the bottom. Others may say in the center and others may say climbing back up the Wheel. This is a great insight for you in the reading and a great visual for the client.

I also understand that climbing back up or climbing back on the horse may be really hard to do. Falling from grace can be quite hard for some to experience, it is so easy to fall and it is twice as hard to stay on top.

The descent is the most valuable part of the journey. But when we come back up we have learnt something about ourselves and therefore we change. We have looked into our unconscious, our internal level, we have consulted with our inner Hermit and we have discovered it ourselves, and that is what I call Fortune.

SHADOWS	KEYS
Overly optimistic	Cycles
Roller-coasting	Lay-back
Ups & downs	Big time
Hiding behind fate	Believing
Same difficulties coming again & again	Gifts
Can't be bothered with details	Opportunities in disguise
Drinking or eating excessively	Charity
Big promises	Sense of humor
Setback	Abundance
Diminishing	Popular
Obstacles	Coincidence
Temporary bad luck	Synergy

SHADOWS	KEYS
Unpleasant surprises	Destiny
Entropy	Movement
Non action	Vision
	Good Luck
	New Cycle
	Synchronicity
	Fortunate
	Sociable
	Uni-verse
	For-tune
	Fame
	Possibilities
	New developments
	Expansion
	Bounty
	Fame

Tarot in Action

Buy a lottery ticket.
Give to charity.
Go to a sociable event.
Learn from the lessons, no matter how dark.
Actively change jobs.
Be proactive.
Enjoy the ride.
Ride a bike.
Go on a Ferris wheel.
Say Yes to a No and maybe No to a Yes.
Change of residence, job or outlook.
    Sit back and wait.
    Think bigger.
    Think positive out of a bad situation.
Things turning for the better.
Celebrate it.
Don't sweat the little things.
Turning point.

Quote

"We shall not cease from exploration
And the end of all our exploring,
will be to arrive where we started
And know the place for the first time." – T. S. Elliot, *Four Quarters 1*.

Books to Read

Many Lives Many Masters by Dr Brian Weiss.
Life Between Lives by Dr Michel Newton.

You will notice that the next cards are less personal; the cards have now become more universal or collective.

Chapter 15

As an adult The Fool encounters the trail of his world with Justice...

XI JUSTICE

SUMMARY

We are now at the halfway mark, in the middle of the Major Arcana journey. Now the Fool can use the sword that the Sphinx in the Wheel of Fortune did not use.

In summary, this card is about truth. Finding out about our truth. What is your truth? At the bottom of the Wheel of Fortune we discovered some truths about ourselves that we may not like. We really have a good look at ourselves. We may not like our thoughts, our actions, our habits, etc.

Basically, we get in our own way and we need to amputate those parts that we do not like, or that we do not need any more. This card says "Get your house in order." Use the sword to cut away that which is no longer of use to you – an adjustment needs to be made.

NUMEROLOGY

The number eleven is a master number, connecting us to a higher order. Master number people are light workers; they are here to help others. The two ones are demonstrating a balancing act, they are symmetrical and working in tandem.

The number eleven adds up to two. Number two is a feminine energy; it is about balance and equality. The number two also connects us to the High Priestesses' energy. The High Priestess connects us to the inner truth, the inner way law, this is why she holds the Tora.

ASTROLOGY

The scales in Justice connect us perfectly to the astrology sign of Libra, ruled by Venus. Venus operates in Libra in a harmonious and peaceful way.

Libra is all about balance. Librans like to have a balanced perspective and they want everything to be fair. They do not mind giving; their challenge is to get some back.

Libra is an Air element; therefore, the balance needs to be foremost in their mind. Librans analyze everything all the time. They also may go through the paralysis repertoire and not make decisions.

MYTHOLOGY

Goddess Maat judged the hearts of man by weighing the hearts of the dead against a feather and then judged their needs. In some tarot cards you can actually see a heart and feather in the scales.

Long ago women were the judges until they were called witches. In medieval times, during the 1500's there was a holocaust against innocent women and from this, the judicial system was born. How else were they going to feed them, house them and torture them in jail? They would take their houses and land to pay for their crimes.

The female part of the card connects us back to the Venus aspect, to the Empress and the High Priestess; the feminine emotions, female power. In Justice, the decisions are based on the open. What is seen and the factual. The questions we have to ask are: How much have you loved? How did you love?

Today, we have the *Judge Judy* show with Judith Sheindlin and *People's Court* with Judge Marilyn Milan on TV. It is great to see women back in power and in these shows you really see the intellect vs the emotions playing out; the balancing act of the heart and the head.

You can see the female in the Justice card is not blind-folded like our images of the Justice is usually today. In the Justice card, the veil is hanging behind her, suggesting that the "Truth is the same today as it is tomorrow."

She has the third eye for all knowing and all seeing in the crown.

In mythology we have the Goddess Athena. She is usually displayed with an owl on her shoulder. Goddess Athena was born out of her father's head and intellect. This is why

she is always dressed wearing masculine armor. Goddess Athena wins all her battles through strategic means. Athens in Greece is named after her, the model for justice. Goddess Minerva is the Roman equivalent.

Justice connects to the reasoning and the rationale on a mental plane. The sword she holds belongs to the Magician. The sword represents the mind, the symbol of the intellect, our thinking function and the air element. The scales represent balance.

We need to internally balance before making proper decisions and this card is telling you to get back in balance. This is where you decide mentally to make decisions to get rid of the old ways that do not work for you anymore. Time to prepare the check list, mentally prepare, review everything before the action, really start the ball rolling, getting rid of attitudes, ideas that are no longer valid, that no longer support you; no longer serve you. But they do not go until the Death tarot card.

Justice is about taking responsibility for your own life, no one can be responsible except you. It is time for growing up; you cannot blame Mum and Dad anymore; no more pointing the finger at anyone. When you point the finger at someone, remember that there are three fingers pointing back at you...look at yourself.

To Get Your House in Order

SYMBOLOGY

The Blue Sword

The sword of discrimination can cut through the forest to see the trees. The sword is in the right hand, suggesting conscious, rational, masculine, active and clarity energy.

The color blue connects to our throat chakra. The blue sword can cut through the emotions; standing by your word, your principles. Speaking your truth and being responsible for yourself.

The Scales

The scales are in the left hand, the feminine, unconscious, passive and inactive energy. It suggests the feminine intuition has to be balanced, internally balanced.

The intuition has to be supported by logic mind, the sword and the scales give us two choices and two sides.

The Crown

The crown connects us to the head chakra, the crown chakra and the masculine ego. The intellect, the ego and the mental plane needs to be acknowledged.

The feminine third eye can cut through the ego, the ability to see the unseen.

Red and Green Outfit

The red outfit that the Justice wears connects us to the Emperor, Mars and the masculine energy.

The green cape connects to the Empress, Venus and the feminine energy, suggesting the energies between the masculine and feminine needs to be balanced.

The broach over the heart area connects us to the Heart Chakra. Love is the Truth, and love conquers all. The heart connects to the Leo zodiac sign and the lion in the Strength card. We tap into our inner strength when you come from the truth.

White Shoe

You can see one white shoe poking out from underneath her outfit. The color white connects us to inner purity. It also looks like a pivot point between the scales and the sword.

Yellow Hair

The yellow hair connects us right back to the Fool, our innocence and pure mental forces. There is also yellow above the veil connecting us to the source, love, truth, and higher forces.

Magenta Veil

You can see the magenta veil behind the figure. The color magenta connects us to the higher authority, higher power, royalty and power.

In ancient times only royalty, bishops and the wealthy could afford to wear these colors. The cost of purples, magenta and violet colors was far too high for ordinary folks to afford.

Grey Pillars

The color grey represents wisdom. She is the pillar of strength.

The grey platform, the strong foundation connecting us to the Goddess Maat and the stable base on which order can be built.

Justice looks similar to the High Priestess tarot card. You can see many similarities, i.e. they both have pillars; they both have a veil stretched between the pillars. Both are sitting on a simple stool, no thrones. The number eleven adds up to the number two. I like to think that the High Priestess represents inner truth and Justice the outer truth.

Always Remember You Make Proper Decisions from a Rational Place, Not from the Emotions

IN A READING

This card is saying it is time to weigh up, measuring and adjust your life. To believe in yourself, to take responsibility for the next stage of your journey with wisdom.

Some wrong doing needs to be made right. Something in the universe needs to be put back into balance. When there is something out of balance in the environment it is usually an indication that something also needs to be balanced within.

The sword in the right hand totally displays accountability!

Of course legal matters are possible with this card. All types of legalities are possible including legal documents and contracts that need to be signed. Dealing with lawyers and settlement cases for example title of houses, wills or a visit from the sheriff.

Court appearances may be required over car parking or unpaid speeding tickets through to relationship marriages or divorce cases.

You will get what you deserve with this card because we are dealing with universal law not just man-made laws based on factual evidence. Divine Justice, karma and just desserts.

People know in their heart what they will get. Heavy heart. Fair distribution, work cover and compensation.

SHADOWS	KEYS
Indecision	Witness
Evil purpose	Trial
Chaos	Diplomatic
Unfairness	Code of conduct
Disease	Decisive
Blind justice – mandate	Morals & ethics
Propaganda	Prosecution
Seeing only one's own way	Penalty
Manmade justice	Sentence
Karma - good & bad	Nature's Law
Agenda	Readjustment
Biased	Integrity
Revenge	Principles
Prejudice	Integrity
Injustice	Balance
Bad judgment	Arbitration
Bad advice	Responsible
Coldness	Fairness
Criticism	Harmony
Insensitivity	Partnerships
Severity	Contracts
	Impartiality
	Intellect
	Analysis
	Curiosity
	Rationality
	Evaluating
	Strategy
	Planning

Tarot in Action

Report a crime.
Don't take sides.
Don't accuse without knowing the facts.
Make long term plans.
Look at your own short comings.
Don't judge.
Fair play.
Look at truth instead of listening to gossips.
There are two sides to every story.
Legal and financial considerations.
Learning to get along with others yet be true to yourself.
It's ok to change your mind.
Practice what you preach.
There are two sides to every story.
Being clever.
Logic and reason.
Be prepared to take drastic measures.

Quotes

'People who live in glass houses shouldn't throw stones.'

'Justice has to be seen to be done.'

'If the truth be known.'

'The truth shall set you free.'

'Honesty is the best policy.'

'Tell the truth because people know the truth.'

'The truth hurts.'

Book to Read

Power Versus Force by David R. Hawkins Ph.D.

Chapter 16

...The Fool now undergoes some sort of loss and crisis, surrender and acceptance with The Hanged Man...

XII THE HANGED MAN

SUMMARY

There may be some form of panic after Justice.

I think the Hanged Man is the hardest card to work through – the hardest act. It is about letting go of everything you know, all the things that you listed in the Justice card. Some things you may need to surrender, some things you may need to sacrifice and accept the new to be able to move forward.

NUMEROLOGY

The Hanged Man is the number twelve. 1+2 =3.

The number one connects us to the Magician, you can see the red pants he wears connecting us to the Magician card. The number two connects us to the High Priestess and the blue top he is wearing connects us to blue of the High Priestess.

The number three connects us to the Empress energy, you can see the green leafage and the living tree, which connects us to all her potential and growth.

Yet there is stillness about this card.

ASTROLOGY

The planet Neptune rules this card and Neptune rules the Pisces' zodiac sign.

Pisces is illusive and can easily fall into victim mentality and become the martyr. Neptune is about illusions, transcendence and universal love. Learning how to sacrifice, surrender and accept the new.

MYTHOLOGY

We connect with all the dying God myths and stories with the Hanged Man card.

Odin from the Norse. He hung himself from the Tree of Life for eight days and nine nights, so he could learn the secret of the runes. But there was an exchange; he poked out his eye for his third insight. This was his sacrifice; he sacrificed something to open up to the higher form. Maybe this is where 'eye for an eye' comes from.

Prometheus hanging upside down from the mountain as punishment from the Gods, for stealing the fire from them and giving it to humans, connects to this card.

Of course Jesus dying on the cross also connects with the card, as does St Peter. St Peter was actually hung upside down because he felt unworthy to be hung the same way as Jesus. St Judas also hung himself after he realized what he did when he betrayed Jesus.

Here is another reason why I like the Justice card in this position, and not the Strength card that originally was in this position. Justice represents either King Herod or Pontius Pilot. The Hanged Man represents Jesus dying on the Cross and the Death card represents death and resurrection.

Hanging from one foot is an old ritual called 'the stocks.' In the old days if you did something that was not bad enough to go to prison for, you were placed in stocks for a period of time in the public square where people would ridicule you. The idea was to inflict public humiliation. People would throw rotten tomatoes at you. Maybe it also gave you an opportunity to take stock of your life.

We still have initiation rituals in all areas of our life today; these initiations are like an acknowledgment of achieving a level in your life.

We have rituals at our universities, weddings and traditional buck and hen's nights, heckling at twenty first birthday parties and roastings. When we enter the armed services, apprenticeships, entering into a gang, or are initiated as a monk and having to shave your head. We also have reality TV shows and Facebook that have taken public humiliation to a whole other level.

With the Hanged Man, we are being initiated into change. Some people do not like you to change. Some people do not want to see the change.

Joan of Arc, the martyr died for her beliefs, associates with the Hanged Man. Martyrdom is about giving up the personal life for a greater value. A sacrifice is made, willing to let go of something in the present to gain greater value later in the journey.

Here is one of those cards that I like to ask the client questions about, such as "What happens when you hang upside down?" Undoubtedly the answer is always "Blood rushes to your head". To which I agree and add; that hanging upside down is a yoga position, the idea being it brings blood and oxygen to the brain that aids concentration.

I then ask more questions, "What else happens?" the client may not respond, but I quickly add that when you hang upside down, money falls out of pockets, suggesting you have to let go of something or something needs to be released, maybe sacrificed before you can move on.

You also become still when you hang upside, giving you the opportunity to reflect on something. Children love to hang upside down on monkey bars or the couch reflecting on their navel.

We are also born upside down. By hanging upside down, your spine naturally aligns.

This is About Surrendering Your Ego Control over the Situation

You are suspended from activity. You can see the Hanged Man's hands are tied behind his back, you cannot see them. This suggests there is no action needed here, no hands, no actions. This is not a card of activity.

The handless maiden is a beautiful myth that connects beautifully with this card.

I think the most important thing that happens when you hang upside, is that you see everything from a different point of view, a different perspective or angle. It can be a long wait for some people but all this inaction allows you the time you need to reflect and trust, letting go of things. You will then make space to take in new ideas to move in a new direction.

People may get impatient with this card. When you go through a process you want to see the progress immediately. In today's western living we get impatient just waiting in a queue. We get impatient waiting in traffic; look at all the road rage going on. It is a drag waiting for public transport or when we get a headache we quickly want immediate remedy and take medicines to make it go away. The medicines are being advertised as being able to heal quickly.

This card says you have to go through this process. The Hanged Man is a major arcana. It is a major step even though it is a card of no activity. You first got the ideas in the Justice card and you want to change everything quickly, but your soul is saying no do not run, walk.

Aborigines here in Australia walk everywhere, this is an important part of the journey. If there are any issues by the time they arrive at their destination they have worked through the issues and resolve them.

This card connects to the law of 'Lag.' Lag is a fundamental law of the universe and suits every case scenario. Everything has a lag time. On average, there is about a year and half engagement period before the wedding day. In the car industry there is approximately a five-year lag period from the blueprint of the new car to the showroom. In the education system there is a ten-year lag period before a new system is integrated in the schools. With mobile phones I think the latest lag period is two weeks.

This waiting or Lag acts like a trial, and this trial will go on until you surrender. Surrender what you may ask? Surrender the Ego. The Ego part of you has no control; it is your spirit or soul that will take you forward. You have to surrender your ego control of the situation over to your spiritual side.

Surrender Ego control of the situation. Surrender and let go of your opinions and your attitudes. Remember it is only one person's point of view, one person's perspective. Also remember that the Ego does not want you to wake up to your spiritual side and this may hold you back.

You need to look at your life from a different perspective, and when you do, some things take a complete flip. Put yourself in other people's shoes to open up to a greater view.

Positive

A real positive with the Hanged Man is looking at your thought patterns and then looking at the total opposite. This will activate the Hanged Man's energy, and when you 'get it,' everything lights up, and you may even hear yourself saying, "that's it!" This is the energy of this card.

Negative

The negative is the eternal martyr because of Neptune's influence. That self-sacrificing, inflexible and righteous energy. When a person is righteous they might as well be dead right.

SYMBOLOGY

Hanged Man's Legs

You will notice that is legs are in a reverse shape of the number four. The number four usually suggests order and being in control. But being reversed means we need to reverse our normal way of dealing with reality, to look outside the box.

The Tree

Known as the Tree of Life. The color green is about potential and growth and connects us to the Empresses' ever abundant energy. There is green leafage on both sides, but the Hanged man is not using the creativity. It is not that he has lost the growth energy, because everything is growing around him as it should.

The tree is alive with living wood and leaves, but he is stationary, not struggling. Suggests life is in suspension.

The tree is in the shape of a 'T-junction.' He may be contemplating which way to go. I also like to mention to my clients that it does not matter which way you go because it is green at both ends.

Gold Rope and Gold Shoes

You can see that the Hanged Man does not feel abandoned. He is not struggling, he is just suspended. He is still connected to the Higher Source with the gold rope and the gold shoes he wears.

Golden Halo

The yellow hair connects to the Fool card. Yellow has to do with the thinking function, the mind and the rational use of this energy.

The golden halo represents the enlightenment that comes from when you surrender. Looks like a halo or the light bulb moment when you break through, like when you have a BFO (Blind Flash of the Obvious).

The Hanged Man is About When the Penny Drops and the Light Comes On

IN A READING

This card says you need to keep faith in the power of self. Just accept that where you are is exactly where you are meant to be and that this process is an important part of the journey, even if it is painful.

Remember the lag part of the journey. Gandalf from *The Lord of the Rings* said, "A good wizard never arrives a minute too soon, or a minute too late, but precisely when he means too".

You need to get yourself out of the way, put your ego in its proper place. Let your inner light shine through and just surrender to the process, trust the process. Connect with your Neptune Universal Love energy.

This card may represent a Mexican "stand-off.' It is hard to say, "Sorry I'm Wrong". What this really means is that you are afraid of moving forward, fear of change. By keeping them at arm's distance keeps your ego in control of the situation. Just surrender the ego.

Remember that ego always wants to be in charge and always wants to be right. Ego does not want you to wake up to your spiritual side.

Some people may have to be really angry before they will move on in a new direction. Some people will hang there until they cannot stand it anymore before they will let go. We will all work through this Hanged Man in our own peculiar and particular ways.

This card allows you to be true to your higher self. It is a purification process, so you can get ready for the next card or the next level or the next chapter of your life. Taking stock of your life, the trial and the initiation.

Another example is like when someone is dying of cancer. The process they go through is the purification process. It is a slow process. Some people may take six months, others six years.

It is time to do a major cleanup of your life, a spring clean to shift the chi energy from the inner level to the outer level.

SHADOWS	KEYS
Impressionable	Visions
Resigned	Unselfish
Illusive	Sacrifices
Predisposed	Mysticism
Misleading	Transition
Victimized	Period of delay
Living in fantasy	Transcend
Malleable	Stillness
Listening to gossips	Delay
Too absorbed in one's own problems	Suspended activity
Inflated Ego	Lag
Lack of willpower	Being quiet
Easily influenced	Forgiveness
Martyrdom	Release
Limbo	Postponed
Suspension	Flexibility
Detour	Rebirth
Apathy	Deliverance
Self-sacrificing	Attitudes
Alcoholism	Beliefs
Addictions	Dedication
Limbo	Sacrifice
Fear	Liberation
Stuck	Surrender
Traitor	Adaptable
	Contemplation

Tarot in Action

Do yoga classes.
Mediate while you are waiting in a queue.
Don't be swayed by public opinions.
Stop playing the role of the martyr.
Trust that things will turn around.
Take a nap, sleep on it.
Take a break, go for a walk.
Hang loose.
Say you're sorry.
Surrendering your Fixed Ideas.
Handling your hang-ups.
Hang loose.
Spiritual initiation.

Quotes

'There are no victims, only volunteers.'

'Look at it from a different perspective.'

Movie to Watch

Joan of Arc.

Books to Read

The Handless Maiden by Dorothy Black Crow.
Dying to be Me by Anita Moorjani.

Chapter 17

...The Fool now has the opportunity to let go of some old attitudes and habits that no longer serve him...

XIII DEATH

SUMMARY

This Death card is almost like a relief for some people because the Hanged Man process can be too hard.

The Death card can be a very scary card for some. Most clients I have are in fear of this card popping up in the reading. Many often say to me prior to their reading, "Please do not tell me if I am going to die". I would then proceed to inform them that the Death card is about a transformation of all sorts, an end to a relationship, a position at work, or an interest and moving on to the next stage with immense self-awareness.

NUMEROLOGY

There is no coincidence that the Death card is the number thirteen. There are so many associations with the number thirteen.

Some hotels in the United States do not have a thirteenth floor. They say it is unlucky to have thirteen guests for dinner because it connects to Judas being the thirteenth apostle.

In fact, Friday the thirteenth or Black Friday as it is known dates back to the French Government when they ambushed and killed the Knights Templar because they began to wield too much power, or they knew too much. The government of the day actually owed them a lot of money and couldn't pay, so they decided to call them heretics and get rid of them that way. But I somehow do not think they killed all of them!

Just recently, France experienced another Black Friday on Friday 13 November 2015, when terrorists blew themselves up at six different venues and killed over 130 people.

Today, many people like to view scary movies on TV or set up scary video night slumber parties on Friday thirteenth.

The number thirteen is a good luck number for some. I remember my mum having a little number thirteen charm on her bracelet. And my dad was born on the thirteenth of January.

The number thirteen also adds up to the number four. The number four connects us to the Emperor card and he represents order, boundaries, structure and control. The Death card may be suggesting the end of the old order, an old structure and the transition into the new order with new rules and new systems.

One major thing I have learned about the Death card is that if change is hard for you, it will be a hard process, and if change is easy for you it will be an easy change process.

ASTROLOGY

Scorpio ruled by Pluto connects to the Death card. Scorpio is about death, rebirth and regeneration. Scorpio is very intense and this comes from their ability to transform on an immense personal level, just like a butterfly transforms from a caterpillar.

Scorpio is the only zodiac sign that has three levels. You have the Scorpio as one level, they can rise up to become the eagle (you can see the eagles representing Scorpio in the Wheel of Fortune and in the World Tarot cards), and then they can rise up again to the dove level. Just like the Phoenix rising out of the ashes.

In many other cards you usually have the grim reaper on the Death card. Here we have a skeleton in armor sitting on a white horse. How unusual. The skeleton connects to the planet Saturn. Saturn rules our base foundations and our skeleton is the base foundation for our bodies.

MYTHOLOGY

Hades is the God of the Underworld. He dug in the underworld for the buried treasure.

All the grim reaper stories connect to this card.

The two great change cards are Death and the Tower. With the Death card you can feel the change coming, it is expected for example, when someone is dying of Cancer. With the Tower card, it is unexpected, a sudden impact, a quick change, just like being hit by the lightning bolt, a car accident, a phone call or even that dreaded knock on the door that changes your life forever.

Dying of a particular issue has three stages:
1. Actual ending, to which we experience the pain of loss. You can see in the card that the King is dead; his crown has rolled off to the side. This is a significant tragedy with the horse trampling the king.
2. Middle stage, where we grieve and mourn. This is represented by River Styx.
3. Rebirth stage, where we have the new life, the spring. You can see the Sun in the distance representing rebirth.

It may be hard to understand in what stage the person can be in.

I remember when Princess Diana split from her marriage; there was a lot of immediate pain for her, the loss of her family, moving away from the love of her boys, and her position. Her grieving went for about a two year period and then one day on TV, I remember seeing her step out of the car with that gorgeous bright blue off the shoulder dress, and her hair was swept off her face, and I knew she was in her rebirth stage, she was back.

The Death card may represent autumn, winter and spring. We need to keep pruning our lives, just like we do our gardens, to make way for the new growth and for the new relationships. We do this by doing a spring clean. Whenever people move out of my life, I know that I have learned those lessons and I am ready to meet new people and ready for new relationships and new challenges.

In the work place they go through reorganizations. This gives the organization an opportunity to get rid of the driftwood on the ground level, and replace old equipment and bring everything up to speed with the latest technology.

Death may represent of an old friend. When someone close to you moves interstate or immigrating overseas, the distance grows and grows and this may be painful, dramatic and, traumatic for some.

Death may also represent a marriage in trouble. The decaying period but there can also be the rebirth again. I find it interesting that when a woman does end a relationship she quite often cuts her hair or styles it differently. This is symbolic of nurturing herself and letting go of what is not working anymore.

This card may actually represent the marriage, the death of single life and the rebirth of duality. Also a birth of a child, and then the couple mourn the loss of their space.

All these examples are life changing experiences.

It is interesting that the word orgasm in French is pronounced Petit Mort, meaning Little Death. To have an orgasm you have to let go, this may be hard for some that like to keep in control. Some women may actually cry when they orgasm, again symbolic of letting it all go.

However, irrespective as to how it may be or play out, change is inevitable with this card, a transformation will take place. Letting go of old patterns, behavior, attitude, clothes, books, that broken thing, everything that you weighed up in the Justice card, now has to change.

You sat with it long enough in the Hanged Man card, the lag time has now come to an end. Now is the time of letting it go. Things will shift.

Death is About Transformation and Transition

SYMBOLOGY

River Styx

You can see the boats on the water, on the River Styx; this is the river of mourning, the river of forgetfulness. It is an emotional journey.

Here you can see you have to go through the transition from one side to the other side, from one state to the other state.

You have to go across the river, and pay the ferry man to get you to the other side. Have you ever seen movies when they put coins over the eyes and the mouth?

The Sun

The Sun in the background represents rebirth. The Sun connects to the Sun card and the feeling of being born again.

You can also see the two pillars, connecting us to the High Priestess and her connection to the two ways of duality. Death puts an end to separateness. Death ends duality and we go back to the source.

White Horse

The black horse was used for funerals and is still used for funerals today. Here the horse is white and connects us to the Fool's dog. White represents purity, suggesting purified by the death experience.

With the four Horsemen of the Apocalypse, the white horse represents death.

Horses are also symbolic of your vehicle through life, they represent movement, action energy, and it is currently happening!

The pink saddle connects us to love and peace, suggesting peace comes with death, and death through love.

Skeleton

You can see the Fool's red feather in the helmet, but it looks wet and limp.

The helmet that the skeleton wears suggests hidden thoughts, and that is correct, we do not really know what death knows.

The Skeleton in armor suggests not even armor will protect you, it is written, we will all experience death. Death strikes everyone. For example, Princess Diana, people were saddened by her death and just could not believe she died, millions of people watched her funeral from all around the world.

The dead person is the King, his crown has rolled off his head and to the side; you can see it under the horse. Next is the Bishop, he knows death is there and maybe he is praying for forgiveness, the child is offering up flowers, symbolizing a child's naiveté and how children can look at death in the face. The young girl is facing away, I would say she represents most of us, she is showing us that side of us that partially acknowledges death.

The Black Banner

 Very Gothic looking. You can see the white flower of purity. The white flower represents the, "Rose of England" also known as the, "Tudor Rose".

This Rose of England connects us to the two main houses of England at the time they were at odds with each other. The House of York versus the House of Lancaster, the Stuarts (James 1st) versus the Tudors (Henry 8th). Read more on this if you like as it is very interesting.

This rose symbolizes the two houses coming together, sorting out their differences and ruling together, then peace reigned thereafter.

The red rose versus the white rose. We see this red and white colored theme throughout the whole tarot deck. The flowers in the Magician card; even what the Magician wears is red and white. The cross in the Judgement card; this also connects us to the union of opposites.

The horse and reigns, the skeleton, the flag, it is all black and white and together they make grey, grey represents wisdom. Death is very black and white, very matter of fact, the end period.

Death is Inevitable, A Change, a Shift or an Upgrade Will Take Place

IN A READING

The Death card represents a death of a painful unproductive time or thing in our lives and/or a transformation on an internal level.

You need to look at Death in its widest form, death of anything that is cherished. For example, end of a life as we know it like when migrants move to another country, having to cross over the River Styx, and having to grieve the loss of their homeland, their family and friends. Today, we have boat people arriving to new lands, truly heart breaking situations on all counts.

Retirement, whether it is retirement from work and your career or moving to a retirement village and the end of your beautiful home that you worked hard to pay off for years and years and all of the life as you knew it.

Could be a physical change of life like menopause, or growing old is painful for some of us, or even a loss of a limb and learning how to cope with that. Working through all the grieving and mourning that comes with all of this.

Narcissus and the end of the ego. We all need our ego in our lives, we also need to learn to move forward with wisdom. Not so much the death of the ego but the transformation of the ego.

Metamorphosis and the caterpillar turning into the butterfly. This is truly a magical occurrence because there is nothing in a caterpillar to tell it that it will turn into a Butterfly. It is a complete transformation. When the Caterpillar is in the cocoon, you cannot see the change but the transition is going on on the inner side, and when the cocoon breaks open the butterfly has metamorphosed.

One thing is for sure with the Death card, change is the only thing that is constant.

SHADOWS	KEYS
Addictive	Resurrection
Bad tempered	Pain and Pleasure
Can't let go	Release
Won't let go	Secret
Poison	Metamorphosed

SHADOWS	KEYS
Inactivity	Orgasm
Selfish	Shift
Apathy	Determined
Compulsive	Fascinating
Hostile	Sensation
Undertakers	Synthesis
Stagnation	Endings
Loss of opportunity	Transformation
Loss of friendships	Clearance
Fear of change	Sweeping change
Pain	Regeneration
	New beginnings

Tarot in Action

Give up a bad habit and replace it with a good one.
Don't be afraid of change.
Learn to cut your losses and move on, then you may win it all.
Tell someone you love them.
Spring clean.
Get a haircut.
Forgiveness.
Cut through outworn forms to allow for new growth.
Examine things to their full potential.
Letting go of something.

Quotes

'Change is as good as a holiday.'

"When I let go of what I am I become what I might be." – Lao Tzu.

Book to Read

On Death and Dying by Elisabeth Kubler-Ross.

Chapter 18

...The Fool can now balance his emotions and regenerates with Temperance...

XIV TEMPERANCE

SUMMARY

Healing, rehabilitation and reconciliation. Re-stabilizing oneself after the death experience.

A great analogy I like to use is after you have changed to new tires on the car, you need to do the realignment. You let go of the old tires, replace them with new tires and realign all four of them together.

An inner alchemy takes place where you can blend the new with the gold you already have to ultimately create a new you.

NUMEROLOGY

1 + 4 = 5. Five is the number of progress and change. It is what I like to call the upgrade number, and the number of freedom. You have changed. The adjustments have been made.

The number five also connects us to the Hierophant card. To really hear what your intuition is trying to tell you, you have to listen to your inner side, and when you do you hear it and you change. There is some angelic presence or a connection to the angelic realm.

ASTROLOGY

The zodiac sign that connects to this card is Sagittarius. Sagittarius is a fire energy and all about the fire experience and renewal energy like when the Phoenix rises out of the ashes.

Sagittarius is all about breaking through the boundaries, that is why he holds a bow and arrow pointing up into the heavens.

MYTHOLOGY

In mythology, we have the Goddess Iris connecting this card; you can see the iris flowers in the card. She is the Goddess of the Rainbow. We see rainbows when the storm has passed and we have the peace after the storm. The rainbow is also God's promise to us. This also connects us to the Phoenix and renewal energy.

Goddess Iris was a messenger. She delivered good tidings and good news. She connects to Love and the heart. You can see she holds two cups and mixes the water, which sort of looks like a rainbow connecting between the two cups.

Temperance comes from the Latin word temper. Temper suggests tempo or time. Having time for or taking your time, giving it the time it needs and being patience. Other words like temperature, temped, temperate and temper your temper come to mind. Temperance is also a girl's name.

When you make a sword or kitchen knife you have to temper the steel. It starts off being just a blob of molten metal and you have to heat it up, hammer it, stretch it and fold it and cool it back down. Repeat this process until the sword or knife takes shape. When the process is complete the sword is stronger, sharper, shinier and more flexible. I also love how you need all the elements to make this happen. The metal comes from the earth; we need the fire to melt it, and the water to cool it down.

When I explain this process to my client in a reading, they can really relate this analogy to the hammering and pressure they are under in their life. But they also get that this tempering process does make them stronger.

In the Temperance card you can see the Angel holding two cups. One cup has the good stuff in it and he has emptied the other cup with things that are no longer needed. He now has to fill the empty cup with new things, then blend and mix and blend the two cups together, and with patience, wait for the new personality and new ways to then emerge.

For example, when you bring new people into the work place you need the time to restore the harmony and bring the balance back in the work place.

Note that it is the masculine energy that initiates change and the feminine energy that gets it together, blends it, mixes and molds it all together.

When there has been a huge change in your life, you need time for it to settle internally first. I understand it like an inner alchemy process has to occur, and I like to see this example as an hour glass.

A lot of people think they have arrived when they see this card. That is why there is a false dawn or false hope associated with it. If you have a look at the Angel, he has only just reached the other side of River Styx, there is still a path on his right side leading towards the sun in the distance that he has to walk down. Many people think as soon as they have reached the other side that they have made it, but they have not.

This suggests; do not go from one relationship to another, no rebound relationships, it is about finding your own feet first, stand on your own before getting straight into another relationship. Control your own cups, your own emotions.

On a psychological level, Temperance is about creating harmony and peace within. Stabilizing and adjusting oneself on a deep psychological level.

The Justice card is about balancing yourself on the mind level, creating harmony in the rational intellect level. Temperance is about balancing the emotions in the feeling level. Tipping the water from one cup to the other until the right mix is met.

Temperance is About Giving Yourself the Time for it to Settle Internally First, till it Feels Right

SYMBOLOGY

Archangel Michael

Here in Temperance we have Archangel Michael wearing white and grey, the colors of purity and wisdom. He was a Mortal Soul liberated by death.

Archangel Michael is the Patron Saint of the Army and of the Police. Call upon Archangel Michael when you have a fight on your hands, problems with a technical situation or a car problem, he can assist you and fights your battles for you.

The Red Wings

The wings connect us to the Air element, the intellect and to Angels, which are the messengers of the Gods. They are Red in color suggesting renewal energy and, once again, the rising of the Phoenix from the ashes. From Death comes new life.

Circles and Squares

When we see circles, they represent the feminine energy, squares represent the masculine and the triangle represents the Trinity.

You can see that the Angel wears a circle on his brow. This often reminds me of what a Doctor wears when examining patients, also a symbol of healing. The circle is over the masculine intellect area. The square with the triangle is over the feminine heart area.

This signifies a balancing and blending of the outer masculine with the inner feminine worlds. Adjusting the head, the intellect area with inner awareness and the heart.

Feet on Land and Water

You can see one foot is on the earth, signifying self-knowledge and standing on reality. The other foot is in the water signifying a connection to the unconscious world and that there are more unconscious issues to go through, a testing of waters so to speak.

You are connected to the higher self as well as self-knowledge, self-realization and self-actualization. It also reminds me of the connection between the High Priestess (the blue water) and the Empress (Green meadow). You become a stronger person when you combine these two energies together.

I remember watching an interview with Dame Elizabeth Murdoch before she passed away in 2013 aged 103. A reporter asked her, "You must be so proud of Rupert" referring to all his wealth. She answered, "Yes I am proud of what a good father and role model he is". Here you can see how bright she still was at age 103, how she brought these two worlds together. We often only want to see the material physical world, but it is the inner spiritual world that truly makes the difference.

Yellow Iris Flowers

The color Yellow connects us with happiness, the mind, intelligence, thoughts, ideas, intellect with awareness. Also connects with Goddess Iris and the messenger of good tidings.

Golden Sun

The Sun is in the background, just like it is in the Death card. The Sun also looks like a Golden Crown. The color golden connects us to the source, the ultimate force.

Having the Sun in the background suggests there are still more tests and lessons to go through. The Angel is just stepping out of the water, you have not arrived yet.

The path on the right hand side goes up and down, over hill and dale, heading towards the blue mountains in the distance, meaning there is a spiritual aspiration and outcome.

This path is not a straight path. I often say to my client that it is not right foot, wrong foot. It is right foot left foot till you get there. As long as you have a goal that you are aiming for, this will keep you on track.

The Water in the Cups

I always see the magic in this card, look how the water flows from one cup to the other, reminds me of a rainbow. The water does not go straight down; it arches across from one cup to the other.

It is the Tempering Process that Brings about the Integration

IN A READING

This card represents that the storm has passed, and the timing is good. They say that timing is everything!

It does feel like it is a good place to stop, a comfort zone! But remember it may be a false dawn, there are more tests to go through, you think you have arrived but you have not really.

This is the last card of the second row. A lot of people choose to remain in this energy, and why not, the storm has passed, right? For example, I always like to remember my folks here; they worked hard to own their own home and reach pension age, as they see it they arrived at their destination. Now they are happy that the Church is around the corner, the Doctor is up the street and they have coffee with their friends and plan what to eat every day, that's it for them. This is how I think 80% of people are like out there in the world.

But for people like you and me, we want to know more, we believe there is more than just that. But look at the tarot card in the next line, it is the Devil. This card is just too scary for some, so they choose to remain in the Temperance energy.

You may need to tip the cups a little this way or a little way to keep the balance.

SHADOWS	KEYS
Stuck in the past	New teachings
Duty	Alignment
Nothing wrong with me	Style
Too Delicate	Spiritual evolution
Refused to learn from past traumas	Bridge
Afraid of being hurt	Exploring
Looking for the easy way out	Enlightenment
Sensitive to pain	Mission
Impatience	Fusion
Lack of foresight	Straight forward
Conflict	Harmony
Quarrels	Health
Domestic Strife	Moderation
High maintenance	Compromise
Stagnation	Self-control
	Inner Alchemy
	Abstinence
	Self-restraint
	Tactfulness
	Art
	Blending
	Balance
	Integration

Tarot in Action

Practice self healing, using alternative healing modality i.e.: reflexology, massage, aromatherapy, ear candling, Reiki, etc.
Join a support group.
Take time out.
Spring clean, make space for the new.
Think outside the square.
Stand on your own two feet.
No rebound relationships.
Testing and trying out your beliefs and philosophies.
Creative combinations.
Have an objective outlook.
Finding a balance in your drinking.

Movie to Watch

Michael with John Travolta.

Quotes

"Follow your bliss." – Joseph Campbell.

"Good things come to those who wait." – Anon.

Book to Read

Radical Forgiveness by Colin C. Tipping.

Chapter 19

...The Fool's Journey now leads him into the underworld in order to discover what is responsible for his crisis...

XV THE DEVIL

SUMMARY

Our deep desires, our shadow. Connects to our fears, our hang ups and drama hooks. We create an emotional web and then we are caught in that web which we cannot escape.

Issues with bondage, limitations and relationship dependency, only through self-realization and knowledge are we then released and experience a personal rebirth.

NUMEROLOGY

One plus five equals six. The number six connects to the Lovers' card. In the Devil card we see the couples together again. When you look at both cards they look like the positive and negative of a photo.

In the Lovers' card the woman looks up to the Angel to a higher purpose, they have choice and they are committed to each other without chains. In the Devil card, the Lovers are both tied up in chains and in the dark.

ASTROLOGY

The two planets that connect well with the Devil tarot card are Saturn and Pluto.

Saturn is the ruler of Capricorn. You can see the zodiac sign of Capricorn on the Devil's uplifted hand. Also, the Capricorn Goat connects to the Devil, you can see he wears the goat horns. Saturn is well known for being a hard task master and the controller. When we have too much restriction we see the dark side of the Emperor, which is the Devil.

Pluto is the God of the underworld. Pluto rules the zodiac sign of Scorpio and Scorpio rules sex, money, and commitment in relationships, which are the main areas the Lovers may have issues to deal with in their relationships. The Devils feet are the claws from the eagle, the eagle connects to Scorpio.

MYTHOLOGY

The Greek God Pan also known as Bacchus, or the God of Wine, connects to the Devil card. He enjoyed himself with wine, women and song.

The Satyr from Shakespeare's *A Midsummer Night's Dream* is a wonderful example of how the Devil plays out. He plays the flute, which has seductive influences and temptations and made incompatible people fall in love with each other.

The *Pied Piper of Hamlin* is another perfect example for this card. The Pied Piper said he could help the villagers get rid of the rat plague by playing his magical flute in exchange for money. When he returned to collect his payment the villagers said they did not have to pay up because the rats were gone, they thought they could get away with it. In the morning, when the villagers awoke they realized all the children had disappeared. The Pied Piper said he would gladly return the children after they paid up what was promised and agreed too. It gives another perfect meaning to the saying, "Pay the Piper".

Which brings up a really important point about the Devil card, you will always know what it is that you are dealing with the Devil. There is an exchange made; a deal is brokered, as they say, "Doing a deal with the Devil".

Tarot is also a very seductive tool and many people can get caught up with calling or visiting the same psychics over and over for answers. As a good reader you need to be aware of this and not get caught up with their high need.

The shadow side of God is the Devil.

The God Pluto dug in the earth for buried treasure. When we dig in the ground we find gold, diamonds, precious jewels, oil, water and minerals, etc. All this suggests that the best part of you is buried.

Many various cultures acknowledge the dark side by having a Shadow Altar. It may be smaller in size than normal but it is still acknowledged.

Our other half is down in the Shadow. Before you can fully understand yourself and be successful, you have to accept your shadow self.

If you are not aware or acknowledge what is down in the Shadow, it has the strongest influence over you – having you hooked as if you are hoodwinked.

The paradox is that it is our own fear that stops us from confronting what is down in our shadow. This fear holds us in bondage. It is self-imposed. Bondage is fear and we hold ourselves back, we become frightened to move forward. A classic example is when you hear someone say, "I hate my job". They are too afraid to leave so they stay. My thinking is, you are already metaphysically out of there, so you might as well physically leave – you will find another job and be less stressed.

The Devil card connects to sexual obsession in relationships, which could lead to bondage in another form, for example, S and M. Guilt around sex brings up fear, which leads to bondage.

The positive side to this card is commitment in relationships and good sex with a positive reading, which gives meaning to the "ball and chain" in marriage.

In yesteryear, man used to control the money and woman controlled the sex. Today, both parties work, both are making their own money. They work so hard that they do not have time for sex, which can bring up other issues surrounding money and sex.

This card rules all the taboo subjects that we do not like to talk about: sex, money, abuse, pedophilia, politics, depression, gay and lesbians, religion, abortion, racism, affairs, death, suicide, dementia, divorce and cancer to name just a few.

Because of the Capricorn energy of this card, we could make any obsession a God-like reality. Money, gold, sexuality, drugs, alcohol, food; any addiction like gambling, smoking, food, any temptation, any obsession, all can be hungered for. We need to feed the fix, anything in excess to the point of destruction. And with most of these obsessions the church has taught us to feel guilt.

The Devil rules our world through animal instincts or bestial senses. The three base chakras are known for their animal survival instincts. The first or base chakra rules our sexual urges and passions, this is also the strongest of all the chakras. Then we have the second or sacral chakra in the lower abdomen, below the navel. This one rules our creativity and reproduction. The third chakra rules the solar plexus and represents our hunger and confidence.

Some movie metaphors to illustrate these bestial five senses are:
- *Fatal Attraction* with Michael Douglas and Glenn Close. This is the movie where Glenn Close's character goes too far and boils the bunny. Today, this is well known as the "Bunny Boiler".
- *Seven* with Brad Pitt and Morgan Freeman. All the murders were animal related.
- *The Mask* with Jim Carey. When he wore the Mask his alter ego would override him... smoking!
- The classic *Godfather* with Marlon Brando where the horse's head is found in the bed.
- Another classic *Scarface* with Al Pacino when he became obsessed with drugs, money and power.
- *SpiderMan 3* was another movie that brought out the ego and power. The Black outfit had total control over him and he had to fight against this power to remove it.

Something from the Unconscious is Going to Become Conscious

SYMBOLOGY

The Devil

The Devil is Lucifer, God's number one archangel. Lucifer is also known as the Fallen Angel. Lucifer comes from the Latin meaning the light. Therefore, he is known as the Bringer of Light or the Light Bringer. The Devil puts light on the situation, shines the light on it and you uncover something. The Devil is the Revealer of Knowledge. When you accept your Shadow parts, it allows you freedom. Like a big plunger, it brings everything up so you can see it, deal with it, and then heal it.

The Devil has many names:

Beelzebub, Pluto, Lucifer, Fallen Angel, Satan, Hades, Diavolo, Diablo, Auld Nick, Baphomet, Prince of Darkness, The Evil One, Horned One, Demon, Evil Twin, Methuselah, Mifostofoleez from *Faust*, Perzuzu from the *Omen*, Horny Devil and the Scapegoat.

His feet are the talons of an eagle, which connects to Scorpio and all that sexuality issues. Usually the Devil is depicted with goat's feet. These feet can suggest a misuse of this energy.

His body is quite orange in color, suggesting courage and vitality and he has hairs covering the lower part of his body, covering his sexual parts. The Capricorn's sexual energy suggests a Horny Goat. You can also see his navel suggesting he still has human fragility.

The Torch

The Torch is pointing downwards, which is very wasteful and you can scorch yourself on it – it is not a useful creative way to use this energy. The Devil looks like he is lighting the man's tail as if it is a wick, as if he wants to see how much heat the man can withstand. Maybe he is trying to get the man to move on. Also, while we are down there, learn something from it.

Blacksmiths were seen as doing deals with the Devil. They were seen as Magicians because they worked with fire, where they turned bland blobs of metals into precious things.

Adam and Eve

Adam and Eve from the Lovers' card once again appear together in the Devil card. You can see the man's tail is a little flame, which connects to the Tree of Life, and the women's tail is a pomegranate and also to the Tree of Knowledge in the Lovers card.

The chains are loose around their necks, so they know what they need to do to get out of their situation but it is fear that keeps them stuck here.

Bat

The black background depicts darkness, the unknown and un-manifested light. Fear of the darkness, fear of the unknown and of the shadows. The Devil wears bat wings not the normal angel wings like the other Archangels cards. The bat as a nocturnal creature lurks in dark places, using sonar as an instinctual sense to move around. The wings are grey in color suggesting wisdom.

The Pentagram

The Star over the Devil's head is a reversed pentacle, known as a pentagram. Pentagrams are not symmetrical like the Pentacle – the bottom point is usually longer and it stands on this single point, rather than the two points of the Pentacle, suggesting the issue is not stable, it can easily topple over and it may be way too big for one person to handle.

The Pentagram is often seen as a satanic symbol. Today, the pentagram is understood to be a protection symbol, from Wicca and other Pagan beliefs.

The Box

The box or cube the Devil is balancing on looks too small for him. It may also suggest that he is too big or that the situation could be too big for some to handle alone, where you may need help with the situation.

The box is the half cube of knowledge or reality. You may be unconscious of what is in the box, our shadow is in the box or you are boxed in.

For example, you are an alcoholic and you tap into AA groups to help you face what you do not want to see. By doing so, it is acknowledged that you are on your way to recovery. Remember the Devil works in our lives as a light bringer.

Things that We Value Are Initially Hidden From Us or in the Darkness

IN A READING

If we do not know our shadow side we are only half complete. For example, you unlock something when you have a one night stand. Sexual encounters can reform you, it can shock you back to reality. You may have been drunk or under the influence, which got you into this situation.

This card suggests, that you put yourself in this position through fear, guilt, obsession or fear of consequences.

What you need to experience in life is the Spirit or the Universe will push in your face until you deal with it. This card tells you that you are stronger than what you think you are.

One of my favorite sayings is, "What you resist will persist". A movie that exemplifies this point beautifully is *Groundhog Day* with Bill Murray.

When the Devil shows up I like to ask to my client the question, "Where does the Devil live?" and I answer, "He lives in the underground". I follow on to say, "that I like it when the Devil shows up in a spread because it tells me that you are now ready to see something that you were not ready to see before. You are ready to heal with it and let it go and bring about peace. This is the sign he makes with his uplifted hand, the sign of peace".

Something is about to be uncovered and the Devil is saying you are ready to face it. Simply stated; this card means something from the unconscious is going to become conscious. The gift from the Devil for you is to see it yourself.

You need to look where this guilt, fear or obsession has come from, it is in your shadow, and you need to get to the root of the problem.

Doing a deal with the Devil, watch that you do not get burnt. There is always a price to pay, remember there are no free lunches.

Evil reversed is live. Devil reversed is lived.

SHADOWS	KEYS
Ignorance	Prudent
Manipulation	Change of view
Stubborn	Comparing
Complex / web	Respect
Greed	Discipline
Hatred	Mirroring
Denial	Future
Devious	Structure
Misery	Conventional
Envy	Responsible
Suppression	Commitment
Perverse	Permanence
Power struggles	Discern
Control	Truth
Power issues	Keeping a sense of humor
Entrapment	Strong sexuality
Lust	Authority
Anger	
Tyranny	
Obsession	
Restriction	
Frustration	
Stirring up unrest	
Darkness	

Tarot in Action

Don't play Devil's advocate.
Don't invalidate.
Don't impose your will or views on others.
Learn to laugh at your own problems.
Develop higher self-esteem.
Seek help.
Don't feel the need to test others.
Don't prove people wrong.

Movies

Spiderman 3. The one with the black outfit controlling and overpowering him.
Bruce Almighty with Jim Carrey.
War of Roses with Kathleen Turner and Bruce Willis.
Devil's Advocate with Al Pacino and Keanu Reeves.
Death Becomes Her with Goldie Hawn, Meryl Streep and Bruce Willis.
The Witches of Eastwick with Cher and Jack Nicholson.
Misery with Kathy Bates.

Quotes

'A problem well stated, is a problem half solved.'

'There's always risks in freedom, the only risk in bondage is that of breaking free.'

'Liberty is what other people give you, freedom is what you give yourself.'

"What a tangled web we weave when first we stumble to deceive." – Shakespeare, *A Midsummer Night's Dream*.

'You can't heal what you don't acknowledge.' – Dr Phil.

'Someone once gave me a box of darkness, it took me a while to realize that this too was a gift.'

'Misery loves company.'

'Better the Devil you know.'

Books to Read

Own Your Own Shadow by Robert A. Johnson.
The Seat of the Soul by Gary Zukov.

Chapter 20

*...Any issue that The Fool is struggling with
The Tower will help him resolve it...*

THE TOWER.

XVI TOWER

SUMMARY

This card often scares people or they see it as a negative card, but there is a lesson of enlightenment through some sort of cataclysm.

If you can allow the process to flow through without struggle it can be a very positive experience

It is the awakening, for some the Mack Truck experience, the big bang or put simply, the shit that hits the fan. A sudden disruption or sometimes it is just the straw that breaks the camel's back.

NUMEROLOGY

Number sixteen adds up to the number seven and connects us with the Chariot card. Remember you cannot sustain the energy of the Chariot for too long, the false façade will erupt. You hold everything together and then one day the explosion of anger energy from the unconscious to conscious is so strong it has to burst up and out.

The number seven is a powerful, analytical, spiritual and magical number. It is also a spiritual number, the number of faith and belief.

ASTROLOGY

There are two planets that connect well with this card.

The first card is Mars. Mars is known as the God of War. He has to do with revenge, aggression, competition and assertiveness, which could bring out the negative energy and expression of this card. The positive side is assertiveness, determination and courage.

Planet Uranus and Moons

The other planet, Uranus is the best planet that connects well with this Tower energy. The planet Uranus is actually tipped on its side and rolls around on its orbit around the Sun. They say an asteroid knocked it off its axis. All the moons also roll around Uranus.

No wonder Aquarians, which are ruled by Uranus, are radicals, revolutionary, and like to follow their own path. They actually spin and think differently. This can be tricky for some, if they cannot stand in their power, they may feel alienated, abandoned and never quite fit in anywhere.

Quite often Aquarians may set up their own business, where they can create the space they want and feel equality with their peers, they understand that everyone can bring something to the table. Aquarians are real team players. Even though they are strong enough to become leaders, and people want them to be leaders, if they do they will lose their freedom and individuality.

Uranus actually turns things upside down so you get a broader big picture, it is a revolutionary experience. You might pick the taps given, intuitively or emotionally, mentally, and if you do not get it that is when it will explode into the physical world, you will eventually get the message.

Uranus takes eighty-four years to get back to its natal position in the chart, so around the age of eighty-four, people may actually feel a new lease of life, as if they are reborn, others may choose to leave this world. But for those who choose to stay on, how many times have you heard an eighty-four year old taking a parachute jump?

At forty-two years of age, this is when the planet Uranus is opposing itself and will trigger this radical or revolutionary energy. It can be simply known as the midlife crisis, but I like to call it the midlife correction, because you just have to make one degree shift in the present to arrive at a new destination in the future. For example, if the egg is empty it will finally crack open and set you free. It may not be a pleasant experience but when you have worked through this experience, it is a release and you will feel freedom.

The Tower can be a negative or positive experience. Sometimes it is that day when you did not plan anything in particular and you washed, vacuumed and cleaned, shopped and dropped off the kids, answered your emails and messages, picked up the kids, cooked dinner for a dinner party and entertained, and wonder how you did it all in one day. Where did you get that energy from? It is that burst of energy from within.

Sometimes when we need to leave a bad relationship we need this energy, the adrenalin to get up and just go. The energy needs to be like that terminal escape velocity, like when the rocket leaves Earth's gravity.

MYTHOLOGY

The myth behind the classic Tower of Babel built by the Babylonians connects well with this card. The myth says that all humanity spoke one language, they decided to build a tower and challenge God. God spoke and struck the tower which fell down and everyone fell to the ground, afterwards they spoke in different tongues.

On September eleventh, 2001 we explored this Tower card with my tarot class. Later that evening while I was watching the *David Letterman Late Show*, the TV automatically started screening the atrocities that unfolded with the World Trade Center, Twin Towers in New York.

The Twin Towers were a symbol for the United States, of their prestige and status. If you look at the Tower card, the lightning bolt does look like a plane hitting at the crown and knocking it off the top of the Tower. The crown is symbolic of the ego and this act represents the loss the ego.

The lightning bolt hits at the ego, of not only the United States, but to the whole world, because the Twin Towers were known as the World Trade Centre and many people from all over the world worked in the towers and spoke many languages.

The September 11 experience has been an enlightening experience for the whole world. We have woken up to a new level of consciousness.

Over the years I have made a list of these monumental experiences that really shift us into new levels of consciousness. I see all these events as an opportunity for us to raise our vibration. Some say new portals open and others say new dimensions open up.

Some of the items in my list are:

- in 1950, the Chinese People's Liberation Army over ran Tibet. The knowledge and teachings that had been hidden in Tibet for hundreds of years was released and opened to the world. Just look at what a marvelous example of love and peace the Dali Lama is.

- 1966 – The LA riots were happening, the Vietnam War, the Hippie movement started. I see the 1960's as the beginning of the Age of Aquarius.
- 1980 – We had the Harmonic Convergence and the fall of the Berlin Wall. During this time we also had the end of the Cold War and Mikhail Gorbachev created the State of the World Forum, where hundreds of people were invited to discuss what came next for the planet.
- 2000 and 2001 – We had the turn of the Century, Y2K bug and all the fear that this caused and of course September eleven.
- 2012 – December 2012, we had the end of the Mayan calendar and the end of the Egyptian calendar, and many believed it would be the end of the world.
- 2014 – The beginning of the four Blood Moons marks; another significant shift for our conscious. And we have the rise of ISIL in Syria and the evacuation of the hundreds of thousands of refugees.

No matter what the situation or the story may be, if the foundations are not built right, the tower will always crumble. Why? Because something is out of integrity, it is just not built right. Whether this happens in the physical world or in your internal metaphysical world, a breakdown from within or a physical falling apart without will occur.

>"Integrity is the essence of everything."
>-Dr. R. Buckminster Fuller

Here in the Tower card we see the Lovers blasted out of the Tower through some catalytic experience. It is not just about losing the ego but also putting it in its proper place. This awakening gets us in touch with our Higher Self and gets our ego in its correct perspective.

Historically, we have the Roman Empire having its day and then its demise. Other classic myths that connect with this card are the stories of *Rapunzel* who was locked up in her tower, and Cassandra of Troy was also locked up in her tower by her father because no one believed her any more – whether it was to protect or shield her, she was secured in the tower.

A Breakdown of Ego or Divine Intervention

SYMBOLOGY

The Lovers

We see the Lovers from the Lovers' card. They were chained in the Devil card and now they are together again in the Tower card. Together the Mother and Father's energy has been flung out of the Tower through the lightning bolt.

I find it interesting how one of the lovers is falling face down as if they knew this was going to happen. And the other is falling backwards as if in total surprise. In a relationship, how often one of the partners seems oblivious to what is going on in the relationship?

The Lightning Bolt

The lightning bolt brings the fertile change. Lightning is a masculine energy, the bringer of light, of new life. It is electrifying, the bolt out of the blue, and it is a shocking experience. It breaks down existing form. It starts fires and represents the renewal energy and the Phoenix rising out of the ashes.

The bolt connects us with the Fool's staff, the Magician's wand, the Chariot's wand, the Hermit's lamp light or his staff, and the Devil's torch.

The flash of inspiration, which breaks down an old way works two fold. From the inside out, you cannot hold it back; it is a personal experience like a mental breakdown. Or from the outside, like the universe pulling the rug from under your feet. For example, you are sacked from your job forcing you to change things. This may be a shocking experience.

Yods

On the right side of the Tower there are ten yods representing the ten planets. On the left side there are twelve yods connecting us to the twelve zodiac signs. These twenty-two yods also represent the twenty-two Major Arcana.

Yods are cosmic side benefits, gifts from the universe, blessings in disguise, however hard the experience may be.

The black background highlights the yods as well as the grey Tower and the grey clouds. The black background represents the unknown un-manifested energy. The Grey represents wisdom; I like the enlightenment connection with this card. Something will be revealed, the getting of wisdom.

The Tower is a spirited force that frees us from the physical structures that we built around ourselves, it releases us and sets us free. It helps us to break through the chains.

On a Psychological Level

The Tower experience tears down structure or the patterns of the past and our castles in the air.

An iconoclastic experience where we have that breakthrough through the illusion of how we see ourselves and we see ourselves as we truly are.

The Tower Brings Enlightenment

IN A READING

An upheaval will occur, either on a physical, emotional, spiritual or mental level. This card really sticks a mirror in your face and if you do not face it, you will cop it one way or another until you get it. An epiphany, enlightenment or a bolt of revelation will arise, a breakthrough will occur.

Change of job or a sacking? You may experience a career change through to being inspired to write a book.

An announcement, a quick death, an unexpected end, a sudden change, an unexpected surprise, an unexpected pregnancy, even a car accident, a knock on the door, someone visiting you unexpectedly or a phone call, something will happen that will turn your life around.

Breakdown in a marriage or in a business partnership. Some people will actually create an unconscious drama to get out of their marriage – create affairs and then get caught out, or a runaway bride on the day of the wedding.

This Tower card is like a cleansing explosion of anger. Unexpressed anger is forced up. Some people are totally out of control, they are like a gasoline can waiting for a match to fall in, any opportunity or excuse to explode. Look at road rage! Some people are totally out of control.

Some people want to get rid of the rubbish in their lives. Some people want to see this card in their reading.

I liken this card to a blind pimple. You know those pimples that hurt when you touch them; they can hang around for a while too. But when it bursts and all that toxic pus is released it does not hurt anymore and the healing process can begin.

This card represents a breakdown of structure built on feeble foundations. Whatever is built on weak or unsteady foundations simply will not last.

I like to discuss with my clients ways in which you can build stronger foundations. For example, if you have cracks in the walls and you just keep patching them up, the cracks will still keep showing. You have to actually re-stump the foundations and get everything level and then you can build a solid house and build it as high as you want.

If you do not heed the warnings yourself, remember that the Universe will step in and do it for you, like that lightning bolt hitting the ego. On some level you have not acknowledged the taps that you have been receiving all along, and if you keep ignoring them and do not heed the call and wake up, you leave the Universe no choice but to do it for you. And if you still don't listen, the next lesson will be harder.

SHADOWS	KEYS
Vandalism	Sudden
Crumbling down	Tension
Destructive	Striking
I know everything attitude	Speed of light
Turmoil	Agitation
Building castles in the air	Warning / Testing
Fury	Fire
Violence	Impetuous
Rage against the machine	Catalyst precipitates change
Holier than thought	Compression
Sudden change	Chaos & order
Misogyny	Inevitable
Misandry	Perturbation
Harsh	Re-evaluation
Tempestuous	Necessary change
Downfall	Blessing in disguise
Disruption	Revelation
Disaster	Unveiling
Anger	Liberation
Shock	Insight
Pain	Illumination
Danger	Awakening
Crisis	
Upheaval	
Confinement	

Tarot in Action

Get something off your chest.
Be prepared when problems arise.
Don't suppress your anger, don't fear it, direct it.
Be willing to change your old ways.
Build stronger foundations.
Cleansing – bodywork, diet, fasting, housecleaning.
Tearing down or burning out old structures no longer necessary.
Face your fear and do it anyway.

Movie

Tower of Babel with Brad Pit.

Quote

'The truth shall set you free.'

Books to Read

Cassandra by Kerry Greenwood.
How To Make Your Thoughts Disappear by Gary Cox.

Chapter 21

...The Fool now encounters the celestial bodies, reaches peace and harmony with The Star...

XVII THE STAR

SUMMARY

This card is about connecting with your inner calm. We achieve the star energy when we make peace with ourselves. During midlife we tend to accept ourselves more as we are, not as what we should be, and so we make peace with ourselves.

We are renewed, rejuvenated and regenerated. Be kind to yourself and practice self-love.

If the Tower card represents the heart attack, the Star energy is the recovery.

NUMEROLOGY

The number seventeen adds up to eight and the number eight connects us with the Strength card. The Strength card is the symbol of balancing; you can see the lemniscate or the infinity symbol, which demonstrates there is power in balance.

The large eight pointed star, once again, connects us with the Strength card. It is gold in color and connects us with the source, the symbol of our soul. It is a large symbol of our growth and what we have been though, showing our potential growth.

ASTROLOGY

This card is ruled by the zodiac sign of Aquarius. Aquarius is known as the water bearer, and you can see here in the Star card the figure is pouring the water. Many people get mixed up thinking that Aquarius is a water sign because of the water, but in fact it is an air element.

This pouring of the water is symbolic of forgiveness and letting go of pent up emotions, an expression of an out pouring of emotions and feelings. She is consciously pouring out her emotions in a calm and controlled way. She can express herself emotionally.

MYTHOLOGY

The Goddess Ishtar of the earth and the sea connects well with this card. Goddess Isis bought light through love and regeneration.

You can see seven white stars in the sky. They connect with so many things:
- with the seven Goddesses in attendance, and symbolizing the constellation or the asteroids that we use in astrology, i.e.: Pallas Athena, Juno, Ceres, etc.
- The seven sages of Arabia.
- The seven pillars of Wisdom Kabbalah.
- The seven chakras.
- The seven metals of alchemy.
- The seven days of the week.
- The seven colors of the rainbow.
- The seven musical notes.
- The seven muses.
- The seven deadly sins.
- It is known as a good luck number and spiritual number.

The Star Asks Us to be Not to Do

SYMBOLOGY

The Feet

One foot is on the earth representing the conscious connection. The other foot is on the water representing the connection with the unconscious. You will notice the foot is on the water but not in the water. She is not stepping into water to do work down there, which is very Aquarian.

Naked Maiden

Being naked represents freedom and vulnerability. She is open to the influence of nature. The card is about being grounded, back on earth, balanced, and getting back to basics.

The Star card is a meditative card. It is about being still and regenerating. Reflection and meditation, you can see the naked maiden gazing into water. Water is mirroring the self, being receptive, recouping, the recovery, relaxing and exhaling.

She is using the water, which is the High Priestess energy, calmly in her life at the moment. A lot like the Temperance card but letting go of the water and pouring it into the pool.

This card always reminds me of floating down the stream in a canoe daydreaming with your hand touching and playing with the water while you gaze up at the clouds going by.

The Water

Represents the unconscious world. She is gazing into the water and her reflection, the water mirrors her soul. You can see the rings are moving out in a ninety-degree angle. This water is not stagnating.

She is pouring one jug into the water and the other jug on the earth. Notice the one stream flows back into the pool, which signifies that all manifestation flows back into the source pool. As they say, ashes to ashes.

True power comes from connecting your personal power to that of the source. Getting back to nature is the best form of healing.

The Ibis Bird

The Ibis bird connects us with the mentor of arts. An Egyptian God called Thoth, this is where Crowley got his name for his tarot deck.

Thoth was worshipped in the form of an Ibis – representing artistic abilities, an ode to pottery and the pursuit of natural talents, e.g. terracotta, handicrafts, aromatherapy, crystals, reflexology, singing, sculpture, the arts and all those hobbies that we love to do and nurtures our soul in some way. It is about smelling the roses and allowing recovery to happen.

Temperance versus The Star

Let us look at the similarities and differences between these two cards. The archangel Michael is clothed, showing control as he mixes and balances the water between the two cups, whereas the maiden is naked and free and lets the water flow freely onto the earth and back into the pool.

In Temperance, the Angel is standing and looking at you, in the Star she is kneeling and looking into the water. In Temperance it is daylight, in the Star it is evening and the stars are out. In Temperance, the Angel has his foot in the water and in the Star the foot is on the water. Temperance has the Iris flower and the Star has the Ibis bird.

Both cards have to do with healing and restoring balance; they both connect to nature; nature is the biggest healer; and they both come after the two greatest change cards, Death and the Tower.

As I Heal Myself I Heal Others

IN A READING

Suggest mediation and reverse the flow of life. Stop, stand still and smell the roses. Connect inwardly and then give to the world. The sea-change that we often talk about in today's living. More people are giving up the bigger wage to have a better relationship with their partners and families.

This Star card is the perfect woman. We have the combination of the High Priestess, which is represented by all the blue colors and the water, with the Empress energy is represented by the greenery and nature connecting us with all that earthly passion. The greenery symbolizes peace, healing, growth and adaptability. It is the equilibrium card.

You do not have to work to achieve the Star energy, you are just in it. It is a being energy, not a doing energy. We are all connected to nature, the flora and the fauna.

The Star also connects beautifully to the Ace of Cups, both demonstrating an abundant and unending overflow of water flowing from the cups, connecting us with the importance of self-love, self-respect, healing and letting go.

This card connects to the quite part of ourselves, our own inner sanctuary, our inner special place. Through meditation we connect to this special place. We need to nurture ourselves.

The Star represents inner calm and hope, peace of mind, healing and wholeness. After the physical energy of the Tower, this Star energy is the calm after the storm, the relief that you do not have to live that lie anymore, and the beginning of regeneration.

Because of the giant star, it connects us with our realization of our hopes and dreams. The wishing card, when you wish upon a star, and day-dreaming. The pool also represents the wishing well.

It is also known as the wishing you well card or the get well card. When I see this card, I often ask my clients, "Have they been feeling unwell lately". This card connects us with all those alternative healing methods, like massage, hypnosis, essential oils, mud baths – anything to do with nature and relaxing and restoring the peace and calm.

The Star represents a peaceful death of a situation. It has proceeded calmly and constructively without drama.

It does connect with the Hermit, the natural healing, and all those alternative therapies, which is the opposite of the Hierophant's traditional medicines and methods.

NEGATIVE

There is a negative to this Star card. One may go overboard with being idealistic, where they may take the phone off the hook and remove themselves from reality, and become lazy. If this happens, they need to mobilize themselves, to get real because they have been 'off with the fairies' for too long, complacent and can lose touch with reality. It is time to take the rose colored glasses off.

SHADOWS	KEYS
Disconnection	Dreams come true
Suppression	Magic happens
Wastage	Conquest of different spaces
Pollution	Serenity
Idle chatter	Anchor
Wasting time on endless discussion	Community
Experimentation on animals	Innovators
Following like sheep	Other forms of life
Nuclear bombs & waste	Humanitarians
Having faith in drugs & politicians	Synthesis
Racism	Communion
Self-doubt	Ideals
Lack of trust	Superior forces
Cynicism	Hope
Pessimism	Generosity
Feeling blaaa	Optimism
Apathy	Spiritual awareness
	Good health
	Good wishes
	Idealism
	Peace
	Rest
	Healing
	Mother nature

SHADOWS	KEYS
	Self-esteem
	Self-love
	Respect

Tarot in Action

Learn about organic farming and permaculture.
Recycle, cut wastage and compost.
Think what you want to think.
See the universe out there, be part of it, better still, be a star!
Look up at the stars tonight.
Make a wish upon a star.
Visit the local planetarium.
Support humanitarian and environmental projects.
Be concerned with worldwide issues.
Take up a new hobby.
Try being vegetarian.
Grow sprouts.
Consciousness of the earth as a living entity, with the desire to heal her.
Go on a retreat.
Go to the beach.
Go for a drive in the country and have a picnic.
Concern for humanitarian and environmental issues.
Treating yourself.

Movie to Watch

Contact written by Carl Sagan starring Jodie Foster.

Quotes

'We are all made out of star stuff.' – Carl Sagan.

'We are star dust, we are golden, we are billion-year-old carbon and we've got to get ourselves back to the garden.' – Crosby, Stills, Nash and Young, Woodstock (August 1969).

Book to Read

Jonathan Living Seagull by Richard Bach.

Chapter 22

...The time has come for The Fool to face nature's dark side with the Moon...

XVIII THE MOON

SUMMARY

We are still hanging around the pool with this card. The Moon is about the deeper unconscious material and illusions. The crustacean that live at the bottom of the water suck everything up, like psychic vacuum cleaners, thereby symbolizing it is time to clean the bottom of the barrel.

Here is one more opportunity to clean up in the unconscious, to clear away in the shadows.

For some people the Moon card can be an uncomfortable card, because things from the past might be coming up that you thought were already handled. For example, you may feel the difference between walking through a familiar park in the daylight or at night. Its familiar, but the shadows are around and you can feel spooked.

NUMEROLOGY

1+8 = 9. The number nine connects us to the Hermit. The number nine is about completion, resolution and healing. The healing happens when you work on the inner level.

When you complete something properly you have learned from it and gain wisdom, knowledge and understanding. You understand responsibility.

The lamp from the Hermit also connects us to the glow of the moonlight. It will provide the light that is needed.

ASTROLOGY

The star sign of Pisces Neptune connects to the Moon. It connects to the spiritual realms and intuitive ability, but also to alcoholic, drug problems, addictions and the illusive side of Pisces. We can get caught up in the victim martyr. We can either sink or swim here. We need a helping hand to pull us out of the deception.

The crab or crustacean connects us to the sign of Cancer, which is ruled by the Moon. Cancer connects us with Moon Mother, the High Priestess energy and all the realms of the Moon Goddess.

Cancer connects us with the home and mother, mothering issues, emotional issues and mental illness.

MYTHOLOGY

Moon Goddess

All the Moon Goddesses, like Diana, Artemis, Selena, Lilith, Hecate, Kaali and Morrigan, to name a few, they all connect with the Moon Card and they are all the feminine aspects of the life power.

The High Priestess bridges the gap between the unconscious and conscious. Remember, she is about the dual aspects and rules the light and dark.

The Moon Mother accepted souls and sends them back to be born again, therefore we are looking at renewal, growth and life. The Trinity represents life, death and rebirth.

The Many Faces of the Moon

The Moon has phases and you can see all the faces are visible on the card, also eclipsing the Sun. There is the full, half and last quarter faces. It symbolizes that we all go through stages, through to final realization. Like stages of the Moon, we wax and wane, develop through all levels of consciousness.

The feeling the Moon gives is like the time just before a woman gives birth. It could be fearful and exciting around the new arrival.

The Moon allows us a final cleanup of our act before the sunshine returns.

Full Moon

I often recommend to my clients to not to make any decisions on or around the full moon. The planet is seventy percent water and when there is a full moon we have high tides. We humans are also seventy percent water, therefore the Moon must affect us also. Our emotions are at their peak and we are not making that clear rational choice.

People do feel irrational around the full moon. Luna is Latin for moon. Psychiatric nurses report the lunatics at asylums. The police are also aware of more heightened activity around the full moon period. There is a higher sense of paranoia and we do take things more personally.

I am especially more mindful when the full moon falls on a Friday night or over the weekend. People usually have weddings, celebrations and parties over the weekend and the full moon could blow things out of proportions.

Look at how many stories and movies there are about werewolves. When there is a full moon the werewolves' claws come out.

There are people that cut their hair according to the cycles of the moon. If you want your hair to reduce its growth, then cut your hair during waning time.

The Blue Moon

This is when we have two full moons in one month. The moon has a twenty eight day cycle. When there is a full moon on the first or second of the month, there is another full moon on the twenty-eighth or twenty-ninth of the same month.

Moon Tents

As mentioned earlier, the Native Americans and other cultures have moon tents for the woman of the tribe, often set up down wind and well away from the community. The menstruating woman would reside in the moon tents and be looked after by the family.

During the women's menstruation, it is believed this is when the feminine is at her most powerful. In today's society it is still seen as a curse, snubbed and not talked or acknowledged as it should be. When we women acknowledge and accept this powerful time only then will society do the same.

Note, that the women have thirteen periods in the one year, because the feminine is in sync with the cycles of the moon. The period has a twenty-eight-day cycle.

Interesting to also note is that the pill was introduced in the United States on 12 May 1960. Since this time, women have taken back the power of their own bodies. They decide when they want to have children, and it has only been since this time that women have been able to climb the corporate ladder, get involved in politics, become prime ministers or achieve high status positions in sports. They have been able to dedicate their time to pursuits that were not an option before.

There are other interesting facts that correspond to the menstruating woman. I have accumulated these from my students over the years. I have listed a few:
- In Croatia, women are not allowed to pick lemons, otherwise the tree will not bear fruit.
- In New Zealand, Maoris are not allowed in cemeteries because it is sacred land.
- Hindus, Jewish, Muslims and Balinese are not allowed in temples.
- Italians are not allowed to make tomato sauce nor make sausages.
- Chinese woman are not allowed to burn incense as it is disrespectful.

I have also been told by some students that work at Sexyland and other same industries, that sales go up around Full Moon time.

Confusion

During the full moon, many Cancer people, in fact many of us are often in confusion. I always mention to my clients and students that confusion is a blessing in disguise. When you are in confusion it actually stops you from saying one thing or committing to the other thing and then being disappointed later.

When you are in a position of confusion, your emotions eclipse your logic. But all the options are open or available for you, therefore you can go in any direction. It is a very powerful position to be in.

There are fifteen yods that look like dew drops. Yods are blessings in disguise, a gift from the universe. It tells me to just sit through the confusion, that the night passes as the confusion passes, just like the cycles of the moon. One morning you will wake up and be very clear about what you need to do and exactly when you need to do it.

But for some reason, in our society today, and with many clients that I see, they believe that confusion is a negative attribute, rather than a time to rework your idea or simply wait for that missing piece of the puzzle to show up.

The Moon corresponds to the dark, the night and the shadows. It symbolizes that our life and our direction is unclear. But it is a good time to put your hazard lights on, to be more alert, and be aware, to use the Hermit's lamp while you are in the dark and to take your time.

The Moon does not have light of her own, she reflects the sunlight. Therefore, it is a good time to reflect, rethink, just to feel it, or better still to sleep on it. Remember it is not a good time to make a clear decision, but it is a good time to reconsider everything.

Sleep Deprivation

Another important thing to note is when we do not have enough sleep, it impairs your body's ability to fight off illness, you will get sick. Not resting, allowing the body to rejuvenate and to process the day's activities raises the chances of your health to suffer.

The Moon Throws Light on Deep Unconscious Issues

SYMBOLOGY

Wolf and Dog

The Wolf represents the untamable, the wild side, the instinct and the primal. This connects us to the werewolf and our shadow side. The Dog is tamable, loyal, domesticated. Marriage is seen as being domesticated and a form of being in control in society.

The Crustacean

The shellfish or crustacean signifies universal fear in the unconscious. It connects to all those drug experiences, old time doomsday stories of the Apocalypse, Armageddon and the end of world. Look at the zodiac sign of Scorpio, ruled by Pluto God of the underworld – scorpions are so intense.

The shellfish can spend a short time on land. This represents that things are not right. It suggests that something from way back or way deep down from the depths is coming up for us to look at and to clear away. And this is enough to bring fear up for people, just look at all the mother daughter issues and how deep do they go?

The shellfish, being the scavenger, crawls along bottom and eats everything in its way, like the crusts, crumbs and the residues.

But for some people the fear that is attributed with this shellfish feels like the world is about to end for them. They are drowning in water; it is way too deep and they are caught up in a whirlpool. They may suffer from depression, eating disorders or many other emotional issues.

You need a counselor, a witness or a helping hand, you need someone to bring you back, to pull you out of the whirlpool.

Interesting to note, that depression is looking at the past with fear, and anxiety is looking at the future with fear.

The Devil versus The Moon

Let us look at the similarities and differences between these two cards.

The fifteen yods also connects us with the Devil card, which is the fifteen card in the Major Arcana.

The Moon is the feminine aspect of the Devil. The Moon is passive energy. It may come out in your dreams, through your intuition, or you may pass it and not know what it was all about. It could go back many years, you may feel uncomfortable about something, you just do not know what it was all about and you cannot put your finger on it.

The Devil is masculine active energy. You can name it and clarify it clearly. Representing the drugs, food addiction or the alcohol, you can bring it into consciousness clearly.

Water Pool

The water pool brings in unconscious issues and aspects of the unconscious mind. Our deeper illusions. How deep do our emotions really go? Sometimes the water is flowing other times it is still and deep.

Remember, the Moon rules the tides symbolizing our emotions and how they wax and wane.

The Path

The road is symbolic of our gateway through our nooks and crannies, to the unknown area of our unconscious, our shadow. We see this path in the Temperance card also. Remember, it never is a straight path, it never is right foot wrong foot, it is right foot left foot until you get there, just keep on track towards your goal, don't give up and you will get there.

The shellfish looks like he is coming out of the water and straight onto the path, but he never quite makes it.

The path is worn by the feet of others that have traveled this path already. The path goes right through the middle of the two pillars. The path rises and falls like the moon and ends on a rise.

This path symbolizes the dark night of the soul where angels fear to tread. For someone it could feel like the darkest hour just before the dawn.

Note that when we are at the most desolate, that is when we make the most progress. This also connects to the Hermit's energy. Desolate is when we are left alone, abandoned and destitute.

Also note that the moon and the sun work as a pair. They operate in unison, it is a twenty-four-hour cycle and they operate quickly. The most powerful thing to note here is that the desolation is short lived.

The Grey Pillars

We first see the pillars in the Death card, but they are so far away on the other side of the River Styx, they are so much bigger in the Moon card. They are just there. The grey pillars represent wisdom.

Take the Time to Reflect on the Matter, Sleep on it, be Open To Receive

IN A READING

The Moon brings up all those unconscious issues. Remember that insight could come through your dreams, your psychic abilities, your intuitive senses or even through astrology. It is about receiving messages from your unconscious world. So tune into your dreams, your inner Hermit through other ways like meditation, open up to what your inner self is trying to tell you.

It is definitely not a good time for making decisions. Maybe wait twenty-four hours.

Feelings from the past could be frightening for some. Old memories and feelings come flooding back and can make them feel uneasy. Some people may suffer through nightmares.

Song analogies are:
- *Memories* from the film *The Way We Were* with Barbra Streisand.
- *Memories* from the musical *Cats*.

- *Auld Lang Syne*, the New Year's Eve anthem.
- Moon River from the movie *Breakfast at Tiffany's*.
- *Blue Moon*.
- *Moon Shadow* by Cat Stevens.
- *Dark Side of the Moon* by Pink Floyd.
- *Bad Moon Rising* by Credence Clearwater Revival.
- *Memories* by Elvis Presley.
- *Silvery Moon* by Judy Garland.
- *Fly Me to the Moon* by Frank Sinatra.
- *When the Moon Hits your Eye like a Big Pizza Pie, that's Amore* by Dean Martin.

The key to this card is that it is a state within every person. The conscious purpose is to examine our hidden agenda and bring it into alignment or consciousness. Ask yourself the question, "What is the crustacean bringing up for me to look at?" When you work on it you can heal it.

Mother daughter issues can come up or need to be looked at. This is the Cancer and Moon aspects of the Moon card. Heal with your mother or the feminine. I often ask my clients, "Do you have a good relationship with your mother?"

Your spiritual path may be discovered during this period, within your heart, mind and spirit. This again connects us to the Hermit energy. Using that lamp light to search for and find the answers that you are seeking; seeing the light within.

Positive

The positive energy of this card is that it is a healing card. If we work with these feelings. Today we can erase the tapes, restructure and become more in charge.

Negative

The negative energy of this card is that we could block our actions because of the fear and bog ourselves in this card to dwell in the past. We indulge in the addictions, food, drink, drugs, gambling, etc. and then we get stuck in destructive addictive behaviors. Becoming the victim and being depressed about being depressed.

Deep water can become very deep, stagnant and smelly. It brings up all those primal fears and instincts like judgment, brooding, paranoia, fear, shadowy and a lack of clarity.

This card asks us to reflect. It is not an out there action energy. When the moon is out, it is dark, you may see something that is not really there. You could delude yourself.

You also need to be aware of the romantic aspect of this card. Romance under the full moon is it an illusion, or did you plan it? Be mindful of kisses under the moonlight.

The Moon is the gateway card into a good run home. Next comes the Sun, Judgement and the World cards, all about the regeneration of the self and creating the world you really want to live in.

SHADOWS	KEYS
Fear of deep water	Sacrifices
Vague	Mothering
Asylum	Link
Complaining	Acting
Drama	Triggering
Jekyll & Hyde	Rehabilitation
Living in a dreamland	Sensitivity
Psychosomatic illness	Emanation
Aberration - out of character	Nurturing
Abuse	Instigating responses
Touchy	Luminous
Moody	Intuition
Immature	Illumination
Lunacy	Inner Glow
PMT / ME	Imagination
Madness	Unexpected possibilities
Absorbing people's negativity	Healing
Escapist	Magic
Weak-willed	Enchantment
Subliminal	Dreams
Delirium	Mystery
Impressionable	Psychic activity
Afraid of the dark	Meditation
Distress	
Seduction	
Hallucination	
Dis-ease	
Bi-polar	
Fear	
Confusion	
Bewilderment	

SHADOWS	KEYS
Lies	
Deceit	
Confusion	
Depression	
Morbid fantasies	

Tarot in Action

Keep a dream journal.
Listen to your inner self.
Remember that most of your fears will never happen.
Accept the way you are.
Nurture yourself, have a spa, bath or massage.
Allow yourself to cry.
Do something once in a blue moon.
Very strong imagination and dream work.
Sense of being drawn by an unknown desire.
Be aware of highly charged emotions.
Seek counseling.
Connect with your Moon energy.
Completing a cycle.

Movies to Watch

The Way We Were with Barbra Streisand and Robert Redford.
Cats – the musical.

Quote

'Your girl is lovely Hubble.' – Barbra Streisand, *The Way We Were*.

Books to Read

The Mists of Avalon by Mary Stewart.
The Red Tent by Anita Diamant.

Chapter 23

...The Fool is now rebirthed and transformed with the power of The Sun...

XIX THE SUN

SUMMARY

The Moon is feminine energy. It is moody – you are in the dark, everything is in the shadow, and you have to look hard to see where you are going. You may be in fear and you might get lost. The Moon connects to the unconscious world.

The Moon connects us the past; for example, when your mum first left you alone, you understood that you were not connected with your mother. Meanwhile, your mother just went into the kitchen to make a cup of tea.

The Sun is masculine energy. It is direct, you are now in the daylight and everything is bright, clear and shining. As the saying goes, "it will be better in the morning". Or "What a difference a day makes."

In the daylight you can see where you are going, there is no fear, and you feel confident, enthusiastic and energized. The sun warms you up and melts stress away. You feel reborn again, it is a new day and you feel renewed. It is about being fully present in the moment.

NUMEROLOGY

Number nineteen equals ten, which equals one and the new beginnings. Ten connects us to the Wheel of Fortune, those things that are turning round again. Nine connects us to the Hermit and all the knowledge we learn from things completing and healing. There is the zero of the Fool and the feeling of being reborn and starting a new level. You can see the red feather in the child's hat clearly showing us that this is the Fool reborn. The number one connects us to the Magician and the willpower to manifest the new.

The essence and experience of the Sun equals joy, pure bliss, and the regeneration of the Spirit. This wonderful feeling does not last – it is like a sunset; it takes your breath away for a moment and then it is gone.

ASTROLOGY

The Sun is the ruler of this card and the Sun rules the zodiac sign of Leo. Basically, Leo is all about me, myself and I or the ego. Leo's are very playful, they have no inhibitions, and they are creative, self-expressive, the most optimistic of all the zodiac signs, the most generous and the most positive.

In fact, most people do not like Leo's, but we need Leo's in our lives because they are the leaders, very enterprising and entrepreneurial. Whenever they go for something, their energy is almost like a child's, big-eyed with naïve energy and because they commit with enthusiasm they always achieve their end result. This is what annoys other people.

The sun makes things grow. We get vitamin D from the sun through skin absorption but the majority of the vitamin D we get is through our eyes. I learnt about this when I returned from a Hawaiian holiday very tanned, but when I went to my naturopath for my annual tests, I was still lacking in vitamin D and I had to up my intake for a while.

Today, because we do not hang the washing outside as much as yesteryear, we lack vitamin D. In a survey I recently saw, veiled women are suffering a high rate of rickets, which is a disease from lack of sunlight and that vital vitamin D.

Today, we are told to slip slop slap, to wear hats in the sun and how much the sun can cause us grief through melanoma cancers and so forth. But we still need the energy of the sun. We just have to learn to be responsible.

When we have a little color we do look healthier, we dress prettier, we are more outgoing, sociable and we shake off those winter blues. They say people in England have pastier skin and suffer from SAD or Seasonal Absorption Disorder. People in Alaska suffer from cabin fever because they have six months of daylight and six months of darkness.

In many surveys, it is believed that there is a high rate of depression in countries with little or no sunlight.

MYTHOLOGY

Apollo the Sun God rules this card. He drove his golden chariot through the sky.

Tutankhamen's father was the first Pharaoh to make the Egyptians worship a single God, the Sun. They worshipped The Sun God RA. He had the head of jackal and body of a man.

It was the Mayans that created sun dials.

We emerge from the womb of the darkness, Mother Moon, and we are reborn into the light. The Sun is a personal rebirth for us. We have freedom from all the heavy energy of the moon and you feel positive with the sun.

Note that you have to embrace both the light and the dark. You need the contrast to see where you are – this gives us a feeling of wholeness.

The Sun is the Birth of Wisdom and Innocence

SYMBOLOGY

The Sun

The Sun is the center of our world, our solar system. Remember that Leo's want to be the center of attention. Leo rules the solar plexus and the heart area, which is the center of our body system.

You can see the friendly face in the Sun card looking straight at you with eyes wide open. In the Moon Tarot card, the Moon is looking side on, facing downward with eyes closed.

The straight and bent rays or beams are the blending of our conscious (straight beams) and our unconscious (wavy beams).

The Horse

The horse is grey in color. Grey is the color of wisdom. We are reborn with wisdom. Our human physical self has now become wise through our life's journey. Through wisdom we have controlled our ego.

The horse represents our vehicle in life and how we are traveling. It is a masculine, active energy and it suggests it is happening right now. We first connected to the horse in the Death Card, which was white, symbolizing purity.

The Child

The child is naked and vulnerable, suggesting a return to a more natural state of being, to whom we truly are, connecting us to the child within and that Leo naiveté.

I like how the child holds no reigns but sits balanced on the horse, trusting the journey. His outstretched arms show inner balance.

The red feather is from the Fool and is the birth of wisdom and innocence. The color red is about passion, life desires and connects us to Angelic forces.

The Sunflowers

There are supposed to be five sunflowers connecting us to our five senses. Sunflowers turn to face the sun; they are heliotrope plants.

Everything on this card needs the vitality of the sun to grow. We have the child, plant life, which are the sunflowers, and the horse, which is an animal.

The Grey Wall

The wall in the background represent the material world and the child is in front of the wall, suggesting we are no longer held back by unconscious conditions, we are free. We have self-mastery. We can set our own limits. As a wise man once said, 'A man must know his limitations'.

The Fool went from those wide open spaces to a controlled environment. The wall reminds me of boundaries, like a playground for children, a containment in which we can create the space to feel safe and have everything we need to survive.

The Orange Flag

The orange flag represents the Lemniscate, the infinity symbol, unfurled, showing its vitality and energy, representing that life itself is joyously unfurling.

The rod the child holds belongs to the Fool, the Magician, the Chariot and the Hermit. It is like he has discovered something and is about to mark his territory with his flag.

Major Arcana 211

Being Open to the Joys of Life with Passion and Enthusiasm

IN A READING

The regenerated self, our personality is renewed. Your faith is restored. A transformation, a rebirth of self-fulfillment, a time of feeling alive. A time in your life when you hear yourself say, "Gosh, it's great to be alive!" It is a wonderful buzzy feeling.

Total optimism plus trusting in life and in the self, you accept that the buck stops here. Understanding and taking responsibility for the self. Freedom to do what you want and be whatever you want to be. Freedom to be me.

In a health reading, the Sun card is about healing. It represents good health, good energy, vitality, good vibrations, and bouncing back. A feeling of becoming confident and strong.

The Sun card may represent the birth of child, which always excites us.

Song analogies are:
- *Zip-a-Dee-Doo Dah* released by *Walt Disney.*
- *Happy Talk* from the movie *South Pacific.*
- *Here Comes the Sun* by *George Harrison.*
- *Walking on Sunshine* by *Katrina and the Waves.*
- *High Hopes* by *Frank Sinatra.*
- *Celebration* by *Kool and the Gang.*
- *Happy* by *Pharrell Williams.*

SHADOWS	KEYS
Sunburn	Open-hearted
Skin cancer	Happiness
Blindness	Recognition
Waste of energy	Alive
Things drying out	Harmonious
Major holiday resorts next to beaches	Ultimate love
Burning one's bridges	Authentic
Desert	Creative
Sun lounges in the sun	Birth

SHADOWS	KEYS
Blinded by the light	Penetration
Sun Stroke	Radiating
Solariums	Beauty
Misjudgment	Celebration
Love is blind	Vacation
Delays	Joyful
Potential failure	Good health
Inflated ego	Vitality
Immature	Enlightenment
Pessimistic	Greatness
Burning the candle at both end	Optimism
	Loyal
	Youthful
	Love
	Fulfillment
	High ideals
	Personal achievement
	Marriage
	Healing
	Expressive
	Confident
	Vibrant

Tarot in Action

Hang your washing outside on the clothes line.
Do cartwheels in the park.
Seize the day! Carpe Diem.
Don't overdo or you will burn out or burn others.
Don't abuse the sun.
Retail therapy.
Walk in the park if you want to know the sun.
Fall in love.
Have a positive attitude.
Have faith.
Look at the sun a little every day and get vitamin D.
Achievement of a major goal.

Sense of self-worth.
Set boundaries.
Play like a child.
Rejoice in the moment.
Don't worry be happy.

Quote

'Our Vocation becomes our Vacation.' – Dr. John Demartini.

Book to Read

Happiness by Frederic Renoir.

Chapter 24

...The Fool now results in triumph over darkness with Judgement...

XX JUDGEMENT

SUMMARY

Liberation. When you do what you are supposed to do, it feels like you are liberated. This card is about listening to the call. Hearing the call and making a stand. Making a stand for something you believe in.

Summoning and healing or reassessing a past issues in order to move forward with purpose and meaning.

The Archangels are always there to give you that much needed spiritual support.

NUMEROLOGY

The number twenty equals two. The number two connects and completes the processes of the High Priestess, to the forces that are universal like High Priestess' energy.

The number zero connects to the Fool and that deeper knowledge and understanding that are spiritual and from the source.

The number twenty also suggests that we are experiencing something that could well have started twenty years ago. Dealing with issues that take twenty year cycles to come back around. It connects to something that we first experienced twenty years ago. Maybe a decision was made and twenty years later you are experiencing it again. I like to say we are experiencing the same theme but a different story.

ASTROLOGY

The planet Pluto and the Moon Vulcan connect with this card. Vulcan is known as the part time moon of Venus, interestingly enough Venus was married to Vulcan. He was a blacksmith and was also crippled, but through his work he was able to create beautiful things.

For all the Star Trek fans out there, the Vulcan character of Spock is well known. He is logical, has integrity and wisdom, he understands and believes in his knowingness. He is always serious and loyal.

Vulcan is known as the God of Fire and the God Pluto. Pluto has to do with transformation. We also have volcanoes and Vulcan heaters. Vulcan is also a bird of prey which connects us with the Phoenix and rising from the ashes, to do with renewal and rebirth.

We are all psychic and we all experience these understandings, you may not even know why you know, but you do know.

MYTHOLOGY

God Hades and Goddess Kaali of the Underworld connect with this card. In the western world, we know Goddess Kaali for being the destroyer, but in India Goddess Kaali is also known for being the creator as well. Goddess Kaali would threaten people that if they did not do it right, she would destroy the world.

Hermes also connects with card. You can see the red and white in the flag that we first see in the Magician card. Hermes is an Emissary of the Gods and an underworld Deity.

This card connects us with all the doomsday myths: Armageddon, our final judgement day, our final reckoning, Revelations and all those end of world prophecies.

You can see the angel blowing his horn, and we rise from the dead and have our sins read out – representative of our Judgement Day. In the Kabbalah, we have to walk the gauntlet and answer fifty questions before we can atone for our sins.

When you rise from the dead, it is regeneration and a new life, a liberation. With Judgement you are being asked to rise, to transcend and connect to your soul, to your higher self. It is like an inner calling to rise to a more meaningful existence. I will always remember Wayne Dyer's words, "You are a spirit having a human experience".

You now have to transform the soul to fit your life and create your new environment where your life fits your soul's urge – aligning your personality to serve your soul's purpose or your sacred contract.

This is a calling in a certain direction. When you see this card you cannot deny it, the horn is too loud. This is that knowingness that connects with this card. Like a tap on the shoulder, the wakeup call from the soul, calling you back to the path that you agreed to take in this lifetime.

With this card you reap what you sow. You will get what you deserve, cause and effect. If you deposit, then you can withdraw.

It is the card of Karma and the card of second chance. The Soul knows where it has been good and or bad. It is time to clean up your act. You have to go through it. You have to face the music or that trumpet, and you will probably know the words to the tune.

All this will bring about a new consciousness. An internal knowledge that you know you are not the same person anymore and you have to adjust your external world or life to make it more meaningful, but you may not know how.

Judgement means Being Accountable for Your Actions

SYMBOLOGY

Archangel Gabriel

You can see the Archangel Gabriel blowing his horn. Archangel Gabriel was the herald that appeared to the Virgin Mary to tell her she was with child. He was God's messenger and he is telling us that something new is about to happen.

He is calling us to rise over our current circumstances, to transcend and to look at the bigger picture – to build a bridge (as the youth say today), to free yourself and get over it and to be the bigger man.

An example: I was invited to an event but was hesitant about going. I decided to turn over a card and Judgement showed up, so I sucked it all in and went and proceeded to have the best time.

The Horn

Archangel Gabriel is holding and blowing the horn. Horns are representative of calling to a new life.

Horns are like an alarm clock; it wakes you up to something you cannot ignore. Like the alarm clock that wakes you up, you have no choice but to pay attention to it. It demands attention.

When we hear church bells, they call us back to the churches and temples, to connect with our spiritual side, our higher calling. It is the bugle call asking us to charge, alerting us to something. It is the loud speaker, an announcement, the town crier calling us to pay attention.

The Grey People

The people are grey, which connects us to the grey horse of the Sun. Grey is the blending of our consciousness and wisdom. They are now reborn with wisdom.

The female with long hair connects to the High Priestess. The male on the left connects to the Magician and the child in the middle connects to the Fool, our new self.

The Sea

You can see the coffins floating on the sea. The coffins represent the boxes we put ourselves in, may also suggest our previous life.

There are huge mountains in the background or are they tidal waves? These may be a reference to the sea giving up its dead on the Day of Judgment, as described in the Book of Revelation.

The sea and all the blue colors, once again, connect us to the High Priestess. The knowingness to rise from sleep, from the sea of the unconscious. This is how we rise from one life to the next, like a resurrection, from one level to the next level, where we up the ante.

When you see this card you recognize that you are no longer who you once were. It is time to rearrange your external life to fit the new you. To stand up and be counted. It is time to put it into practice. Practice what you preach, walk your talk and put the money where your mouth is. To be accountable and to be the model. Understanding things from a transpersonal level.

The realization that you are not just responsible for yourself any more but also for other people. The collective, everybody and everything. It is time for you to be the demonstration. A saying assigned to Gandhi, "You are the change you want to see in the world, so be that change!"

Your backyard is just not that area fenced off in the rear of your house. The whole planet is now your backyard. All the trees belong to you, the whales, the rivers, everything. What are you making a stand for?

Understanding the effect of our personal life on others such as The Precessional effect, therefore we need to watch the gradient when we are sharing something we love with others. Learn to speak to others like we are melting chocolate, and you have a better chance of getting their attention and listening to what you have to say.

St George's Cross

The cross on the banner hanging from the horn is St George's Cross. The cross represents the meeting of opposites. It is also the symbol of the Crusaders and the Knights Templar. It was St George that killed the dragons.

St George is the Patron Saint of England.

Represents the daytime, eternity, the now and forever. Draws our soul back to the promise we made before we were born. Today, we recognize this symbol as the Red Cross. They aid those in need and it is a symbol of healing.

The colors of red and white also connect us back to the Magician card to the outfit he wears. The cross also connects us to the High Priestess and the cross she wears symbolizing the Christian beliefs, the union of both sides and living the duality that we agreed too.

Destiny Card versus Fate

Fate for me has a negative connotation, like a divine decree. For example: people get up for work every day. Something that takes you off your course and particular events happen as a result or consequence. Things that are fated.

Destiny has a positive connotation, a lot of fortune, there is a course of events, for example, what happened with Mother Teresa, Dalai Lama and Princess Diana, they all had a destiny.

Special workers also connect with this card. Master number people, volunteers who look after others, animals and the environment; they know it has to do with doing more than just looking after themselves. Everyone can make a difference. A vocation and a calling, like what Sir Bob Geldof was called to do with Live Aid in 1985. It was a miracle Live Aid happened at all.

This again connects to the liberation and the release of this card. When you do what you are supposed to do and wake up to your potential. Liberation from a restriction we place on ourselves. Shaking off the coffin or the box we put ourselves in.

When we see the Judgment and the World cards together, it is like how we leave this life and enter a new life, a new job, a new career, a new house, a new family, a new country, a new world.

When You do What You are Supposed to do
You Feel a Sense of Liberation

IN A READING

Judgment emerges from the past. Judgment is paying back a debt, a period in our life summoning our past and healing it.

Cause and effect. Consequences of our actions. Confronting what we have created in our life and it may have taken a twenty-year cycle to come back around. Remember same theme, it is just a different story.

Responsibility versus Accountability

I wanted to make a distinction between these two words. Words are tools and when you understand them you have more power.

In the dictionary Responsibility means:
The state, quality, or fact of being responsible. The ability to respond. Something for which one is responsible; a duty, obligation, or burden.

And Accountability means:
The state of being accountable, liable, or answerable. A policy of holding public officials or other employees accountable for their actions and results.

Everyone can make a difference. An example I can give you, is when I go for my walk and I can see a bin just ahead of me, and I notice a plastic bag or broken glass along my path, I will pick it and pop it in the bin. This is being accountable. Someone has to pick it up, I am so aware of the environment and not leaving a footprint, and by my action I will trigger someone else to do the same and all this will make the world a better place.

There are many things that we can all do that will make a difference, for example, using natural cleaning products, no SLS (Sodium Laureal Sulphates) in your toothpaste, shampoo and other cleaning products. Every little bit makes a difference to you, to your home and to the planet.

Our soul or our Fool must now answer for our journey, for the creative efforts and for all those mistakes. To be accountable for our actions, not just be responsible. Time to pay the piper – remember there are no free lunches.

All will be processed and paved to make way for the next life, the next stage or the new relationship. You have to heal and clean things here first before moving on to the next so we leave this world with no regrets, and we don't bring the old baggage with us.

We arrive to a clear distinction that this process may not always be pleasant. We now know our good and bad sides. The question is what are we going to do about it?

It is not about denying yourself or others to grow through this experience. Sometimes someone is born in one generation that can clean up something for the whole family that could go back for three generations if not more. The television show, *Who Do You Think You Are* can go back seven or eight generations, and then they can heal something in the family lineage.

Once you are on this path you cannot go back, a trap door shuts behind you. They say, 'a little wisdom is a dangerous thing and ignorance is bliss.' But do you want to know or not know? Like in the *Matrix* movie, when Neo was asked, "Do you want the red pill or the blue pill?"

Because of the horn, when you say or do things you know you should not be saying or doing, it feels like a pin in your bottom forcing you to listen to your true self. Maybe next time you will refrain.

Integrity is the essence of everything. Remember you are still human and you are perfect in your imperfection.

SHADOWS	KEYS
Manipulation	Turning point
Guilt	Resurrection
Shame	Cataclysm
Fanatic	Overcoming obstacles
Cannot be stopped	Urges
Phobias	Self – discovery

SHADOWS	KEYS
Elimination	Alteration
Imposing	Emigration
Obsessions	Assimilation
Too much pleasure	Awakening
Loss	Alignment
Self-reproach	Healing
Delays	Responsible
Fears	Recycle
Obstinacy	Atonement
Disgrace	Understanding
Self-blame	New potential
Criticism	Absolution
Immature	Rejoicing
Non-compliant	Rebirth
Challenging	Integrity
Defiant	Accountable
	Impeccable
	Evaluation
	Assessment
	Satisfaction
	Compensation
	World View
	Maturity
	Evolution
	Liberation

Tarot in Action

Pick up after yourself.
Don't judge others or yourself.
Be more adaptable and flexible.
Try hypnotherapy or self-hypnosis to get rid of your problems.
Listen and trust your inner-knowledge.
Heed the taps.
Dealing with judgment.
Breakthrough to new beliefs.
Dealing with death and transitions.
Rewards for past efforts.
Declutter.

Quote

'With great power comes great responsibility.' Said Spiderman's Uncle.

Books to Read

The Four Agreements by Don Miguel Ruiz.
It's All Too Much by Peter Walsh.

Chapter 25

...It is time for The Fool to celebrate victory in The World which then leads him back to the beginning...

XXI THE WORLD

SUMMARY

Wholeness, completion and self-realization. Individuation is what Carl Jung said we are all striving for and this is what this card is about.

In Jungian psychology, individuation means the gradual integration and unification of the self through the resolution of successive layers of psychological conflict.

Integrated, integration and a sense of achievement. We are born dependent, we want to become interdependent, and to achieve interdependence or be mutually independent is what it is all about.

NUMEROLOGY

Number twenty-one equals three, two plus one equals three. The number two connects us with the High Priestess, number one to the Magician and number three connects us to the Empress.

In Australia, we celebrate our twenty-first as a coming of age.

The Hanged Man Connections

There is a strong connection to the Hanged Man and the number twelve. It is as if the Hanged Man is the reverse energy of the World card. In the Hanged Man, he is upside down and stationary whereas in the World card, she is upright and moving.

The tree in the Hanged Man card connects us to the Empress and all her growth potential as does the Wreath in the World.

Their legs are both showing as crossed. In the Hanged Man, he wears red leggings which connect to the Magician and the blue top connects us to the High Priestess card. In the World card, she wears the purple sash. The color purple is made up of the colors red and blue combination, once again demonstrating integration.

ASTROLOGY and MYTHOLOGY

Saturn also known as Father Time is the ruler of this card. The story goes that the God Saturn devoured his own children because he heard that they were going to overthrow him and his throne.

This story suggests an expression of absorbing back into the self. Going back to the source when we have completed our journey, back to the beginning but to begin again on another level. We have come a full circle and are ready to go round again.

It reminds me of the classic T.S. Elliot poem from his classic *Four Quarters*, 'We shall not cease from exploration, and the end of all our exploring will be to arrive where we started, and know the place for the first time.'

The Goddess Athena was born from her father's head, from that intellectual masculine energy. That is why she is always seen in her warlike outfit, holding her sword, ready for battle. In fact, she wins all her battles because she uses strategy and is always prepared. Goddess Athena connects to the Justice card.

The World card is the last card of the Major Arcana. It is about a successful completion. Success in completing a part of your journey. Because it connects us to the world, we have to look at this card in its widest form.

It may represent an outer world acknowledgment for example, like a twenty-first birthday party. A celebration of a new stage of life. Celebrating a rite of passage, a homecoming.

A wedding where we have the union of a couple coming together in perfect balance and ready to create their new world. A successful business partnership on the world stage.

We also have to look at world travel or traveling to a new world.

The World Represents a Successful you, Happy in your World that you Created

SYMBOLOGY

The Victory Wreath

The Victory wreath is the ultimate symbol of success. It also connects us back to the zero of the Fool card. We have now come full circle.

We see victory wreaths everywhere such as on kings' crowns. Nero used to wear the laurel wreath around his head, it symbolizes power and authority. We see the wreath at horse races for winning the race, as well as Formula One grand prix winners. It symbolizes success, triumph and achievement.

We also see the wreaths on the front doors at Christmas time and angels wear wreaths too. At funerals and ANZAC Day and other war memorial events, they celebrate the circle of life.

We have gone through the process of individuation and everything is now open and balanced. You have earned your stripes.

Nirvana

Nirvana means no longer living your life through your ego. Nirvana is the ultimate utopia and bliss. In Buddhism, it is the symbol of wholeness, the emergence of individual spirit with supreme spirit.

This is what the Judgement card has awakened you up to do, to rise above the ego.

The Dancing Spirit

This figure in many other tarot cards is androgynous looking. You usually see the union of the masculine and feminine to the characteristics that connects us to the High Priestess and Magician. In the Rider Waite we have what we call The Dancing Spirit.

The purple sash represents the unfolded lemniscate. The color purple is made of the colors red and blue, which are the colors for the High Priestess and the Magician. Purple is the color for spirituality and wisdom, and the merging with spirit. The celebration, the victory of blending the two halves and now becoming whole.

The Red Bindings

You can see the two red bindings; the infinity symbols are lemniscates. There is one above her head chakra and the other at her feet chakra. They encapsulate her whole. She is the one in between Heaven and Earth.

The Four Guardians

The four Guardians also connect us to the elements of fire, air, earth and water. We first encountered these four fixed signs in the Wheel of Fortune. In the Wheel of Fortune, they were still writing their Gospels, but now they are matured, fully grown and wholesome, they have arrived.

A Feeling of Wholeness within Oneself

IN A READING

On the inside we have the coming together of the masculine and feminine aspects of the self, an internal balance. A successful union.

On the outside, we are who we are and we are doing it successfully. Happy with who we are and have found your place in the world.

And our internal and external worlds are in balance also, like the two wands she is holding, as if she is a cheerleader and twirling her wands successfully. Burning candles at both ends. The acceptance of I am OK, you are OK. It is all OK. Achieving independence and individuation.

The World a successful completion and it all begins again but on another level, representative of the many layers of the onion. It is the last Major Arcana card where the cycle completes. We have ended one part of our journey successfully, ready to begin another.

We have become liberated by understanding a peak in our life. The Dancing Spirit in the middle of the zero. It looks as though she is dancing to keep the wheel of life turning. Life is continually moving.

Integration, achievement, and accomplishment. A successful attainment of the goal and this goal has been reached through hard work and effort on the internal and external levels.

This card always reminds me of that spiritual saying, 'you chop wood before enlightenment and you chop wood after enlightenment.'

Success of whatever you are doing; in the work and career reading, it may be a promotion in the work place. A success in the outside world and reward for efforts.

People who mainly work in the media like actors on the stage, in films or who play sports are frequently recognized on television and get rewarded for their efforts at awards nights.

In a relationship reading, we are looking at perfect relationships. Balance in partnerships in business as well. A beautiful union.

Remember to look at this card in its widest form, from traveling or becoming widely exposed, such as writing a book and selling it on the world stage. World exposure like a speaker at a United Nations conference.

The World Tarot card is one of the best cards in deck – a totally positive card without any negatives. It is the card of wholeness and balance. The world is your oyster. You have the world in the palm of your hand.

SHADOWS	KEYS
Martyrdom	Labor
Heavy burdens	Track record
Can't fulfill	Reliable
Lack of confidence	Duty
Carrying the world on their shoulders	Wise
Can't grasp money or material issues	Up-holding
Stagnation	Worldly success
Lack of will	Atlas
Impatience	Fulfillment
Delays	Completion
Stress	Success
	Satisfaction
	Joy
	Understanding
	Wholesome
	Integration
	Recreation

SHADOWS	KEYS
	Victorious
	Individuation

Tarot in Action

Complete a project, you can do it.
Reward for your efforts.
Act with confidence.
Believe in yourself.
Acknowledge what you have achieved.
Count your blessings.
Be thankful and grateful for your success.
Take a world trip.
Learning to dance to your own limitations.
Working within limitations or structure.
Sense of endless potential.
Just rewards.
Going back home.

Quotes

'The world is a stage and we are merely players upon it.' – Shakespeare.

'Life is meant to be lived as play.' – Plato.

'Your world is your oyster.' – Shakespeare.

Books to Read

The Biology of Belief by Dr Joe Dispenza.
Abundance by Diamnadis by Kotler.

Section 3 - Minor Arcana

ACE of SWORDS.

Chapter 26

THE FOUR ELEMENTS

We will first look at the four elements and start to bring in more of the astrological and the zodiac signs associated with the tarot.

There are four main groupings of zodiac signs: fire, earth, air and water. Each category has three zodiac signs that all have strong fundamental characteristics in common.

The zodiac signs of Aries, Taurus, Gemini and Cancer are known as personal energies, in that they are personal to them. I think of these guys as the baby signs. For example, Aries fire may not be able to control their energy, their anger, their fire, and what is in it for them? They could quickly burn everyone like a blow torch without thinking.

The zodiac signs of Leo, Virgo, Libra and Scorpio are interpersonal energies, meaning they are interested in you, me and the cat; my immediate family. I think of these energies as the teenage fire. You see, the Leo fire needs to look good in front of their friends and peers, a lovely looking flame, like a camp fire.

Whereas the zodiac signs of Sagittarius, Capricorn, Aquarius and Pisces are the transpersonal signs, they look at things from a collective point of view. What is in it for the whole community, if not the nation, or even the entire planet? Here we have the adult fire. For example, Sagittarius is like a simmering flame, like when you slowly cook a yummy curry sauce, that's when you get the best flavor.

ELEMENT and ZODIAC SIGN	Carl Jung PSYCHOLOGY TYPE	TAROT SUIT
FIRE • Aries • Leo • Sagittarius	INTUITIVE	WANDS
EARTH • Taurus • Virgo • Capricorn	SENSATE	PENTACLES

ELEMENT and ZODIAC SIGN	Carl Jung PSYCHOLOGY TYPE	TAROT SUIT
AIR • Gemini • Libra • Aquarius	**THINKING**	**SWORDS**
WATER • Cancer • Scorpio • Pisces	**FEELING**	**CUPS**

FIRE

WANDS - Work, Career, Skills, Talents, Efforts and Ideas

ASTROLOGY - Aries, Leo, Sagittarius

ELEMENT - Fire, Masculine energy

Fire people are inspirational and have a lot of courage, but they need courage to move through life. They love drama and are energized and spirited.

As soon as they get something they move on to something else. They need the next new exciting thing because they need the challenge.

POSITIVE

The positive side is that fire people are an inspirational force. They are creative and courageous. They are warm-hearted, charming and courageous.

Fire energy people can be idealistic, tomorrow always looks better than today. They are future oriented, looking at tomorrow. Therefore, they are not grounded in the now just like the Fool card, look at his stance, it shows how he is moving forward, about to step off the ledge, not looking at where he is going, displaying an enthusiasm of life, a joie de vie.

Fire people enroll people, they have contagious energy, may be controversial and provocative. Look at Madonna, she is a Leo. Jennifer Lopez is also a Leo, Lady Gaga is an Aries and Tina Turner is Sagittarius, so is Cristina Aguilera and Miley Cyrus.

Fire people are creative in the work place. They make great team players and traveling sales people. They will always prepare or invent something that will just need some tweaking, until the final report. Unlike an earthy person that may not know where to start in fear of doing it all wrong.

As fire peters out, things may never get done. There is a trick to harnessing fire. Fire needs to be stoked, it needs fuel to burn. Look at the preparation needed to start a camp fire.

People like to gather around fire at camp sites. Fire mesmerizes, look at how people stare at the fire, wondering what is it going to do next.

Fire people are action oriented. They have plenty of initiative, are resourceful, enterprising and always lead busy lives. Being fiery they have a hot temperament, are impatient, outspoken and assertive, and may boil over sometimes.

They are confident, believe in themselves and in their abilities. They will take a risk and go for what they want in life with courage, passion and spirit.

NEGATIVE

The negative side to fire is that they are selfish, egotistical and have impulsive energy. They may be self-centered, arrogant, reckless and impatient. They can burn out or burn others.

IN A READING

If there are a lot of wands in your reading, you are looking at a lot of energy. Remember that fire burns fast, so it all may be short lived. Just like a volcano when it erupts - exploding but then fizzles out. Fire can leap and it could also burn itself out.

Fire is at its most positive when dealing with your **WORK, CAREER, SKILLS, TALENTS, EFFORT AND IDEAS**.

You first have the creation of the idea, and then it is your masculine energy that puts it out in the world.

WARNING

Do not burn yourself out or burn others.

Important to come down to earth or ground yourself. I always like to use the example of when lightning strikes the ground; it neutralizes, so it is important for fire people to earth themselves to feel more balanced.

Take drives in the country, do some gardening, visit the park and arrange a picnic or just have lunch under a tree. Connect with nature. All these examples are a great way to bring in some overall balance and trust.

OVERALL

Fire people are laborers and workers.

You will notice that all the people in the Wands tarot suit are wearing work uniforms or ordinary folk wear. They are the ones with the energy and always working at something.

KEY WORDS

Adventure, adventurous, sporty, pioneers, action oriented, activity, loves doing something, enterprising, healthy, robust and healthy, doers, leaders, growth, invention, energy, progress, advancement, entrepreneurs, loves spending money, generous, and courageous, movement and struggle, optimism, engaging, spirited, challenges, vitality, strength, sovereign, creation, catalyst, achievers, arrogant, snobby, entertainers, aloof, passionate, proud, ego, workers, peasants, ideas, skills, how we work, career, talents, common workers, blue collar workers.

QUOTES

'Necessity is the mother of all invention.'

'Strike while the iron's hot.'

'Fast forward and total burnout.'

EARTH

PENTACLES - Material and Spiritual Wealth and Values

ASTROLOGY - Taurus, Virgo, Capricorn

ELEMENT - Earth, Feminine Energy

Responds to the physical outer world and our inner value system. Deals with money, currency and possessions. Wealth in the outer world and in the metaphysical or spiritual inner world. Earth people put a value on everything; they would not do anything if it had no value in it for them.

POSITIVE

They understand what is of value to us, whether it is on the material physical level or on the spiritual inner level. They like to build their empires and then relax and enjoy themselves later on in the journey.

Let us have a look at some outer and inner ways:

Outer Material

They will invest in money, possessions, property, antiques, heirlooms, inheritances, shares, stocks, gold, currency, horses, houses, cars, bonds, jewelry, collectibles, artworks, workshops, all outer world values, etc.

Inner Spiritual

Your personal value system, the value of self-confidence, self-esteem, self-worth, morals and ethics, health, integrity, love, family traditions, religion, principles, charity work, etc.

The energy of the Hierophant Major Arcana links these two inner and outer worlds together perfectly. That is what he asks us to do – bring in and to work these two sides of ourselves together.

Earth people plan and create things of value. They also work for things of value; they may even choose a position or a career that not only is of value to themselves but also to others. Earth people are very hard workers and have committed energy.

Earth people can see the magic and value in everyday life. People show you their struggles in life.

How often do we put a monetary value on ourselves? Such as when we go shopping, we always look at the price tag. What this says about ourselves is that we are not worthy of spending much money on ourselves. When a disaster happens, the media always gives us the monetary value of the loss – a million dollars went up in smoke at the factory fire.

How much am I worth? What do you do for a living? All these are value judgements. Another question may be, where do you live? All place a judgmental value on ourselves.

Earth people are realists; they are down to earth with strong practical values, seeking security and stability. Ultimately they want to put down roots and establish a settled home and family situation.

They analyze their emotions and experiences rationally and make careful, logical choices. They can seem unemotional or controlled, but they are deep, sincere, emotionally constant people who do not blow hot and cold. They are consistent.

NEGATIVE

They may be too greedy, jealous, possessive, materialistic. The energy of amassing things to prove they exist and are of value. Social status becomes important.

There may be a malfunction in the value system. They think they have to have possessions to be someone. Suffer from self-doubt, self-centered, vanity and pretentiousness.

IN A READING

Pentacles or Earth energy works best when dealing with the **MATERIAL AND SPIRITUAL WEALTH AND VALUES.**

Remember earthy people only have one speed, the other speed is slower. They are committed to whatever is of value to them. They would not get involved unless there is a result or outcome. They would not waste their time, resources, money or efforts. They want an outcome and a realized result, a physical outcome.

WARNING

Earth people need to trust themselves. They plan and strategize everything so much and they still do not trust themselves to follow through with their plans.

They are like a rock in the sun. They need that push to roll down the hill.

OVERALL

Here we have the merchants and tradesman. They are the business owners, the landlords and the bosses.

KEY WORDS

Steady people, stable, grounded, practical, material, financial, occupation, sensual, sensitive, strategy, earthed, sensible, security, wealth, responsible, white collar workers, reliable, status, planners, common sense, fixed, stubborn, even keel, approachable, tenacious, static, methodical, rules, comfortable, conformity, routine, loyal, stick in the mud, do not like change, systematically, realistic.

QUOTES

'Slow and steady always wins the race.'

'Stuck in a rut.'

AIR

SWORDS - Mental Conflict Energy

ASTROLOGY - Gemini, Libra, Aquarius

ELEMENT - Air, Masculine energy

Swords have to do with the mind and the thinking function. Mental energy and conflicts. The mind has lots of thoughts; this is often called a Monkey Mind, the monkey forever on your back, a chatterbox.

Sometimes our thinking is foggy or it could be with great clarity. It is the thinking function that is revered most in our society.

Important note. The air and water elements are opposites. Therefore, when you are not thinking clearly, you are in the emotions. You need a rational clear-thinking mind to make the correct and clear decision because emotions can change so quickly.

You will always hear an air person say, "I think this", where as a water person will say, "I feel that".

The mind is the only tool in our head. The left brain is the logical side and controls the right side of your body and your conscious, masculine, active energy. The right brain is the creative and receptive side and controls the left side of your body, your unconscious, black, feminine and passive energy.

POSITIVE

Air people are linkers and are switched on. They are great connectors; it is easy for them to bring people together.

They think to evaluate, rationalize and analyze everything. Great linkers and connectors, they can put things together in the mind and actually solve issues. They can even think backwards, they are great people to help you retrace your steps and find things that are missing.

Air people are 'people people.' They are friendly and sociable. They value their friends and are natural networkers who will have contacts from all walks of life.

They have quick, open minds but get bored easily as they love variety and spontaneity. With a desire for independence and freedom of movement, they need emotional space and breathing room, even in a relationship. They can be flirtatious and are innately optimistic too.

NEGATIVE

On the negative side they are the worriers, confused, suffer from headaches, indecisive, pessimistic, fearful, paranoid and overall negative and suspicious.

They can actually split off and have abandonment issues. Often they feel that they come from another planet and no one understands them.

IN A READING

Air works in the most positive way when dealing with **MENTAL CONFLICT ENERGY.**

The mind can quickly surmise the end results but it can also trick you. It is important for air people to deal with facts.

WARNING

May suffer from headaches and worries.

It is important for them to learn to mediate and learn how to control the mind and how to switch it off. Learn breathing exercises or do yoga, maybe even read books to bring about more balance.

Some air people may enjoy going for a run or a drive in the country to feel the fresh air on their face. All this will assist when in need in making the right decision.

OVERALL

Air people are our leaders and warriors in society. In fact, society is geared for this top twenty percent.

KEY WORDS

Head, rational mind, rational thinking function, ambitious, wind, logic, teacher, writer, PR, bold, common sense, analysis, airhead, persuasive, argumentative, media, author, disc jockey, trickster, manipulators, singers, orators, airy fairy, charming, detached, intelligent, change their mind a lot, talk a lot and talk fast, con artists, problems solvers, good Listeners, fickle, journalists, flittering mind.

QUOTES

'Better to wear out than to rust out.'

'I think therefore I am.'

'Jack of all trade, master of none.'

'Communication with a capital C.'

WATER

CUPS - Feelings and Emotions

ASTROLOGY - Cancer, Scorpio, Pisces

ELEMENT - Water, Feminine energy

We are now to deal with the internal feminine energy, the feminine receptive quality. Our feelings and emotions are fluid and movable; they are always changeable.

This person may feel strongly about something but it is not real. It is how they feel right now, in the moment, yet it is the most unrealistic suit because the feelings shift and change so much, so quickly. They tend to go with the flow.

It is easier to change your feelings than to change your mind, and you may need to use mind to change your feelings. There is a method called Rational Emotive Therapy that helps with this process.

Remember that the water (feelings) element is opposite to the air (thinking) element. For example, if your relationship is finished, the mind will accept this but your feelings and emotions would still be high or low about it all. We are dealing with two different realms, the head versus the heart.

If you use feelings and do not listen to mind, you may be pushed around a lot, or be taken advantage of, or assume other people's feelings. You may tend to be the scapegoat or a doormat for others.

People may tell you that they know things and may even have a way with words, but the body's reaction may be saying something different. They say actions speak louder than words.

If it is difficult in understanding your feelings, I recommend doing a Body Language workshop or a Neuro Linguistic Program (NLP) to assist you and to stand in your power more.

Another process is to listen to your body which responds in many ways: through your heart beat, twitches, your breathing, facial reactions, sweaty hands, head wobbling, hot face flushes, tears, eyes rolling up towards the sky, making a fist, etc. All these reactions are clues.

Cups processes human feelings and through these feelings we can access the unconscious, which is the world of the High Priestess and what is she trying to tell us. When feelings are activated we can penetrate the unconscious world.

Cup cards connect us to human emotions. We all experience happiness, joy, love, grief, disappointment, etc. We all feel these same emotions through different stories and circumstances and we all understand them because we all experience them.

Cup cards work on the inner level energy, they deal with reflection, contemplation, passive and introspective energy.

Water people are emotional and live life from the heart. They have a deep capacity for love, and through it they can find inner strength and purpose. They are complex, insightful, perspective and intuitive.

They can be over-sensitive and get easily hurt. Inclined to be private, they can retreat into their shells, into their caves or go down deep into the dark abyss.

IN A READING

Water energy works the best when dealing with **FEELINGS AND EMOTIONS.**

The planet is seventy percent water. When there is a full moon we have high tide or king tides. We humans are seventy percent water as well and when there is a full moon our emotions may be at their peak. We need to be mindful of making proper decisions during a full moon time. Maybe it is better to wait until the full moon passes before making that decision.

WARNING

Not to make decisions on or around the full moon.

Not to have too much alcohol – especially during full moon time, but to have a spa, a foot spa and a relaxing bubble bath instead.

Not that long ago, if you had asthma, it was advised to take up swimming. It helped to regulate the breathing and open up the lungs.

OVERALL

The humane person. They deal with tenderness, compassion and empathy, are psychic healers; the medicine man or woman.

KEY WORDS

Passions, dreamer, sensitivity, pleasures, memories, emotional, deep feelings, empathic, counselors, drips, nurses, sympathetic, old age carers, young child minders, moody, romantics, artistic, poetic, intuitive, alcoholics, healers, detectives, insensitive, forensics, private investigators, creative, musical, psychics, mystics, telepaths, guilt, molly coddle.

QUOTE

'Dreamer, nothing but a dreamer.' – by *Supertramp*.

Chapter 27

No. 2 - CHOICE and BALANCE

2 WANDS - Choice in Work, Career, Skills, Talents, Efforts and Ideas
2 PENTACLES - Balance in the Material and Spiritual Values
2 SWORDS - Choice in the Mental Conflict Energy
2 CUPS - Balance in the area of Feelings and Emotions

2 WANDS - Choice in the area of Work, Career, Skills, Talents, Efforts and Ideas

SUMMARY

The man is dressed for traveling. He is wearing brown clothing and standing on a balcony. The brown cloak signifies a hard worker with a practical and committed energy. He is wearing orange underneath, signifying inner vitality, warmth, pride and confidence.

His left hand is holding onto a wand, representing a skill or talent. Because it is in his left hand, this suggests the skill is still in the unconscious world. It also suggests he does not know how to direct the energy or know what to do with it yet.

In his right hand he holds a globe, representing success and achievement. You have got the whole world in the palm of your hand. Because it is in his right hand, it suggests he is conscious of this worldly success.

Another thing that shows he has made it and he is successful is the balcony he is standing on. The balcony is grey indicating he has wisdom. Balconies are also a symbol of social position, you are elevated, you have social position, you have power and you have the advantage.

There is a wand behind him and he has turned his back on it, yet he has kept it. You can see he has shackled it or secured it to the wall. It may have made him successful and perhaps he does not need it anymore. But by keeping it, he can always fall back onto it if need be. Maybe it was this skill that elevated him to his high position, which offered him advantage and choice.

But the skill he wants to pursue is in the left hand. This is the choice that he has to make, this is the energy of the card.

He is looking out across the blue lake, looking to the future, towards the purple mountains. The color blue connects us to emotions and the purple mountains represent aspirations, conquering your goal, aspiring to new heights. Everyone wants to climb their mountain. The color purple suggests spiritual aspirations. Maybe he wants to put more spiritual meaning into his working life.

Put More Meaning in Your Work

The red hat connects us to his passionate thoughts and desires; he has reached a moment in his life to be in the position to create his future. All that greenery in front of him suggests creativity and a very lush looking environment ahead of him.

The St Andrew's Cross on the pillar represents the battle of the lilies and roses. We first met the red roses and white lilies in the Magician major arcana card. The red roses represent passion and desires. The white lilies represent the ideal scenario, pure intentions. Crosses also represent the union of opposites; the challenge is for him to bring these two points together.

Basically, he is trying to make the crossover or choice between these two points. This is his battle or the choice he needs to make. This person is trying to make a choice between the skill they know how to use, and the desire to pursue their new idea or dream.

IN A READING

This person may be going through a mid-life crisis or is at a crossroad in life. For example, he wants to change his career from being a banker and going off to do pottery. This is his dilemma; does he stay with the old or go with the new? This is the choice that he has to make.

The Urge is to Move Forward

The key with this card is that they usually go with the new because of the fire element associated with this card. He is showing you that he has already turned his back on the old wand he has already achieved. The urge for him is to go forward; the energy of fire is that they will move forward.

In a relationship reading, the question here is; do they stay with old friends or move to the next girl or boy. There may be a 'been there, done that' type of attitude. You know the old one works but the new one is so much more adventurous, challenging and exciting. Exploring the new relationship is exciting for fire people. The urge is that they want to jump into the fire. It is important to not put a foot in both places because it will not get you anywhere.

In a work or career reading, the urge may be to bring a more spiritual meaning into your life. You are ready to take your work out there into the world on an international level. Maybe working on a world trip.

They want to go forward and move into the new energy. The challenge here is do they stay with what they have already achieved, or do they follow their dreams?

2 PENTACLES - Balance in the area of the Material and Spiritual Values

SUMMARY

We have someone practically balancing two pentacles as if they are balancing two values. There is no need for choice in this card.

The green lemniscate or infinity symbol demonstrates he can keep on juggling these two values forever. It reminds me of a bicycle chain. There is no way he can drop the pentacles because he is in motion, it is happening right now, you can see his foot is off the ground as if he is doing a dance to keep the rhythm going. He is in motion to keep the balance.

He wears green shoes suggesting creative steps and foot work to keep it all flexible, moving and flowing. As he dances to his tune, he is also thinking on his toes. The platform is grey suggesting he has wisdom and knowledge.

In fact, the card is full of ups and downs. The foot is up, the sea is up and down, one pentacle is up and the other down, the water and the ships are up and down riding the waves. He is also looking at one pentacle more than the other, and holds one pentacle higher than the other.

Going with the Flow

You can say in the past, he has been successful in negotiating the ups and downs of life and he is still very good at doing it now. Even though it looks stormy with the waning sea in the background, he seems to keep his balance, not caring what others think.

Water represents the emotions, even though the emotions are upset, he seems content and resilient; this connects us to the earth element that rules the pentacles. Also his back is to the water and to all the emotions. Just like the ships are riding the waves, he is going with the flow and keeping afloat. Ships also represent travel.

The saying "Ships passing in the night" also suggests things not really coming together, like an affair or a relationship not really getting off the ground, a fleeting encounter. Or a husband and wife team missing each other throughout the day and playing tag team.

He wears orange and red clothing, demonstrating his confidence, his vitality and passionate energy. His high hat represents high desires and he is passionate about his ideas. It is also phallic looking.

IN A READING

In a financial reading, this person can keep juggling money and is able to make his finances work and keep the books balanced. There is a good balance of money coming in and money going out. Maybe he needs to take a little from here to put over there and vice versa, but it all works. If there is a need to split the finances, this card suggests equal splitting. In business it may not be a huge profit but it all works, it is steady.

Whatever the other values are, this card says you can have your cake and eat it too, putting in the same energy, not necessarily the same time. It keeps him on his toes and it all balances; it is rolling along smoothly.

To Perfectly Balance Two Things of Value in Your Life

In a relationship reading, this card says you can stay married and have other relationships as well, being able to perfectly juggle two women or men in your life. Remember he has his back to the water, therefore emotions are not involved.

Remember the two ships passing in the night; this often refers to a brief interlude, a fleeting encounter or two things never really coming together. Two people are able to make their relationship work or we are looking at balanced relationships.

We can also have a mother balancing her family and work; she is able to manage the two.

I also like to mention that the person seems to have the finances balanced and they may need to bring in more spiritual awareness to create the balance.

2 SWORDS - Balance in the Mental Conflict Energy

SUMMARY

You can clearly see that she does not want to make a choice. She is wearing a headband and blindfold representing restricting thoughts. She does not want to see the choice nor wants to hear anything.

This card suggests that you need to become more emotionally balanced on the inside first, before making a choice in the outer world. She does have a choice to make and she is closing herself off to listen to her inner voice. Some people may think she is meditating and she may come across as being defensive.

Positive

The positive is that you do go inwards; this connects you to your inner Hermit, and to the High Priestess energy. There are a lot of similarities between this card and the High Priestess; there is the number two, the color blue, the moon and both are sitting down on a simple stool. In this card, she is blindfolded. In the High Priestess there is the veil hanging behind her.

The tips of the swords are out of the picture as if she does not get the point yet. The swords are also the same height, suggesting that one choice is just as good as the other.

Connecting Inwardly before Making Decisions in the Real World

Negative

The negative is being over-armed, defensive, will not make a choice, will not listen, see it or hear anything. Not coping, totally in denial and shutting down.

The last quarter moon is saying this is the end of the emotional energy and being in the dark. The moon looks like it is eclipsing the sun.

You can see that all seems calm around her. It seems as though the darkness is passing because the orange mountains are in the background, which suggests a new day is dawning. The color orange represents vitality, confidence and that there is good energy.

Water represents life and emotions; she is keeping a lid on it because you can see she has turned her back to the water so she is not emotionally involved. The water also looks calm.

The grey stool and grey platform connects us to wisdom and the white gown she is wearing represents purity and innocence.

The yellow shoes connect us to our inner soul. She has contact with her soul and third eye and that is where the answer is. Yellow connects us to the intellect and our logic. You need to use your mind to make the right balanced choice. This card is telling us to get emotionally balanced on the inside first before using the mind to make a choice in the outer world.

Note that when all is serene, the smart thing to do is not to bite into the situation. While it is calm let it be – do not rock the boat. A friend once said, while the bear is sleeping "Do not poke the bear".

Feeling Centered Within

IN A READING

Sensing something and sitting with it first to get clarity and to get the point of the situation before moving ahead.

Going inwards and reflecting. Sleep on it one more night. Take your time. Thinking before you speak, thinking before you act.

She also shows you that she can protect herself, protect her ideas and her integrity. She can shield her heart.

2 CUPS - Balance in the area of Feelings and Emotions

SUMMARY

Everything in this card definitely demonstrates that all is in balance, rather than having to make a choice. There is total symmetry in this card. The height of the people and the cups are the same, the wings, the snakes, the feminine and masculine are the same. The general look of the card is showing you everything is balanced.

The two people are ceremoniously dressed; saluting each other as if exchanging cups; exchanging rings, or exchanging vows. There is a sentiment about this card.

The back of the card shows green pastures and a lush environment, a home with a red roof suggesting there is love in the home. Is this their past or future? If they came from this home setting in the past, they can definitely recreate it again in their future.

The Female

Let us look at the female first. Her garments are white with a blue over tunic, demonstrating her purity, spirituality and feminine intuition. The green wreath around her head connects to her feminine quality, her creativity, celebration, fertility and growth.

The red shoes poking out underneath her garment represent her inner passions and desires; her sexuality. The symbolism of a female wearing red shoes in the tarot represents the hidden female sexuality.

The Male

With the male, his sexuality is boldly displayed around his head as the red wreath. He wears white underneath his garment demonstrating inner purity. The floral dress he wears reminds me of the male peacock and also of the Fool's outfit. You can see he looks like he is buff and strutting his stuff. The yellow and orange colors represent his vitality and that he is keen. The yellow stockings shows his positive intellect.

The Soul Mate Card

He is stepping forward and his hand is reaching out, joining, touching hers, which is clearly showing the masculine active energy. The male feeling level, the masculine reaches out with his right hand demonstrates his conscious and that he is in motion. The female shows the feminine side which is the receptive passive quality. He makes the moves and she is the one that accepts or receives him.

The bottom color of card is golden, showing there is a soul connection – they are soul mates.

The head of the lion connects us to the zodiac sign of Leo, which connects to the sun energy, the self and the ego masculine energy. The wings connect us to the dove, the feminine, to peace and the love energy. What we have here is the full force of masculine and feminine energies where the energies are balanced.

The serpents known as the Caduceus represent healing energies. An Egyptian symbol of coherence and balance, connects to the Hermes the Magician.

The coiled snake is also the symbol of the Kundalini or the base chakra. When we talk about raising the Kundalini we are talking about awakening the sexual energy. There is sexual energy or urges between these two.

Equality in Relationships

IN A READING

A relationship between two people where the energies are balanced. A happy union between two people. This is the love card. This is one of those tarot cards you want to see when doing a relationship reading.

Both bring what they can contribute to the relationship. For example, both are working and give their fair share to the relationship. A well balanced relationship, it is nurturing, supportive, caring and loving. It is all about equality.

The relationship is also balanced in the outer world. Both parties are powerful. If one partner is powerful and the other is powerless, the relationship will not work. Both have to be powerful to make the relationship work.

In a business partnership, the friendship between two people is well balanced. The union is balanced and therefore the project will work.

On the personal level, we also have two halves coming together to make a whole, balancing both the inner masculine and feminine energies within. Balancing inner and outer worlds. When you have a balanced inner world you have a balanced outer world.

Chapter 28

No. 3 - Growth and Expansion

3 WANDS - Growth and Expansion in Work, Career, Skills, Talents, Efforts and Ideas
3 PENTACLES - Growth and Expansion in Material and Spiritual Wealth
3 SWORDS - Growth and Expansion in the Mental Conflict function
3 CUPS - Growth and Expansion in the Emotions and Feelings

3 WANDS - Growth and Expansion in Work, Career, Skills, Talents, Efforts and Ideas

SUMMARY

Growth and expansion in the world through the use of your ideas and efforts. Wands represent work and our career life. You have to work for your ideas and efforts.

This card is also a nice follow on from the two of wands, where you can see he has left his home balcony and has advanced a bit further along, moving closer to the work he aspires to do. It also suggests there is more work to do.

We have a calm looking man looking out across a golden sea where you can see the boats on the water. The golden color connects us to the source of life and a great imagination; you also see the ships are moving forward.

This card also connects us to the Death card and the River Styx and the need to move through emotions and to new beginnings on the other side.

The purple mountains in the distance signify aspirations and spiritual meaning. For example, volunteer work brings fulfillment on that inner level. Today many people volunteer their services because they are not getting that fulfillment from their everyday work.

There are two wands on his right side, representing that he is conscious of these two skills or talents that he is holding onto, they are secured in his hand. There is one wand on his left side, representing his unconscious, suggesting it is just not realized yet. He has no idea that wand is on his left hand side at all. He has no connection on the left hand side to it. Therefore, he has no idea and he is not aware that wand is actually there.

Something Will Come in From Left Field, then You Will Adapt

Although he is standing on the shoreline and standing on raised ground, he is not grounded. We can see this because the ground is unleveled and discolored, suggesting he is not standing steady. The green and orange colors bring in growth and new energy. There is a change-a-coming, maybe he has itchy feet, something may be moving underfoot, or he is standing on shaky ground. It is not terra firma.

The band around his head represents restricting thoughts. The black hair means ignorance, and also connects us the Magician's energy and knowing that the knowledge is there but not time yet for it to come through, but to keep visualizing and holding the intention of the new ideas. The brown red cloak represents he is practical and hard working. You can see the blue undergarment showing through, meaning he has an emotional connection and there is an internal need to be more spiritual.

The green mantle over his left shoulder means he is conscious about peace, harmony, adaptability, creativity, flexibility and potential growth. This also suggests the new growth that will come from left field.

The checkered cloth is the key to this card. It suggests at times you feel like you are going two steps forward then two steps backwards, also suggesting he may be indecisive or changes his mind a lot. The yellow represents the mind and intellect, the black representing the unconscious and the unknown factor.

IN A READING

This person is trying to discover his aspiration, trying to give more power to his soul or to put more value in his life, as if he is searching around for things to do. Trying to find his place in the world to put his skill and talents to use, maybe looking at expanding his business overseas, trying to work out how is the best way to accomplish this.

For the clients who draw this card, no matter what they are thinking about, they really have no idea what they are going to do next, because they have no idea what path they will take. No matter what they say to the contrary, the idea just has just not been developed yet.

This card speaks of the Universal Law of Lag. Lag is when you surrender; letting go of the ego control of the situation. It is a way of being happy in any circumstance.

Something new will come from nowhere; from the left field, from unexpected sources, from the unconscious, then you will have to adapt, you have no control over it.

Do not search around because you will not know where to look. It is just not ready, it is not the right time. This should not distract you from looking forward, to keep aspiring, dreaming, visualizing, researching and strategizing just, like the Magician energy would be doing because there will be a development. The Magician is always in a process of manifesting. Remember wands connect us to the element of fire, and fire is enterprising, creative and entrepreneurial.

The best example I like to use for this card, is when you are selling your house. All you can do is pack the big stuff, know who is going to move you, know where you are going to move to and have all the bank papers ready to go. You will have no control over who that someone is going to be, when they will make their offer and exactly how much they are going to offer. You simply have no control over the situation, but you know that eventually and inevitably the house will sell and then you can move forward.

Prepare for the Change

In a relationship reading, this person may be thinking about the other person and they do not know what to do. Should they stay with the one they are with or move to the one they are thinking about? Will they do this or that? Remember the fire element will always want to move forward. With the energy of this card, what will happen is the one they are with will leave them, and they would not have expected that, totally coming from that left field.

Could someone new also be unexpectedly coming into your life or someone leaving? Something will happen unexpectedly and then you will have to change you plans accordingly.

The man in the card is wearing his coat; he is ready for the move. We do not know if he missed the boats or if he is waiting for them to arrive. I always suggest to my clients to get things ready and keep preparing, to start packing and filing things away, so when the boats arrive you are ready to jump onboard, heading towards new growth and expansion.

I feel this is a positive card, that the person has worked hard to get themselves in to this position and now it is time to allow the universe to work for you. A great quote that works well with this card is 'Timing is everything.'

3 PENTACLES - Growth and Expansion in the area of Material and Spiritual Wealth

SUMMARY

In the physical or material sense, this card represents rewards for your efforts. On the metaphysical or spiritual sense, we appreciate the value of hard work.

This is one of my favorite tarot cards, I have a few that I really connect with.

Within the card, we have three individuals, a tradesman, an architect and a monk. The tradesman is building the church, you can see the mason's hammer in his hand. The architect planned and drew the plans of the project for the monk, who had the idea, and you can see the paperwork in the architect's hands. It takes all three to bring this project together.

The tradesman is wearing blue undergarments, meaning his work is a spiritual devotion for him. He is standing on a pink and orange bench, suggesting he is elevated and it also means he puts value in his work. In the olden days carpenters were respected and held in high regard as they had a skill; they could build things and can pass this skill on to others.

The architect's flamboyant garments make the same statement as architects still do today – the hood denotes authority. His outfit and shoes are also pink and orange. Pink is the color of unconditional love and orange is about confidence, vitality and positive energy. Suggesting he values and loves what he does and it is a labor of love for him.

Through our work or the value of our work, we are able to contact or connect to our spiritual side. For example, working for others is a higher deed, has a higher purpose, selfless giving, volunteering services and pro-bono work teaches us an appreciation of the value of giving. The actual physical labor develops spiritual growth.

This is the only tarot card where the pentacles are not gold, suggesting it is still in the planning stage. The reward will come but later as there is still work to be done.

The black background suggests unfinished business and it bring our attention to spiritual growth because this black color highlights the grey lace work in the foreground. The color grey means wisdom, knowledge and responsibility.

There is a triangle pointing upwards and another pointing downwards on the column. In the middle of both triangles are crosses in a circle, suggesting the union of above with below, masculine and feminine and the union of opposites. Connects us to the physical and spiritual worlds, time and space and is also the symbol for Earth.

Reward for Your Efforts

IN A READING

This is the card of planning. The need to work at something, to create and make plans, put the energy and effort into it and only then will your dreams come true.

Time to check the blue print, get back to the drawing board, checking your plans because you may be off track. On a personal level, working on your vision and goals, time to create a vision board and a timeline through to manifestation.

This card is about practical learning, not theory. Remember the tradesman has the hammer in his hand and the architect holds the project paperwork. The job is in hand and they are all on the work site.

Training for example, learning a new skill, like learning the tarot. Tarot is a practical skill, also brings in a spiritual discipline. Other practical skills you may try are Reiki, Yoga,

Meditation, Tai Chi even, where they all open you up to a higher learning. Also you are part of a group sharing the knowledge with others.

The Vocation Card

A vocation card is if they have a vocation to their work. Vocation means love and devotion that is a dedication, like the monk and his life's work and commitment to the church. A calling to be a doctor not just for the money. RPA Dr Chan comes to mind as does Dr Fred Hollows and the legacy he has left behind.

In a career reading, this card may suggest going for further training or it is time to become a trainer or to now become the master, time to teach and go through to the next level.

For young people, this card may represent their VCE year. You have to work hard to complete the course, you may be struggling, but you have to go through the annoying part of life to complete and achieve the end result.

In a money reading, there is a need to work hard to become financially secure. Plan that nest egg, create a portfolio, do a financial workshop, read the books and learn how money works.

In a relationship reading, you both have to work hard in the relationship or you will not get the rewards.

Home renovations, actual practical and physical work needs to be handled around the house, such as, landscaping and painting. Building an extension like adding a pergola, all this physical work will also add more value to the property.

In summary, there is a need to work with others, to plan the ideas and to bring all the talents together, linking everyone together and team work. When I see three people in the picture it may actually suggest three people.

You need to work to reap the awards and all the rewards. There is value in the work. There is reward because of the Pentacles, put in the effort and then the pentacles will turn to gold!

3 SWORDS - Growth and Expansion through Mental Conflict

** This is the first of the Warning cards.

I always recommend having a box of tissues handy when doing readings. Some people may shed tears, not in a sobbing way, just releasing tears as if it is a realization and on some level they have come to terms with the situation.

SUMMARY

The picture on this card is pretty clear for people. There are three swords through a heart. When there is mental conflict, it is usually between the head and the heart.

Remember that number three is about growth and expansion; I like to mention to people that there is growth, or they are growing through an emotional pain. People understand it when you put it to them in this way.

It is obvious we have a conflict between the mind and heart and for some people there is no release. You can see there is a lack of blood flowing in the card, no blood-letting, therefore no satisfaction.

In fact, the key to this card is that the swords have been in the heart for a long time, you can see the sword tips are blunt and discolored.

The grey clouds represent symbolic messages. The darker grey of the background represents confusion and clouded thoughts. The rain represents tears, it is raining down on you. Rain water is cleansing, a release, tears suggest here is an opportunity to clear and wash away something.

This is the Card of Sorrow

Being the card of sorrow, for some people, this can be overwhelming and bring up immediate acute pain. It is not a new pain though, because the swords have been there a long time. The present situation is pricking or pushing all the buttons, triggering a past story like rubbing salt into a wound, taking you back to past sorrows and you remember past emotions. But something may happen in the present moment, and it could be the straw that breaks the camel's back to clear this issue up once and for all.

A question I always like to ask with this card is "Have you experienced this before?" as the same theme may be repeating in a new story. For example, as a baby your father may have abandoned you, as a teenager your boyfriend abandons you, then as an adult your husband abandons you. As a child or a teenager you may not understand abandonment, but as an adult you understand more and you can do something about it.

Another question I may ask (because it is always better if they get the answer themselves rather than you telling them) is, "Why do you think this is happening again?" They usually respond that it is happening again so it can be resolved. As an adult you are able to heal and clear these abandonment issues.

Note that for some people pain can be a long term friend, they like to suffer, they relish in it, mia culpa, mia culpa, as they say "Misery loves company".

Because of the three swords we may be looking at three different people bringing in the same pain over and over or it may be one person giving you grief three times over. It could also be three different issues or may even represent three years of time. The three swords all cross each other creating an acute pressure point.

Dr John Gray, the relationship psychologist and author of *Men Are from Mars and Women Are from Venus*, says that when couples argue they dig up past conflicts and so it is hard for them to stick to the current issue. He says that ninety percent of the argument is past issues and only ten percent is the current issue. Dr Phil says "If it is historical it is hysterical".

Swords connect to the mind, the intellect, therefore all this anguish could all be happening in one's mind, giving grief and heart ache all by themselves.

There is a need for a lot of work to heal the pain. The grudge, each new sword aggravates the pain.

Growth Through a Pain

IN A READING

For the pain to be this strong, the issues may be family related or close relationship issues. You need to deal with it and heal the pain in some way. You may be bringing past relationships into the new relationships.

I have noticed that when people think there is a problem, tarot readers are the first port of call for them to visit, to check if their assumptions are merited.

I recommend to my students to do ongoing counseling or relationship therapy courses and to read many books. (Refer to the Booklist Attachment page 410.) You have to be careful how you word things to your clients; you are dealing with sensitive issues and people are looking for immediate answers where there may be no immediate answers.

For me tarot readers are right brain psychologists. There are some tarot readers that open the floodgates for people and then do not know how to put the client back together again. It is imperative that you keep your training going with counseling and relationship workshops, the further you go the more you will be able to assist your clients. Eighty per cent of tarot readings are on relationships. New insights and understanding of relationships are happening all the time. You need to be able to direct the client in the right direction.

When you see that the client is in need of further counseling, you may suggest a psychologist or some other form of assistance, because of this I suggest the tarot reader creates a referral manual. Start to collect business cards of masseurs, psychologists, hypnotherapists, counselors, acupuncturists, etc. that you can suggest or refer for your client to visit. It may also be good idea to have an experience with these people you recommend, know the prices, give your client the right information and send the right person to the right help.

Also, have books on hand that you can refer them to, or exercises you can give your client to help them let go and work through their issues. There are heaps of things one can do, like writing a letter to the person that has given you pain and complete with that person. Not that they have to post the letter – it is about getting your thoughts out on paper. Writing in a journal is therapeutic. Reading self-esteem books can create a total shift, learning meditation techniques and having a massage is all about nurturing oneself and raising your energy to help ease that pain.

This card could suggest a disagreement, a separation between two loved ones, maybe separated through distance creates pain in the heart. This card does have degrees of pain; it could bring tears up for some people if the pain is acute. This pain will keep happening until you face it and clean it up. One of my favorite sayings that connects well with this card is "What you resist will persist".

This card may be just what the client needs at the time, to realize that they have work to do to let go of something. Discuss the many options.

If this card comes up with the Tower card, it could literally mean a heart attack and immediate surgery on or around the heart area. Sudden and unexpected rift in the relationship, an unexpected split ending in a divorce. Healing deep heart issues, maybe the swords can create a release.

If this card comes up with the Empress card, it may represent a miscarriage. This is a pain that one can hold for a very long time. The loss of an offspring, an abortion, and or a loss of some form of creativity. Learning that you are infertile is painful through to a separation from mother and child and adoption issues.

GO GENTLE WITH THIS CARD!

3 CUPS - Growth and Expansion in the Feelings and Emotions

SUMMARY

Here we have the three Faiths, or the three Charities, or Faith, Hope and Charity, just like the Botticelli painting of the three graces in white – in other paintings they are displayed naked. Today we have the modern day Charmed Ones, the power of the three and connecting to the Holy Trinity.

This is known as the Celebration Card. We have three maidens celebrating the harvest. It is a time of abundance. The three maidens are dancing, rejoicing and having a merry time with others. There is fruit and flowers everywhere, it is a fruitful time in your life.

This card reminds me of the first of May and dancing around the may pole. The song that comes to mind is *Love is the Air*, an upbeat song. It's very uplifting and engaging and you cannot help but tap your foot, clap and dance along to the music.

We know they are maidens because their hair is unbraided, demonstrating that they are free and unmarried.

The woman in red is more dominate. She is in front of the others but her cup is not the highest. The highest cup is from the women in white.

Faith, Hope and Charity

Often seen as charms for a bracelet. Faith Hope and Charity were known as three sisters and three saints. Their mother is known as Sophia (Greek for wisdom). The names are also the words designating the three key Christian virtues.

It is a card of equality because of the growth aspect and due to there being three people in the card. The number three is all about growth and fertility, especially in the area of love.

Abundance of love because of the cups and the water element associations.

The Celebration Card

IN A READING

Sharing a good time with family. There is happiness and joy and sharing these good feelings with friends and or loved ones.

It may be a social event like a birthday, a wedding, or depicting a formal social life. A formal gathering on a social level like celebrating the birth of a baby, and celebrating it with the christening or name giving. So ask the question, "Is there a special family function coming up like a wedding or a birth of a baby?"

We could also have someone who has had a difficult time in life and is now ready to come back out and enjoy themselves with others. They have come back and everyone is celebrating their return.

Perhaps they are celebrating a homecoming of some sort, like returning from army duty, a honeymoon or from being sick.

Celebrating a Good Time with Loved Ones

NEGATIVE

The negative is if you are not putting in the effort with your studies, or having too much of a social life and not studying enough.

POSITIVE

The positive is celebrating the end of year final exams. A very positive card indeed, celebration and sharing with friends that love you. You will get a lot of support from friends and are sharing a good time.

In a relationship reading, we have growth in the emotional life. May be public recognition, for example the first time you introduce your partner to your family and celebrating this. The engagement with family and friends, this is the growth in the relationship, taking the relationship to the next level, or could be announcing the wedding date.

In a career setting, we have a celebration around the completion of the successful project. End of year Christmas function. It is a business social time like a promotion, a launch of a project or maybe the celebrating of finally leaving work. Finally reaping the rewards!

If you have the three pentacles and three cups together we may have a celebration of a job well done and getting paid off. Or a house renovation finally completed and having a house warming party to celebrate it.

Chapter 29

No. 4 - Foundation and Stability

4 WANDS - Foundation and Stability in Work, Career, Skills, Talents, Efforts and Ideas
4 PENTACLES - Foundation and Stability in Material and Spiritual Values
4 SWORDS - Foundation and Stability in the Mental Conflict area
4 CUPS - Foundation and Stability in Emotions and Feelings area

4 WANDS - Foundation and Stability in Work, Career, Skills, Talents, Efforts and Ideas

SUMMARY

Here we have people celebrating the harvest; you can see the floral garland secured with ribbons to the wands at the back demonstrating stability.

Fruit and flowers are held high in celebration. The four wands remind me of goal posts that are there for us to aim towards our dreams, ideas, hopes and our visions.

In the background is a castle representing security or maybe security gone too far if there are too many restrictions. The walls are grey in color, representing wisdom and they are made of stone, showing us how solid it is, strong foundations and security for all that live there.

It looks like a lot of people live there, a big community. You can see some people walking back towards the castle and two people are walking towards wands in the front. You can see a bridge depicting a link between the two.

The two figures in the front; one is dressed in blue, connecting us to the feminine energy and the High Priestess card. The figure in red connects us to the masculine energy and the Magician card. They are both holding bouquets and pointing to the garland above. There is also a red turret between the two figures and perhaps their goal is to reach the top of the tower and to remain there.

Celebrating the Harvest

The garlands are joined to the two wands in the back, once again representing security. The two wands in the front are not yet joined, held there for their future – there is more to come.

IN A READING

This card reminds me of a marriage in that you can see how the wands look like a podium or a gazebo, and the figures holding bouquets is another giveaway.

The four wands look like they are laying down new foundations for their future and actually look like the new framework. The figures are leaving the security of their past, and their family home, with another person moves forward to start a new life together.

Moving to a new house with joy, happiness and anticipation, a move to a new life or future with a significant other.

Creating a Solid Future with a Significant Other

If this card shows up with three pentacles, we could have a move to a new home, one where they make it their own, perhaps through a renovation. Using the practical and reasoning together.

In a work or career situation, there could be a beginning of a new business partnership which will be a fruitful enterprise. They left their secure paid employment to start their own new business venture. With this card you are never alone; it is you and someone else laying down foundations for future.

4 PENTACLES - Foundation and Stability in Material and Spiritual Values

SUMMARY

We have a man sitting down demonstrating that he is stable.

There is a city behind him suggesting he has reached his destination and now he has turned his back to the city. His back towards the world may also symbolize his vulnerability.

The black shawl he is wearing in some way suggests the unknowing energy, his ignorance or the unconscious energy he covers himself with this. He may want to be invisible, or maybe he is discreet, reserved or contained, not exposing himself, although he wears other rich colors.

The brown garment he wears represents he is hard working, could be too practical, too stuck or too cautious. The strip of blue represent his emotions and spirituality, this strip of color is low on his outfit, low on his list of priorities, for now.

The crown represents ego and the orange boots represent his vitality. It also looks like he has bloodshot eyes. It takes a lot of energy to build an empire; he looks stressed from working so hard and achieving all his ambitions.

Committed to What is of Value

The placement of the pentacles shows he is closed off, he has blocked himself off, or he is holding on to the pentacle tightly, perhaps closing himself off to spiritual awakenings. He has the pentacles placed over his head, heart and feet chakras.

IN A READING

This person does not like to share his money, possessions or his emotions with others. His personal and financial securities are somehow linked and both needs are met. It is as if he is saying "I know where I am and I know my values and I am happy with my lot".

Sometimes we need to hold on to our values so as not to lose our identity. Although at times, it may make us feel isolated and alone, I believe there are always two, three or four core inner values that are down deep that we will never compromise on.

NEGATIVE

Quite often this card gets a bad rap. He is often called a snob, Uncle Scrooge, a tight-arse, a miser, arrogant, narrow minded, a petty tyrant, possessive and greedy.

Too much attention is paid to the material possessions and not enough energy is paid to the spiritual awakenings, but the opportunity is always there to see the spiritual.

POSITIVE

The positive with this card is that he has secured his finances and it makes him feel at ease, safe and secured. He must learn to become a spendthrift. For example, when one goes overseas they tighten their money belt and watch their spending. They have become self-sufficient and do not have to work anymore, so they leave the big smoke and go back home.

Secured Finances

In an emotional reading, this person has become contained and does not want to give or share with others; it may be all about setting boundaries. Or the other hand, you may need to open up and share.

In a spiritual reading, we could have simply blocked chakras and you may need to do work in this area to realign them.

In a health reading, this person may be constipated, digestion is blocked or they may be emotionally dysfunctional. They simply cannot stomach or digest what is going on around them. Once again, some healing work in this area will support them and help them work through the issues.

4 SWORDS - Foundation and Stability in the Mental Conflict area

SUMMARY

This card is mainly about reflection and looking at the foundation of the problem.

His hands are keeping the energy together as if he is praying, keeping the faith, keeping the hope alive and quite possibly meditating.

It connects to having a day off work, what we used to call a 'Mental Health Day' in my day or today it is referred to as a 'Doona Day.' It is about having time out, letting it all go and having the time to nurture yourself.

You can choose to either have a rest for a longer period by going on a holiday. If you do not consciously and voluntarily take some time off, it may be enforced upon you through illness or disease.

Note, that stress is one of the biggest killers today. The body does not need to know specifically what you are worrying about; it could be not having enough money to pay the monthly rent or completing a report for work. The body produces bad hormones and we suffer the consequences.

Looking at the Foundation of the Problem

The scene on the card depicts a church scenario. The yellow-gold connects us to the intellect and to the higher source. Asking us to rest, connect with Spirit and wait, give yourself time.

There are three swords hung up on the wall or placed on a hat rack or simply put on the shelf for now. They are in order; they may be the present sores, inner conflicts or wounds, where all point to the head throat and heart areas. They are mounted as if to say "Time Out" from this inner conflict and I will handle you later.

The sword lying down underneath the person may be the underlying cause and it looks like it is set in stone.

The picture in the stained glass window, you can see someone receiving communion from the priest as if spirit is feeding your soul. Stained glass windows symbolize hope, having faith and looking up, connecting to your inner sanctuary, receiving wisdom from the source. Windows are also a way out and represent brightness of the future.

Connecting with Spirit

IN A READING

Having time out from the mental conflict and laying the worry down to rest. This card touches on the energies of the Hermit, an inner journey and reflecting inwardly.

It touches on hibernation, a retreat or hiding from the outer world in order to get it all together and rejuvenate.

Meditation, giving yourself time to refill your cup and let it overflow unto others. As they say, take time to smell the roses.

You can choose to have lunch under a tree, walk in the park, do something and just keep it simple to renew your flagging spirit.

A time to forgive oneself and time for self-healing. Resting is healing.

4 CUPS - Foundations and Stability in Feelings and Emotions

SUMMARY

His legs and arms are crossed and he is ignoring the cup that is offered to him.

Being crossed suggests he is blocking off the energy flow, and blocking anything new coming in. Some people say he is protecting himself, sitting in a yoga position, maybe sulking or being defensive.

He sits on raised ground so he feels OK about himself or his expectations could be too high. The purple mountains in the background are low on the horizon, suggesting he may have low aspirations, plus he has his back to them.

He is sitting with his back against the tree showing he does have contact to life and is grounded. The tree is green representing creativity, growth and represents the tree of life.

The red undergarments suggest his desires are on the inner side and it connects us to the Magician energy. His blue leggings connect us to the spiritual inner world and the High Priestess energy. His green overcoat connects to the cloth of peace and harmony and the Empress energy.

This is the Contemplation Card

His black hair may represent ignorance, maybe not disclosing his true inner feelings. Brown shoes represent practical steps; he could be too practical or stuck.

He looks at three cups in front of him but he does not see the fourth offered to him from a hand in a cloud.

IN A READING

This card is commonly known as the contemplation card. Basically, he is at the halfway mark and considering what is next.

May also be emotional boredom, apathy or a feeling of indifference. Apathy means he does not care, cannot be bothered with it or may even feel withdrawn. There is dissatisfaction with his emotions in his life, therefore he is not looking at what is being offered.

There is a hand coming from a cloud. This is the hand of Mercury, the messenger of the Gods. But the man is simply not interested in any new offerings. He thinks it is more of the same that they have already. This is sad because they have come from a place with no steady foundations and so they cannot make a new foundation with the new offering.

For example, a woman who has had three marriages and another guy comes along, may not be interested because of the past experience — once bitten twice shy. Therefore, apathy towards love and relationships, they hold themselves back or are stuck in the past.

They think it is futile, becoming a self-fulfilling prophecy so as to prove themselves right. Or they are happy in their current position and do not want a relationship, for now.

But you need to consider what is being offered because the message is from the Great Spirit, how can you dismiss this?

Consider What is Being Offered

IN A READING

If the relationship is in rut and the partner is offering you a weekend away, consider it. If they say sorry, do not say, "Oh no not again I am sick of it," consider that this time they truly are sorry and give it one more go.

Consider anything you may be offered, this can even be a new position in the work place.

Or you may be at a party and someone offers you another drink, maybe there is too much of a celebration going on and you need to just hold back or stay back a bit. You may have that one drink too many to tip you over the edge and then suffer the consequences later.

Whatever the offer may be, this time it could really be "The Offer." Consider it because this is the energy of this card.

Chapter 30

People are all fighting for their change in the fives. We are now looking at hard times and any change we make in life usually is hard.

No. 5 - Change Process

5 WANDS - Process of Change in Work, Career, Skills, Talents, Efforts and Ideas
5 PENTACLES - Process of Change in the Material and Spiritual Values
5 SWORDS - Process of Change in Mental Conflict area
5 CUPS - Process of Change in the Emotional and Feelings area

5 WANDS - Process of Change in Work, Career, Skills, Talents, Efforts and Ideas

SUMMARY

We have a group of friends all jostling on uneven ground, which suggests they may not be sure of themselves.

They are all testing and competing against each other. Many people think this card is aggressive, I would say it is more of a competition card. The five of Swords is more aggressive or the conflict card.

No one is really the leader, even though the one in red is in the front, his wand is not the highest. Each wand represents their talents, their ideas, a skill or contributing a gift.

They all want to bring their energies, all wanting to have their say, all putting in their two bobs worth.

The red one is bringing vitality and energy, motivation, enthusiasm and passion.

The yellow one brings logic, intellect energy, new ideas, knowledge and awareness.

The blue one brings intuition and spirituality, feelings, compassion, caring abilities and ethics.

The green one brings harmony, creativity and awareness of today's environmental issues.

The black one in the background brings in the unknown energy, the unknown factor, ignorance, the unseen possibility, the potential and the synergy of everyone coming and working together.

What we have here is rivalry or competition within a group of people. Everyone is coming from their own point of view, opinion, perspective, need, agenda, having themselves heard or their ego.

Competition within a Group of People

IN A READING

In a family situation, we may have a child fighting for the attention of the parents, especially if there are teenagers in the family or there are many siblings and there is sibling rivalry going on.

In a relationship reading, we may be competing for the attention of the partner, for example, the wife versus the mates.

We may have rivalry between families, such as a family wedding; there are always issues in the family around a wedding. Or where to have the next Christmas Day celebrations and who is bringing what.

Wands rule work and career issues so this card may suggest a work group or a staff meeting where people are insecure and they are stepping in to have their say. There may be a brainstorming session in the work place. Also, it may just be someone going for a job interview and competition against others all going for the same position, as in an audition.

Selling Yourself

Some form of competition like a football match or even a jury deliberating.

Bidding for a house at an auction or even online through an eBay auction for a much needed item.

I do not think this is a bad or negative card, I see this card as a form of healthy competition. For example, a football match.

5 PENTACLES - Process of Change in Material and Spiritual Values

SUMMARY

Basically, this card speaks about the process of change through impoverishment. Commonly known as the poverty card. Unless everything is ripped from you, you won't change.

We have two miserable people walking in the same direction but not supporting or reaching out for each other. They are not helping each other. She looks like she is leaving him behind.

Both are in emotional pain, like when you are in bed with your partner and you are not touching or reaching out for each other because you have argued. There is a feeling of hopelessness and you are giving each other the silent treatment.

The man is on crutches, representing he is lame or wounded. He wears a bandage on his head suggesting mental constriction. There is a leprosy bell around his neck, representing emotional poverty. Yesteryear, one would wear a bell and no one would come near you, you were ostracized, emotionally shunned, a social outcast known as a pariah. The blue garment he wears also connects to emotional and spiritual feelings of depression and despair.

Change Through Impoverishment

The lady is wearing an off-yellow ochre color; meaning banishment or an outcast color. Her clothes also look raged and frayed and she is not wearing shoes, depicting material impoverishment.

They are both walking in snow and they are out in the cold. Water represents the emotions, suggesting it is a cold time in their life; it is uncomfortable for them. The white snow may also suggest purification.

The background is black, depicting the unseen, maybe they did not realize what they had, or there is an unknown future.

IN A READING

This card means there is a lack of self-esteem, lack of self-confidence, feeling unworthy and it is this lack of that prevents them from reaching out.

Neither are looking up at the stained glass window. Windows symbolize hope, growth, a way out, faith and brightness of the future, a future of possibilities. All they need to do is to look up.

The Pentacles are Placed like a Mini Tree of Life

Church windows especially mean that these people could be going in to a welcoming place for nourishment, but in the olden days the church was also a place for the rich – this further adds to their feeling of poor self-esteem.

This couple needs to look up at the church window. They need to build their self-esteem. They need to build faith to see that there is a way out.

A question you can ask your client is, "What did you do last time you felt this hopelessness and what did you do to get out of it?" It is healthy to open up a conversation about this, no matter what the circumstance.

If someone wants to sell a house and this card comes up, I would suggest not to sell it. If this card comes up in a relationship reading it may suggest this relationship is not a healthy relationship and I would, once again, not get involved in it either.

They need to work around the 'Lack of' their self-esteem, and to build their self-confidence. Selling the house or getting in a relationship will not help if they do not build their own self-worth.

I like to finish this card off by saying "Tough times never last, but tough people do!" "When the going gets tough, the tough get going!" This card also makes me think of "While you are down there, what can you learn from this situation?"

This couple may represent going on a pilgrimage. The Beatitudes, "Blessed are the meek".

They are being forced to change, it cannot get any worse than this – they have hit rock bottom. This is the exact opposite to the Ace of Pentacles. Not to lose their faith because things will turn around again.

5 SWORDS - Process of Change in the Mental Conflict

** This is also a Warning Card.

SUMMARY

We have three figures in what looks like conflict. One is the winner, you can see him up front holding three swords. One is walking away and the other is the looser crying by the lake.

The clouds look angry, stormy, ominous and sharp, as if they are blowing past very fast. To me, they actually look like sharks. The water looks choppy, depicting that we are looking at stormy emotions and they are changeable.

Let us look at the man in the front first. He is wearing red undergarments; therefore he may have a desirous or an underlying agenda. He has orange fiery hair, suggesting he may be a hot head or has anger management issues. He looks willful, may have an ulterior motive, he looks like he is sneering, snickering, and has a shifty smirk on his face.

The green overcoat he wears may suggest jealousy, envy and greed. His orange boots suggest ambitious ideas, an overall control streak.

You only need one sword to hurt someone but you can see he is holding three swords, suggesting he is over-armed, over-powering and selfish, may be a greedy entitlement. He does not look like he is using them; he may have already won the battle.

This Card is Very Straight Forward Assertiveness, an Up-Front Energy

If we are looking at a woman in a reading, the woman needs to be over-armed, to be tougher, and to be prepared for battle. To put the effort in to make the phone calls, get clear with the facts and figures, understand exactly what she is dealing with and feeling confident before starting.

The man walking away is saying "I don't want to play your game" and has thrown his sword down in disgust. He is wearing white boots as if he has pure intentions; he is neutral and innocent in the matter.

The crying man by the water looks dejected, he looks like he is defeated, maybe his pride is hurt, and feeling inadequate.

A great question I like to ask my client is, "Which position would you be in, in a conflict?" This question opens up a great discussion. I find the person I am usually doing the reading for is the one crying by the water.

Depending on the situation or circumstance, many feel they are the one crying by the water, other times they are the neutral one and sometimes they have the need to be the one up front and in control. Women especially tend to give their power away.

Another good question to ask is, "Are you having bad communication or fighting with someone?" You may have received a nasty letter or email, had a disturbing phone call, experienced bullying of some sort or heard some rumors.

Swords rule the mind and your mental conflicts, so this mental torture could be happening in the mind, having negative thoughts and feeling paranoid.

IN A READING

This is a very aggressive male way for getting what one wants. The male energy is more aggressive and it is harder for woman to stand up to their power so they have to learn to stand in their power even more and be over armed.

This is the classic triangle: the victim, the rescuer and the persecutor roles. The person being made redundant is being blamed and made to feel he is the victim. The person in the middle, who is not affected is the rescuer. The person up front is the aggressor, the persecutor. Note that the aggressor could end up becoming a victim of his own actions because he can lose respect from others.

For a male, this card suggests they are over-armed, over powering and they need to rethink and relax their actions.

For a female, this card suggests they need to learn to stand in their power more. I often mention how tough Lara Croft is, that she needs to be strong to get herself out of this particular situation.

A leader is someone that does what they want to do.

Stand Up and Fight for Your Rights

Whatever the agenda, you have a fight on your hands and this card tells us that you may have to stand up and fight for your rights.

Usually you are doing the reading for the defeated person down by the water, and looking at ways of working through this situation to get them out of their predicament. It is about making a stand or walking through it.

The number five is about change. Something has to change. It is time to put down all the swords. Not to be a victim any more. One of my favorite sayings that actually opened my eyes is "There are no victims, only volunteers". So why are you volunteering to be a victim? Something needs to change.

The warning part of the card is the emotional or physical abuse associated with this card. We could have a very aggressive man, or a woman for that matter, afflicting or being afflicted with mental mind games, sexual violation, domestic violence, rape, victimization, violation, ruthlessness, bringing fear, verbal abuse, manipulation, control issues, etc.

GO GENTLE WITH THIS CARD!

5 CUPS - Process of Change in the Emotions and Feelings

SUMMARY

This is the card of loss. We are looking at pain and conflict.

There is a person looking dejected, rejected, closed off, mourning the loss, and feeling disappointed. In fact, we are not sure if it is a man or woman standing there because they look androgynous.

The black cloth he wears suggests depression and cutting himself off from the world – you can see he is showing us his back. Some people call it the black pits.

There are three cups down in the front, with two cups still standing behind him. There is a blob of red amongst the cups that represents blood and the life force that has been lost. The blob of green represents the loss of peace and harmony.

There is a bridge behind him, he does not see it. Bridges represent a link to the other side, a crossing over, a way out, a link to the other side. A bridge over troubled waters and as the youth of today say, "Build a bridge and get over it".

This is the Card of Loss

Also, there is a river running through the middle of this card, like an emotional barrier between him and the castle on the other side.

The castle on the other side looks like it is in the front; usually castles are in the background and behind the people. It is a funny grey color that almost looks like the grass. The background color is grey in color. Usually grey means wisdom and in this card I reckon it means confusion.

He does have the choice to pick up the cups and fill them in the river or at the castle. He can also cross over the bridge to the community and get support from castle.

IN A READING

This person is extremely depressed. They feel low about themselves and cannot snap out of it, so we are looking at a total victim; they are thinking *poor, poor pitiful me*. They feel lost forever, although this card suggests a temporary loss. This is because of the water element associated with the card; that feelings are so movable and flexible that things will always change, therefore things will improve; that they have not lost what they feel is gone forever.

But still the person is feeling hopeless so it is important to acknowledge their sorrow and disappointment in the matter. Assure them that they have not lost everything like they think they have. This too will pass, like the water passing under the bridge.

What is before is now moving on, it is just a temporary loss. Validate their grief and loss, whatever the situation may be. It has more to do with feelings of loss than the physical loss.

We could have someone feeling alone, feeling home sick, thinking of family overseas and planning a trip. Maybe they are dreaming of building their dream home.

Look at the Bigger Picture

Maybe they are comparing what they have to what someone else has, and this makes them feel like they are under achieving, this makes them feel lowly about themselves, because the other person has more. But what really is going on is that people just have different values in a different order to what you have.

It could be this person is feeling the loss of their family; the divorce really hit them hard. They lost the house, the family, the dream. What they need to look at now are the two children they have from the marriage, the children represented by the two cups still standing behind him.

It is now time for change, time to look at the bigger picture, not just looking at their feet or at themselves. That there are always bigger wheels turning in the background, this is what this card is asking you to do.

I like to finish this card by saying that "Change is the only constant".

Chapter 31

After the fives you want to restore the harmony and protect that harmony so that everything feels secured and settled again. Sixes are the most layered cards, and as such the most difficult cards.

No. 6 - Harmony, Protection and Balance

6 WANDS - Harmony and Balance Work, Career, Skills, Talents, Efforts and Ideas
6 PENTACLES - Harmony and Balance in Material and Spiritual Values
6 SWORDS - Harmony and Balance in the Mental Conflict area
6 CUPS - Harmony and Balance in Feelings and Emotions

6 WANDS - Harmony and Balance in Work, Career, Skill, Talents, Efforts and Ideas

SUMMARY

In this card, we see a victory parade or a victory march and someone is being cheered. They may have brought in a new leader, like in the work environment and the harmony and balance is now restored.

This card follows on nicely after the five wands where we had the five people jostling for their position and now in the six of wands we have the winner.

The horse is grey in color depicting wisdom and knowledge. Horses also signify your vehicle through life – they represent masculine active energy, therefore it is presently happening. You can see the rider is dressed for traveling; thereby suggesting it is currently happening right now.

The green cloth covering the horse suggests adaptability, peace, prosperity and the ability to change to new circumstances. He has come out on top; you can see he is sitting on the horse above everyone else. He is the winner.

The red brown cape represents his practicable and committed energy to this endeavor, and the yellow undergarments represent his intellect and his intelligence. The orange leggings and boots he wears reflects vitality and confidence.

Using the Right Skill and Talent to Win

The wreath on his crown demonstrates he is a winner. There is also a wreath on the wand in his right hand, his conscious side. Holding the wand in the right hand suggests he knows what skill he has used to be successful.

There are two wands crossing over each other making the 'V' for victory sign.

IN A READING

What we are looking at here is someone who has used his skills in the right way to win. He was conscious of exactly what skills he had to use to win over this situation. Success comes from using that right skill or talent, and the harmony is then restored through the use of using the right skill, talent or strategy.

We have victory, especially in careers, a job or a promotion in the work environment. It is a card of leadership, success in the job is at hand. The job is in the hand; after all he is holding the wand in his conscious right hand.

The Job is in the Hand

Reminds me of the Ace of Wands where the right hand holds the Wand.

In fact, whatever you focus your attention on, for example being pregnant, working on a relationship, anything you do you will be successful and come out a winner. All the efforts, forethought, planning and focus are all working well together for you to achieve your outcome.

I often think of this card as the king's messenger, bringing good news that everyone has been waiting for.

The news is good and everyone is cheering the messenger. Also reminds me of the saying 'Do not shoot the messenger.'

6 PENTACLES - Harmony and Balance in Material and Spiritual Values

SUMMARY

This card is about receiving something unexpected from the universe. The universe provides for you somehow. We receive good value from the universe.

There is a man standing in the middle. He wears a brown cloak, which depicts he is hardworking and he has practical desires which he has achieved, he seems to have abundance. His undergarments are striped blue, grey and white suggesting he is spiritual, sincere, genuine and an authentic character.

He wears a fancy red hat denoting prestige and status; he also has many more desires to achieve. In ancient times, people who wore fancy hats usually had wealth and prestige.

In his left hand he holds scales. The left hand is the unconscious side, suggesting he understands innately this unconscious balance and is instinctively spiritual.

The scales connect us to the Justice card, discovering your own truth and weighing it up. That is why he reminds me of a successful lawyer, a CEO, a Rotarian or someone doing pro-bono work for the community. People in these positions understand the value of giving.

Receiving Good Value from the Universe

There is a beggar in blue depicting emotional poverty and the beggar in yellow depicting mental poverty. These two figures also connect us to the two figures we first encountered in the five pentacles that were impoverished. But in the Six of Pentacles it looks like their luck has changed because they are now receiving support from the lawyer, from the universe, or an unexpected source. Look at the little ticket hanging out of the pocket of the beggar in blue, this may be symbolic of the winning ticket.

The pentacles also seem to be balanced around the card.

IN A READING

There are two meanings to this card:

First meaning

The universe is giving out an unconscious balance to you; receiving something unexpectedly from the universe. The universe balances the energies to then restore the balance.

A classic saying is "What goes around comes around". This card also speaks of karma, tithing or pledging to a worthy cause. In the book *Richest Man in Babylon*, tithing and pledging is explained in more detail.

The universe or someone may be giving to you in an emotional, mental, spiritual or monetary way, so it does not just pertain to finances, it is an unexpected gain, whatever is of value to you.

If this card shows up with the Wheel of Fortune it is a good indication of wining some money, an inheritance or property. Maybe winning in the tattersalls or winning a raffle. Note that for some people, learning they still have a job is just as good as winning the tattersalls.

From my experience that unexpected financial support, or whatever that gain may be, always tends to come through at that eleventh hour, just before you are about to throw in the towel.

Second Meaning

Because there are three pentacles on the left side of the card, and two on the right side, things may be off balance, which begs the question, "Who is meeting whose needs?" "Which one are you in the picture?" "Are you the giver or the receiver?"

For example, in a relationship, there may be someone who is always giving more than the other. Talk about who is giving and who is receiving in the relationship. Open it up for discussion. This may be what the client wants to explore.

> "Tarot cards are about the exploration of the self and of the issues."
> - Ruanna

Someone in the relationship could be giving because they may have the need to be needed. There are strings attached, co-dependency and power issues going on, keeping one partner poor and the other in control.

Also note that it is hard to receive. People always find it easier to give. We also give what we need to receive.

This card shows that we all see ourselves as givers, just like the man in the middle is displaying. What we need to talk about is what is out of the balance. Things may be too much one way and balance needs to be brought back to consciousness.

The scales in his left hand could be displaying a negative energy because it may all be happening in an unconscious way. Unaware that it is out of balance.

Need to discuss the exchange. What needs to be exchanged? This could be anything, for example, if you like to drive the car, it is ok to ask others to pay for the parking or for the fuel.

Another question we have to ask here is, "Do you give to meet your own need or give for their needs?" If you give and give and receive nothing in return resentment may set in. You may start to feel used and not want to give anymore. Open it up for discussion.

Note that parents may give financially and not emotionally.

The other thing I have learned from this card is that most people only give to a point where it does not hurt. For example, they may only give $5, which really is not that much. Well, people give emotionally like that as well, but your true friends will go all out for you; we know unconsciously who will be there 100% for us.

This Card Speaks of Adding Value

IN A READING

Six of Pentacles and the Wheel of Fortune are a good combination for winning money or receiving good value from universe. Going for that loan at the bank and receiving it!

This card may also speak of giving in the form of giving service or a healing. The scales connect us to the zodiac sign of Libra. Libra has to do with service, healing, beauty and creating harmony.

This card may also connect you with the health industry, professional care services, nurses, councilors or giving care to others; this could be locum doctors or volunteer workers, donating their time or their money.

The combination of the Six of Pentacles and the Three of Cups may also suggest catering services for others; for example, singers at an event.

This card also reminds me of that saying, "Give man a fish and he will eat for a day, teach a man how to fish and he will eat for the rest of his life".

I usually like to ask the client; which one on the card do they see themselves as. This may give you some insight into what role play they are playing out.

Another lesson I have discovered is the person that you give too is not the one who will necessarily give back to you when you are in need. They do not know how to give to you; they need you to give to them. You will receive the total support you are seeking from someone from left field.

The other lessons I have learned that connects well with this card are when you make others wealthy, that is when you truly become wealthy. The same goes for happiness, when you make others happy you understand the meaning of happiness.

6 SWORDS - Harmony and Balance in the area of Mental Conflict

SUMMARY

We have a boat moving on the water and there is a quiet silence about the card. The blue color gives a serene feeling and everyone is showing you their backs.

This is another card that follows the five of swords quite nicely. The conflict is still happening but the boat is moving forward. We do have progress through change but it is a slow progress.

There are six swords stuck in boat and if they are pulled out all at once, the boat would sink. We have the time to pull a sword out one at a time, heal and patch that hole and then we can move onto the pulling out the next one, and so on.

This card depicts a quiet progress through a difficult time. The person is recovering but very slowly. Some people take two months to recover; others may need two years or even more.

Water represents our feelings and emotions; the water on the right hand side of the card shows bottled up emotions, and you can see that they are still churning. On the left hand side we see vast peaceful water and the boat is heading through this calm water towards the island on the other side, to solid ground and to the safety of the land.

This is Known as the Grieving Card

The women is wearing that off-yellow ochre color and she also wears a hood suggesting she is consumed with grief, probably still holding a grudge or the charge. This outcast color connects us to the past, it suggests that her energy is not good, she feels defeated in the matter and it may be hard for her to leave it or let go of the issues to restore harmony.

Children in the tarot represent the future. The child is wearing that violet color which connects us to healing energy and higher knowledge, or that he may be the one to restore the problem and resolve the issues in the future. Children are our future and he is the new beginning.

The man represents the present; the masculine energy of action and movement. He holds the black pole and he shows you that he is initiating the change. He uses the pole to move the boat through the water, through all the emotions. The pole is black in color suggesting he does not even know what he needs to do to get to the other side but it involves manual labor.

IN A READING

The people are moving towards calmer times and there is still work to do to restore the harmony. They are moving from rough water to calmer waters as if moving from one state to another state, the emotions are subsiding but very slowly.

There may be a physical movement away from something, such as, literally moving interstate or moving away internally. It is a quiet process through a difficult time.

Moving from One State to Another State

A trip across water, therefore an emotional trip; for example, a weekend away from the stress, or a sad journey like going interstate for a family funeral. The Ten of Swords has more to with traveling overseas internationally.

We could have someone walking away from a marriage, and grieving the loss, maybe they were forced to leave to protect themselves. Or maybe it is that sea change we all look forward too.

The common term for this card is grieving what was lost in the Five of Swords, meaning it is a time of grief and working through the grief to get to the peace and harmony, which was brought about by a conflict or loss.

Connects to the Death card, these people may be in one of the boats on the River Styx. River Styx represents the grieving and mourning, and you may have to journey through the emotions and grief of loss to get to the other side.

If this card shows up with the Star card, it suggests a peaceful death of something, to proceed calmly and peaceful through a stressful situation. If this card shows up with the Tower card, it may suggest that you are grieving for something that was snatched from your life unexpectedly.

6 CUPS - Harmony and Balance in Feelings and Emotions

** This is another warning card and is one of the most involved tarot cards.

SUMMARY

This card would suggest creating harmony with the past.

It is as if the glasses worn are rose colored. The building is painted with a golden glow. This hazy golden yellow harkens us back to a golden age, a golden era where we remember the good times, as if we have enshrined the past. Like our childhood days when we seem to only remember the happy times.

It connects us to the past, but it is the past, not seen in reality. This card connects us to our childhood because that is when we were most protected. It also connects us to a past country, past friends, past family, a past marriage and a past home. Even an overseas trip can be a nostalgic trip for the person.

In many books and documentation, this card is looked at as a lovely card, but when we break it down, all is not as it seems to appear.

The building looks shabby and the roof tiles look like they are falling off. The building is huge and all encompassing. When we are children, our views are distorted, things always look bigger than what they really are. There are tiny black windows, unusually found in country homes. Normally, the windows are large and open like the French doors onto a patio. The color black suggests the unknown or unseen so no can see inside.

All is Not as it Appears to be

There are six flowers and all the flowers are in cups. This is most unusual and unnatural as if they are controlled, restricted or looking artificial. You would expect green pastures and rolling green hills, but this is not the case in this card.

We have a dwarf handing a cup to the child. The symbolism of the dwarf represents a mischievous being as stunted growth was seen as abnormal in those days. Dwarfs connect us to past memory, a protector, as a child we learnt about dwarves in fairy tales. He is wearing a hood, which denotes hidden thoughts. He is also wearing the color red, connecting us to the Magician energy. The blue undergarments connects us to the High Priestess energy.

There are six cups signifying our inner senses and especially our sixth sense. The dwarf is offering the little girl the sixth sense, which is the doorway to the High Priestess energy, as if he already knows something and he is trying to tell the little girl.

If we breakdown what the little girl is wearing; first of all, she is wearing gloves. Gloves represent a covering and a symbol of protection, as if she is armored herself against something. You can only see her left hand. The left hand connects to the feminine and the unconscious side, suggesting she is covering up her deeper feelings.

She is wearing a lot of layers of clothes; the pinafore is covering up her outfit and her shawl over the top of her head, are also another symbol of protection. The red connects to the Magician and the blue of the dress connects to the High Priestess — and you can see her shoes just peeking through underneath.

The real tell-tale is that there is another face in the girl's yellow hair. The face is looking towards the left and downwards. This is shown as she is being two faced, or is she in two minds.

She is looking at the dwarf and not at the cup. This means she is not accepting the sixth sense that he is offering her. All these extra clothes and her looking away suggest she is definitely covering up something. Maybe she does not understand what he is offering her and this is why she is covering up her inner feelings, guarding herself because she does not trust what the dwarf is offering her.

In the background, there is a guard and this guard is not protecting them either. He looks like he is walking away and does not seem to care. He is wearing blue. Blue connects us to our feelings and emotions. And who is he really? Does he represent society and how we turn our backs on some circumstances that we do not understand?

St Andrew's Cross

There is also a shield on the column, a shield is another protection symbol, sitting underneath one of the cups. This is known as the cross of Martyrdom, or the St Andrew's Cross.

The victim or martyrs would suffer extreme penalties and be tied to the cross in a spread eagle position. When Jesus carried his cross through the streets, it also made this shape.

There are two meanings to this card:

First Meaning

This is called the affair card. It takes a third person to disturb or nudge the protectiveness of the affair because affairs are usually hidden. The affair does not come out unless someone or something like the sixth sense has picked it up.

Open it up for discussion. What have they seen that makes them think there is an affair? It is important to deal with the facts and not to talk about the suspicions. You are dealing with people's emotions here, also they maybe not be open to hear the truth.

This is Known as the Affair Card

Second Meaning

The other side to this card connects to the past and maybe the childhood stage was NOT protected. The child's feelings or child's sixth sense was not acknowledged. The concerns of the child in the past were not validated.

We may be looking at abuse in childhood, especially if this card comes up with the Devil card.

Flashbacks or memories can occur later in the adult stage about what happened in the past or childhood stage, especially if this card comes up with the three of swords.

POSITIVE

If this card comes up with the six of wands, we may be looking at efforts of the past, at long last will be rewarded. But it may be an offer given too late.

A peace offering of some sort. We remember the good times. You can guard and protect yourself in a stressful or deceitful situation. Someone from the past may reappear or you may bump into a past friend.

You do have the opportunity to heal the past, get present and finally get over it in the future.

NEGATIVE

Memories of the past which were unrealistic could be intruding into the present as a flashback and could be giving you conflicting feelings and emotions in the present situation.

Some people live in the past. People come and go but the past can be like a long term friend.

Someone may be deceiving you. Someone from the past may reappear, which could summon some past concerns and feelings.

Chapter 32

The sevens are about assessing the situation, so you do not know which way they are going to go.

No. 7 - Internal Assessments, Reassessment

7 WANDS - Reassessment of your Work, Career, Skills, Talents, Efforts and Ideas
7 PENTACLES - Reassessment in Spiritual and Material Values
7 SWORDS - Reassessment in the Mental Conflict area
7 CUPS - Reassessment in the Emotional and Feelings Level

7 WANDS - Reassessment of your Work, Career, Skills, Talents, Efforts and Ideas

SUMMARY

He is reassessing his skills, talents and career and is not sure which way to go just like he does not know which shoes to wear. The shoe laces are undone on one shoe and he wears a boot on the other foot.

Typical fire sign, they are always ready to fight. You can see the wand is crossing his body as if he is ready to defend himself.

He is standing on raised ground. It may represent a position of importance, he may be there for a long time and he is now defending his position. Standing on higher ground suggests he has more authority or the upper hand; he is elevated and has more advantage.

The person defends himself before he can see the basis of the problem. He cannot see the basis or the bottom of the six wands, so he may jump to conclusions, but if he reassesses things first, he may not need to defend himself after all. Because he does not know the full story, we are looking at a typical knee jerk reaction.

Reassess the Situation Before Jumping to Conclusions

The green ground where he is standing is all over the place, there is also a patch of blue. It suggests he is not standing steady and may be emotional attached to the situation. This suggest insecurity or things are shifting under foot, whatever the case, he needs to be aware.

He also wears green. Green suggests flexibility, creativity, flexibility and growth. He has the adaptability or he may need to be more adaptable. He needs to listen to the other person first, perhaps they have something important to say. Have your say or your opinion if you need to, then you may not need to defend yourself like you think you do.

His yellow undergarment connects us to the intellect and may be that jumping to conclusions energy. So it is important to think before you act and think before you speak. This is what you need to reassess.

IN A READING

In a career reading, you may be defending your position because someone may want your position. Maybe the heads of the company want to shut your position down and you are defending your ideas, your project, your budget, and supporting your team.

Positive

The person should defend their position and they are doing it very well. They are successful and they have the strength to do it. With all that fire element energy, they have the stamina to proceed. They are winning because they are on top of the situation.

Negative

In a work situation, the person on top may be scared of new people coming up the corporate ladder, so they are defending their position and this stops others and themselves from moving on up. They may be afraid of change. Whatever the reason is, they are stopping the flow.

When You Move on Up You Let Others Move Up Also

Some people think they are or own their positions. I remember a friend's father who was a school principle. When he retired he lost his identity, did not know what to do with himself. It was as if he lost his power.

Talk about how to make themselves redundant, this is the distinction they need to make and what needs to happen, so that they can move on to a better position or totally retire and enjoy what life has to offer.

I always bring up the Steve Jobs Stanford University speech. He speaks about joining the dots and how every bad situation he encountered opened him up to something better. Check him out on Youtube.

7 PENTACLES - Reassessment in Spiritual and Material Values

SUMMARY

Here we have a person reassessing the value of the harvest.

The vine was expected to produce a harvest and there is an offshoot but he is ignoring it. There is a pentacle at his feet but he is not looking at it. This offshoot is the new beginning.

We can see purple mountains in the background. Mountains represent aspirations and challenges to conquer and the color purple connects us to spirituality and a higher purpose.

The pink and blue ground that he stands on represents the basis of project. It suggests he has put a lot of love, devotion and emotion into this project. He has put his heart and soul into it, a labor of love.

He wears an orange overcoat and blue undergarments, suggesting he is a man of practicality and that he has put a lot of emotion and effort into a career, a love prospect, etc.

Did he set himself up to fail? Some say he looks defeated. Nothing usually lives up to our expectations. Sometimes we put all our eggs in the one basket and it does not pay off.

You Have the Energy Needed, Just Reassess Things so that You can Make the Best Moves

IN A READING

He is looking at the harvest or at his project and reassessing it before he keeps going because it will only make so much, he needs to work out if he wants to continue.

Some of the questions he may be asking himself are:

"Do I still want to continue this project?"

"Do I want to stay here and go again to the next round or level, or do I pull the roots out and begin again somewhere else?"

"Was it worth all that effort?"

"Am I the best person for this position or how can I make it work more effectively?"

The project did not fulfill his expectations. Like the two different colored boots he is wearing, he is reassessing the situation, looking at both sides before he goes the rest of the way.

Half of the vine leaves are discolored as well, another demonstration of his indecisiveness. Remember with the 'Sevens,' they do not know which way they are going to go?

In a relationship reading, he is reassessing the long-term relationship. Do I want to keep going? Maybe it is the seven-year itch?

In a financial reading, maybe his investments have not fulfilled his expectations. Does he cut his losses?

It relates to something that you have established for a long time and you reassess it before you go the rest of the way. The fruit on the vine did not happen overnight, it takes years to produce a good quality fruit. The vine shows that it has produced fruit, but you expected more of a return.

Reassessing the harvest of your wealth. Whatever it has produced, is it of value or spiritual value to you. It is an internal energy or an internal process only you can resolve.

One great example I can give you is whether one should renovate the house or sell and purchase a new house? Well if you love the house, the neighbors, the shopping center around the corner, etc. Then it is worth to remain and invest in an extension. But if you do not love the house any more, if you have outgrown it, and you do not want to live across the road from the school anymore because all the children have grown and left home, then it is worth selling and move to something new.

If you love to do what you are doing, no matter what the return is, then you will tend to continue with this project or investment.

This is probably why they have come to you for a tarot reading, to exhaust and explore all the possibilities before making their decisions.

7 SWORDS - Reassessment in the Mental Conflict Area

** This is another Warning Card.

SUMMARY

Straight away there is a negative connotation to this card. This card is commonly known as the theft card.

This could mean taking from someone else or someone taking from you. You could also be ripping yourself off and limiting yourself by some sort of self-sabotage.

Swords rule the mental mind energy and mind games going on. Taking what you want with stealth. Interesting how the word 'steal' is in the word stealth.

We have a man sneaking away with five swords. He leaves two swords behind, which he has reassessed and realized he could not take them all. But he does have a part victory here. He prioritized the taking of the swords and he may return to collect the remaining two swords at a later date.

What would have happened if he did take them all? He may have dropped them all and then risked being caught out. If he took them all he may have been seen as being too greedy. He may be weighed down by his conscience. He would have reassessed how to mentally handle the situation.

Being Able to Take What You Need and Realizing that You Cannot Have It All

The people did not really want the swords. Swords are taken from the people in the tents, you can see the tent doors are open. There are a group of people at the back of the card that do not seem to see anything; if they were guards they are not doing their job because the swords were not being guarded or protected by them.

There are grey clouds hovering above the people in the distance as if a storm or trouble is about brew. The ground in the background looks uneven, displaying an unstable and insecure situation.

What we have here is taking something from somebody that really was not valuing it. Therefore, they are taking advantage of the situation.

This person is making it work for themselves, they may have an agenda. There has been a strategy set here. Therefore, he has premeditated the situation with cunning and conniving energy.

SYMBOLOGY

The red high hat suggests high passionate thoughts and high desires. The red boots suggest courageous steps and action. Both the hat and boots have fur trim that connects us to animal instincts and animal cunningness.

The garment he wears has spots on it, like a leopard or cheetah, therefore cheating something from someone else. Cats usually stalk and then pounce on their prey, whereas cheetahs catch prey by chasing them relentlessly, wearing them down and then taking them.

This card always reminds me of someone tapping you on the shoulder and asking you if they can wear your coat. They tap, tap and tap, pull and tug at your sleeve, which can become quite annoying, to the point that you give up and say, "Take the coat, I do not want it back!" This is a manipulative situation so they can take something from you.

Wearing someone down so you could it take from them. Another example is, a verbal fight until one person drops out, therefore you win. This too is manipulation.

IN A READING

In a career reading, it is an unfair advantage when someone steals your job from under you. Someone is stalking your job. Someone may be headhunted or poached in the work place.

Be mindful that someone is not taking credit for something you did. You put all the work and effort into it.

You may be ripping yourself off because you are worrying yourself for nothing. Mental mind games can make you worry. Worrying does wear you out, or stresses you. Insomnia may not allow you to sleep properly, whereby you do not regenerate and replenish your energy; therefore, you are not operating normally not at your optimum.

Known as the Theft Card

Remember this is the theft card. Reassess the way you protect your money and all your valuable things. One of my favorite sayings today is, "triple check everything".

Some things to be aware of are:
- If you are worrying about the car, check it again to make sure your car is locked.
- In a divorce settlement, people may be going for what they can get, instead of working it out and being fair.
- Read the fine print and copyright issues before signing a contract.
- Read the instructions.
- Stealing people's thoughts and ideas or your intellectual property then they say, "They said It". Don't leave it open for plagiarization. Take and use another's thoughts and ideas, writing it as one's own.
- Keep to your agreements.
- People sneaking money from your credit card. Today, people may sneak $20 at a time and you may not even notice it.
- Person doing your head in.

- When you argue with someone, they can wait for that spot, that moment or that gap, to point something out to you and they get you.
- Someone stalking you.
- Someone plotting against you.
- Backstabbing, sneaking, being underhanded or undermining you.

7 CUPS - Reassessment on Emotional and Feeling Level

SUMMARY

The blue background brings in the spiritual connection. The black person in the front, who looks like a silhouette, represents the unknowing self, the shadow self, the unconscious self or the spiritual self. Black is the color for the unknowing, the unmanifested, the feminine and the intuitive side.

The unknowing self or the spiritual self is focusing on the fluffy grey cloud and reassessing the seven cups. The clouds represent symbolic messages, the seven cups are all holding that something of value and special to you.

The unknowing or spiritual self is making an unconscious choice. The unconscious self will always make the right choice because there is an alignment between your soul and the universe. You really do not have any idea which cup you will choose but you will (somehow) choose the right one.

Remember with the 'Sevens,' they do not know which way they are going to go. This card is about reassessment and trusting the universe to make the right choice.

Reassessing What is of Value to You

Each cup holds something that has an emotional value or emotional fulfillment to us:
- The Dragon represents power, conquering conquests and something magical.
- The Wreath represents victory, winning, and triumph. If you look at the cup there is a skull on the cup which may suggest that victory is not good or suggests a bitter victory. It may be a warning that it is not all about winning.
- The Jewels represents riches, wealth, materialism and abundance.
- The Castle represents fame or security, maybe a high position. Your home may be your castle.
- The Head in the cup represents choosing the loved one, dealings with a partner, a beloved, physical beauty, vanity and ego.
- The Snake represents wisdom, and temptation. In fact, the snake points towards the divine choice that you will ultimately choose.
- The Veiled cup in the top center is highlighted; there is a red light, like a halo or aura around it. This is the cup that you will unconsciously choose.

IN A READING

This person does not know what direction they are going in, they unconscious and totally directionless.

Maybe they are facing too many options. Too many pies in the sky? For example, like a small child that cannot choose between all the candy in the candy store, and they take forever.

This card taps us into those day-dreaming days. For example, you look at what you are going to do when you retire, you think you may buy this or buy that, do this or do that, but what you WILL do is pay off the mortgage.

I often talk about creating vision boards. Allowing one to create an intention or thinking bigger than what they are doing at the moment.

Thinking Bigger than What You Are

I remember seeing Dr John Demartini when he described and redefined the seven main areas of your life, I totally related to these, and they connect beautifully to this card.

You cannot just be successful in only one area of your life; you have to look at your life holistically; be successful in all these areas.

The Seven Areas of Empowerment are:
1. Financial – creating stability in your financial area. Are you saving? Are you creating a nest egg towards a project? Creating wealth and studying how money works.
2. Family – Keeping in touch with family. Resolving issues with family because we need the intimacy with loved ones.
3. Social – Making your friends happy as well. This will empower you as well.
4. Fitness – Yes working out and getting fit and having a good vitality.
5. Health – Eating right for you, seeing a naturopath if you have to.
6. Mental – Reading, learning, doing workshops, it is important to keep stimulating oneself.
7. Spiritual – Understanding meditation is just as important, it's one of the most important things you can do in your life. Having a mission and purpose in your life.

Having balance in all these seven areas of your life, will give you a good attitude to then serve others.

Trust your higher self. Trust in the Universe. Connect with your inner Hermit, going within before making a choice. Just choose because it will be the right choice.

Chapter 33

After all the internal assessments and weigh up of things you have more power with the eights.

No. 8 - Power and Success

8 WANDS - Power and Success in Work, Career, Skills, Talents, Efforts and Ideals
8 PENTACLES - Power and Success in Spiritual and Material Values
8 SWORDS - Power and Success in Mental Conflict Area
8 CUPS - Power and Success in Emotions and Feelings

8 WANDS - Power and Success in Work, Career, Skills, Talents, Efforts and Ideas

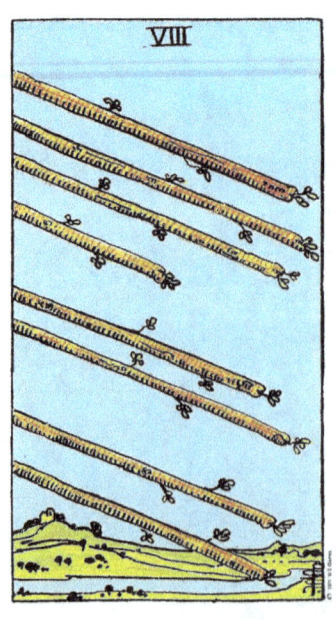

SUMMARY

Wands connect us to the element of fire. Fire is very spirited energy. All the wands cards are direct, exact and quick to work through.

This card may represent many ideas with the practicality of earth because you can see that the wands are about to land. Our ideas are about to be practically manifested. You are about to plant your ideas.

Your ideas have been set off and they are about to be manifested or become real. It is happening right now because they are flying through the air and are on their way.

Swift progress in a project, with fast results and outcomes. This is the most reliable timing card and it is imminent.

The other interesting fact about this card is that there are no people nor animals in this card.

This Card is Known as the Fastest Timing Card

IN A READING

Wands represent work, career, skills and talents. This card may suggest travel with your work. An unexpected quick work trip interstate.

The wands also look like a ladder of success, therefore suggesting moving up the corporate ladder. A successful move. There is movement in the workplace, quick movement, unexpected movement, maybe sideways movement but there is still movement.

Out with the old and in with the new. You may be in the crossing over stage.

In a relationship reading, we have arrows of love and things are moving very quickly, progressing successfully in a relationship. It is time to take the relationship to the next level. The relationship may be with someone interstate, an internet romance, a love through the airwaves or a quick fling.

Maybe Going Sideways but There is Movement

In a health reading, we are looking at physical fitness, rapid improvement and recovery after an operation or illness. This is a good card to suggest quick recuperation.

There could be swift travel or an unexpected trip – an unexpected interstate trip because the wands are literally flying in the air and across water. There is a little water referring more to being interstate rather than a big overseas trip.

8 PENTACLES - Power and Balance in Spiritual and Material Values

SUMMARY

Here we have a tradesman producing the same thing over and over, which is not necessarily a bad thing because he could be making a mint.

Pentacles connect us to the Earth element and earthy people like their routines, they have pride in their work.

This card relates to perfection because he is taking the pentacles off the post to perfect them again. Also it connects us to the zodiac sign of Virgo and how they think that things are never good enough.

This is the apprentice at their trade, whatever the skill may be. Practice makes perfect. Apprenticeships usually take four years to complete their training and because of this, you would have to be serious about your work and your commitment to doing it.

The blue undergarment connects to spiritual work and the High Priestess energy. The red leggings connect us to the Magician energy and something that he is passionate about. But it is all kept under wraps by the black apron worn over the top – keeping it in the unknown and under protection as long as he stays an apprentice. Maybe he does not know how good he is.

Practice Makes Perfect

In the background, there is a city with a yellow brick road leading towards it. That is where he should be going – to the city. But he does not risk taking his work to town; he also demonstrates this by having his back to the city.

We could be looking at the fear of rejection or fear of success, fear of failure, fear of change, fear of growth or fear of the unknown.

He is sitting on a wooden bench, suggesting practicality and a commitment to training and bettering himself at something that is of value to him. He first must be the apprentice before he can become the master. The brown bench shows he is committed to whatever he is doing.

IN A READING

Basically, this card is saying that it is time he goes to the city because there is no more room left on the post, you can see there are two pentacles on the ground. Take the plunge.

But it is a big step to put yourself into the market place. It takes commitment, responsibility and also learning a whole new set of skills, such as marketing, management even financial, among other things.

He may be saying, "I'm not good enough". But who is the biggest critic of you? YOU! Therefore, it is time to face your inner critic. Become open to criticism because feedback or constructive criticism allows us to correct. If you do not give people feedback, how can they correct? And you are denying them this opportunity to correct. I remember reading about Madonna and how she felt she made it when she read her first bad review, she knew she made it!

This card is Known as the Career Card

You need to find out where the client is in their career. Either they have all the skills they need to make it, or it is time to now become the trainer, or the master.

I love how big the strings are at the back of the apron, inviting you to untie them. This is what they should be doing, remove the apron, that unknown factor and move off into the next stage of development.

Here are a few books that I can recommend and should be on every professional's bookshelf. Also refer to my Bibliography list at the back of the book.

- *The E Myth* by Michael Gerber. This book relates to working on the business and not in the business.
- *In Search of Excellence* by Thomas J. Peters and Robert H. Waterman Jr. This book is about various lessons from America's best run companies.
- *Maverick* by Ricardo Semler. The success story behind the world's most unusual workplace.

- *7 Highly Habits for Highly Effective People* by Steven Covey. Covey brings in spiritual and material aspects of business.
- *Midas Touch* by Donald J. Trump and Robert T. Kiyosaki, This book is about why some entrepreneurs get rich – and why most do not.

I can also recommend playing Robert Kiyosaki's *Cashflow* game to understand the energy of money. There are also many Dr John Demartini books as well as CDs that will help you. You can also subscribe to many Youtube listings, especially Tai Lopez where he recommends other books you can read and how to create wealth. Note that today, the top CEOs in the workplace read a minimum of one book per week.

Back to the Eight of Pentacles, he is so absorbed in his work that he is not looking outward. Sometimes it could be safer to keep doing what you are doing rather than to look up. This position may well be known as the comfort zone or safety zone.

The energy of this card suggests you get on with it because things are perfect, it is a perfect time to move onto the next level. You have asked for this right now, you have worked hard for it and you cannot make it any better. Remember there is no more room on the tree.

If the Tower card comes up with this card, it may be the universe giving you the helping hand, you may lose your job, pushing you on to the next stage of development.

8 SWORDS - Power and Success in the Mental Conflict

SUMMARY

We have a woman in orange blindfolded and standing on marshy ground.

The color orange suggests she has courage, confidence and vitality, even though she is bound. The binding represents some form of restrictions but they look lose around her, suggesting she can get out of it if she wants to.

The blindfold indicates she is not thinking clearly, mental bondage and restrictive thoughts. The black hair represents unknown thoughts or even ignorance, and she cannot see her way around. The grey background adds to her confusion.

The marshy ground she is standing on is soft and pliable, swampy and not solid or stable representing emotional insecurity. It is a sticky situation.

She looks like she came from the castle, down the hill and traveled to the marshy ground to where she is standing now.

Maybe she left the castle of her own accord, and it took a lot of courage and strength to leave. She now has her back to the castle – this looks like it was an emotional trip for her. She had to leave everything behind, which takes a lot of courage.

To Stand in Your Power and Not Look Back

There are eight swords all around her. Five swords are on her left hand side representing the unconscious and connecting us to the past. They look like they are covering the castle on the hill, like bars from a prison cell. She has surmounted these conflicts or has already fought five battles in her life's journey.

The two swords on the right hand side are held there for her future meaning there are more battles to come ahead. Life has a way of throwing wobblies at you. I remember hearing Oprah saying, "What happens to you happens for you".

There is one sword in the front, suggesting this is the only battle or hurdle remaining that she needs to work on or get around.

IN A READING

What this person is feeling is powerlessness, thinking they are not able to move forward in a particular situation in their life, they feel they cannot go on.

This person needs encouragement to continue. They need validation to go on. Talk about the fact that the person is just not in touch with their own power and that they do have the power to continue. The orange outfit connects to the Strength card, showing them that they do have the vitality, confidence and energy to go on.

They already have come a long way, down the hill and across the swampy ground, which has been an emotional journey that they have already endured. It is now time to pat themselves on the back and to count their blessings.

This is the Acknowledgement Card

To acknowledge how far they have come and to take stock of where they are. Look at what they have accomplished already. Against all the odds, look at how far they have come. Most of the hard work is behind her already. Keep going forward and do not look back.

They feel they cannot go on but this card tells them that they can go on, take back their control, take back their power, it is time to stand in their power.

Your beliefs are your greatest restrictions. This could be self-sabotage. It is about making the victim into becoming victorious. Remember, 'There are no victims, only volunteers.' So why are you volunteering to be a victim?

8 CUPS - Power and Success in Emotions and Feelings

SUMMARY

The figure in red turns away from the cups that are spaced out in front of them. They are spaced in such a way that it looks like there is a cup missing.

The color red is prominent, suggesting he has desires and passions. Also that there is still love there but he is cutting himself off from his emotions. You can see he is showing you his back, and heading towards the unknown; the unchartered territory of the black mountains. Mountains represent aspirations and personal challenges. People are always climbing and conquering their mountains.

He is heading towards the mountain alone, the Hermit lives on a mountain. You can see he is holding the staff that belongs to the Hermit. This is an inner journey. He is looking for what is missing inside, looking for the Holy Grail, looking for that missing cup.

Mountains have caves and tombs, which connect us to wombs, symbolizing rebirth. John Gray from the famous book, *Men are From Mars and Women are From Venus* says that men go into caves. If you follow them, they go further in. Women go up and down in wells.

Notice he is not heading towards the green mountain. The color green is about creativity, flexibility and adaptability. He is heading towards the taller black mountain, it is a whole new unknown territory to explore, he is running on or trusting his instincts.

In order to leave the cups and those he loves, he has taken a giant emotional step across the water, to go off and to start looking for what is missing. This journey has not been an impulsive decision.

The energy of this card is when you say, "Is this all there is?" Or "What if this is as good as it gets?" Just like what Jack Nicholson says in his movie *Good as it gets*.

Looking for a Deeper Meaning in Life

IN A READING

This person is looking for a deeper meaning in life. Looking for the missing cup or missing bit in his life, a need to feel good inside again.

It may involve a spiritual growth, spiritual quest or a pilgrimage. This is what the Holy Grail or Grail Quests refers to. A symbol of spiritual wholeness that leads a person to union with the divine. In old legend, this is what the Knights of the round table went off to search for after the fall of Camelot. A search for a desired ambition or goal.

In other legends, it refers to Sangraal, meaning holy blood. The search for the lineage of Jesus and Mary, and their blood line.

The Full Moon or the Eclipse connects us to emotions and feelings, a feeling that your life is being eclipsed. The waxing moon represents attainment and a need to begin anew. The waning moon suggests a lack of fulfillment. The glow of the moon is like the Hermit's lamp – he is not totally in the dark. It also suggests a time of reflection.

The person is trying to find their own emotion that they feel is lacking and trying to balance it internally and this could be hard for others to understand. You have a wonderful loving supportive family but you also need to withdraw and love yourself. A need to be alone and find your own space.

People around you may think you do not love them anymore, which threatens them, but this situation is not about them. It is about you.

This card is about dissatisfaction with the self and an inner search to find yourself again. It is an emotional withdrawal, a time out, or a rite of passage. The person will come back; they just need time out alone. You get your own nurturing from within.

You Get Your Own Nurturing from Within

Women go through a process of withdrawal and renewal every month. Men do it by going hunting, fishing or playing sports like football and cricket.

This card is mainly seen with people in relationships. The other person may feel threatened and it may be hard for others to accept you want to spend time alone. No one can do this for you.

This card is not about judgements. It is a way of being, spending time alone, time out, going inward to check in with the self.

In a relationship reading, there can be a moving away from the relationship, a withdrawal, leaving the relationship as something is missing in the relationship.

There may even be a death in the relationship but death also suggests a transformation, an ending of the old way and the rebirth of the new relationship.

Chapter 34

Now we prepare for the ending.

No. 9 - Attainment and Completion

9 WANDS - Attainment, Completion in Work, Career, Skills, Talents, Efforts and Ideas
9 PENTACLES - Attainment and Completion in Material and Spiritual Meaning
9 SWORDS - Attainment and Completion in the Mental Conflict Energy
9 CUPS - Attainment and Completion in the Feelings and Emotions

9 WANDS - Attainment and Completion in the Area of Work, Career, Skills, Talents, Efforts and Ideas

SUMMARY

There is a man with a bandage on his head. The bandage symbolizes he has fought a lot of battles; it may be covering battle scars. It could also represent that he has restrictions or is single minded in his thinking.

In his hand he is holding a wand as if he has chosen a particular skill to use; it also looks like an emotional crutch. In fact, he has a lot of skills behind him but it seems he depends upon this particular skill when it is time to cope or when his back is against the wall. It is like he chooses the same routine; for example, fight or flight. It is skill that is tried, true and tested.

It is a skill that you have used over and over again and now it is worn out and time to look at other skills to cope with life. In the background, you can see how green and lush the ground is. There are eight other wands – he is not using all this creativity and here is the opportunity to do so.

I like to call him the wounded old soldier, the reliable one; he will remain there until he completes his mission, like he said he would. He is wearing an orange top, suggesting he is committed to the role, or he may be in a rut or even battle-weary.

It is like this card is saying; "I am a secretary" and when you are looking for a job you only look for secretarial positions, forgetting that you do have other skills that you could bring to the community. You tend to limit yourself and your choices and options. You can pigeon hole or type cast yourself. It could be seen as being narrow minded.

This Particular Skill is too Well Used and is Now Tired

You may play the same 'being' in the different groups; you may be the joker in one group, the challenger or a controller in other groups, etc. If all of a sudden you decide to be a different 'being,' they will pull you up and say things to you like, "What's wrong with you today?" "Are you alright?" Once a joker, always a joker.

Also, it is hard to say that you are different if your family always sees you play the same role. This role play feels comfortable; it could also be your safety zone.

It could be your ego? For example, going from being a manager with responsibility to being a barperson; you still have responsibility but it is more relaxed. It could take time for you to get your head around this. This is exactly what happened to me; I thought being a barperson was not a reputable position and was below me. Boy was I wrong. When I did the bar work it was one of the most rewarding careers of my life.

IN A READING

This card asks us to look at yourself. Why are you always choosing the same career attributes or 'being' the same role play? They may well be the same role play as when you were a child. It is time to check that it is not the victim role play.

It does suggest you have very committed energy but it is time to create new habits. Time to find new ways of doing things, for example, delegate and let go of some duties that are unnecessary for you to do, hire a cleaner and lighten the load a little, buy a PC or a laptop. Yep, there are still people out there that do not have a laptop or a mobile and do not realize how these technical gadgets can make their life so much easier.

When I found my house cleaner it took me about six months for me to allow this possibility to occur. I would say to myself, I used to be married, do all the shopping and cleaning all by myself. Now that I am single, how come I need a cleaner? Then there were other questions I went through like, "Can they clean as good as I can?" "Can I trust them with my personal things?" I did eventually find a cleaner, and they were the first cleaners I allowed into my space, they are a husband and wife team, this same couple have been looking after me and my home since 2011.

This experience showed me that it takes time for people to resolve and move through what they need to get through to achieve their outcomes and goals, and that you do not have to do it all on your own. Time management is also very helpful, just book it in and do it!

Time Management is Integral

Do something different because what you are currently doing is not working for you anymore. People can be doing or playing the same old same old, expecting a different result. This card tells you that you can break old habits, that there are other options.

Einstein's theory of insanity is, "Doing the same thing over and over again and expecting different results."

The number nine is about completion and attainment; this card is saying that you have already grown in this area and it is time to make new things grow in other areas.

9 PENTACLES - Attainment and Completion in Spiritual and Material Meaning

SUMMARY

We have a woman of nobility standing in a beautifully flourishing garden, covered in lush greenery. It is rich in color and there is fruit everywhere. There is a castle in the background and she is holding a falcon on her arm.

Here is another one of my favorite cards, I like to think that I am like this person, abundant and understanding, independent and giving.

We know she is a married woman because she is well groomed and her hair is braided and up under her hat. Her sleeves are wide, showing you she is generous and open. The red and gold colors on her gown bring in all her desires and her connection to the divine. There is a strip of blue trim around the collar of her garment connecting us to the spiritual source.

There are Venus symbols all over her gown, which connects us to the Empress card, her abundant and unconditional energy.

The falcon sitting on her left hand represents that she has internalized the falcon's energy instinctively and has disciplined herself with this energy. The glove also represents protection; she can protect herself if she has too.

Only nobility can afford to train falcons. You can see the hood is over the falcon's head to stop it from swooping down on prey. Falcons are shrewd, skillful hunters, have keen eyes, are birds of prey and trained pursuers. They can swoop over 300km per hour and fly as high as they want – real mavericks.

This Person is Abundant and can also Protect Themselves

There are three pentacles on her left hand side, her unconscious side. She has worked on the self, she is self-disciplined and applies these learnings intuitively.

On the right hand side, the conscious side, there are six pentacles. Her right hand is resting on these pentacles. She is conscious of her success; she understands the balance of giving and receiving.

She has worked on and has attained spiritual and material learning. She has worked hard and has made the best of what she has had in life. She is self-confident and self-aware, attained and has achieved much success.

Also has attained security, you can see there are trees in the background; they are balanced on either side of her demonstrating perfect symmetry, she is in control of her life.

The grape vine is a symbol of abundance, a lush plant with edible fruits. The vine is sturdy and tough and can creep along a surface or rails. The roots like to be in shallow and do not need much watering. You can eat the juicy fruit; you can dry the fruit or you can make delicious wines. Often seen in victory wreaths, or over a pergola in an outdoor eating area.

There are also purple mountains in the background, suggesting there are still more aspirations and goals to conquer

The snail on the bottom right hand side of the card suggests she is humble and is aware of the fragility of being human. It also says she did not get this success overnight; it has developed at a snail's pace. The threads or the snail trail connects her to past threads and heritage, suggesting she does not forget where she has come from, she remembers her past roots and she does not forget the people she has met along the way.

What a contradiction; the speed and shrewdness of the falcon versus the slow and steady commitment of the snail. The falcon flies very high in the sky and the snail crawls along the ground.

IN A READING

This person has attained what they have worked for in life. They have reached a high level of independence. They are self employed or financially independent.

This Person is in Control of their Environment

The earthy energy associated with this card suggests steady growth, whatever is of value to you, be it finances, growing a business or building, a relationship or your spiritual wealth.

Even though there is a picture of a woman on the card, it could represent either a man or a woman in their own business, living a successful and independent role.

They are creative and abundant. They have control over the condition of where they work and control over their environment. They are out of the rat race and living their dream.

I often see the garden as something that they have made or grown like a business; it could also represent their family, like the family tree. Therefore, I think that this person has a beautiful family.

I like to complete this card by saying, "It is nice to be important but it is more important to be nice".

9 SWORDS - Attainment and Completion in the Mental Conflict Energy

SUMMARY

We have a person crying in the bed with nine swords going across the card. You do not see the points of the swords. Some may say there is no need to worry, no point to this worry.

But there are three swords going through her head, throat and heart. The client may need to do some clearing around the crown, throat and heart chakra's.

In the background, there is a black sky signifying confusion and uncertainty. When you are stressed in the middle of the night, you wake up and begin to blow everything out of proportion. It is usually three am when we wake up – this is what they call 'The witching hour.' In the morning, the sun is shining and you know that you blew it out of proportion. In the light of day things never look so bad.

This card is commonly known as the card of worry. To worry this much is often worrying about someone else and things are just out of your control. If it has to do with you, you know that you can do something about it.

Card of Worry

The mattress is pink; the basis of worry, denoting a love and devotion to someone, usually a family member or loved one. To worry this much about someone means that they are usually a loved family member, a partner or children.

The blue blanket has red roses all over it, suggesting love once again, and there are all the signs of the zodiac all over it, suggesting the answers are always right there in front of you. Maybe you do not want to see the answers. Take your hands away from your face.

There are two people fighting in the carved section of the bed. One looks defeated, suggesting you may feel defeated in this matter. You can see she is humped over as if she is tired and carrying all the weight on her shoulders.

IN A READING

It is an upsetting card; it is a worrying time so pay attention to your client. When this card shows up, I often ask my client, "Is there something keeping you up at night?" "Are you not sleeping well?"

Talk to the person because the person is feeling low; allow them to talk it out so they can see something that they are not currently seeing. Swords connect to mental energy. The person may be stressed out, thinking like they do not know what to do, and that's why they have a tarot reading, to open it up for discussion, exploring the possibilities and find out what to do.

The person could be feeling defeated and overwhelmed because they feel they cannot make it better. They need to quieten the mind, rest and connect with their inner Hermit.

A Mental Breakthrough

Even though they may not know what to do, they are still worrying. Worry does not achieve anything; we know this yet we still worry. Worry today is one of the biggest stress killers. They need to break the cycle or transfer the worry into something more positive and one of possibility.

I like to mention to my clients that you only have one energy source, like a battery. It is 50/50 how you use it. You can use it creatively and constructively or the battery will corrode and destroy itself. If it is me, I can change this or if it is someone else, I cannot, so let it go.

The person is tired because worrying does wear one down. There is a saying that goes, "Worry is like a rocking chair. It gives you something to do but does not get you anywhere".

But the number nine suggests a completion, an end to the worry and all that mental anguish.

If this card shows up with the Tower card, it may be a breakthrough of some sort. A nightmare has finally ended and with it the end of the worry.

9 CUPS - Attainment and Completion in the Feelings and Emotions

SUMMARY

This person sits comfortably in front of nine cups. Some people say he looks smug.

The cups are displayed like they are trophies and there is a blue veil, which suggests he has put an emotional veil between him and the cups, like a barrier. He also has his back to the veil so maybe he does not want to see or feel it.

His legs are open inviting the energy in; he is willing to receive, but his arms are crossed, therefore he is guarded and not letting the energy out.

You can say he has a lot of love to give because all his nine cups are on show. It is just that for whatever reason he does not connect it to the heart. Somehow he is not letting the energy out as if he has blocked his heart chakra.

There could be various reasons, maybe he has had a bad relationship, suffered past hurts. Therefore, there are fears and he does not want to put his heart and soul into it any more.

Basically, he does not want to know about the deep and meaningful. He does not want to hear anything bad; he is firm about this. Do not tell him bad news. You do not have to air your problems to others. You cannot tell him any emotional news, no negativity and no drama please. For example, it reminds me of the father of yesteryear, with the belief that children should be seen and not heard, or had to look clean like angels for when dad came home. The children did not talk to dad about their day, he would find out about everything through mother and they will learn that he loves them through mother as well.

Good Provider just not Emotionally Involved

Still he is a very good provider. He would ask, "How much money do you want?" He just does not need to know the details.

He sits on a brown bench. The color brown represents the practical and grounded, keeping it simple and down to earth. The red hat represents desires – maybe he is full of himself, or he has many dreams and goals.

The fancy hat also suggests pride, status and prestige. The white gown represents a sincere wisdom.

Quite often this person is a business man; he does look like a man selling his stock in a shop. He does not give out a lot of energy, maybe he has learnt from past experiences so now keeps himself busy in his business. He is so caught up in his business that he does not have time to dwell on dramas, or loving relationships.

You know what you are dealing with here; remember all his cups are on show as if he has laid all his cards on the table. What you see is what you get. He is not intimidated.

You know you have all this love, maybe he does not know how to return it and also does not want the negativities. He does not need to hear "I love you every day". Notice the veil is up. This could be saying that he does not want another relationship. You do hear today that some people prefer to live alone.

He just does not know how to demonstrate or tell you that he loves you. Not emotionally demonstrative.

IN A READING

In the olden days, this card was known as the 'Wish card.' If this card came out in a spread your wishes would come true.

It demonstrates emotional fulfillment without any dramas, receiving and attaining all the good things in life without hassles.

Life is Good

If you put the card on its side, you can see there is a Lemniscate or the infinity symbol in his gown around his knee area. His crossed arms are making the same infinity symbol as well. It suggests acknowledging what we have and to put more balance in your life and to open up your heart.

This card is saying this is a good life. Life and hope are returning.

This card follows on nicely from the Eight of Cups; he has found the missing cup and is now satisfied with what he has and displays it for all to see.

In a relationship reading, he is holding himself back cause of prior hurts and pains. If they keep going on like this the relationship will eventually fail. He is protecting his softer side and not giving one hundred percent any more.

Chapter 35

The recycle, the planting of the new seeds to go round the next level.

No. 10 - Beginning a New Cycle

10 WANDS - Beginning a New Cycle in Work, Career, Skills, Talents, Efforts and Ideas
10 PENTACLES - Beginning a New Cycle in Spiritual and Material Values
10 SWORDS - Beginning a New Cycle in the Mental Conflict Energy
10 CUPS - Beginning a New Cycle in Feelings and Emotions

10 WANDS - Beginning a New Cycle in Work, Career, Skills, Talents, Efforts and Ideas

SUMMARY

Here in this card we have someone that looks like he has struggled all his life. He carries a heavy load because he has so many talents and responsibilities that weigh him down.

The orange garments he wears shows he has vitality and the white undergarments shows he has committed energy and stamina. Even though he has good intentions, he is doing it the hard way.

This card may suggest we take on too much before we know where we are. Your energies may be scattered and there are no goals. He may tend to be the 'One Man Show,' someone working on their own like the 'Lone Ranger.'

What this person needs to do is to put all the wands down and rearrange them or they will drop. He also cannot see where he is going, cannot see the trees for the forest.

Also, the wands are long and awkward and he may be feeling overwhelmed, like he is carrying the world on his shoulders. Maybe he has bitten off more than what he can chew.

IN A READING

You quit work to be free, but in no time you are so busy, you have taken on too much and need to rearrange a few things that are not working for you anymore. Let go of a few ideas so you can be free to pursue the ones that are of real interest and value to you.

Sometimes people think that when you want something done that you have to ask a busy person. Or vice versa – no one can do it as well as you can so you stay back and do all the work yourself.

Literally Cannot Find a Job

In a work or career reading, you may have taken on too much work in an effort to retain your position. Others do it as they build their image through their work and like to hear things like, "Oh, he works so hard".

You keep yourself very busy at work and therefore not give any attention to the family. You may have too many skills; in fact, some are over-qualified and literally cannot find a job!

For a student, this could be becoming overburdened with school work, going through the VCE year and there is a lot resting on their shoulders.

Number ten is about beginning a new cycle. This person needs to stop, put all the wands down and prioritize things. It is time to pick the wands up one by one to see if they are valid in your life, and if they still support you.

Or learn to carry the burden in a different way: delegate, have better time management, get a better car, employ someone to assist you or simply think smarter and not work harder.

An Opportunity to Sort, Clear and Lighten the Load

This card is about the ending of an old way of doing things and the beginning of a new cycle. The load is too heavy; reorganize things and lighten the load or it will collapse around you.

In a health reading, we are looking at back problems, shoulder and neck problems as you are shouldering too much of a burden. It is bad karma to carry heavy burdens.

In a health reading, I actually ask my clients the question, "Do you suffer from any back problems?" And I am always surprised how many times the answer is yes. I then proceed to explain what the back issues may symbolize and open it up for discussion in how many different ways one can support themselves.

Basically, your back is the support mechanism for your whole body. When you have back problems it is saying that you do not feel supported, you are not being supported by loved ones and you feel you are doing it all alone.

You now have no choice but to do something about it. Take action in a new direction. Step into it now or keep walking blindly.

10 PENTACLES - Beginning a New Cycle in Spiritual and Material Values

SUMMARY

I love how the pentacles are placed like the Kabbalah Tree, which is symbolic of the Tree of Life or your Family Tree.

There are people under an archway; an old wise man, a child and dogs, a lady and a man. We are looking here at an established family.

The man is looking towards the outer world and the woman is looking at the man. The woman is dressed in red and the man in blue. Usually it is the masculine that is in red that connects us to the Magician energy, and the feminine is blue, tapping us into the High Priestess energy. This interchange of color is offering us an interchange of energies.

They are only looking at each other and we do not know if they are arguing or sharing. For example, he could be going to work and she is returning from work, they could be a tag team.

There is a tall tower between them, symbolizing what they are working towards, aiming to reach it or wondering how to remain on top. Maybe this is what they are discussing.

The mother is not looking at the child. As mentioned earlier, children represent new beginnings; they are our future.

The child's left hand is on the dog. Dogs represent animal instincts and those instinctual parts of ourselves. The dogs are grey in color suggesting wisdom. The child is getting the wisdom unconsciously and by osmosis from the old man.

The old man's right hand is on the dogs. Only the dogs are looking at the old man who is the wise one – he has the grey beard, he has the magic and all the wisdom. Just look at his cloak, it is the cloak of riches and it looks fertile. It is a cloak of many colors.

The Card of Family Wealth

There is a great Greek myth that connects well with this card. It is the story of Ulysses (Roman name, Odysses is the Greek name) from the movie *The Odyssey*. *The Odyssey* carries on from the *Iliad*, written by Homer. Ulysses had a wife called Penelope and she wove a tapestry during the day and undid it every night.

One day Ulysses decided to go fight at Troy, so he rallied his friends and off they went. To get past the Sirens they had to blindfold themselves as well as tie themselves to the ship's mast so they weren't seduced. He was away for many years and after the war, he was kept under a spell from Circe, a very powerful witch. After seven years the spell wore off and he realized that he had a wife, a home and country to get back too.

When he arrived back home, there was a competition to take Penelope's hand in marriage. They conducted this thinking that Ulysses was dead. When he returned home no one recognized him because he looked like a beggar but the dogs recognized him. The competition was coming to an end when Ulysses shot his arrow and split the winning man's arrow in half and then everyone knew he had returned, for only Ulysses had that accuracy. Penelope was most happy and so were the people.

So just like in the card, the dog recognizes the magic of the old man that the others are not paying attention to.

IN A READING

This card is about keeping up with the Jones's. We are looking at family money, family property, a family business. A well to-do family, a well healed family, a well off family, a well established family.

This is so because their priority is to look to the outside world and make the family materially secure, for example, to reach the top of the tower and to remain at the top. Keeping up appearances.

The child is clinging to her mother and the mother does not pay attention to the child. Often children end up emotionally insecure, emotionally immature, neglected and dysfunctional. This is what happens when no one pays any attention to the children that they so desire and deserve. They can also be over compensated with material things.

This family is always 'Seen as doing the right thing.' I often say these people are looking good but going nowhere, because they are more focused on the material side of life and what people think of them. Later on they will realize that all the material things have not fulfilled an inner calling. Nor are they emotionally supportive of each other, like they are in the Ten of Cups card.

There are many family crests on the wall. A specific one hangs just above the old man's head and it is of scales. Maybe he is the one that brings balance to the family or the family needs to create more balance, just like how the pentacles are placed on the Kabbalah Tree.

The old man (or the old Merlin, as I like to call him) has a full rich and symbolic cloak, but is being ignored. The magic is still there, waiting within; they are just not paying any attention to the inner world of knowledge, to the inner values for now. No attention is being paid to the magic.

The man under the archway is holding the wand in his left hand; this wand connects us to the Magician card. Suggesting the magic is there, they only need to pay attention to it. The man is holding the Wand in his gloved left hand, the unconscious side; it is also black, representing the unknown or unmanifested energy. Perhaps they are too caught up in life and too busy to look at the magic.

The Opportunity to Break Free from the Old Family Patterns

The number ten is about beginning a new cycle and a new generation, the re-patterning of the family. It is always the new generation that opposes the old ways, breaking down the old fossilized structures and break the old cycles to make way for the new. And thank goodness for that.

This card reminds me of Queen Elizabeth with her family's traditions and standards. Prince William and Prince Harry are the new beginnings and they surely have broken some old ways. Prince William married outside of royalty, unheard of before. And Prince Harry has let his hair down and shown what a fine man he is. All this brings about the new balance in the family.

If this card shows up with the Six of Pentacles, it connects to family money, maybe a family inheritance being given. There may be family money to buy a new family home.

If this card shows up with the Ace of Pentacles, we could have the money from selling a property or having money to buy a property.

10 SWORDS - Beginning a New Cycle in the Mental Conflict Energy

** This is also a warning card.

SUMMARY

This card has to do with regeneration. This person is so far down the only place to go is up.

The danger with this card is that this person looks like he has been stabbed in the back. You can see the ten swords in him are all in a row along the chakra points.

This card says that it has ended in defeat. Swords rule the mind; it may have all ended in the mind; or the mental torture is finally over. The mind is flat.

They feel they cannot cope and could give up; this is the danger with this card because it may suggest they lose the plot and decide to jump. The person is depressed. They need to get help.

If we break down the symbolism; in the background we have the black lifting with day break. The black sky represents depression and darkness, the yellow sky represents the hope of a new day, the new dawn.

There is Light at the End of the Tunnel

The water in the background looks calm, symbolizing that emotions are flat, there is no charge left. We have calm emotions – they have lost the fighting instincts; the batteries have run out, the charge or the energy is gone around whatever issue there was. He has surrendered, there is a rebirth and as they say, there is light at the end of the tunnel.

We can clearly see that the man is dead – there are ten swords running along the chakra points and the sword in the heart is the deepest. He is covered in orange which represents vitality and confidence but in this case because he is dead we have death of pride, ambition and all that vitality. You can see the red blood or life force running out of him. We have a loss of ego, loss of the will to fight and a loss of the fighting instincts.

He is making the peace sign with his right conscious hand. Another symbol suggesting this is the end. All the worries are finished and dead and gone. Rest in Peace. He is at peace, the matter is at rest.

This is as bad as it is going to get – you have reached the bottom of the well, and it can only get better from here, the only way is up. He has reached rock bottom and will come out the other side.

IN A READING

The number ten has to do with renewal and new beginnings. For some people, they need you to tell them to stop the struggling, to just free yourself and move on, to finalize the divorce once and for all, sign the papers and leave, to let it go.

There may be a connection with overseas. You may have to die to old ways before you cross over to the other side. Crossing over the River Styx, which is the river of forgetfulness, and represents the mourning and grieving energy. This also connects us to the Death card. Death is a journey, a cycle and a rebirth.

The Release of the Mental Conflicts

It may also represent going on a trip or journey. Going on a holiday overseas to regenerate. Time to let it go here, and create new aspirations and a new life over there.

Can connect with migrants leaving the old home, old family, old country and traveling across the big seas to get to a new land, therefore creating a new home and a new life. There is nothing left and everything available to you is in the lucky country. Australia is still seen as the lucky country.

In a relationship reading, the person may be coming from overseas, a relationship with someone from overseas. If this card shows up with the Nine of Cups there is romance coming into your life, possibly someone from overseas but it could be a little bit flat.

If the Tower shows up with this card, we could be breaking down mentally, cracking up mentally or having a mental breakdown. It could be a nervous breakdown or finally, a breakthrough.

10 CUPS   Beginning a New Cycle in the Feelings and Emotions

SUMMARY

This card is about happy families, a happy marriage and happy relationships, happy times and a happy ending.

It connects nicely to the Two of Cups because there is the same gold on the bottom of the card; hence it suggests there is a soul connection between these two, or all of them.

We have a supporting partner; you can see the man's arm around the woman, demonstrating his support, giving emotional and nurturing support. She looks like she is in his nook.

Both are wearing a combination of red and blue colors. Both are connecting to the energies of the Magician and the High Priestess. They both have integrated the interchange of these energies. Both are facing the same way unlike the couple in the Ten of Pentacles.

The man and woman's arms are open to the energy of the rainbow. Their upheld arms make the symbol of the cup. Rainbows symbolize hope and the promise of tomorrow. We usually see rainbows when the storm has passed. Also they bring hope; when you wish upon a rainbow, the pot of gold at the end of the rainbow, all those bright colors represent a bright future. Like the song says, "Somewhere over the Rainbow".

There is a stream running past the house which connects us to emotional support. The water is free flowing. Totally rich, lush and healthy environment to be in and to grow a family.

Loving Supporting Partners and Families

The number ten represents a new beginning and children are the symbol of the future. I always like to say there is a future in this relationship because of the children. The children are the by-product, the offspring of this loving relationship.

One child is wearing blue and the other red, representing a lovely balance of masculine and feminine energies. And to me, the woman looks pregnant again with another child.

IN A READING

This may mean being in a supportive family environment where they support you and make you happy; they love and trust you. We all hope for this type of relationship. There is an emotional closeness between these people.

A country feeling depicting a close family bond that reminds me of those television shows like *Little House on the Prairie* and *The Walton's*, when they all said goodnight to John boy. The *Brady Bunch* even, and today we have new types of family shows like the show *Modern Family*.

The female in blue connects us to the High Priestess, she also wears some red, the man dressed in red connects to the Magician card, and he also wears some blue. This represents a well-balanced emotional relationship.

And They Lived Happily Ever After

The green and lush garden environment represents a fruitful and creative existence. There is a red roof suggesting there is love in the home. Is it their past or is it their future? If it is their past, it was a very supportive and lush environment and it is easy to recreate again in their future.

In a relationship reading, this card says that there is a future here, one of emotional fulfillment and happy family relations. The number Ten of Cups is about the renewal in the relationship.

This is that Walt Disney's picture perfect family.

I like to end this card with saying, "And they lived happily ever after".

Chapter 36

ACES - Cards of Triumph

In the Rider Waite Tarot cards, the Aces are cards of triumph rather than new beginnings. They are too strong for a new beginning. They are the full force of each particular suit.

They represent a striking success, elated energy, exaltation of victory. I always think of Aces as number elevens. They are super-sized and amplified.

In the ordinary playing cards, the Aces are called Trump Cards. They come after the kings or before the twos, neither a beginning nor an end.

What we have here is the full force of the energy of the particular suit. I will say it again there is too much force for just the beginning. For example, look at the Ace of Pentacles – the archway is completely covered over and the red roses and white lilies in the garden look lush, fully grown and completed.

All the Aces have three things in common:
1. They are all coming from a cloud.
2. It is the hand of Hermes, the hand of the divine; you can see a glow around the hand. The white color represents purity of that particular symbol, this is pure energy.
3. They are all the right hands, all positive cards for the person or situation. The right hand represents the conscious side and a powerful active energy.

If you place the wands and swords together you will see masculine energy. You can see this by the fist holding the wand and the sword; the clouds are darker grey in color.

If you place the cups and pentacles together, they are feminine energy, they represent the receptivity quality of the feminine, and you can see this by the open hand holding the cup and pentacle; also the clouds are lighter grey in color.

Another interesting point is that the wands and cups are coming from same right side, and the swords and pentacles are coming from the same left side.

ACE OF WANDS - Triumph in the area of Work, Career, Skills, Talents, Efforts and Ideas

SUMMARY

The element of fire and masculine energy.

We are looking here at a pure fertility symbol; you can see it is a living growing energy.

Sexual energy, the wand looks like a phallic symbol. Fertile energy, this energy gives birth to something. You can see actual branches growing, the new shoots.

We are looking at enthusiasm, courage, initiating energy, spirited, drive, enterprise, the full force of fire, optimism, engaging, contagious and renewing energy.

The leaves falling off are Yods. Yods represent unexpected magical benefits or gifts coming from the universe.

IN A READING

This is the card of triumph in any particular area – whatever area you put your effort, energy and ideas into. If you want to fall pregnant, this card says you will be successful with all your efforts.

This is the energy of this card: the surge, the injection of enthusiasm, the turbo button, the boost, and the warp speed.

This Fertile Energy gives Birth to Something

In a career reading, this card represents double energy because wands relate to work, career, skills and talents. It says your career will take off like a rocket! The job or the promotion is in hand, success in the work place, two thumbs up.

When I was doing a reading for a friend about her pregnancy situation, this card showed up with the Empress, I was confident enough to say, yes she was pregnant, and possibly with twins! My friend had quads! Two boys and two girls.

ACE OF PENTACLES - Triumph in the Material and Spiritual Values

SUMMARY

The element of earth and feminine energy

Triumph in the value of the Spirit of Man and the spiritual world, as well as the value of money in the material world.

The pentacle is held over a beautiful garden. It is the most beautiful pentacle and it is the biggest pentacle. You can see the spirit of man spread eagle in the pentacle.

The pentacle is also used as a symbol of protection; the symbol of man. The circle around it represents the universe protecting the man.

Success and triumph of the forethought and effort that we have to put into our lives. This is what we have to earn; we have to work for it. For example, like planting a tree, you prepare the soil first, put in all the nutrients to give that seed the best chances to grow and produce the best fruits.

This is the Magician's garden in full bloom. You can see the lilies that represent pure ideals and the red roses representing desires.

Through the archway, you can see the Blue Mountains in the background, they represent spiritual aspirations because they are blue in color, from all the work and effort you are putting in.

This is the Top Dollar Card

There are no Yods in the Ace of Pentacles because earth has its own magic. Like the beautiful story *The Secret Garden*.

IN A READING

Triumph in whatever it is we hold of value, no matter what the reading is about and in whatever area. Everyone has a different list of values. In any area we hold of value, we will be triumphant and successful.

In a finance reading, business or property, things will turn out triumphantly. This is the money card for the most money, an abundance of money; this is the card you want to see when dealing with money, finance and business. Positive success in financial and material matters, this is the top dollar card.

In Feng Shui, they say twenty-five per cent is Heaven Luck, meaning you can be born in any particular country, and twenty-five percent is Earth Luck, meaning you can be born in a wealthy family or not. The remaining fifty per cent is Man's Luck, meaning the effort you have to put in to achieve your goals. If you have a strong Man's Luck, it doesn't matter where you were born and whether or not you have family money, you will succeed because your intention is strong.

This card is the exact opposite of the five of pentacles. This card is all about abundance in the material world and also in the world of spiritual matters.

If this card shows up with the Wheel of Fortune, we are looking at some financial gain, a Tattersall's win, an unexpected bonus, etc.

If this card shows up with the Ten of Pentacles, we would be looking at family property, family money, and or family inheritances.

ACE SWORDS - Triumph in the Mental Conflict Energy

ACE of SWORDS.

SUMMARY

The air element has masculine energy.

Note that the swords suit can be the most troublesome. But this card suggests no more mental conflicts.

The Ace of Swords connects us to positively expressed mental energy. Look at the sword – it is straight up and the point is in the picture. We get the point.

The swords represent the power of the will, the power of the mind. Your mind is your sword, a sharp mind with sharp logic, sharp as a tack. This comes from the Magician energy, being straight up, that is conscious, active, masculine energy.

What we have here is the full force of the mind piercing through the ego or any confusion or doubt that is around. The crown is symbolic of the ego and you can see the sword cutting right through it. The Ace of Sword has quick full force energy, an action like a guillotine chopping off a head – it is a clean cut.

Full force of energy in the intellect. We have clarity in the mind, clarity in communication, clarity of thoughts, ideas and strategy. Like that light bulb moment, you get the picture, clearly.

Through clear writing and communication within yourself or with others, there is no misinterpretation. It is easy to make that decision; it is precise. Clearly expressed, it is succinct, to the point, sharp and swift, like a samurai sword.

It is easy to cut the rubbish out of your life and to cut to the chase. The sword is good for cutting through stuff; you can see the trees for the forest. Cut away what is not needed anymore and no longer serves you. Cut the ties that bind, that which is holding you back or cutting away the dead wood.

The sword connects us to the truth, true perception, true conviction; you know it is the right thing to do. This card connects us to the Justice card, to the sword of discrimination and detachment.

Represents Clear Thoughts and Making Up Your Mind

If you have been confused and this card comes up, it is saying it is time to go for it. This is the card of the mind, making up your mind. Once you have made up your mind, then you can move on. When we use the sword in our lives, we know this is how it is with no doubt, no confusion.

A negative would be becoming caught up in diabolical, inhumanly cruel and wicked thoughts, being fiendishly clever, or having cunning or annoying energy.

The palm of triumph is hanging off the crown, connecting to the calm feeling after making the right decision. The olive branch of peace connects to the peace of mind after making the decision. The crown represents the ego and connects us to the crown chakra.

The Yods represent pleasant surprises, blessings from the universe and extra special benefits.

IN A READING

This card may come up when someone leaves a marriage or a partnership. For example, you put up with things, then one day you say, "That's enough!" and there's no turning back. No if's, no but's, you have decided and you just go. When you know you know. All has been said and done and there is nothing left to say.

It is a quick decisive energy, a cutoff point, a trip switch, like the master switch that goes off. You sever the ties; it is over and a done deal. It is one of the best cards of the deck.

If you are having exams, this card would suggest excellent results; students doing very well with their studies.

In a health reading, you can say having successful surgery. If you are going under the knife, we are looking at positive outcomes and a quick recovery.

If this card shows up with the Hanged Man, it suggests he can cut himself down and set himself free from all that hanging around.

This card always reminds me of Zorro; doing good deeds with his sharp sword.

ACE OF CUPS - Triumph in the Emotions and Feelings

SUMMARY

The element of water and feminine energy.

The Ace of Cups has a far calmer, much quieter energy and is almost a religious or spiritual looking card.

I would say it is a more spiritual love than emotional love.

We are looking at God's Love with this card. We have a golden chalice which connects us to the source and the Holy Grail. There is the white dove – the symbol of purity, spirit, peace, love and God's messenger. In its mouth he holds the bread or host as if the Spirit is nourishing our emotions, feeding us, having communion with God, the last supper, eating the body of Christ and drinking his blood.

The cup is overflowing and there is no ending to it, like the flow of abundant rain.

The water lily represents love and devotion. It connects to the Indian worship of Buddha sitting on the water lily. From the muddiest water comes the most beautiful flower, the lotus. It is white and pure in color, succulent and divine.

There is another spiritual connection to this card. *My Cup Runneth Over* is a religious prayer from 23rd Psalms. Religious love, spiritual love, there is a gentleness and devotion to this card.

The cup is held in an open hand suggesting you cannot ask for love, it comes naturally, you cannot manipulate it. Like they say, "Let it go," if it comes back it is yours. If it does not, it was never meant to be. For example, a vocation comes to you, it drives you, you cannot force it.

IN A READING

Triumph in the area of feelings and emotions, a spiritual love. Be happy within yourself, content in peace and love, inner contentment, fulfillment and satisfaction. Your cup is full.

This card connects also to the Star card. The water is representative of feelings and emotions as free flowing, a demonstration of an out-pouring of the emotions in a loving, caring way.

This card just does not have to be about romantic love. It is not just about predicting a relationship; it is about being happy in yourself, having peace within and contentment with the self.

You cannot love others until you love yourself first. Fill your own cup then let it overflow unto everyone else. Love yourself first then others will love you. The same goes for trusting yourself first – only then will others trust you. When you allow yourself, you then allow others.

The Yods speaks about special gifts from the universe, a blessed gift.

The W on the cup looks like an upside M. This is the Jewish symbol for God's name, YHWH, Yahweh. The three bells under the cup connect us to the Trinity and the church bells ringing in old times – a spiritual calling, like that alarm clock that wakes you up to your vocation.

A Spiritual Devotion

You hardly see this card, and if you do it is a gift. It holds feminine unconditional and abundant energy.

This card may represent the birth of a baby and mother's love and her devotion to her baby; it is more than love, its unconditional and abundant love just like the water free flowing from the cup.

It may also represent a marriage and all the love that is there on the day of the wedding, love is in the air at this union of two people in love.

Blessed be!

Chapter 37

First, let us look at a Summary and then the Overview of what the Court Cards represent in a Tarot reading.

Through all my years of teaching Tarot, my students moan how hard or tricky it is to read the Court Cards. They need to be seen from two points of view. Basically, they are representing either yourself or someone around you, remember projection!

We will slowly enter the world of the Court Cards and hopefully I can dispel some of the myths associated with them.

COURT CARDS - SUMMARY

Court cards are people cards. They live out their particular trait and experience of their suit. They connect us to the energies within a person that are at work in that particular situation.

Court cards may represent yourself or the other person in the situation. The energy is either coming from yourself or from them. Whichever way you look at it, this is the energy that is working around you or is reflected back at you. It can bring in projection issues.

The court cards are the energies of ourselves – they show us how we are mastering or dealing with a particular area or a particular situation. For example, wands deal with work and career, pentacles deal with spiritual and material issues, swords deal with mental conflicts, and cups deal with feelings and emotions.

If there are a lot of wands in the spread or reading, we are looking at a lot of fire energy and it is about their energy in the work place or a career issue and their skills and efforts involving a project or an endeavor.

Court Cards are People Cards

We are looking at the energy within a person whom you are reading for or we could be hooked into that developing energy ourselves. It may be a new energy and it may be slowly unfolding or we have already experienced it in the past. Or that it is our current energy and that is why we have attracted this person and this reading into our world. Our client is there to mirror our needs; they balance what we are looking at or are dealing with. Like-minds attract like, as they say.

Note that it is easier to see your stuff through the other person via projection. You may be so far into it, you cannot see, but through the other person you will see it or make the distinctions you need to make. Remember, you are a healer, you heal yourself every time you heal another. The reading will always belong to the client but on some level there is always a reflection back on you.

For example, when I was going through my IVF procedures, I attracted a lot of readings around mothers and their relationships with babies: women wanting babies, their issues with infertility, whether they really wanted the baby and so on. In my case, I was fertile. It was my partner who was infertile; it still brought up all the issues around having or not having a baby for us and having a family. Unfortunately or fortunately for me, at the time my IVF procedure was not successful.

Now that I am in my mid-fifties, I am attracting a lot of women going through menopause issues. Interestingly, I have a wealth of knowledge and experience with natural hormone replacements, naturopathy tests and a myriad of knowledge around supplements. Check out *Suzanne Somers*, read her books if you want to know more about this subject.

Additionally, I am doing readings about having relationships but on another level such as second marriages and so on. These are all issues that I am currently exploring and through all these readings with my clients, they are allowing me wonderful insights, understanding and making finer distinctions for myself.

Court Cards Symbolize Stages of Our Development

The Court Cards could symbolize stages of development or stages of action; they show us our growth within the situation, the growth of the development. For example, the page usually shows up in the beginning of the spread, the knights show up half way through demonstrating the movement or growth we have, and the kings showing up at the end of the spread, shows how we have mastered the outcome.

Court Cards can show us an emotional situation in a reading. If all the cup cards show up, we are looking at a lot of feelings and emotions. The Queen of Cups may represent a loved one or you may be a young man represented by the Knight of Cups in shining armor, demonstrating movement in the relationship, or the King of cups representing you taking control of an emotional situation.

The Court Cards show a particular energy in the reading such as how you are handling the situation. An older man usually shows up as a king but he could also be a page because of his behavior in the situation. Instead of being a man in charge, he is carrying on like an adolescent in this particular situation.

If a court card shows up in the environment position, it would represent someone else in the outer world that somehow may be influencing you. Court cards in the environment may also represent how other people see you in this particular situation, or their attitude towards you. If a page shows up it could be a child in your life or someone with childlike behavior. If a queen shows up, she represents a woman in your life. If a king shows up, he represents someone with adult and mature behavior.

Note; if a Court Card is the last card in a spread, this may represent your resulting energy of the situation or you can take it further to see what the energy of this person is going to do or how it will develop and how it is going to impact on you, by doing another spread on this court card.

Families in their Element

Let us now work through each suit and see what their impact symbolizes.

As we work through each suit, they may remind you of a particular family or particular friend that behaves in this way. This is a good way to remember this energy, through association we can sympathize with the energy.

Also, we all have these four elements in our astrology charts, and so on some level we all understand and connect with these energies. Remember, it is always easier to see the energy working through the other person.

I will now bring in more of the astrology through the learning of these Court Cards. Many of you will become interested in learning and understanding astrology a lot more after exploring the court cards. Astrology definitely assists us with the personality types.

The three modalities that work well together are astrology, numerology and of course tarot. Every card is numbered and there is either a zodiac sign or planet that connects with each card.

WANDS FAMILY - Wands rule the area of Work, Career, Skills, Talents, Efforts and Ideas

The element is fire and it is a masculine energy.

The three fire zodiac signs are Aries, Leo and Sagittarius.

This family probably would not be at home a lot, a very outgoing family, therefore they would hardly eat together. If they do, the kids would be eating in their rooms and the parents will eat in front of the television with their plates on their laps.

They are open and honest with each other and with others. They are warm and friendly to everyone.

They would encourage each other to pursue their ambitions and goals. They are enthusiastic with projects, enterprising, have impulsive energy and are always encouraging to each other and saying, "You can do it".

Yet everything is left until tomorrow. Why? Because typical fire element leaps. If it is not exciting they move onto the next best thing or project – they get bored easily. They need to keep it exciting and challenging. A classic fire saying would be, 'Strike while the irons hot.'

Very community minded, they are always involved with activities. They are sports-minded, love; football, cricket, skiing, motorbikes, horse riding, etc. They love physical involvement with outdoor activities because they are adventurous and spirited. And because of all these outdoor activities, they are usually sturdy and of robust health.

Open and Honest, Warm and Friendly with Everyone

There may be a lot of ego clashes because of their competitive nature with each other, especially if there are a lot of young children or teenagers in the family, fighting for the attention of parents, especially with young children. The Five of Wands displays this healthy debating, jostling, sparring and playful energy very well.

They also get over tragedies quickly because they are optimistic. They do not wallow in their emotions, unlike the water element where it can sit and brood. Fire people do not hold grudges and they get over things quickly, they can get it out and move on. Using their typical fire energy, they get on with living.

This family would live in the suburbs because of the community involvement and especially if they have young children.

KEY WORDS

Self-growth, spirited, inspiration, energy, creativity, initiation, enthusiasm, desires, passion, perception, action, movement, optimism, courageous, intuitive and hot tempered.

PENTACLES FAMILY - Pentacles rule the area of Material and Spiritual Values

The element is earth and a feminine energy.

The three earth zodiac signs are Taurus, Virgo and Capricorn.

The pentacle's Court Cards are the only Court Cards with a yellow background.

The house is always freshly presented, neat and tidy, and they are house proud and may even be house bound. They spend time around the home, gardening, decorating and cooking; this connects to their earthy, natural and grounded aspects.

If they are not at home, they are at work. A hard working family – remember the ten of pentacles? They could actually become workaholics, always striving to better themselves and their pockets.

Earthy People Believe There is Value in Hard Work

Making money or spending it; if they are not at work making the money, they may be spending it, or could be at the pokies or shopping (which is a negative use).

A positive use would be to save their money, be aware of budgets and be careful when spending their money. They send their children to the best schools that they can afford. They are also aware of doing things of value like self-development workshops, working at the library or volunteering at a church.

Earthy people love bush walking, picnics, camping and spending time in the country. They probably own a country home or may have a caravan in Torquay, visit every year for the holidays, and build relationships with other families there. They get to know the community and the environment really well, and eventually retire there.

Earthy people know how to make things grow. They are patient and repetitive. They usually have pets because they too keep you in a routine: walking them and feeding them at the same hour every day.

Because of their value system they are socially conscious about developing countries like Somalia, Ethiopia and Afghanistan or with people less fortunate than themselves.

It may be hard for them to communicate with you on an emotional level. They are not emotionally attached, therefore it is easier for them to give money or adopt, sponsor or even foster children.

They would also be aware of environmental issues: they recycle, may even invest in the green technologies.

They give practical assistance to each other, give practical advice and give practical presents.

Remember the image of the Ten of Pentacles? Family traditions, family wealth and values. They would aspire to live in Toorak in Australia or on 5th Avenue in America. It is about building their empire; their castle is their home.

KEY WORDS

Result - oriented, outcomes, actualization, sensation, security, grounding, centeredness, manifestation, skills, craftsmanship, rewards for accomplishments, sense of achievement, fruits of their labor, traditions, physical, material, appreciation, and spiritual endeavors, conservative and concerned.

SWORDS FAMILY - Swords rule the Mental Conflict Energy

The element is air and a masculine energy.

The three air zodiac signs are Gemini, Libra and Aquarius.

These are very busy people – half would be home and the other half would be out. People coming and going, just like the wind, real gadabouts, social butterflies, they should have a revolving front door. Air people tend to arrive late, miss the appointment or may cancel altogether.

They link with each other through the telephone, emails, and through the airwaves. Communication is with a capital 'C.'

This family would be a noisy family; playing loud music, doors slamming, people screaming at each other and the Television is always on.

They would have enquiring minds, and will ask a lot of questions. Healthy debates always go on, a lot of gas bagging, quite talkative to the point they can justify anything and even talk back to the Television. They are great with general knowledge as well; they talk fast and probably talk to themselves.

They Would Know a Lot of People from All Walks of Life

There would be family conflicts because their strong opinions could be volatile, especially if there are strong adolescent. The kids could also be volatile and there are a lot of upsets because they can get it out in the open. They can say what is on their mind, speak their mind or maybe spit the dummy. Then it is ok if they move out and leave home. Sometimes these upsets are so they can cut the apron strings from mother.

The lawn could always be in the need of mowing; the garden in the need of watering because there is never enough time. The rubbish bin is always left out the front on the street.

They probably move a lot because they are not grounded, therefore it is OK to move. The air element is not emotionally attached to a community like the earth element is.

KEY WORDS

Thoughts, struggles, conflicts, decisions, wit and cunningness, analysis, discussion, communication, mental processes, acuity, sharpness, criticism, pessimism, whirlwind, analyzing, linking and evaluating.

CUPS FAMILY - Water Rules the Emotions and Feelings

The element is water and a feminine energy.

The three water zodiac signs are Cancer, Scorpio and Pisces.

Water has strong emotional links and ties. They are probably always at home. It is a home not a house – they are real home bodies. They may have a sign in the entrance that reads 'Home Sweet Home.' Or a cross-stitched cushion on the couch that they created themselves with the words "Home is where the Heart is".

They are caring, loving and pay attention to each other, making each other happy. They are nurturing and supportive like in the Ten of Cups cards but could drag each other down with too much molly-coddling and too much pampering.

Sentimental feelings and memories are huge; the family photos are on the wall, they keep nostalgic and memorabilia items, they are most probably still have the baby booties.

The do-gooder family, the female may leave her work or career to be there for the children and support the children from the whole street, including looking after the pets. Supportive mother energy, baking cookies for everyone, an aunt to everyone so everyone may call her, "Nan".

Always There for Each Other Because of Their Loving Supporting Nature

Always there for each other especially in hard times and they never forget birthdays, anniversaries etc. And they may feel guilty if they forget to call home.

They can manipulate each other through guilt or emotional blackmail issues. They do not cope well with adversity as they tend to take it personally. It is hard for them to get above their emotions, they may not take feedback well and they need to look at it as constructive criticism.

These guys get sick the most because they take on a lot of negative energy in their bodies. Worrying could be over the top.

Children may never want to leave home because of the nurturing space, tender, loving care—remember they create homes. And if they do leave home, they would live close to each other like around the corner or across the road.

They tend to live near water. If they do live near water its best for these people to live in a solid house of brick or stone, bringing in more stability and a sense of grounding.

KEY WORDS

Unconscious, imagination, intuition, psychic, dreams, visualization, inner processes, relationships, receptivity, reflection, carers, creativeness, actors, musical and poets.

Chapter 38

COURT CARDS - OVERVIEW

PAGES - Represent Beginning Stage

In the form of an idea, a feeling, a thought, a conversation, a communication, a deposit, a birth, things that begin something,

A beginning of an action, the first steps in a project or endeavor, baby steps, a newbie and that junior level stage — even a relationship can start with a kiss.

The Pages are Qualities in Their Most Simple or Childlike State

We are looking at the childlike state or quality. The pages' qualities are in their most simple or childlike state. Most basic and natural manner.

Pages suggest being open to new experiences, having childlike behavior, immaturity and naive energy.

AGE GROUP

If it is a child or people still with children, we are looking at a youth up to sixteen or eighteen. Remember, the parents still see their twenty-five year olds as children. And also remember that our brains keep growing till at least thirty-years of age.

We are looking at an immature person or someone with childlike behavior, mentally or physically.

Pages can be either sex but I tend to use pentacles and cups for girls because of the feminine energy, and wands and swords for boys because of the masculine energy.

KNIGHTS - Represent Action Stage

This is where we take action. We are in motion, the situation is in motion and we are in pursuit or in progress.

They are charging towards something in their own specific way according to the suit. For example, earth energy will be slow and steady, whereas fire energy will jump with no hesitation.

The knights are the most important of the Court Cards because they are active and have motion energy. They are happening right now – you are in the midst of it. They have momentum.

The Knights are the Most Important of the Court Cards Because of Their Active Energy

All knights are wearing armor, suggesting they are ready for battle, dressed for traveling and ready for any action. They are dressed ready for change and ready to charge. The armor they wear is a symbol of protection.

Horses represent vehicles through life; they are symbols of movement and change.

Therefore, translate the quality of each suit into doing and movement words. For example, jumping, running, galloping, speeding, prancing, slow and steady, racing, pacing themselves, charging, demonstrating, chasing, pursuing and challenging.

A knight in a spread can be either sex in the reading because we all hold that energy but traditionally they represent a male because it is an active, action energy. Typical masculine energy to want it right now and to move towards it.

AGE GROUP

In a relationship reading, knights usually represent a young man.

The age group is between sixteen to fifty years of age.

We are looking at a young man, a mature adolescent or a youthful immature man or a person who acts without thinking and acts in a youthful impulsive way.

QUEENS - Represent Reflection Stage

Queens reflect our progress of a situation. They are all looking inwardly and evaluating. Queens have femininity, passiveness and a receptive quality.

They are the receptive quality of each suit. The energy is translated into feelings and understanding.

Interpret the queens using words of feelings, for example, pondering, wondering, sitting, reflecting, reviewing, revaluating, questioning, compassionate, contemplating, reassessing, thinking, mediating, integrating and considering.

Queens are All Looking Inward and Evaluating

AGE GROUP

The age groups for the queens are women over the age of sixteen years.

Women usually show up in a reading as queens.

The queens represent the four different aspects of the Empress.

I have broken them down as the following:

QUEEN OF WANDS

This queen shows up as two different types of personalities.

Wands has to do with work and career, skills and talents, efforts and ideas.

Therefore, one aspect of this queen is someone you work with: a work colleague, a career woman, your boss, a manager or supervisor in the workplace or someone like a friend in the workplace. We usually connect with someone in the workplace and become good friends; we spend a lot of our time at work place.

The other side of this queen represents our friend. Someone you have outside fun, activity and adventure with this person. They bring sunshine into your life as well as good times and fun times.

QUEEN OF PENTACLES

Once again this queen has two sides.

Pentacles has to do with material and spiritual values.

Therefore, one aspect to this queen is the business woman. She has a professional role. She may have great wealth or great morals and values. She is aware of ethical investments.

The other type of woman is earthy, into alternative lifestyles, a healer, a woman with earth mother energy, maybe a hippie, a pagan or into Wicca.

Both of these types of women have maturity; they are stable and have grounded energy. Both are in command over their garden. They are practical, sensible and concerned about money.

QUEEN OF SWORDS

Yep, this Queen has two sides to her as well.

Swords has to do with the mental conflict energy.

Therefore, if she represents the other woman in your world, we may be looking at an ex-wife, ex-friend, ex-girlfriend, ex-lover or that nasty mother-in-law.

She may represent a viper, a real gossip woman, a hag or a witch. Someone you have crossed swords with. She has used the sword in some way to hurt you as she knows how to use her tongue. Her tongue is as sharp as her mind.

If a man has been hurt by a woman, the queen of swords usually shows up.

If this queen represents you, she is positive. She represents that things are clear and she has made up her mind about things. Knows how to use the sword in a positive and constructive way.

QUEEN OF CUPS

This Queen also represents two sides.

Cups rules the emotions and feelings.

Here we have the woman of feeling. She represents your sister, mother, a daughter, your cousin, your favorite aunty, your wife, your grand-daughter, good mother-in-law, your grandmother, a female relation.

This queen may also be your lover or close friend, someone you have intimate feelings with, close family relations or family concerns and relationships with.

When a man is in love, the queen of cups usually shows up. She represents the love interest in a relationship. A man would be in love with this type of woman – she is a loving, caring and nurturing woman.

KINGS - Represent Resolution Stage

The kings show us that we have mastery over the situation. We have mastered it. We have completion and an outcome.

They are rulers who rule over their domain. They have maturity and authority and they wear a badge of success.

If You Get a King, You are Successful

They are in charge. They have social responsibility in the area that they rule. He now has authority in the area of his particular suit. He has mastered it. He is now the master.

Kings can also represent women, as a successful woman in her environment.

AGE GROUP

The age group of the kings may start anywhere from fifty years upward.

We are looking at the mature man or personality that has responsibility and who understands responsibility. Also note that today a thirty-year-old may be a king if they have responsibility and are in charge of their company.

Kings represent the four different aspects of the Emperor.

I have also broken them down as follows:

KING OF WANDS

The King also has two sides.

Wands has to do with work and career, skills and talents, efforts and ideas.

We are first looking at the work colleague, a friend in the work place, a boss, a team leader, director of sales or a project manager.

As the king, he most probably would run his own business. He would be the professional man, a teacher, a dentist; other professions would include an architect, a builder. He is entrepreneurial and enterprising and would love his sports, maybe a sports coach or team captain.

If sports-oriented, he would be healthy and robust or he would also be a great entertainer.

This king is also your buddy, your best friend, someone you have outside fun with. You connect on that outdoor activity level, get together to play rounds of golf, tennis, football, follow the grand prix, go sailing and fishing.

KING OF PENTACLES

This king also represents two different aspects.

Pentacles has to do with material and spiritual values.

First type, we have the one who is money oriented and works with money such as a banker, the business man, the accountant, a broker, a solicitor or involved in real estate, which is a perfect business for an earth element to do. He understands stocks, shares and bonds on an innate level.

This king is the wealthiest of all the kings therefore he would have his own business and it would be a very wealthy business. He knows how to make money grow; this is so natural to him, it is innate.

He could well be a CEO, Manager Director or have a corporate status. Usually people in these positions could be involved with an organization like Rotary or on the board and fundraise for a charity organization.

The other side of this king is the farmer; he would own acres of land and heaps of cattle. He could be involved with mining, own a vineyard, canola oil or involved with green technology and be environmentally conscious.

KING OF SWORDS

Once again we have two different aspects to this king.

Swords has to do with the mental conflict energy.

The first type is responsible for making a lot of decisions; he is accountable, like a judge, a doctor, dentist, a lawyer, scientist, politician, a chemist, a professor and a justice of peace.

They use words and their mind a lot, are decision makers and involved in media, communications, public relations, journalism, an author or even a policeman.

The other side of this king is the ex-husband, the ex-lover. Someone who you have crossed swords with like a feuding neighbor. They have a sharp tongue and have hurt you in some way. Be mindful – we could have mental mind games going on or mental abuse.

KING OF CUPS

Once again we are looking at two sides of this king.

Cups rules the emotions and feelings.

First, we have that emotional connection with someone you love, someone close or a friend or relation that supports you, like a father, a brother, a boyfriend, a son, a husband or a lover.

They are nurturing, caring and supportive of you. They are emotionally connected with you.

The other side of this king is someone that usually works from home like a consultant. They too would be professional and have their own business. They could work as a psychologist, naturopath, social worker, a psychologist, a counselor, healer, priest, a masseur.

They are also artistic and creative such as a singer song writer, poet, actor, musician and artist. They understand emotions and know how to tap into them and bring them out in a positive and constructive way so that they can heal themselves and also heal or assist others as well.

Chapter 39

Now we will go through each of the Court Cards in more detail as well as explore the symbolism of each card, their positive and negative traits and what they particularly need to excel.

PAGES - BEGINNING STAGE

The age group is up to sixteen or eighteen years of age. We are looking at someone with childlike naïve and immature qualities.

PAGE OF WANDS - Beginning Stage in the area of Work, Career, Skills, Talents, Efforts and Ideas

SUMMARY

The element for wands is fire. The three fire signs in the zodiac are Aries, Leo and Sagittarius. Wands hold a masculine energy.

I believe that the page of wands are males or have a masculine, active and courageous energy.

POSITIVE CHARACTERISTICS

Fire energy personalities are enthusiastic, outgoing, warm and friendly.

This child is a genius, a dare devil, he has leadership potential. He is energizing, creative, engaging, enigmatic and a force to reckon with.

Fire sign children are determined and self willed as well as resilient. Typical fire energy always renews itself because they have enterprising energy. They have a strong sense of self. They are the optimists of the world and the most generous.

It may be hard to parent this child because they know what they intend to do about a situation or they are very determined, knowing what they want from a young age.

NEGATIVE CHARACTERISTICS

Attention seeking, jealous, impish and temperamental. They have fiery tempers and tell big whoppers because they have a wonderful imagination.

The negative side of this energy always reminds me of Bart Simpson from the TV show *The Simpsons*. He has a great imagination and always gets himself in trouble and either burns out or burns others in the process.

Very Inspirational Energy

WHAT THIS CHILD NEEDS

What they need from the adults is praise. Praise will assist them to develop their healthy sense of self-confidence and courage. This child needs the self-confidence and courage to follow their road or pathway through life.

What we are looking at here is your cowardly lion from the movie *Wizard of Oz*. Be careful not to lose courage and heart. They say to let a child run free (within safe boundaries of course,) not to break their spirit and to not put out their spark of life.

SYMBOLOGY

Here in this card you can see all the colors of fire. The yellow and orange colors connect us to the dry, hot and barren environment.

Dressing in yellow and orange colors leads us to his vitality, his confidence and his will power; this child has a cut and dry personality, is fully conscious, aware and full of ideas. He has the typical Leo energy that is full of life, abundant creative expression and has much strength.

You can also see the pyramids in the background as symbols of hopes and aspirations. Mountains represent challenges – he is a spirited adventurer and someone that is creative and pursues their goals with vigor.

The grey hat that he wears has a spark or a flame in the front like he is having a light bulb moment that comes when you have a great idea. I like to call this fellow Sparky; he has a wonderful imagination and it is alive and well. He knows what he wants to do.

He holds a wand with both hands. The wand represents an idea or a skill and he is looking at his skill or talent wondering what he is going to do with it or how is he going to apply it. He is conscious of what he has in his hands; he is just too immature to do anything about it.

Salamanders

There are salamanders on his garment. Salamanders live in the desert and can withstand fire, extreme heat or pressure. The salamanders are telling you what type of character we are dealing with here. Salamanders can change their color, they are versatile and adaptable to their environment and they can camouflage themselves.

They are feisty and can spit poison at their enemies. Their tails can drop off and they can also re-grow their foot if it has been chopped off. This process is called transmutation and it connects us to the regenerative process of the fire element, like the phoenix that rises out of the ashes.

To Nurture This Child with Praise so They Feel Confident to Pursue Their Path

IN A READING

We are looking at a beginning of a new project, a new venture, a development of a new skill, a new development in career or a new career in self-employment.

Learning to use a new skill or utilizing a new skill or an interest in a new hobby.

New beginnings in a creative or adventurous area, especially in developing new skills and talents in work and career.

Creating something new – it may be a new stage, a new development, a new chapter, a new idea or starting a new adventure.

May even be making new friendships through a sports activity.

PAGE OF PENTACLES - New Beginnings in the area of Material and Spiritual Values

SUMMARY

The element for pentacles is the earth energy. The three earth signs in the zodiac are Taurus, Virgo and Capricorn.

Pentacles are feminine and have a softer, gentler and understanding nature.

POSITIVE CHARACTERISTICS

This child is patient, contemplative, careful and respects authority. He studies quietly and if you show him how to do something, he will do it due to his own practicability, at his own pace. Note that their other pace is much slower.

They say that a Virgo child may not even need a bib. I have tested this theory and asked many of my students over the years about this and they have all agreed that their Virgo babies and toddlers did not need to use a bib while eating or while in their high chair.

This child has a particular love of nature. Loves to be outdoors, may have a pet, believes in fairies and loves jumping on the trampoline.

NEGATIVE CHARATERISTICS

Timid, shy, so committed to the point they are self-centered, do not want to budge, do not want to change, stuck in the mud, stubborn and you can never get them to do anything.

They may have a tendency to rebel against parents or authority, are always testing the limits and pushing the envelope.

May be a slow learner, therefore suffers from learning difficulties and can be late bloomers. They need to feel and experience things for themselves; therefore there is the tendency to learn the hard way.

There may be a lack of self-esteem, self-confidence and self-worth and so they may need to learn how to build up their self-confidence.

Thinking of New Ways to Secure Something of Value

WHAT THIS CHILD NEEDS

What this child needs from adults is the need to feel needed and valued, and then they will feel like they have a place in the world to build their self-worth and self-esteem.

Earthy people use their five senses, so give reassurance, love and lots of hugs. Affection is important to them. They have a need to feel physical closeness. They are tactile and like to be tucked into bed to feel secure.

This is the child who wants to do things for you all the time so they feel necessary in the world; this is because they are an earth child.

SYMBOLOGY

You can see the page is standing in a field. In the background there is a plot planted already and the trees are already grown. In the front there is a new plot ready for planting.

She is wearing the color green and with so much green around her, this shows you the connection to the earth, which suggests she has a lot of growth potential. She is creative, adaptable and flexible. The trees look rich, lush and orderly.

The fancy red hat she is wearing also shows a creative feminine energy, the page of cups also wears this same hat. The color red taps us into her desires and dreams.

This page has her two hands on the pentacle whilst looking at it, which shows us that she is conscious of what she is doing and what she wants to do with this pentacle. It also suggests she is not afraid of getting her hands dirty – she is strong and can stomach things.

Maybe this page is a scout, always ready for anything. This child is happy to wash the car for little money or reward. Yesteryear, these children used to get up early to do paper rounds. They understand working for money and they would also have a plan of what to do with the money they made.

The Blue Mountains in the distance suggests spiritual aspirations and intuition. Maybe she is involved with the church because she understands spiritual discipline.

To Nurture this Child with Understanding and Respect so They Feel Necessary in the World

IN A READING

The page of pentacles is about making something of value grow; developing a new value. This card does not just suggest money; it also connects us to the inner value system. We all have different values; whatever is of value to this person is worth investing in.

This page is also known as the student. We could be looking at a beginning of some form of study. Going back to school to study something of value or we are looking at the perpetual student. Education is an investment in itself – it is something you pay for now and is returned later on. Even a self-development workshop or program is of value.

You have a little nest egg of money. It is not much but you are going to do something with it and make it grow.

We have here a beginning of a new investment, planting a new seed, for example, a deposit on a house or a new business. Investing in stocks or into a 'green' product (green products are becoming a new trend). Typical earthy people have a green consciousness; for example, they may invest in tree plantations.

If it is money we could be looking at a new study in accountancy, or accounting program. Working for a bank or becoming a realtor and learning about Real Estate – this is also a good connection for this earthy energy card.

Investing in health and the beginning or a new health regime and planting a veggie garden is also of value, not only for the self, but also for the whole family.

PAGE OF SWORDS - New Beginnings in the Mental Conflict area

SUMMARY

The element for swords is the air energy. The three air signs in the zodiac are Gemini, Libra and Aquarius. The air element is masculine energy.

I usually like to say they are males or have a masculine, sharp and active energy about them.

POSITIVE CHARATERISTICS

His personality is adaptable, diplomatic and impetuous. He is a moving force and is stimulated and switched on.

He is an easy learner and a quick learner. A good communicator, talks early, is physically athletic and loves competition. Is friendly and talks to everyone and has an inquisitive mind.

NEGATIVE

Can be a scatterbrain and have a flighty and rash energy. May be timid and lacks concentration. Can also be cynical and be impetuous..

Because of the swords we could be looking at a child that can be quite hurtful. They may be a problem child; they could spit on you, slap you, poke their tongue at you and have a real attitude. They may bite you, kick and scratch you; their words can be cutting and hurtful, could be a cheeky little brat or even be a bully.

WHAT THIS CHILD NEEDS

What this child needs from an adult is for you to talk to him and explain things. Because they have an inquisitive mind these are the children that asks "Why?" a lot, and expects an answer.

Having the Confidence to Think Differently

SYMBOLOGY

Straight away you see that the ground where this page is standing on is all uneven suggesting that he is unstable, unsteady, insecure, and not standing steady. He is standing high on a mound, therefore he may have tickets on himself.

The wind is up and he looks like he has just appeared looking for a challenge. Note that the tip of the sword is not in the picture, symbolizing he does not get the whole point as yet.

Magenta connects us to the higher intellect, suggesting he has potential; he is just not mature enough to use the sword and like a child does not understand his full potential yet. The black belt he wears suggests the unknown factor.

He is not even looking at the sword, therefore he is not focused and does not connect with it, unlike the other pages that are looking at what they have in their hands.

The typical young Gemini is the child that blurts out, "Hasn't that lady got a big nose?" while you are waiting in the bank queue. You may think how embarrassing, but they are blunt, have no tact and tell it like it is.

Librans are more diplomatic and understand a sharing consciousness concept. It is the Aquarian child that is the troublesome one, they may lash out, be childlike and problematic. It is the young Aquarian that may find themselves expelled from school.

You can see that his head is in the clouds. Clouds suggest symbolic messengers. There are also birds flying around and there is no formation, suggesting his mind is racing away with the birds. He may even be a bird brain. He is just not focused.

The red boots he wears suggests he has the energy to just jump right in – boots and all. Sometimes he thinks with his feet rather than his head. They may have foot in mouth disease, or takes one foot out to put the other foot in. Typical childlike quality wanting and looking for that immediate gratification.

To Nurture this Child with Understanding, Speak and Explain Things to Them so They Can Make Up Their Own Mind

IN A READING

There are a few ways of looking at this card.

First, we are looking at the problem child. They have the X factor, because of this, this child needs extra attention. He may have ADHD, seizures, be accident prone and hyperactive. He may have speech difficulties, may stutter, be hearing impaired or have a visible deformity. He could have Autism, Asperger's or suffer from mental conflicts and dyslexia.

You need to read with them and discuss things afterwards. Watch videos with this child, engage their mind, and challenge them. Physical activity is attractive for them.

The Page of Swords could represent messages in a reading. There may be a phone call, a letter, an email, a messy or troublesome phone call or a text, etc.

We are looking at the beginning of some form of communication. The first discussions of a new enterprise and it still may all be in the thought process and not even talking about it yet. New ideas, the initial meeting, it could still all be in the research stage.

If the Page of Swords shows up with the Empress, we could be looking at the loss of a child or the loss of a creative endeavor.

PAGE OF CUPS - New Beginnings in the area of Feelings and Emotions

PAGE of CUPS.

SUMMARY

The element for cups is the water energy. The three water signs in the zodiac are Cancer, Scorpio and Pisces. The water element is feminine.

I usually say they are females or have a feminine, creative, compassionate and loving nature.

POSITIVE CHARATERISTICS

They are dreamers and have a responsive nature; they are gentle, sensitive, imaginative and loving, a loving child and a much loved child.

They are artistic, creative and work quietly by themselves. These are the children that are happy to sit there and color in for hours.

NEGATIVE CHARATERISITCS

They are insecure and may run away from reality via day dreaming and having imaginary friends or playing make believe all the time. They dream their life away.

They may be emotionally unbalanced, dysfunctional and therefore could withdraw from society or the family. This character always reminds me of the brother from the movie *Little Miss Sunshine*. He was so awkward and stayed in his room all the time, yet was supportive and caring of his little sister. He did not talk for years because he wanted to show his parents that he could get into the air force, only to discover at recruitment time that he was color blind.

They tend to be a thumb sucker and carry a security blanket like Lionel did from the cartoon show *Charlie Brown*.

To make them feel secure at bedtime, you may need to check under the bed and the wardrobe for the 'Boogie Man' and probably leave the light on all night.

Bringing in New Ways to Love Yourself and Others

WHAT THIS CHILD NEEDS

What this child need from adults is a lot of love to develop their sensitivity and to feel safe in the world. Their nature needs to be nurtured with love.

They need to feel emotional closeness, need you to be close to them and understand their sensitive needs. If it is a male child, they need even more special attention. If you have a male child, allow him to cry, to be sooky, allow him to show his emotions, express them in a safe environment then he can handle the emotions as he grows older. Otherwise he may turn to alcohol, drugs or food to drown the pain because he can't handle it.

They have sensitive needs; they are a sweet child, known as the koala baby – clingy and dependent, the kind that wants to lifted and hugged all the time with a need for physical attention. Allow them this attention; they will pull away from you when they are ready.

SYMBOLOGY

This child wears a lot of blue, signifying spiritual and emotional energy. This connects us to that enchanted child within all of us, that part of us that we call the inner child or the old soul.

The psychic experiences associated with this card are because of the third eye you can see in her feminine shaped hat. She is a dreamer; no wonder they can see imaginary friends. I always think of that young child in the movie *The Sixth Sense* when he says, "I see dead people".

Daniel Johns from the band *Silverchair* used to have an imagery friend and his folks would even lay out a place setting at the table at dinner time for his imaginary friend.

Because of the psychic ability connection, no wonder he can see the fish in his cup. The fish represents spirituality. Fish live in the water and the water represents another realm, the unconscious world. Therefore, he has intuitive powers and religious energy. The black belt signifies the unknown factor.

The pink shirt and leggings also connect us to love, devotion and unconditional love. This child brings a lot of love in to your life. The lotus flower on her outfit also represents a much loved child and the divine child that lives within us all.

The water in the background is swiftly flowing; you are looking at one emotional package and possibly a sooky-lala.

Nurture this Child with Love so They Feel Safe in the World

IN A READING

We are looking at the beginning of our psychic abilities. This may develop as a new spiritual awakening, for example, learning Tarot, Yoga, Reiki, massage or all sorts of creative arts. A creative outlet that also has a spiritual connection for us.

This is not just representing a new love but is the beginning of something you really love to do, something that you are passionate about or have an emotional connection with.

In the relationship area, it may well be a new love, a new feeling, a new emotion, a new friend, a new relationship and a new romance.

It could be a much loved or much-wanted baby or bonding with baby. Universal world child energy, an old soul or even a love child.

If the Page of Cups and The Empress show up together we could be looking at the birth of a child or a birth of a new creative endeavor.

Chapter 40

KNIGHTS - ACTION STAGE

This age group is from sixteen through to fifty years.

Also remember that traditionally, knights are usually seen as males because of their conscious active motion energy.

KNIGHT OF WANDS - Action in the area of Work, Career, Skills, Talents, Efforts and Ideas

SUMMARY

The element is fire, masculine energy and the three fire zodiac signs are Aries, Leo and Sagittarius.

POSITIVE CHARACTERISTICS

The colors are the same as on the page's card but now you can see the salamanders are larger on his tunic.

This knight has matured into an honest, outspoken, adventurous, competitive, courageous, ambitious, spontaneous and charming man.

He is spirited and has a moving force. He is cheerful and good fun to have around.

We could be looking at Sir Lancelot, the first knight of the round table or his son Sir Galahad. Both outshone everyone and were most gallant.

This knight would be athletic and involved with various sports such as: golf, football, tennis and horse-riding. Maybe he owns a motorbike, goes skiing, yachting, camping and hiking. He likes challenges and because of the outdoor activities, he would also be healthy, tanned and robust.

He takes pride in the way he looks, could be vain or have a huge ego. He would own a little red sports car and take you to the best restaurants – he would know his way around town.

NEGATIVE CHARATERISTICS

On the negative side he is selfish, impulsive, egotistical, dogmatic, jealous and pushy.

He may be difficult to tie down because he is always off doing his own thing.

Getting Fired Up About a New Project Venture

SYMBOLOGY

There are flames coming off his grey helmet as well as flames coming off his elbow; he is a real trail blazer. Even the horse's mane looks like flames. He leads and lights the way.

The horse is orange in color suggesting vitality, stamina and confident energy. Horses are symbolic of movement. This horse is an Appaloosa, which are bred for distances. It is not a fast looking horse but the horse will carry him a long way. It has endurance for the long haul.

The knight sits well on the horse; he looks comfortable and it suits him well. He is enthusiastic and ready. He is going at a good pace and the progress is good. He is positive, paces himself well and has rhythm.

This knight is in charge of his crusade. You can see the wand is in his right hand suggesting he knows what he is doing and is aware of his skills. He actively uses his skills to achieve goals. He is charging towards his goals and makes it look easy.

This knight always reminds me of that person in the old cowboy movies that leads the caravans across Indian country and to the new lands.

Once again, we see the pyramids in the distance – hopes and aspirations are still luring him.

This Energy is Active, Ready and on the Move

IN A READING

We could be moving house or we are on the move. Maybe it is a career move, for example a transport worker or even working interstate.

If this card shows up in a career reading, there may be movement in the work place, maybe sideways, but still movement. It could be moving to a new building, to a different position or to a different company altogether.

You may travel with work as a long distance truck driver, for the food transport industry, as a train driver or even a bus driver. Perhaps they work as a traveling salesman, have a mobile business, are an electrician, a fireman or a taxi driver.

Also, this card may suggest work or a project that is growing and moving forward. He is fired up and all systems are going well. The progress is good or it is going at a good pace. He sits well with whatever project he is doing, it suits him and does it comfortably and easily.

He is driven to action for this venture, particularly using skills, strategies and his talents.

In a health reading, you can say his health is progressing well and he is on the mend. Remember this knight is usually fit, tanned, healthy looking, robust and feisty.

KNIGHT OF PENTACLES - Action in the Material and Spiritual Values

SUMMARY

The element is earth, feminine energy and the three earth zodiac signs are Taurus, Virgo and Capricorn.

POSITIVE CHARATERISTICS

His energy is practicable, dependable, conservative and he is concerned with his material security. He is considerate and thoughtful, loyal and responsible.

He can be possessive of those he loves and of his material wealth. He is reliable and stable as he likes routine.

He commits with caution. He is a plodder, taking one step at a time but eventually gets there; a slow and steady wins the race sort of person. It always reminds me of the story of the tortoise and the hare, where the tortoise always wins.

Earthy people usually do not get involved unless there is plan and a likely result. They will not waste their energy, their money or effort on anything that will not give them a return, an outcome or a desired result.

They are hard to tie down because they could be at work and focusing all their attention on their goals.

He is proud of what he owns rather than what he does. There is a real appreciation of things of value. He does not really have a talkative personality, nor is emotionally demonstrative yet as he matures he will. His actions speak louder than his words.

They are very interesting characters because they will do things for you as that is how they show you they love you. Remember, they do things that are practical and of value. For example, they give you a filing cabinet, typewriter, an iron or today may give you an iPad, or wash your car for you – all very practical actions.

They watch their money; only spending when value for money. They are aware of budgets. Also, they will remind you that they bought two dresses for you at a thousand dollars each ten years ago. They keep things forever like old clothes, they will recycle t-shirts and old sheets, etc. They are hoarders and real bower birds.

They also use their five senses; they really know how to take care of you on a physical level. Their challenge is to develop their spiritual side; they need to learn to give a bunch of flowers and as they mature they will.

They usually work with money in positions such as a banker, accountant and in stocks and shares. It is in their nature. They are often professionals such as vets, agricultural workers, organics, green thumbs, landscape gardeners, bricklayers, electricians, plumbers, leather workers, craftsmen, tradesmen, farriers and chefs.

They would tend to work with their hands – real DIY guys. You would always find them at Bunnings Hardware stores or at home in their sheds. It is important for them to have their space such as a shed or workshop.

I would not be surprised if they are farmers because they are the earthy characters and would probably have heaps of animals around – dogs, dogs and more dogs.

During a midlife crisis they look for something more. This is when they develop their spiritual side and become a king. They develop when they realize they need to help others.

Action Around Financial or Spiritual Matters

NEGATIVE CHARATERISTICS

He may be greedy, irresponsible and afraid of change. He is very earthy and to the point. He may be stuck in mud or be stubborn. He could have insecurity issues, be in a rut or bogged down with bureaucracy.

He is slow to take the opportunities that life has to offer because he plans everything and therefore finds it hard to sidetrack from his plan so often he misses out. As they say, he could be set in his ways.

SYMBOLOGY

Here we have the black horse therefore this knight is known as the Knight of Death or the Black Knight. In the old days and even today, black horses are used for funerals. The color black suggests his energy still needs to develop or transform or once again he may be a late bloomer.

The saddle on the horse is built for comfort not speed and it looks like he has had it for a long time. It looks like heavy leather – it is of sturdy quality and there is no way he will fall off this horse.

This horse is a Clydesdale; you can see the hairs around the hoofs. Clydesdales can pull large things. It was the Clydesdale horses that pulled the Carlton Draught kegs. They are strong, reliable, plodders and real work horses.

There is a bush on the knight's helmet and on the horse's head as well – this is a fertility symbol. It represents the growth potential. It connects to the acorn and the oak tree; it is also a hard nut to crack.

If he were to drive a vintage car, it would be a 1939 car or an e-type Jaguar.

The fancy red reigns around the horse and the knight demonstrate how passionate they are about what they are doing. He is very committed to what he does or is that all the red tape they create? Remember they would not do it if it were not of value.

You can see in the background that the field is further ploughed and further prepared than the page card. In his right conscious hand, he holds the pentacle. He plans what to do with his pentacle; maybe he has planted all his seeds already and is now surveying all his work and considering what is next.

You can see his spiritual side is still not developed because you cannot see his left hand. This is what he still needs to develop; it needs to come into the picture.

He is a strong silent type, no idle chatter here. He likes to keep it simple. He does not say much and so you will probably spend a lot of time pondering what is going on inside his head and what is he thinking about.

He is too practical, shy and timid. He probably does not have many friends because he is working all the time, head down bottom up, focused and a quiet achiever.

This Energy is Stable, Planning and Steady as She Goes

IN A READING

There is action that needs to happen in the area of financial planning, money matters or a tax return. Maybe he is set to receive a small return or have a business meeting; meeting with a broker or the bank manager.

Also take action on the practical side of life, for example, cleaning the house and doing all that spring cleaning. Maybe consider where and how to build the pergola on the house in time for the summer holidays – this will also add value to the property.

Creating a new routine and including meditation, yoga, opening up to the spiritual side of life.

Try grounding energy through gardening or just stop and connect with your values and health. Reset yourself by attending a retreat and pushing that restart button.

Place a deposit on the house and take time to actually build it. All systems are go or you are checking on the progress.

KNIGHT OF SWORDS - Action in the Mental Conflict Energy

SUMMARY

The element is air, masculine energy and the three air Zodiac signs are Gemini, Libra and Aquarius.

POSITIVE CHARATERISTICS

This knight is assertive, has a conscious mind, is intelligent and is quick in linking things together. He would have many interests and is a champion of many and various courses.

He tends to lead with his head and he would have many ideas. A dashing young man, a persuasive talker, he could be over opinionated so be mindful of this.

He would crave mental stimulation, even on a relationship level, because he needs to exchange ideas with you. He can read the paper, watch TV, listen to your conversation and talk on the telephone all at once. With his intelligence, he is dexterous.

Being smart, they make wonderful lawyers. They can be mesmerizing and charismatic as an orator, storyteller and someone that has to talk their way through life. They can talk their way out of a paper bag or repeat things to you verbatim. However, because of the air element, they may be all words and no feelings.

Often they have a beautiful voice, a distinctive voice, are a singer or a radio disc jockey. They could work as a newspaper reporter, a pilot or a car salesman.

They could be a risk taker and interested in extreme sports. They could be a racing car driver, a crusty demon motorbike rider, long distance runner, tri-athlete, skier and sky-diver.

Time to Get into Action Around Your Ideas

NEGATIVE CHARACTERISTICS

He is going so fast that he could fall off the horse.

He would feel insincere, unreliable, never arrive on time and may be manipulative. He does everything quickly, such as eating fast, walking fast, driving fast, talking fast and even have verbal diarrhea.

He could have an overbearing nature and hates waiting around; therefore it could be tricky when you go shopping with them, especially if a Gemini, because they can be impatient. He may be cruel in his words or actions towards you in the mental, the physical and emotional areas.

Sometimes this personality just does not think, may have no tact and comes across as quite callus. They could be bad tempered, impulsive and fly off the handle – a bad loser. Often they only see the situation from their own point of view and can be one-eyed.

He could create whirlwind relationships. At times it would seem he leaves your life just as quickly as he arrived. It is easy for them to split off quickly because they can cut from their emotions easily. Fickle, very fickle. He may also have a total logical behavior, like a Vulcan character from the *Star Trek* series, or have no heart like the Tin Man from the movie *The Wizard of Oz*.

SYMBOLOGY

This horse is a racehorse as they have tiny saddles and therefore it is easy for this rider to fall off. The way he is sitting on horse looks uncomfortable and even the horse looks scared.

Racehorses are usually highly strung, skittish, flighty, and swift yet they are purposeful sprinters and their racing life is short lived.

He could ride like a bat out of hell or like a bull at the gate or maybe behave like a bull in a china shop. He has real gun-ho energy.

This knight looks like he is running, flying and jumping on the horse all in one movement to get there no matter what. His energy is just like that of a page; going against the wind, running like the wind. But if your house was on fire, you would want him to race this fast to get there to help.

This is of course the impulsive side of this knight. You can see the tip of the sword is still not in the picture, suggesting he does not have or understood the full point or meaning, yet.

You can see the horse is in midair, suggesting this personality type is a high flyer or he is flying high, also connecting us to the high achiever.

Interesting how the knight's boots have a pointed toe and what looks like a sharp spur. This connects us to his sharp tongue or how, inadvertently, he can hurt you and also hurt himself.

The birds and butterflies connect us to the air element. He has a feather in his helmet, connecting us to spirit messages from above. His head is still in the clouds and the birds are still scattered all around the place.

The brown cloak he wears represents the great instigator, the troubleshooter. He arrives, sorts it out and then leaves. I suppose this energy gets bored once it comes down. These people need challenges and stimulation although his real challenge may well be to be more practical.

This Energy is Assertive, Intelligent and can Change Their Mind

IN A READING

This knight suggests we need to get active to pursue a project. We need to get focused, we need to get the point. Otherwise we are running around and wasting our energy.

This may be the warning aspect of this card to slow down as you are going too fast and you could fall off your bike. Think before you speak, think before you act. You may be out of order, you may receive a speeding ticket or you are moving aimlessly, blindly and recklessly.

You can see the gloves are off his hands, suggesting he is open. He also knows how to protect himself. He is ready to get in there; he is charging through life with initiating energy.

We need this energy to get motivated. It is like a breath of fresh air.

Various forms of communication need to happen to get things to the next level or progressive meetings: a project needs to occur or an endeavor needs to progress. The project could now take a flying leap forward, moving in leaps and bounds.

Itinerary and agendas should be put in place. Messenger bringing news, sharing an announcement. Expect to hear some news.

He can be an exhaustive energy so be aware he can be clever when arguing because they may never stop, always wanting the last word. This could wear you out.

KNIGHT OF CUPS - Action in the Feelings and Emotions Area

SUMMARY

The element is water, feminine energy and the three water zodiac signs are Cancer, Scorpio and Pisces.

POSITIVE CHARACTERISTICS

This knight is emotional, sensitive, has a receptive nature, idealistic, is dreamy, caring and loving.

His energy is artistic, musical, creative and spiritual. A romantic at heart, this is the knight in shining armor. Maybe gay in nature, he is a sensitive new-age guy. What we have here is an emotional soul.

If he has developed positively, women fall in love with him. He may have the capacity to turn into a Casanova, a real man about town. This could be troublesome for a young male because if he feels the need to end a relationship, it may be hard for him, because he does not want to hurt the partner, therefore they end up creating emotional webs.

Other possibilities are that girls fall in love with him and he does not stay. As a result he gets a bad reputation as a heartbreaker or a coward. Then girls think there are no men of integrity, and so can lose their faith in love.

It is also interesting to note that sensitive men like this often attract woman that tend to trample them. They attract the strong forceful woman and may end up being hen-pecked.

Society still thinks men like this should not exist; a man should be a man and not show feminine qualities. This is the man that sits and talks with the women in the kitchen and so the men and boys dislike him. We are looking at a beautiful youth like a Leonardo DiCaprio.

They should dive into their work or project for that release as an outlet for their emotions – when they are helping others they can heal themselves. Some sympathetic healing professions are good for them and they may be drawn to becoming a counselor, medic, lawyer, a Good Samaritan, a musician or poet, a Hare Krishna devotee, a psychic, a priest, a masseuse, a naturopath or a psychologist.

They need a lot of love and space to feel safe and to nurture and release their emotions in a constructive way. They should be allowed to or encouraged to play an instrument, act and do martial arts; all constructive outlets to express their creativity in a positive way.

NEGATIVE CHARACTERISTICS

May be insecure and unable to deal with feelings, and so display an emotionally immature or emotional dysfunctional personality.

If he has not developed emotionally, he may tend to be an escapist and use drugs, alcohol or indulge in food and other addictions to hide behind. He hides in the addictions.

He may well say things he knows you want to hear so as to get away with something – a sweet talker, a gigolo, a real sleaze and manipulator.

Action Around Creative or Artist Endeavors

SYMBOLOGY

This horse is fire-bred like a highly strung Arabian. They are superb looking. It is a real show pony, like the Venetian Dancing Horse, the equestrian horses or like Barbie's horse, which is called Dancer. The horse is grey in color, displaying emotional wisdom.

The color blue and the water on his tunic display an emotional life or a beautiful, understanding and compassionate soul.

The fish connects us to the spiritual life. In the Page of Cups, the fish was in the cup, now the fish are all over his garment.

He is not wearing any gloves; he is open and vulnerable. His quest is for a spiritual life or love.

The wings on his helmet and his feet connect us to the wings of an eagle or the element of air. Maybe he needs to develop more air qualities; this is his challenge – to become more rational. Also, he may be psychic, angelic or he could easily fly off into dreamland.

The spur on his boots connect us to his destructive side, his escapism side. This knight inadvertently hurts you but hurts himself even more.

Look at how he carries the cup. He holds it gingerly and carries it very carefully.

Straight in front of him is a river. He has to go through the water, which is representative of the stream of life. The emotional side of him needs to grow for him to become the King of Cups.

On the other side of the river are the cliffs. He has to climb up and get over these cliffs and may need a helping hand to climb out of his emotions.

This Energy is Gentle, Patient and Understanding

IN A READING

We have here movement in the affairs of the heart, love, feelings and the emotions.

This knight is the knight in shining armor, offering you his cup of love, the cup of life. Or it may be you offering the cup to someone else.

The relationship is in progress; it is definitely making head way. There is action in the affairs of the heart.

In a romantic reading, this is the knight that symbolizes a partner to fall in love with for all women. He is the lover, the love interest in a relationship reading. You can see he is making that offer of love with his cup.

What you are passionate about is in progress – you are moving towards something you love to do. You are passionate about it and it fulfills you on the spiritual level and this balances your emotions, for example Tai Chi or martial arts classes, massage, yoga or even tarot classes.

Someone cares about you and is offering you a helping hand. This card demonstrates that you are working through an emotional situation.

Chapter 41

QUEENS - REFLECTION STAGE

All the queens have a feminine quality and therefore a reflective and passive energy. Note that you may also be dealing with gay people.

Queens represent the internal reviewing process, hence reflection, reevaluating and reassessing is associated with these cards.

The age group for all the queens is a woman over the age of sixteen years.

QUEEN OF WANDS - Reflection in the Work, Career, Skills, Talents, Efforts and Ideas

SUMMARY

The element is fire, masculine energy and the three fire zodiac signs are Aries, Leo and Sagittarius.

There are two ways of looking at this queen. Firstly, she is a woman you know through the work environment. The other represents a friend that you socialize and have fun with.

POSITIVE CHARACTERISTICS

The queen of wands has a warm and friendly nature and is generous with her time and resources. She is ambitious, enterprising, assertive and creative in her career – all fire signs are progressive and entrepreneurial.

She is also competitive in nature, positive with an adventurous spirit, independent and courageous. She makes a good leader, is confident and is not to be threatened. This queen will take on the school principle to defend her child if she needs too.

This queen comes from personal self-experience and has a social conscious, especially if they are Sagittarius. They are true leaders and use personal charm to influence others. Once again, all the fire signs are the same. They will all have strong feelings for you if they are close to you.

Good to have as a friend in the work place; they may be a manager, supervisor or even a personal assistant.

NEGATIVE CHARACTERISTICS

They may not even notice that you exist if you are not close to them. For example, you have to be a family member or in their social group to be noticed. They can come across as snobs or demonstrate an arrogant energy. For instance, Leo woman are often seen as snobs and only interested in their own pride. Not that they do this on purpose, it is just that they are self-absorbed.

May come across as jealous, inconsiderate, egotistical, dogmatic and vain, and enact a philosophy that says, "My way or the highway".

They have an attractive and charming personality that people get sucked into, but not for long.

This Queen has Wisdom, Strength and a Strong Sense of Self

SYMBOLOGY

You can see the lions on the backdrop and on the throne arm rests. Lions demonstrate her courage, pride, royalty, loyalty and regal energy. There is a lion clasp over her heart area which holds her grey cloak.

There is also a grey platform that her throne sits upon. Grey is the color for wisdom. It shows she has wisdom, strength, a strong sense of self and a strong base. The pyramids in the background show us that even though she is reflective, she still has creative aspirations.

There is a black cat in front of the queen, suggesting she can be as strong as a lion and as soft and sweet as a pussycat that just wants to lounge around in the sunshine. Cats also connect us with the Goddess Bast – the Egyptian protector of cats. Cats and sphinxes were known and understood to be a protection symbol. They have magical and intuitive powers. The cats and lions are showing us the powerful and intuitive side of this queen. In fact, we still see lions on either side of pillars, drive-ways or entrances of properties today.

The sunflower connects us to the sun's fiery energy. The sun is the planet for Leo and Leo is all about the self, me, myself, and the ego. Sunflowers are heliotropes because they follow the sun – rising in the morning and sleeping in the evening.

Her golden gown also connects to the sun as a source of energy. This shows her exciting and warm energy that is very attractive to be around. Her red shoes poking out underneath her gown shows she may have creative drive and be sexually active.

This queen does not sit in a very ladylike position. She actually looks athletic and tomboyish. She is independent and open to life's possibilities, full of life and not a typical lady. She often follows male pursuits, such as horse riding, rock climbing, canoeing, and may even be a football presenter.

The crown is fertile; you can see all the leaves and growth suggesting she has a creative mind, she is enterprising and entrepreneurial. She is approachable and open – that is why she sits like that and she is not intimidating and approachable.

A Time to Reflect on Your Creative Aspects

IN A READING

Time to reflect on your skills and talents in the area of work, career, a project or organizing an event, etc. Possibly thinking of a career change.

Think about teaching yourself a new skill and researching what is out there and available for you to do. Think creatively and laterally.

She is often a woman you work with or someone you associate with on the social scene; she may represent a friend, a companion, an acquaintance.

Reflecting on a friend. She represents someone you go out and have fun with, someone that brings sunshine into your life.

QUEEN OF PENTACLES - Refection in the Material and Spiritual Values area

SUMMARY

The element is earth, a feminine energy and the three earth Zodiac signs are Taurus, Virgo and Capricorn.

There are two aspects to this queen. Firstly, she is the business woman and the other is the woman that lives an earthy alternative life style.

POSITIVE CHARACTERISTICS

This queen is productive and creative.

She feels close to nature; you may always find her in her garden. She enjoys long walks in her beautiful garden and being in the environment. She has an earthy quality, is grounded and a liberated woman. She is pragmatic, possibly feminist and/or a lesbian.

She may be that alternative life style person who does not shave her armpits or her legs and who cooks on a wood stove and makes bread. She does not mind getting her hands dirty, may have possibly been a girl guide when young because today she can handle many basic things of life, such as changing the nappies, cleaning up the vomit, etc. She has a very domesticated quality.

She can take care of herself, mend the fence, replace the light globe, tow a trailer and even try her hand at welding to repair the boundary fence. She can shovel manure and is not afraid of spiders. She is independent and self-sufficient.

Of course they are good at managing money and here we have the business woman. She is aware of budgets and knows how to stick to them. She knows how to build on her resources.

She attracts anything of value; this is the queen that ends up with grandmother's furniture, and antiques and absolutely loves all the traditional family stories and hand-me-downs.

This is quite possibly the reason why a lot of people talk to this earthy queen because she comes across as level-headed and grounded. When you are going through a hard time, this queen sits with you and listens all the pros and cons to give you practical guidance.

Reflecting on Things of Value and How to Make Them Grow

The three types of queens are:

TAURUS

They love to touch and always expect cuddles and hugs.

They are mature and trustworthy from a very young age. Security is important to them so it is important for a Taurean to purchase their own house. This builds their stability and security, and things of value are all part of building their self-worth, self-esteem and confidence.

VIRGO

They will shake your hand and rate you out of ten.

They could be concerned about perfection, therefore not a hair is out of place. They can be possessive about their things and will tend to do their own washing up, thank you very much.

CAPRICORN

Capricorns are very shy and usually do not ask for what they really want.

We are looking at the high flyers and social climbers. She works very hard from a young age to get what she wants. For example, her house will be huge and quite possibly a mud brick home. This queen likes the house to look like a mansion.

All of them are responsible and creative in the home, as well as creative in business and financial matters.

All types are healthy and consciousness of fitness. Their food is always of good quality; this has to with their earthy nature.

NEGATIVE CHARACTERISTICS

Here we are looking at insecurity, dependence on others if they are very insecure and this is sad because they lose the plot and find no satisfaction at all.

They can be materialistic, mean, stingy and can be hooked on power and money. They are attracted to men with money.

On the social scene, they think more about what other people think of them and are always comparing themselves against others.

This Queen is Pragmatic, Practical and a Patience Quality

SYMBOLOGY

The most mature and most rounded queen of them all, this queen is wealthy and achieves her goals in a practical and steady way.

The Blue Mountains in the background connect us to the High Priestess energy and her spiritual aspirations. Her challenge is to become more spiritual and less materialistic.

In fact, this card reminds me of the Magician card. They both have the yellow background, the red outfits with the white undergarments, the red roses above their heads are complete and beautiful. Just like the Magician energy connecting us to the positive creative desires with inner integrity. She can manifest just like the Magician can.

She wears the green mantel bringing in the Empresses' feminine peace, harmony, practical and healing qualities.

A conservative crown demonstrates a conservative queen and therefore conservative aspects. The red growth on her crown, like in the Knights of Pentacles, suggests growth, enterprise, creative ideas and desirous thoughts. All this shows she is able to manifest with practical steps with real outcomes.

She holds the pentacle with ease; it is large and looks perfect and she is not afraid of losing it.

The card has a lush garden, just like the Magician's garden. There is a rabbit on the bottom right corner, which is the symbol of fertility, new life, and new ideas. Also rabbits are gentle and show their attachment to nature.

On the throne there are apples and pears, demonstrating fruitfulness. Her lush rich garden also symbolizes a beautiful family environment. Even the grass looks trimmed and is rich and fertile.

There is also a goat connecting us to Capricorn energy. A bull's head on the side of the throne connects us to Taurus energy. There is a cupid angel on the top of the throne connecting us to Mercury that rules Virgo.

IN A READING

Reflecting on things of value to her.

Earthy people appreciate things of value. Health and the home are usually at the top of the list.

Maybe this card says to have time out, reflect and meditate, spend some time in the garden to smell the roses. This taps us into the spiritual side of life.

On the material front, we are reflecting on material and financial issues and ethical investments. This is a great business woman.

It is a time to ground ideas and make them real. Manifest these ideas after much consideration on what to do.

QUEEN OF SWORDS - Reflection in the Mental Conflict area

SUMMARY

The element is air, masculine energy and the three air zodiac signs are Gemini, Libra and Aquarius.

The two main ways of looking at this queen are: if she represents yourself, it suggests you know the direction you are heading and can be decisive and can make excellent decisions.

If she represents another person, we are looking at someone whom you have crossed swords with and is a real trouble maker.

POSITIVE CHARACTERISTICS

This queen is keen and has a sharp mind with strong mental abilities. She is independent, self-reliable, opinionated and analytical.

She makes fair and well thought out decisions. She analyzes her feelings and does not show her emotions. Her mind is her weapon in life and she knows how to use it too.

This queen may symbolize past hurts, difficulties, loss and grief or someone who is much troubled.

She is found in areas of education, communication, journalism, PR, acting, media and as a performer or singer, she would have a distinctive voice. In HR, a teacher, a lawyer, judge, doctor and politician.

NEGATIVE CHARACTERISTICS

The negative side of this queen could affect someone who can live in the past and use past hurts as an excuse to not get on in life. She may go through life with a huge chip on her shoulder.

She may represent someone who is a widow and or who may be childless.

She can be cunning, uses cruel words, can back-stab and is known for her sharp tongue. Can be someone who is spiteful, a plotter and is conniving.

Her mind is always somewhere else and she is not listening because her monkey-mind always chats away. She can be a procrastinator and therefore puts things off because of worrying about the consequences.

This is the card for the ex-wife, the ex-lover, that bitchy person in your life. It may be that nasty mother-in-law we always hear about. She may be the biggest gossip, a nag or that problem person in your life.

This Queen has a Sharp Mind That Can Make Clear Decisions

SYMBOLOGY

There is one bird flying around overhead which may represent an old tale, the same old story, for example, the widow, spinster or someone who is alone. It may be a bitter betrayed woman. The tassels at her wrists are known as Victorian marine bracelets. They were worn if one was a widow or if a relationship had broken up and they could also represent a symbol of holding onto past hurts.

The clouds in the background are still and low on the horizon yet it looks like there is a storm brewing or there may be underlying issues going on. The clouds are grey and there are clouds also on her cape. The throne she sits on is also grey; grey represents understanding, knowledge and wisdom.

The butterflies are a symbol of a freedom and being free in the mind. Her crown is made of butterflies, therefore she has free flowing thoughts. They say butterflies are free, a symbol of transformation and metamorphosis and this suggests her potential intelligence.

There are moons and cherubs on the throne suggesting she is capable of loving and also able to protect herself. But when the hurt returns, she uses her sword to cut you out and then leaves. She finds it easy to split or detach herself from emotions.

Her left unconscious hand is up and it looks as though she is inviting you in. The right conscious hand holds the sword. She is conscious of her surroundings, of what she is doing, saying and her decision making process. She also knows how to defend herself.

Unlike the other queens she is sitting sideways so she can act without hesitation and that sword may come down hard and fast.

Because of her ability to detach herself from her emotions, she can make proper decisions.

It may be hard to show her feelings; her challenge is to be more like the Queen of Cups in being more balanced. Remember that the element of air and water are opposites.

The sword in this card connects us with the Justice card. Both swords are straight up and the tips of the swords are in the picture suggesting getting straight to the point and no nonsense energy.

Note that we need this energy or we get walked on all over. This queen may be someone that directs you or shows you the way.

Being able to stand up for yourself

IN A READING

Time to reflect on the decision making process.

This card represents someone that can make the right choices. Remember this queen is a positive card if she represents yourself. She says there are decisions to be make, to get focused, do the research and only then can the right decisions be made. Or she has already made her choice.

She has the total point; you can see the whole sword is in the picture and standing straight up. The sword connects to our rational thinking function.

Think about discussing your probable decisions. Reflect on things before you speak or act. Review how you are handling this situation.

This queen knows how to stand up for her rights. The pen is mightier than the sword; this is a more positive way of using the sword. For example, composing a letter, which will be to the point.

This card may suggest you may need to see a professional to assist you in making the right decision, for example a solicitor.

Remember the problem person? Or is there worry over someone? This queen symbolizes someone with past hurts and difficulties. It is hard to let it go in the mind.

QUEEN OF CUPS - Reflection in the area of Feelings and Emotions

QUEEN of CUPS.

SUMMARY

The element is water, feminine energy and the three water zodiac signs are Cancer, Scorpio and Pisces.

Either she represents the love interest in the reading or a loved one, such as a daughter, mother, partner or someone you have an intimate connection with.

POSITIVE CHARACTERISTICS

This queen is emotional to the point that she could be totally immersed and assumes the feelings of other people. She picks up on surrounding feelings, Pisces are known for being psychic sponges – they have a chameleon quality.

They are supportive and understanding of nature and love harmony and peace. She spends a lot of time meeting the needs of others, such as visiting folks and old friends.

She treasures the memories of those she loves, has sentimental and nostalgic feelings and is a romantic at heart. She needs time to dream and contemplate and has to have an escape of some sort, for example, a need to watch movies or to indulgence in a good book.

She shows interest in the creative artistic pursuits: music, poetry, dreaming, dancing etc. She demonstrates intuitive feelings and psychic abilities, possibly studies astrology, tarot or other esoteric and occult studies.

She is usually found working in the areas of psychology, mysticism, counseling, religion, or with the sick and ill, in the health industry as a nurse or even an overseas aid worker. She is sensitive and sympathetic and is a nurturer with an empathic nature.

She quite possibly will look after elderly parents or look after others and she loves to work with children as a carer or is involved with working with youth as a kindergarten or a primary school teacher.

Reflecting on Sentimental Memories

NEGATIVE CHARACTERISITCS

Can be over sensitive, easily hurt, unforgiving and can take it on personally, either because they are insecure or are emotionally unbalanced, depressed, etc. Therefore, they can become resentful and have unrealistic expectations of others. They can hold a grudge.

They are moody and manipulative, have addictive personality behaviors, can use emotional blackmail, guilt and passive aggressive techniques.

She is prone to being a martyr, a doormat, and often thinks the world is against her. She is a victim. If she becomes a doormat, she would often think like one.

She can become withdrawn and can become tired of giving if her feelings are not acknowledged, easily becoming disenchanted.

This is the woman who finds a lump in her breast and will not do anything about it, nor tell anyone. She keeps a lid on it and does not want to face the pain, for herself or her family. She is totally in denial – it will go away.

This is the queen that needs the qualities of all the other queens:
- The challenge to be more like the Queen of Swords—to become more whole and balanced. The Queen of Swords says, I think.
- The challenge to be more like the Queen of Pentacles—to be more practicable and earthed. The Queen of Pentacles says, I sense it.
- The challenge to be more like the Queen of Wands—to get moving, to get over it and move on quicker. The Queen of Wands says let's do it.

This is the only cup card with a lid on it. This refers to denial—if I don't give it any attention, it will go away. She knows that the feelings hurt so much that is why she keeps a lid on them.

If this card shows up, I will always let my client know that I understand they are dealing with a lot of pain. I will always acknowledge them. A comment I would propose is, "You have been through a lot and there is a lot of pain down there".

This queen needs to learn to contain the pain and not be swallowed or overwhelmed by it, otherwise they may drown in the water, in all their emotions. They need to look at and face these emotions in another way, to look at the lid on cup in a different way. This is her challenge.

This is the woman who knows her husband has had an affair for years and does not say anything, nor wants to face it so she suffers in silence. She does not want to upset herself, her family or others around her and does not want to rock the boat because she knows the Titanic will sink.

Scorpios need to trust you first before their lid comes off. Scorpios are the most intense energy sign of the whole zodiac – their pain may be acute. But note, people may relish in their pain and find it hard to let it go.

This Queen is Sensitive, and has a Nurturing Loving Nature

SYMBOLOGY

She is sitting in the middle of the ocean with all the jewels of ocean around her feet. This queen is the High Priestess of women.

Her throne is in the middle of the water, suggesting she is in the middle of her emotions, as if she is floating on top. She is showing you she can surmount any emotion, but that it has been an emotional journey. When she reaches the land, there she faces huge cliffs to climb up all over again.

This cup is the most richly adorned of all the cups in the deck. It looks like something much loved and treasured, almost spiritual looking with the little cross on top like the Holy Grail. Or is it a trophy?

There are black angel wings on either side, which may be handles. The black suggests the unknown so we just do not know exactly what is in the cup. The red spot in middle of cup signifies the sore spot or the bleeding heart.

This cup may represent the loss of a dream or loss of what she was hoping for. It could be the loss of security, the pain of losing a friend, a lover, a past family or the loss of a baby. The cup may be an urn that holds something precious.

Maybe the lid on the cup aids her in containing the pain so she is grounded and keeps centered. The Queen of Pentacle's energy is a good challenge for her to help become more grounded and stable.

Her white gown connects us to her virginal High Priestess energy. There is a shell clasp on her cape and the cape looks like it is made of water. There are bows along her left arm (her feminine unconscious side) suggesting she can reveal her intuition. It is easy to access her psychic abilities.

The cherubs on the throne have fish tails. These connect us to the loving woman energy, a beloved woman and her psychic abilities. Her feet are crossed over, which shows her insecure emotional side.

Her hair is braided, suggesting she is a woman with a partner and her crown looks like a conventional crown.

IN A READING

It is time to reflect on what is in the cup. This queen looks sadly at her cup.

We are now looking at the emotional side of woman. Tread carefully in your approach with this person because they can be very emotional.

There may be much apprehension about taking the lid off the cup. You need to acknowledge them and validate their pain and emotions.

This Queen of Cups may represent a daughter, your sister, your mother, your favorite cousin, your grandmother or someone you have an emotional and intimate connection with.

This is the feminine card for all females. If there is a woman or man in love, the Queen of Cups will show up. She represents the good wife syndrome. Most men want to take this woman home to meet their mum and marry them because she has a submissive energy. They will breed children and be easily molded and will do all to keep the peace and harmony in the family. She could even give up her career for sake of kids and family.

This Queen of Cups always reminds me of Princess Diana, the people's princess, known as the Queen of Hearts. Diana was a Cancer zodiac sign, and a water sign. This queen has the same shy look as Princess Diana did, looking at you from underneath her fringe. Diana was tender and had a caring nature. She was a kindergarten teacher and she assisted in many charities. All along there was a lot of pain in her cup; it all came out after her marriage failed and she moved away from all the royal obligations, faced the pain of leaving her boys, facing her bulimia issues and her dealings with Camilla.

Chapter 42

KINGS - RESOLUTION STAGE

A mature man from fifty years upwards. Remember a mature youth could also represent a successful king.

Kings have mastery over the particular area they symbolize. Kings could also be a woman and have mastery over her life.

KING OF WANDS - Mastery in the Work, Career, Skills, Talents, Efforts and Ideas

SUMMARY

The element is fire, has masculine energy and the three fire zodiac signs are Aries, Leo and Sagittarius.

There are two ways of looking at this King of Wands. Firstly, we have a man you may know through the work environment and the other is your best friend that you socialize with.

POSITIVE CHARACTERISTICS

This king has now matured from the knight's energy and has grown into a charming, warm, friendly, confident, generous person with a good sense of humor.

He is persuasive, has vision and foresight and is now comfortable within himself. He has definite faith and trusts in his gut feelings.

He loves a challenge and often creates one. He has a courageous personality and is a good family man.

He represents a friend in the workplace, perhaps a boss or a supervisor. As a king he would be successful in his career. He would be now the Chief Executive Officer or the Managing Director.

This king is more likely to have a profession rather than just a mere job, such as a teacher, an architect, or a salesperson. He would need room to move in his position to properly express himself.

He is interested in sports and therefore may have a career in sports like the captain of the football team, the coach, a pro-golfer, a master chef or a yachtsman.

He has very enterprising and entrepreneurial skills and qualities. Fire people always know how to reinvent themselves.

Success with Your Projects and Endeavors

NEGATIVE CHARACTERISTICS

Selfish, arrogant, domineering, can ignore the home and family and be totally involved in his own life, this brings out the self-absorbed traits and aloof aspects of the fire energy.

He can become irritated if his enthusiasm and optimism is curved by practicalities. His energy can be abrupt, brash and idealistic.

Some personality types that display this nature are: Alan Bond, Jeff Kennett, Paul Keating, Derryn Hinch, Murdoch, Kerry Packer, Donald Trump and Richard Branson to name a few.

The most classic example of them all is John Elliot, also known as Big Noise or is it Big Nose? He gets irritated when his dream is quashed. He would say, "Why can't I? Sack them all!" A classic line of his was, "Pig's arse".

These personality types are tactless and full of themselves; sometimes they may well have 'foot in mouth disease.' But they are competent, have a never say never attitude and always have many irons in the fire.

Fire is about renewal; these types are not afraid of spending a million dollars because they know what they have to do to get it right back.

SYMBOLOGY

The salamanders on the backdrop have now grown bigger and you can see the tails have joined up like the ouroboros, representing the self-consumed aspects of this king. There are also lions on the back drop which connect us to his courageous energy and the King of Beasts.

The wand is resting comfortably in his right hand; he is conscious about his skills and talents and now feels comfortable with utilizing his abilities.

The fire flames in his gold crown are smaller in size, looking more like a simmering and slow burning fire, which displays he has maturity, is more controlled and more focused. The orange and green outfit represents vitality and creativity.

The chain and the ring around his neck are his only adornments, suggesting he is blunt, straightforward, does not mess about, takes no bullshit and has a 'This is what I want attitude.'

There is also the stable grey platform, displaying all his projects have solid grounding and a strong base to build upon.

He looks to the right side, showing you he is future oriented. Typical fire energy, always creating something.

This king is Ambitious and Enterprising and has the Confidence to Back It Up

IN A READING

He holds great mastery in the area of ideas, inspirations and talents. When you have got it, you do not need to flaunt it. He does not need to prove himself because he has now mastered it.

Resolution in the area of work and career matters.

Their opinion is never wrong. Some may say that his bark is worse than bite.

He has success in his work prospects and career. He has reached attainment and is now sitting back reaping his rewards. Just like the lion king basking in the sun.

He now trusts his intuition and achieves accomplishments galore. He has the knack, is creative, enterprising and entrepreneurial.

He still loves to work on projects and remains sexually active.

If you need to see a professional about work issues and career paths, the King of Wands is the king to see.

KING OF PENTACLES - Mastery in the Material and Spiritual Values

KING of PENTACLES.

SUMMARY

The element is earth, has feminine energy and the three earth zodiac signs are Taurus, Virgo and Capricorn.

There are two aspects to this king. First, he is the business man, and second, he leads an alternative life-style.

POSITIVE CHARACTERISTICS

Most often this king is Capricorn. Taurus and Virgo usually show up as the Knight. Although a friend of mine was in charge of his company by the age of thirty. He showed the competence and all the responsibility of a mature man to lead his successful company.

All that hard work has now richly paid off in investments, property, stocks and bonds. He is literally oozing money.

He is interested in business roles in the material world, such as a banking financier, businessman, an accountant, financial advisor, a broker and could well be a wealthy Arab, an oil tycoon, maybe even a drug lord. This king is the wealthiest of them all.

In other values, he would also be successful in such things as farming and agriculture, a manager in whatever area is of value to him.

His practicable side brings out the engineer, mechanic or hands-on-trade like a wine maker or a realtor or someone like Bob Jane T-marts. Now being the king, he would be the owner of the company.

He is practical and believes in his senses, a real wheeler and dealer. He always reminds me of that Kenny Rogers song *The Gambler* who "Knows when to roll them, knows when to hold them, knows when to walk away and knows when to run".

His energy is traditional and conservative; there is respect for ancestry and old fashion values. He is cautious and shows love by spending money on you. He is a good provider, a good father and takes care of your physical needs but perhaps not your emotional needs. Overall, he is contented with what he has in life and whatever is of value to him.

He likes his walks in the garden, surrounded by pets of course. His home is his castle. He is resourceful; there is always a veggie garden to take care of or an interest in orchids and the like. He does not have trouble with retirement because he takes pleasure in the small things.

This is the only king, who in his later years, starts looking for the deeper meaning of life. For example, the value of giving flowers.

NEGATIVE

Not content with anything in life, stubborn, arrogant and a workaholic.

Impressed with people's status rather than getting to know them.

Possessive, totally materialistic and ignores the spiritual side, therefore it is difficult for him to show his emotions.

This King is now Mature and Confident to See All His Investments Grow

SYMBOLOGY

You can see a city in the background with different colored turrets signifying his successes and him having many fingers in many interests.

He is not holding the pentacle tightly, showing he is not worried about losing it. It is in his left hand (the unconscious side) as if to say it is not his main priority, which is opposite to the other kings. Either he values his spiritual side more or now he has the finances to support what he values.

There is blue in the background that is almost creeping into his coat, like an outline, as if it is a luminous light displaying his spiritual energy. He values his spiritual side; there is self-worth here, he is emanating it. The king should be enlightened.

The scepter in his right conscious hand signifies leadership. It shows he has status and looks good at doing the right thing.

As the most richly adorned king, there are grapes in his gown, displaying a lush greenery and a lush fruitful environment that is still growing. Grape vines are sturdy, tough and clingy plants which show you his style and tenacity in the area of his material wealth.

The crown also displays fruitful flowers and a victory wreath suggesting he is successful. He is creative, resourceful and victorious.

If you look at his left foot, it is revealing armor. He can take care of himself; the foot is resting on what looks like an armadillo – a prehistoric creature that wears plates of armor. This suggests he is thick-skinned, resilient and a hard nut to crack. This armor also connects us to the Emperor energy for he too wears armor and is thick-skinned.

There is a black throne suggesting an unknown factor or that he does things unconsciously. It may also symbolize that we really do not know how he made his money either.

There is also a grey base bringing in his wisdom. Really, we may not know how he has made his wealth but don't be fooled by his riches. He is a smart man and he knows how to protect his interests.

There are Taurus bull heads on the throne displaying his strength. He is powerful, like the bull, nor does he take any bull.

His eyes are closed as if he is aloof from what is going on around him.

Success with All the Finer Things in Life

IN A READING

He represents someone like a father, a husband, a lover or a sugar daddy. A giver, one who looks after your material needs rather than gives emotional support. He is a good provider.

He has mastered his money and his finances. All his efforts have paid off and he is now well off. All is secured. His wealth has been growing steadily and is now bearing fruit.

He has mastered his wealth, health and his well-being. He looks very comfortable.

Resolution in the area of wealth and his resources.

Has more time to enjoy his life now, having built his empire and know he can sit back and enjoy himself and his family.

They say money makes money!

If you need to see a professional about money, stocks, your tax accounts and financial business plan, the King of Pentacles is the king to see.

KING OF SWORDS - Mastery in the Mental Conflict Energy

**This may also be a warning card.

SUMMARY

The element is air, masculine energy and the three air zodiac signs are Gemini, Libra and Aquarius.

The two main ways of looking at this. One is that the king makes clear and decisive decisions. On the other hand, he represents someone you have crossed swords with and could be a trouble maker.

POSITIVE CHARACTERISTICS

One part is cool, calm and collected. He has inner strength and conviction.

He is a lover of truth and justice. He can judge harshly but usually it is fair. An authoritative figure, he is a strong silent type. He has conquered many personal and professional hardships, therefore judges according to his own experiences.

There is a power of determination and discrimination to him. He is a dependable and a wonderful person to have around, especially when there is a crisis. He is not an emotional type and that is why he is strong. He is very level headed.

He can be lawyer, judge, surgeon, scientist, educator, PR, journalist, a magician, a general in the army, solicitor, movie director, a strategist or a media mogul. In whatever area, he is a decision maker in the community.

He has strong beliefs and may be opinionated. If he has power and authority in his position, he will either be happy or he will be a rebel and really angry with a chip on his shoulder.

NEGATIVE

This king has masculine energy that can be harsh and untouchable. He can be cold and ruthless and not allow you to get through. He can cut you off easily. It is easy for him to detach himself and he may suffer from abandonment issues.

The elements of air and water are opposites. When not thinking clearly, you are emotionally plugged and cannot make a clear decision.

Cups and swords personality types both have escapism qualities in them. They both inadvertently hurt you. Cups energy tend to hurt themselves more by getting involved in emotional issues, then develop a drug, alcohol or food addiction to drown the pain. These are toxic dependent outlets. Whereas, the swords' energy comes from that logical rational or irrational head area – they can cut you off and hurt you or abuse you verbally and mentally with cutting words. Both are the hardest men to have around because of this split in them.

This King Uses his Logical Mental Abilities to Make Clear Responsible Decisions

SYMBOLOGY

He looks gentle in the card. The soft blue color brings in the serene energy and connects to spirituality and the High Priestess energy.

The magenta on his cape brings in wisdom and a higher knowledge and a higher mind, hence he is an authentic character. He could be a world class or world renowned astrologer or a polymath character like Dr John Demartini.

The inner color of orange on his cape shows his vitality and confidence. He is not sitting on a real throne, the backdrop looks like a wall hanging, very Spartan looking.

The red shoes show he has inner desires and that he is sexually active.

Unadorned with little gold, his only adornments are a crown and ring; this shows you his personality type. He is blunt, straightforward and has real masculine energy. His crown has the face of the lion and the wings of an eagle, which connect us to the sting of Scorpio and the lion of the Leo zodiac signs. They also represent a fixed intensity and that self-absorbed aspect.

There are butterflies on the backdrop displaying his freedom of thought. Two half moons and two birds flying above show you he is more emotionally balanced and there is a connection to the High Priestess again. The two figures over his left shoulder connect us to the Gemini zodiac sign and air element and another symbol of balance and choice.

In the background, the trees are still black, showing you his cut and dry manner and his sharp mind and thoughts. There is no wind now, you can see the trees are standing upright suggesting he is more settled. There are not so many clouds now showing he has more clarity.

The sword is resting more comfortably in his hand and he is less likely to use it than the queen or the knight. It looks less ready for use and he feels more comfortable with it. He thinks more now before speaking and can temper his temper. The sword shows two colors and therefore his two sides.

He is looking straight at you, suggesting you know where he and you stand. But be aware because the ground looks uneven, the unsteadiness referring to him being an unstable character – remember the escapism quality. Beware where you tread with him because he can change his mind. Get it in writing. You cannot push him too far. Be clear with him.

Powerful and Meaningful Determination

IN A READING

This king has mastery over the decision making process and in making the right decisions. It is a clear card. He is clear headed, clean cut, crisp and has clear energy.

He makes clear concise decisions and choices because he comes across as stable with strength and truthfulness. He is someone with clear thoughts, a clear mind and has great ideas.

It is a good time to put it in writing or write a letter or have a meeting for clear communication and therefore a successful meeting.

This card may represent consulting with a professional, like an Attorney, or signing a pre-nuptial agreement or signing a contract, completing a settlement or closing a successful deal, or a done deal as they say.

Resolution in the area of mental conflicts and decision making.

There is a warning with this card, so please go gently with it. You may be dealing with an ex-husband, an ex-lover or a man acting aggressively towards you; you could be dealing with domestic violence, someone displaying cruel action and who uses cutting words against you. Someone that cuts you down to size, cuts you off at the knees, has a sharp tongue and gives you verbal and mental abuse.

If you need to see a professional about making decisions, legal matters and dealings with the law, the King of Swords is the king to see.

KING OF CUPS - Mastery in the area of Feelings and Emotions

SUMMARY

The element is water, feminine energy and the three water zodiac signs are Cancer, Scorpio and Pisces.

Either he represents the love in the reading or is a much loved special someone such as a father or someone that loves you and supports you unconditionally.

POSITIVE CHARACTERISTICS

If the knight grows up positively, he will have a deep understanding of life. He will have an inner psychological, spiritual meaning and powerful subconscious intuition.

This king is sincere and powerful and has emotional energy with strong beliefs and morals. He is courageous and motivating as well as having a strong imagination and great creativity.

He may not seem intense and passionate but when you get to know him, you will see it. He could come across as shy, quiet and reserved.

He has a genuine concern for loved-ones and society in general. His personality types are like: Bob Hawke, John Denver, Robert Kiyosaki, Dr Wayne Dyer, Deepak Chopra, Anthony Robbins, John F. Kennedy, Martin Luther King, Dalai Lama, Nelson Mandela, Rev. Desmond Tutu, Mahatma Gandhi and The Pope.

He is also found in creative areas, such as the arts, medicine, and in counselors, good Samaritans, ministry, social workers, therapists, poets and musicians like: Paul Kelly, Bono, Sir Bob Geldof, Eddie Vedder and Sir Paul McCartney.

All these personality types understand deep loss and help people deal with these issues.

NEGATIVE

He is emotionally immature and denies his intense feelings, therefore can become defensive.

He often needs substances to drown the feelings, his sorrows and his pain like drugs, alcohol, sex, pornography, food, money problems, gambling, etc.

They are addictive personality types with obsessive compulsive disorder. They could be insatiable and never feel like it is ever enough and also relying on being co-dependent. They can be a frightened soul and can put up a front that looks weak, needy, ineffective and even hostile.

Remember, air and water are opposites and just like the king of swords, we may be looking at two personality types. We could have a wonderful man who can express his feelings and everyone loves him, or have the exact opposite – a jealous, frightened, angry man that takes it out on everyone around him. Passive passive or an aggressive aggressive.

He can be made positive if he works in this area and lets his feelings out in a constructive positive way. A couple of things he can partake in are music lessons or even Taekwondo and marital arts to give him a constructive creative outlet for his emotions.

Some reasons why he would turn negative are:
- A negative relationship experience.
- As a child, he was not encouraged to show his feelings.
- An addiction to alcohol could have turned him violent and he ends up with weak behavior.
- Loss of his dream; life hasn't measured up to his expectations.
- He has grown up with a dysfunctional family and does not know another way.
- He has suffered abuse of some sort in his youth and never handled it or healed it.
- He was conditioned as a child like that crazy Australian movie *Bad Boy Bubby*. In this movie, the child grows to understand why he is the way he is and finally he ends up in a happy, loving family environment.

This King is Sensitive and Has Empathy Towards Your Emotional Needs

SYMBOLOGY

He is perfectly at ease with his emotions. Look at him totally balanced, sitting on his stone throne in the middle of the water, as if balanced, with all the rocky emotions lapping up around his feet. The ships are perfectly balanced on either side of him. There is a ship on one side and a fish on the other side. He is steady as a rock.

The blue garment he wears brings in a positive High Priestess energy, tapping into spirituality and his emotional side. The gold collar connects us to his golden spiritual intellect and soul power. The red shows his strength, passion and positive energy. He is passionate about his beliefs.

There is a pillar on his throne connecting us to the High Priestess and the Hierophant cards. He is a pillar of strength; against all adversity he stands by his morals.

There is a fish around his neck. Fish display spirituality, initiative, psychic abilities and interests in the esoteric side. Fish connect us to the unconscious emotional spiritual world.

The scepter in his left hand (his unconscious side) displays his dominion and leadership qualities in this area. The cup in his conscious right hand side suggests he has mastered it and he is aware of his emotions. He has dominion over his spiritual world.

The crown is fancy showing his feminine, creative and artistic side. He has green fish scales on his feet. Green represents peace, healing and harmony and fish scales represent protection for the fish against their vulnerability.

He looks towards the left and his past memories.

Powerful Emotional Achievements

IN A READING

He has mastery over an emotional situation and mastery over his emotions.

He can represent a loving father and a much loved man such as a husband, a brother, a close loving relation or a grandfather. Remember Merlin who has the magic as the old man in the Ten of Pentacles card?

This king is supportive, loves you unconditionally and is a real nurturer.

He could represent a professional counselor and through his expertise you have now mastered the emotional issues. You are now healed. You have conquered and healed an emotional pain.

Resolution in the area of emotions, care giving and spiritual matters.

Remember the split in this personality type. He looks positive but can have a real Jekyll and Hyde personality. When the horns come out he could break your heart, although woman stay with this type of man because they see the loving side.

If you need to see a professional about psychological issues, healing matters or inspired with musical aspirations the King of Cups is the king to see.

This concludes the cards.

Congratulations you have mastered the tarot!

Section 4 - Attachments

Attachment 1

Recommended Book List - Excel Spreadsheet

ASTROLOGY

Book Title	Author
Astrology Psychology & the 4 Elements	Stephen Arroyd
Astrological Houses	Dane Rudhyar
Relationships & Life Cycles	Stephen Arroyd
The Only Way to Learn Astrology. Vol 1	March & McEvers
The Only Way to Learn Astrology. Vol 2	March & McEvers
The Only Way to Learn Astrology. Vol 3	March & McEvers
Astrological Insights Into Personality	Betty Lundsted
Saturn: A New Look at an Old Devil	Liz Greene
Archetypes of the Zodiac	Kathleen Burt
The Twelve Houses	Howard Sasportas
American Ephemeris for the 20th Century	Neil Michelsen
American Ephemeris for the 21st Century	Neil Michelsen
The American Book of Tables	Neil Michelsen

NUMEROLOGY

Book Title	Author
Life You Were Born To Live	Dan Millman
Discovering The Inner Self	David Phillips
Numbers of Love	Robin Stein
Colours & Numbers	Louise Hay
Your Key to Your Success	Thomas Muldoon

MEDITATION

Book Title	Author
Sacred Space	Denise Linn
Meditation Pure & Simple	Ian Gawler
Meditation For Everybody	Louis Proto
Meditaion Book	Shaki Gawain
Creative Visualisation	Shaki Gawain
Falun Daffa	
Buddhist Chant	
Hare Krishnas	

TAROT

Book Title	Author
The Artistrs Way a Spiritual Path	Julia Cameron
78 Degrees of Wisdom	Rachel Pollack
Care of the Soul	Thomas Moore
The Tarot Revealed	Paul Fenton-Smith
Super Tarot	Sasha Fenton
The Mythic Tarot Set	Juliet Sharman Burke & Liz Greene
The Secrets of the Tarot	Barbara Walker
The Tarot	Cynthia Giles
Tarot Spells	Janina Renee
The Women's History of the World	Rosalind Miles
Tarot For Yourself Workbook	Mary Greer
Wheel of Tarot - A New Revolution Tarot	Anthonology by James Wanless & Angeles Arrien
Tarot	Paul Foster Case
The Mythic Tarot Set	
Mythic Tarot	Sharman-Burke
Tarot Handbook for Apprentice	Eileen Connolly
The Thursday Night Tarot	Jason Lotterhead
Tarot & Individuation	Eileen Gad
Rider Waite Tarot Deck	Arthur Edward Waite
Man and His Symbols	Carl Jung
Tarot Myths & Secrets	Barbara Walker

MOVIES / DOCUMENTRY

Title	Author
The Secret	
What The Bleep Do We Know	
Further Down The Rabbit Hole	
The People Versus The State of Illusion	
Thrive	
Zeitgeist: The Movie	
Zeitgeist: Addenoum	
Cosmos	
Black Hole	Nassim Haremein
From Ambition to Meaning	Wayne Dyer

GENERAL INTEREST

Book Title	Author
Women who run with the wolves	Clarissa Pinkola Estes
Dance of Anger	Harriet Lerner
Dance of Intimacy	Harriet Lerner
Dance of Deception	Harriet Lerner
You Can Heal Your Body	Louise Hay
The Psychology of Romantic Love	Robert A. Johnson
Own Your Own Shadow	Robert A. Johnson
The Masks of Gods	Joesph Campbell
The Inner World of Children	Frances Wickers
Conversations With God. Book 1	Neale Donald Walshe
Conversations With God. Book 2	Neale Donald Walshe
Conversations With God. Book 3	Neale Donald Walshe
The Bodacious Book of Succulence	Sark
Succulent Wild Woman	Sark
The Power of Love	Marianne Williamson
The Course of Miracles	Marianne Williamson
Anatomy of the Spirit	Carolyn Myss
Mists of Avalon	Mary Stewart
Women are from Venus Men Mars	Dr John Gray
Venus and Mars in The Bedroom	Dr John Gray
The Magician's Way	Willem Whitehead
The New Earth	Eckhart Tolle
The Power of Now	Eckhart Tolle
Many Lives Many Masters	Brian Weiss
Intuitive Thinking or Spiritula Path	Rudolf Steiner
Of Gods and Fighting Men	Lady Gregory Smith
Who Moved The Cheese	Spencer Johnson MD
Understanding Jung Understanding Yourself	Peter A. O'Connor
The Alchemist	Paolo Coello
Clestine Prophecy	James Redfield
The Red Tent	Anita Diamant
Dying to Be Yourself	Anita Moorjani

Book Title	Author
Life Between Lives	Dr Michael Newton
Power Versus Forces	David R. Hawkins MD
Breaking the Habit of Being Yourself	Dr Joe Dispenza
The Course Happiness	Frederic Lenoir
The Biology of Belief	Bruce H. Lipton Ph.D.
Eat Pray Love	Elizabeth Gilbert
Real Magic	Wayne Dyer
The E Myth	Michael Gerber
In Search of Excellence	Thomas J. Peters & Robert H. Waterman Jr
7 Highly Habits for Highly Effective People	Stevy Covey
The Midas Touch	Donald J. Trump & Robert T. Kiyosaki
Rich Dad Poor Dad	Robert Kiyosaki

Games

Title	Author
Cashflow	Robert Kiyosaki

Attachment 2

PSYCHOLOGY

ARCHETYPE: Content of the rational collective unconscious consisting of inherited ideas and predispositions. An original model or type after which other similar things are patterned; e.g.: a prototype.

THE EGO: The Self or particularly an individual's perception of the Self. The division of the psyche that is conscious, most immediately controls thought and behavior.

THE SELF: Not a psychological definition, but in context of Tarot and other spiritual disciplines pertains to the Soul or the Spirit of an individual. The total, essential, or particular being of a person; the individual. The True Self.

SHADOW: The unconscious opposite of what an individual expresses in his consciousness. What an individual cannot see about themselves. The Devil represents the shadow in the Tarot.

PERSONA: A mask. The aspect of the personality that is involved in playing a role. The role that one assumes or displays in public or society; one's public image or personality, as distinguished from the inner self. In astrology, this is defined by an individual's sign on the Ascendant.

CONSCIOUS: Awareness or knowing. Pertaining to the process of being aware. Characterized by, or having an awareness of one's environment and one's own existence, sensations, and thoughts. Mentally perceptive or alert; awake. Capable of thought, will, or perception.

UNCONSCIOUS: Characterizing an activity for which the individual does not know the reason or motive for an act. Lacking awareness and the capacity for sensory perception; not conscious. Pertaining to all psychic processes which cannot be brought to awareness by ordinary means, the seat of repressions. Altered States.

PERSONAL UNCONSCIOUS: A part of the unconscious, which arises from the individual's experience, as contrasted with the collective or rational, unconscious. Caused by the environment and or conditioning. Freudian term 'No man's land.'

COLLECTIVE UNCONSCIOUS: Jungian term proposing that part of the unconscious which is inherited and, which is common to all humans. It is the seat of the archetypes.

SUB-CONSCIOUS: Freudian word which means a transition zone through which any repressed material must pass on its way from the unconscious to consciousness. Muscle memory; the Automatic Pilot.

PRECONSCIOUS: A process of which the individual is not aware but can be brought to consciousness. Memories fall into this category. Archive section, where a memory has no effect on you.

SUPERCONSCIOUS: Above our normal way of thinking. Our Higher Self, our Moral Self. Spirit energy. Doing something special and coming from that higher ground. Angelic energy.

Attachment 3

Astrology

First House: Aries
Dates: 21 March – 19 April | Planet: Mars
Fire element, Cardinal mode, Personal, Masculine energy, Positive.
To be, Being, Personality, Self-expression, My impact on the environment, rules the head area. Appearance, outlook, vitality, identity, self image, body type, own birth, the questioner, they forget they have a body, risk takers, fiery, the ram, color red.

Second House: Taurus
Dates: 20 April – 20 May | Planet: Venus
Earth element, Fixed mode, Personal, Feminine energy, Negative.
To use, having, security, stability, sense of self-worth, rules the throat and ears area. Earning ability, finances, capacity for pleasure, the five senses, wealth, resources, earthy, the bull, resourcefulness, self-esteem, money and possessions, food, values, color brown.

Third House: Gemini,
Dates: 21 May – 21 June | Planet: Mercury
Air element, Mutable mode, Personal, Masculine energy, Positive.
To understand, informing, mind, mental attitude, education, speech, talkative, rules the lungs area, communication, concrete mind, writing, speaking/language skills, siblings and neighbors, twins, early environment, movement, early learning, local affairs, color orange.

Fourth House: Cancer
Dates: 22 June – 22 July | Planet: Moon
Water element, Cardinal mode, Personal, Feminine energy, Negative.
Maintaining, source, childhood, mother image, crab, moody, feelers, rules the breast area. Family, family roots, nurturing parent, emotional security, foundations, family of origin, home, heritage, end of life, mother, premises both home and work, basic family unit, color sandy.

Fifth House: Leo
Dates: 23 July – 22 August | Planet: Sun
Fire element, Fixed mode, Interpersonal, Masculine energy, Positive.
Expressing, creative expression, naiveté, positive, generous, optimistic, rules the heart and solar plexus area, love affairs, romance, pleasure, recreation, gambling, hobbies, creativity, inner child, play/fun, children, amusements, lovers, enterprises, speculation in business or gambles, color yellow/gold.

Sixth House: Virgo
Dates: 23 August – 22 September | Planet: Mercury

Earth element, Mutable mode, Interpersonal, Feminine energy, Negative.
Transforming, self-purification, rituals, habits, attitude at work, creative, rules digestion system. Work, health, day to day routine, hygiene/diet, pets, short illnesses, self protection, duty, service, hospitals, bosses and employees, color dark green.

Seventh House: Libra
Dates: 23 September – 22 October | Planet: Venus
Air element, Cardinal mode, Interpersonal, Masculine energy, Positive.
Being, awareness of others, balance, harmony, scales, rules the kidneys and ovaries. Partnerships, marriage, co-operation, counsellor/client, mirrored awareness, decisions, also house of enemies, what they're doing the concern to them, color light green.

Eighth House: Scorpio
Dates: 23 October – 21 November | Planet: Pluto
Water element, Cardinal mode, Interpersonal, Feminine energy, Negative.
Having, crisis, emotional and sexual union, regeneration, rules the sexual organs. Intimate relationships, sex, inheritance, corporate or shared money, birth and death, endings, union/love, re-incarnation, healing, letting-go, deeper side of life, color Aqua.

Ninth House: Sagittarius
Dates: 22 November – 21 December | Planet: Jupiter
Fire element, Mutable mode, Transpersonal, Masculine energy, Positive.
Informing, aspiration, search for meaning, religious views, god-image, rules thigh and knees. Belief system, travel and foreigners, metaphysics, law, cross/cultural awareness, philosophy, religion/mysticism, higher education, outdoor life, color light blue.

Tenth House: Capricorn
Dates: 21 December – 19 January | Planet: Saturn
Earth element, Cardinal mode, Transpersonal, Feminine energy, Negative.
Maintaining, persona, social values, father image, rules, hard task master, rules the knees and calf area. Profession/career, ambition, reputation/social status, authority figures, goals, socializing parent, aims, don't really ask for what they want, Color Navy Blue.

Eleventh House: Aquarius
Dates: 20 January – 19 February | Planet: Uranus
Air element, Fixed mode, Transpersonal, Masculine energy, Positive.
Expressing, group awareness, social consciousness and concerns, highly Intelligent, Rules Ankles. Friend/colleagues, group involvement, hopes/wishes, ideals, social activity, clubs, intellectual, hobbies, organizations, aware of environment, revolutionary, radicals, color violet.

Twelfth House: Pisces
Dates: 19 February – 20 March | Planet: Neptune
Water element, Mutable mode, Transpersonal, Feminine energy, Negative.
Transforming, collective unconscious, self-transcendence, psyche, sacrifice, family fate, rules feet. Places of confinements eg: hospitals, hidden strengths, isolation and retreat, spiritual awareness, meditation, dreams and images, long or chronic illness, mourning, inner self, inner peace/terror, victim/myrtar personality, psychic sponges, creative, artists, poets, color purple.

Attachment 4

COLORS

You can use these same colors for house paints or for the color of your car, be creative. I remember one student saying, "That's why I drove a yellow car when I was at University. It was when I used all the mental attributes, both for study and for the stress."

BLACK Unknown energy, imponderable, unmanifested light and the unconscious.
Black is the source of life as well as its end and absorbs all colors.
Black allows you to deal with your shadow side.
Black and white together make gray and represents wisdom. Black hair symbols ignorance.

GRAY Deliberation, analysis, fear, detachment, aloofness and wisdom.
The Hermit is dressed in Gray; he is aloof and does bring up fear.

BLUE Intuition, awareness, inner peace, emotions and feelings.
Throat chakra.

BROWN Practicality, security, solidity, physical sacrifice, hard work, commitment and responsibility.

GOLDEN YELLOW Wisdom combined with knowledge. Service to others. Selfless giving. The Source, the Force, Divine, God, and Godliness.
Solar plexus chakra.

YELLOW Intellect, ideas, expansion, logic, awareness, mind, thoughts, discrimination and discernment.

GREEN Peace, healing, compassion, harmony, adaptability, fruitful, fertility, creativity, potential, hope, lushness, abundance, harmony, growth and living color.
The negative for the color green would be a lack of judgment, agenda, envy, and jealousy.

MAGENTA Nobility and truth. The blending of spirit and matter on a higher vibration.

PURPLE	Power, authority, regal and royalty.
VIOLET	High ideals, inspiration, intuition. Color of spiritual life. Third eye chakra.
ORANGE	Pride, vitality, independence, confidence, courage, openness and warmth. Sacral Chakra.
PINK	Unconditional love, devotion, tenderness, sensitivity.
RED	Desires, passions, courage, willpower, lust, sexual. We give red roses for Valentine's Day. Base chakra.
SILVER	Cool emotions and Mystical powers. Connects to all the Armor the knights are wearing.
WHITE	Purity, perfection and The Spirit. Just like when you put all white garments on a new born. Crown chakra.

Attachment 5

NUMEROLOGY

Number	Key Words	Other Key Words
1.	Independence Originality	Beginnings, Ideas, Invention, Will, Leaders, Boss, Alone, Masculine, Planting a Seed, Alone, Boss, Unique, Initiative, Birth, Own business, Being Number 1.
2.	Balance Choice	Waiting, Sharing, Patience, Cooperation, Scales, Diplomacy, Peace, Harmony, Receptivity, Feminine, Equality, Fairness, Duality, Equilibrium.
3.	Creative Growth	Expansion, Communication, Fertility, Creative Expression, Scattering, Potential, Green, Busy, Artistic, Fun, Growth, Opportunity, Possibility.
4.	Stability and Foundations	Security, Endurance, Application, Order, Organization, Practicality, Restriction, Boundaries, Control, Containment, Structure, Brown.
5.	Change	Unexpected changes, Freedom, Movement, Self-expression, Excess, Travel, Movement, Unusual, Upgrade, Extrovert, Upgrade, No 9-5.
6.	Harmony	Service, Beauty, Protection, Adjustment, Vulnerability, Discrimination, Family, Love/Hate, Peacemakers, Restoring, Choice, Peacemaker.
7.	Reassessment	Perfecting, Order, Discipline, Aloneness, Introspection, Inner-conflict, Faith, Spirituality, Meditation, Research, Plan, Prepare, Think, Weigh up.
8.	Power and Balance	Strength, Success, Recognition, Withdrawal, Honesty, Emotionalism, Enlargement, Prosperity, Wealth, Courage, Money, Values, Heart, Fruit of Labor, Heart.

Number	Key Words	Other Key Words
9.	Completion	Inspiration, Truth, Magnetism, Introspection, Wisdom, Dissipation, Sensitivity, Solitude, Healing, Healer, Ended, Responsibility, Hermit, Clean up time, Completion, End of a Cycle.
10.	Transcendence	Regeneration, Loyalty, Beginning of a new cycle on the next level, Renewal, Recycle, Up the Ante, Wheel of Fortune.
ACE	Triumph	Purity of Energy, Triumph, Success, Unconditional, Attainment, Fulfilled, Perfect, Aced it, Pure essence, Pure unto itself.
0.	Knowledge	Deeper Knowledge and Deeper Understanding, Infinity, Ohm, Spirit, Infinity number, Cycles, Unity, Wholeness, No Beginning No End.
11, 22, 33, 44	Master Numbers	Special Workers, Carers, Teachers, Healers, Environment workers, Animal carers. Spirit has come to help others or pay back karma. Eventually fall into the bucket, or miss out on making real difference.

Attachment 6

SYMBOLOGY

ANIMA   Feminine energy within a male. Soul. Latin. Soul Mama. Soul Food. Soulful.

ANIMUS   Masculine energy within a female. Spirit. Spirited Energy.

ANIMAL   Representing the instinctual. Desirous nature. Unconscious aspects.

ANKH   Egyptian cross. Symbol of life. Union of Masculine and Feminine. Venus Symbol.

ANGEL   Invisible forces. Protection. Spiritual Messages. Message from above.

BLOOD   Life force vitality, confidence, life.

BELL   Creative power from Spirit. A Spiritual calling. A wake up call.

BRIDGE   Transition from one state to the next. A process of correlating. A Link to the other side. Connecting two things.

BIRDS   Associated with air. Intellect. Spiritual Messengers. Air Head. Flighty or in Formation.

BUTTERFLY   Freedom. Butterflies are free. Rebirth, transcendence, transformation.

BOLT   Victory. Commitment energy such as marriage, shackled, locked up, tied up and secured.

CADEUSES   Dr Snakes. Symbol of healing and medicine. DNA helix. Universal symbol of medicine and chemists.

CASTLE   Security, seclusion, permanence, solidity, set in stone, aa fort, stability and integrity, protection for the whole community, aa Community Lives there, material world.

CAT   Associated with the Moon Goddess Bast who is the guardian of marriage. A symbol of magic, intuitive.

CAVE   Containment and regeneration, symbol of the womb of the Great Mother.

Site of sacred rites, rebirth.

CHAINS   Bondage, restriction, linkages, solidity, in the dark, to harsh.

CHILD   Development stage, children are our future, innocence and purity immaturity and naiveté. Children also represent healing.

CITY   Protection symbol, daily life, routine, a community, sharing, taking your wears to town, making big money in the city.

CLOAK   Sign of superior dignity OR a veil cutting a person off from the world, covering or hiding something inside.

CLOTHING   Outward and external representation of the internal psyche. Denotes position in life.

CLOUDS   **Light Grey:** fertility symbol, symbolic messengers, images, air element.
Dark Grey: confusion and depressed. In the dark, sadness and tears.

COFFIN   Represents the physical world, restriction, death, symbol of boxing yourself in.

COLUMN   Support, positive or negative, self-affirmation, symbol of power and strength, holds up the roof.

CORN   Nurturing, growth, a symbol of fertility, goddess Demeter rules agriculture.

CROSS   The relationship between the spiritual and physical worlds, connecting. Union of opposites.

ST ANDREW'S CROSS   Union of upper and lower worlds, conjunction of Opposites, union of masculine and feminine.

CROWN   Success, recognition as the highest of achievement, ego.

CUP / VESSEL / URN   Feminine principle, receptive, receptacle and receiving, the chalice. God's love, Divine love, holds water and emotions.

DOG   Man's best friend, the instinctual world, your instincts are loyal to you, just like dog's.

DOVE   Spirit, soul, loyalty and higher faith, symbol of peace, God's messenger, spirit.

DWARF   A symbol of the forces which remain outside the orbit of consciousness. A mischievous being with childlike characteristics, a protector. Found in fairy tales. Jung says they can be regarded as the guardians of the threshold of the unconscious. Can be seen as abnormal by man and signifying the blindness or ignorance of man, stunted growth.

FALCON   A ruthless pursuer, like the eagle they are birds of prey, can Fly as high as eagle. Can be Trained, fly over 300 Km's per hour with skill.

FEET   Connects to your soul, support, progress and freedom, standing steady and standing on your own two feet, standing alone, feeling settled within.
>   **Right Foot:** progress in spiritual purity.
>   **Left Foot:** lack in expression of spiritual potential.

FEATHERS   Corresponds to the air element, intellect, contemplation, connects to angels and spiritual messengers.

FISH   Fecundity, fertile, fruitful, fertilize, spiritual world, surge of life force, the unconscious, creativity.

FLAME   Corresponds to fire element and the spirit, spirited, transcendence, burning idea, fiery personality.

GARDEN   A place where nature is subdued and controlled, subconscious mind, also connects to family, beautiful family and family tree.

GLOVE   Gloved hand, Armed against someone, not disclosing mind or feelings, protection symbol like an apron, a covering.

GOAT   Capricorn, use of force rather than higher will, goats climb mountains, they just get on with things, high climber high achiever.

GRAVE   A place where the spirits of the dead rest and rise from, resurrection, rebirth.

TOMB   A symbolic place of transformation, a door between worlds.

HAT   Thought, ideas, thinking and planning, bright ideas.
>   **Red hat:** desirous thoughts
>   **Grey Hat:** thoughts of wisdom.

HEART   Love, the Sun connects to Leo, eternity, center of Illumination, solar plexus. Symbol of courage, wearing your heart on your sleeve.

HELMET   Lofty thoughts OR hidden thoughts if visor is lowered, security in defense, not revealing your ideas.

HOOD   Spiritual world, psychic invisibility, repression, The Hermit, solitude.

HORSE   Your vehicle through life, traditionally represents masculine active energy, it's happening right now.

IRIS   Greek Goddess of the Rainbow, the goddess energy manifested in the world, connects us to nature and the earth.

KEYS   Mystery, a task to be performed and the means of carrying it out, threshold of unconscious, instinct and knowledge, unlocking a mystery or keeping things under lock and key

LEFT SIDE   The Unconscious, feminine, sinister side, receptive and creative side.

LANTERN   Symbol of individual life in the face of cosmic existence, guidance, illumination. The Hermit's lamp, the light within, seeing the light, consciousness, Spirituality and the truth.

LEATHER   Enduring quality, study and long lasting, comfortable and well worn.

LEMNISCATE   Symbol of the infinity and cycles, balancing, the number 8, prosperity and inner wealth.

LIGHTENING   The planet Uranus - Flash of fire, spirited, destruction and/or change. A demand to illuminate, enlightenment, the bolt of out the blue, shocking.

LION   Zodiac sign of Leo, gold, the sun, king of beasts, virility, powerful, willpower, regal and royalty, pride of a lion.

LOTUS LILY   Symbol of Godliness, spirituality, symbol of devotion, usually seen as a white flower, purity and virginity, a symbol of pure religious.

MARSH   Inactivity, water and earth together are both passive feminine elements. Inability to move ahead, swampy condition, stuck in the mud.

MOUNTAINS   Aspirations, conquering and conquests, meditation and greatness, peaks and valleys of life, represents the great mother, womb of mother, to climb, to conquer.
   Purple: spiritual aspirations.
   White: purity and intelligence.
   Orange: confidence and vitality.
   Blue: conquer inner truth.

MOON   Zodiac sign of Cancer, feelings and female principle, Yang energy, strengths and dangers of the world of appearances, imagination world, night principle, full moon symbolizes feelings are at their peak.

NAKED   Exposure, vulnerability, open and honest, back to basics, open to nature, natural.

OUROBOROS   Dragon, snake or serpent biting its own tail, symbolic of time and the continuity of life, self persecution, cycles, Phoenix rising out of the ashes.

OAK TREE/ACORN   Strength and antiquity, hard nut to crack, strong and sturdy tree, resourceful and powerful.

OLIVE BRANCH   Symbol of peace, peace of mind, the storm has passed.

PALM LEAF   Feminine principle, nurturing, symbol of victory, victorious, winning!

PENTACLE   Five pointed star symbolizing a person with arms and legs outstretched who is receiving spiritual inspiration through five points – head, hands and two feet, protection symbol.

PHOENIX   Resurrection, new life, the ability to renew one self, Phoenix rising out of the ashes.

POMEGRANATE   Fertility and abundance, feminine fertility symbol, fruit of love, forbidden Fruit, the reproductive system, the undeveloped creative potential.

RABBIT   Timidity, harmlessness, in need of protection, fertility symbol, connects to nature, fecundity and populate everywhere.

RAIN   Fertilizing agent, life, water, purification, spiritual influence, falling from heaven, cleansing tears, washing and healing.

RAINBOW   Enlightenment, power to rise spiritually, symbol of connecting two levels, the spiritual and the material, brightness of the future. The Pot of Gold, the storm has passed.

RAM   Symbol for Aries, ancient symbol of sacrifice, energy of Mars, aggressive or assertive, powerful and Fire energy.

RIGHT SIDE   Conscious mind, masculine, active energy, logic.

RIVER   Life is flowing, feelings and emotions, irreversible passage of time, water under the bridge, a river runs through it.

ROSES **Red** - desires, passionate love, immortality, lust.
White - purity and innocence.
Yellow - peace and friendship.
Pink - love and devotion.

SALAMANDER Mythological creature, spirit which inhabits the element of fire, can withstand heat and pressure, versatile and adaptable, transmutes, feisty.

SAND Shifting surface, not firm ground, not terra firma, risks involved. shifting sands, about to change direction in Life.

SCALES The sign of Libra, justice, balance, harmony, the symbol of truth, weighing up your truth, balancing the emotions with the rational.

SCROLLS Symbol of knowledge and wisdom, The Tora. Five Books of Moses. Old Testament.

SCEPTRE Light and purification, emblem of fertility, symbol of rulership and authority.

SEA Source of life, the Collective Unconscious, Sea of Knowledge, Sea of Wisdom. Water retains memory.

SHELLS The goodness and wisdom of God, protection of providence, connects to the sea, symbol of protection for fish, crabs, etc.

SHIP Negotiating life, represents the physical body, balanced on the seas no matter how rough, riding the waves, travel and ships passing in the night, process of growth. Change movement.

SHOES **Red:** connects to the female sexual organ, the lower nature. Sexually active. Dorothy's magical red shoes from the *Wizard of Oz*.
Yellow: soul connection, soul mates.
White: inner purity, the answers are within, connect to your soul.

SKULL Skull and cross bones, the dead, be aware, poison, pirates, deadly symbol.

SNAIL The action of a microcosmic spiral upon matter, snail mail, leaves a trail and connects us to our past roots, humble, humility and fragility.

SNAKE / SERPENT Wisdom, transformation and sexual energy, feminine principle. Rebirth, life after life, Kundilini, base chakra, snake sheds its skin, Snake in the Grass.

SPHINX Two faces of birth and death, positive and negative. Symbol of protection. Greatness and power.

STARS Associated with the night, linked with multiplicity, higher level communication. When you wish upon a Star, we are all made out of star stuff.

SUN Light, life, wholeness, consciousness and constancy. Purification and tribulation. Energy and life force, brightness and positivity.

SUNFLOWER Courage, obedience and vitality, connects to the sun, heliotropic plant, fire element.

SWAMP Hidden dangers, instability and deceit, because of emotional issues.

SWORD Connects to the mind, ideas and mental conflicts, air element, clear thinking, can sever easily.

TENT Something which envelopes and hides things from sight, a protection from the elements, veil enshrouding mysteries of the world, protection and good luck.

THRONE Centre, stability, unity, exaltation, royalty and authority, power symbol.

TOWER Structure, consolidation, assertiveness, building castles in the air, also maybe a symbol of restriction.

TREES Consistency, growth, regenerative process, life and living symbol, immortality. Tree of life, connects this world with the next and the previous.

TRIANGLE **Up Right:** transcended consciousness, meditation, the Trinity.
Inverted: Secrecy, dark, evil, perversion, mystery, mystic nature.

TRUMPET Heralding news, declaration, a calling, the alarm clock, a spiritual awakening like church bells.

VENUS Goddess of love, planet Venus, spiritual love and sexual attraction, containment, abundant, unconditional and creative, the cornucopia shell.

VILLAGES Daily life, routine, a community, sharing, taking your wears to Town.

VINE Natural creation, eternal life, symbol of abundance, sturdy plant, fruitful plant. Fertility, sacrifice, harvest, redemption.

WATER Feelings and emotions, Life, he unconscious world intuition and wisdom, potentiality, life, death and rebirth, meditation and dissolution.

WAND   Willpower, embodies implications of direction and intensity, represents your work, career, skills, talents, efforts and ideas, fire element and fertile energy.

WINDOW   Possibilities, consciousness, a way out, insights, looking up, illumination.
   Stained Glass: spirituality, colorful, hope, having faith, brightness of the future.

WREATH   Mandala, celebration of accomplishment, success and victory, completion, coming full circle, the circle of life, fecundity. garland and laurel.

YOD   **Jewish Kabbalah:** tenth Hebrew letter, represents cosmic side benefits, gifts from the universe, blessings in disguise.

Attachment 7

Homework Exercise - Tarot Activation

The purpose of this exercise is to get to know your cards and to put your energy into them. By handling them every day, you notice things on the cards you never noticed before. You will also open yourself up to using creative words, which will make you see the cards differently all the time.

Everyday. I suggest that you get a notebook for your notes and observations.

Shuffle the cards and pick a card every day. Some people like to pick the card in the morning, others in the evening, it does not matter when you decide to do it, just pick the card the same time every day so you will remember to do it every day.

1. Write the name of the card and the date on top of your page in your new notebook.

2. Then list 5 words that quickly come to mind. Do not think about these, just write them. Look at the card and write the first thing that comes up. You might pick the same card every day, three days in a row and different words will come up for you. This exercise is about getting your words out on paper.

3. Look at the card and note what your eyes keep looking at. Write this item down. I call it the Focus point. It may be a flower, it may be the horse, and it may be the road, whatever it is write this down.

4. Now it is time to activate it and put it into action. For example, if it is a flower, buy yourself flowers, or buy them for your mum, or spend some time in the garden, or wear a flower in your hair or a flowery shirt. Be creative. You do not have to go out of your way to do this work, keep it simple and you will do it.

5. Then before you choose the next Tarot card on the next day, write a summary of what you noticed, or what happened, or how you felt, or what you did or what people said about it. Perhaps look at the description of the card in this book as that will help you learn the card. You may also do a Google search and on the symbology or meaning of the flower. It is up to you to do the research as much as you want. The more you do, obviously the more insights you will have.

1. Name of Card: _____ Date: _____

2. 5 words to describe the card:

   _____

   _____

   _____

   _____

   _____

3. Focus point on the Card:

   _____

4. The Action:

   _____

   _____

5. The Summary after activating the focus point:

   _____

   _____

   _____

   _____

   _____

   _____

   _____

   _____

Attachment 8

The Hero's Journey

Attachment 9

Questions and Answers

Here are some questions that always seem to come up about tarot cards and doing tarot spreads. Some of the questions have already been answered, but I include them in case you missed them.

1. Tarot Cards

Q: Is it ok for other people to touch my cards?

A: I personally do not mind if other people touch my tarot cards. But I have had students that do not like other people to touch theirs. Some students have an extra deck and they use this deck for other people to touch. It is up to you.

If I am at an event doing tarot readings, like at a Hens Party for example, and everyone is eating finger food and handling drinks, I would prefer to do the shuffling myself, to cut the cards into three stacks and ask the client to pick between stack A, B or C. Then I would go from there without them having to touch the cards at all.

Q: Can I let another person use my tarot cards to do their own reading?

A: If you do not have a problem with this neither will the tarot cards.

In my classes, my students sometimes forget to bring in their tarot cards; I always have spare decks on hand they can use; or at times my students offer them their own cards to use, which is nice for them to offer.

The cards will always bring up the significant issues in the reading. So whether they are using their own cards or someone else's they will always bring up that important something for you to be made conscious of.

Q: Should tarot cards be gifted to you?

A: This is a myth. Of course it is very special when someone gifts you tarot cards, but this is not the rule.

I have bought many tarot cards for myself over the years. My students, after spending a good six months with me have also purchased many (various) decks for themselves. I have even purchased many decks from EBay.

Q: How to dispose of tarot cards?

A: You can gift them to someone you know that uses or has an interest in tarot, or are starting to learn and are collecting various decks. You can even sell them on EBay and allow someone else to purchase them for a good price.

Trust that the cards will always go to the right person. I would not burn tarot cards; to me this is simply a waste, you have loved them and put good energy into them, allow them to go to a new home, to someone who is going to love them, just like you did.

Q: Why use a scarf?

A: I prefer to use a scarf to wrap my cards in, to keep them all together before I put them away in their pouch or bag. I always feel like I am tucking them into bed for sleep. I also like to lay this scarf out on whatever surface to keep the cards clean when I am doing a tarot reading.

Q: How to store the tarot cards?

A: I suggest to keep them in anything that is natural and breathable. It does not matter if it is the original cardboard box they came in, or wrapped up in a silk scarf and then placed in a cotton bag or kept in a wooden box.

Q: Is it necessary to tap or knock the cards?

A: This is a cleansing act.

I have seen many people do this, some of my students do this and I have also done it at times myself to my cards when I felt they needed an extra hit or tap to release the unwanted energy. Three knocks will do the trick.

Q: Is it necessary to keep crystals with your tarot cards?

A: Crystals are used as a protection or another way to keep the tarot cards cleansed.

I do not think it is necessary to keep crystals with your tarot cards, but I do think it is a lovely thing to do. It does not matter what type of crystal you use; you can change them around as you attract new crystals into your life.

Crystals keep the tarot cards sharp and well protected. I think the best crystal to keep with them is the clear quartz as it has Piezo energy and you can program this crystal to be anything you want it to be. It is always a good one to start with.

Q: What is the best way to clean the cards?

A: Just keep the ritual easy and simple to do otherwise you will not do it.

Tapping or knocking the cards is a simple and an effective way. Some people might want to get a cloth and wipe them down individually, maybe a damp wet cloth if your tarot cards are plastic.

Holding the deck in your hand and simply blowing all over them works perfectly for me too.

Or put all the cards face down on the table and simply giving them a good old mixing up, spreading them right across the table and then bringing them all back in together into one stack, not knowing which ones are up the right way and which ones are reversed is an act I call "washing the cards".

Q: Which are the best tarot cards to work with?

Personally, I started tarot readings using the Rider Waite tarot deck and I have worked with them for years before I came across another tarot deck that I just had to have and I worked with this other deck for a few years and then I went back to the Rider Waite deck.

I found that the Rider Waite cards are the most popular, they are the most recognized and have the best symbolism in them. People are more comfortable with these cards because many readers use them, which makes them open to the reading.

Some tarot decks can really freak some people out. Even though you love the deck, the imagery for some people can really shut them down and this is not helpful when doing a reading.

I worked though many various decks over the years, worked with some longer than others. But, for yourself, one day a special deck may just appear for you that speaks to you, that you believe were made just for you, and you will change again.

Then there are also collector's editions, like the Salvador Dali tarot deck!

Q: Why are a lot of people attracted to the Aleister Crowley Thoth tarot deck?

A: I wanted to answer this question because I do have a lot of people that are interested in doing my tarot class but want to use and learn with the Thoth tarot cards throughout the class. Why are people attracted or interested in this particular deck?

Of course I welcome all sorts of tarot cards in my classes, even though I teach using the Rider Waite deck I do invite my students to bring other cards to see the similarities and or differences between all the cards.

The Thoth deck do work differently from the Rider Waite deck. The Thoth deck uses a different quality and they have a lot of power that people do not understand. When you do a reading with the Thoth tarot cards you really need to know your Astrology, Numerology and the Kabbalah to do the reading. You cannot use these cards in a normal tarot spread way, they work differently.

The Thoth cards are very masculine and have an intellectual energy about them, unlike the Rider Waite cards that have a feminine and intuitive energy. Thoth cards are very intense and for some are quite phallic looking; for example, the Strength card in the Rider Waite Deck is called Lust in the Thoth deck.

Then the court cards are set up differently. It is interesting that they hold this masculine energy, yet the Queen is on top of the pyramid in the court cards, it is the queen that makes the knight a King. Whereas the traditional King is the head in the Rider Waite court cards.

Q: Should I charge a fee for a reading?

A: There is always much debate about this question.

I have always taught my students to charge something, whether it is over a cup of coffee, a lunch or something else. But I like there to be this exchange, otherwise people will not value your reading nor your time. And you do not value yourself either!

I do not give discounts either. For example, if you really want something you will find the money to get it. If you do not want it bad enough, maybe you are not meant to have it. Because of this example, I find when people really want a tarot reading and pay for it, they will have the best reading, they will get their answers they are searching for, and you will put in more effort and energy into the reading because you are getting paid to do so.

I also suggest to my students that once they start charging for their readings, to start small, for example $20 for an hour reading, or pay for a reading and get one free. This is good training and a good exchange. You will intuitively know when you want to up your fees or change things around.

Q: Do readings work at Markets and Festivals when you are surrounded by many people and much noise?

A: I love doing readings at Markets and Festivals and still do so today, this is where I built my confidence and started practicing being with the public. I did not have to do hour long readings, just simple spreads and quick readings. You should be able to give your clients heaps of insights and answers in a fifteen or twenty-minute period.

When I do tarot readings at markets or festivals, I always charge a cheaper rate than when they visit me at my shop. I might charge something like $30 for a twenty minute reading or $20 for a three card spread. I tend not to do long readings at these types of places because I find I do not have the client's full attention, like I do when they come to see me at my shop. They may also have their friends waiting for them or their children.

I like the background noise. Anyway, the noise falls into the back ground, but on some unconscious level, it tells you exactly where you are. It is like when you sleep with the television on, as soon as someone switches it off, you wake up.

Q: Should I always ask the tarot cards a question?

A: Yes! I teach my students to always ask their clients, "do you have a question?" when they want a reading. There is a reason why the client wants a tarot reading, they are not readily going to spend their time or this much money on nothing. And if you only have thirty minutes to do the reading, then let's get to the point.

Asking a question when you do your daily card pull, whilst you are learning and activating the process is a good way to get answers.

If you do not have a specific question, then ask the cards for some guidance or to highlight something that you need to be made aware of.

I also found that people do not trust the cards or sometimes the reader, so they tend not to speak up at first. Then as they become more open, trusting and understand that they are safe they then want to ask all the questions at the end, but guess what, the thirty minutes is up!

It also does not matter when the question is asked. You may have already laid out the spread and then remembered to ask the client if they had a question. Trust your cards.

Q: Does learning tarot open me up to any psychic attacks or invite evil entities in?

A: No, this is a myth.

Today tarot readings are used as a psychological tool to get insights into oneself, to assure yourself that you are on track or not, to change course and get back on track.

Q: How often should you have a tarot reading?

A: As often as you like.

I encourage my students to pick one or two cards per day and to learn, activate and process this card into the day, to see if there are any connections or insights. This also allows you to see the card in many different ways; there are so many levels to each card.

If you have a client that wants to see you every week for a reading, I would consider this a problem, it is not right and I definitely would not encourage this behavior. I would talk to them about referring them onto a psychologist, to someone else professionally that can assist them with their issues.

Some tarot readers are not trained in counselling and psychology matters and can do more damage to the person. For example, they can open people up like opening up the flood gates, but then they do not know how to close the gates again. Professionals know how to open the gates slowly so the client feels in control through every step of the way.

I always recommend to my students to read specific books and do to various counselling courses to become a better tarot reader or what I like to call "a left brain and intuitive psychologist", as opposed to a right brain psychologist, someone that has learned psychology the traditional way.

Everyone does readings differently. My readings go for a year, so I have regular clients that come and visit me once a year. Some people come at the beginning of every year and others come on or around their birthday.

If someone is going through a tricky time, they may tend to visit a few different tarot readers to see if they are all saying the same thing, or if they can give different insights to give them more information, I think this is normal. But it is not normal when they ring the tarot phone lines every day and become infatuated with getting the answers they want to hear, then it becomes a problem.

Q: Is it ok to read my own tarot cards?

A: I believe it is ok to do so but I do hear many people say that they find it hard to do tarot readings for themselves. Or your sister finds it hard to do a reading for you. People say that they are so involved in the issue that they cannot see past it and that it is better to have another person do the reading for you.

Like everything, the more you practice the easier it is to do. This is why I encourage my students to pick a card per day, to train themselves to see more than what the cards appears to be so that they are open to doing readings for themselves and their close friends.

I have also suggested to record yourself doing a reading as if you are sitting with your client, to play it back and listen to yourself. Or simply take out your pen and paper and write down everything you see, put the pen down and walk away and come back to it again, to review it all and see what other insights have come through.

Q: Do I need to perform rituals before and after a tarot reading?

A: I think this is an important thing to do before and after a tarot reading.

Before a reading you can open your third eye, meditate for a few minutes to put you in a calm state, to also connect you with your higher self and then say a few words of power to enable you to do the best reading for your client.

Like in meditation when you take some deep breaths to calm you down, so you are feeling centered; this also tells your body to get ready to go to that special place again. There is also soft background music you can play and candles you can light to create the perfect space. All these are important and simple rituals you can easily do.

Then after the reading, you can close the third eye, tap your cards, like I mentioned in a prior question, in between readings through to washing your hands.

When I do day long festivals, I have various little methods and rituals I use to keep the cards clean in between the readings and the many clients. And at the end of the day having an extra-long shower and cleaning all my chakras is welcomed before a deep restful sleep.

Learning new tricks keeps it interesting and fun to do, as long as it is easy and simple to do, otherwise, if it is too hard, I find people will just not do it.

Q: If I do a reading and see bad things happening, how do I convey this to my client?

A: Firstly, I would like to say that every card has a positive and negative energy about them. And this question is one of the main reasons why I like to use tarot cards in a reading. Every card is full of archetypal imagery and on some level you and your client understand the meanings of these images. So, if bad things are seen in the cards, you both can see these things and already understand what is going on.

As an interpreter of the cards, I would say things may not be working out as well intended and if they keep going the way they are it will only get worse. I do try to relay the information in a sensitive way. Remember, that the client already understands this because the cards are confirming to them that something has to change.

Sometimes we can be so caught up in the issue we cannot see a way out. Sometimes the bad thing has to happen to turn us around. I remember Oprah saying, "that failure is that 'thing,' that gets you back on track." There is no such thing as failure.

Q: Is it ok to lie when doing a tarot reading?

A: I do not think it is a good idea to lie when doing a tarot reading, no it is not.

Personally, I convey the messages as sensitively as possible and as real as I see it, this is your responsibility. The client can see the images just as you do, they will know if you are lying.

I think in reality we all say 'Little white lies' to make a point or bring the idea across to the client, but I do not see this as lying to the client. One of my favorite sayings is, "Fake it till you make it".

If there are a lot of lies being told, there is a thing called "Karma". And as John Lennon put it in his song, "Instant karma's gonna get you".

Honesty and integrity are important, and this is why I love tarot cards. The client will always see the pictures, those archetypal images just as you do, and they will understand on some level what these images are referring too without you even having to say anything.

Q: Is there a good or better time of day to do a tarot reading?

A: Yes of course there is. During the day you are brighter, more alert and the readings will be clearer.

I do not recommend doing a reading if you are tired at the end of the working day. Even if you are at a party and have had a drink or two, people will ask you to do a reading, I would not suggest doing one here either. Even if someone makes you feel uneasy, you always have choice not to do the reading for them.

I have performed many tarot readings at parties, but I do not drink. I always bring my own beverage or I may have a lemonade if I am offered something to drink. If the party starts at seven pm, this is when I will commence the readings, while everyone is still arriving and I will leave after my two hours of work. From my experience the party gets louder and people are not listening to you anyway, they are there to party.

There are people that practice the darker occults and the night time is the best time for them to practice their rituals.

Q: Is it important to be sober when doing tarot readings?

A: Yes, absolutely. Respect the cards and they will respect you.

If you are under the influence of drugs or alcohol you are not honoring yourself, the cards, the client, nor the reading. How can you be? You are not in your right mind. You may think you are but you are not. You may see things and interpret them in an unrealistic way.

This is why there are rituals to center yourself, to be present, meditation to quiet the mind, to open yourself up to your higher self and most importantly, to be there for others. You have a responsibility to uphold.

Q: Is it appropriate to do a reading when the person is emotionally distressed?

A: Depending on how emotionally distressed they are. Sometimes giving them a glass of water, allowing them time to settle down, having a little discussion about what is going on first may help them.

Then you can say, let's see what the tarot cards have to say about this, and do a reading about the issue. You will continue the discussion of course, and bring in the cards to see if they confirm and support the situation or if they suggest something totally new and different.

Q: Is the reverse position of tarot cards really important? Can I ignore them?

A: When I start teaching my students, at first I get them to ignore the reverse meaning as it is tricky for them to tap into the energy of the card without having to complicate the matter.

Remember every card is positive and negative, the card does not have to be reversed to suggest the negative is going on.

I know some people that do not use reverse meanings at all. I also know people that do not use the heavier cards like Death, Devil, five swords, nine swords, etc. They will actually take them out of the deck.

Let us say that there are over ten different ways to read the meanings of the reversed cards. Sometimes the energy is blocked, a piece of the puzzle could be missing, maybe they are suggesting to wait a little while, maybe there is a bump in the road ahead, maybe it is a detour you just have to go the longer way round or maybe it is a flat out no!

Negative cards could sometimes bring in a positive message. It all depends on the question, the placement of the cards in the spread, or it may also depend on whether the client is a risk taker or not. Whatever the situation may be, think twice, take your time, or be mindful of your next step.

2. Spreads

Q: What are the best tarot spreads?

One of the best spreads I like to do is the simple Three Card Spread.

I especially like to do this spread when I am at an event like a Hens Party. There are usually about twenty ladies to do readings for in my two-hour time limit, this gives approximately five to six minutes to spend on each person. Any more than three cards and you would need to spend more time on the reading.

It is up to you how you read the three card spread, you can make up your own version or here are some suggestions for you to work through:

Good Old 3 Card Spread

A	B	C

A: Past	B: Present	C: Future
A: Idea	B: Action	C: Result
A: Her	B: The Relationship	C: Him
A: Focus	B: Challenge	C: Action
A: Parent	B: Child	C: Adult

Famous Celtic Cross

The other spread is the famous Celtic Cross spread. This is the most recognized spread in the world. I tend to lean on this one a lot when I do my hour sessions with clients because it covers so many areas. Once you know the positions off by heart, you can really get into it.

You may also decide to use a particular spread for a particular reading, as well as use particular tarot cards to answer specific questions. For example, you may choose to use the Lovers Tarot cards when you do a relationship reading and use The Lovers Spread.

Celtic Cross Spread

6. Life Lesson
Where are you going? If a Major is here it is more significant.

11. Probable Outcome
If a Major is here it is more significant.

11A. More insights into Outcome

11B. More insights into Outcome

1. Significant
What is significant about this reading. What is it all about.

2. Present Conscious
You should be aware of the energy of this card.

5. The Past Influence
See if this energy connects with the Present.

7. Immediate future
What is just around the corner. End of a chapter.

10. Hopes Fears and Expecta-tions
If a Major is here it is more significant.

3. Crossing Card
Either a Help or Hindrance card. This card gives you insight into what it may be.

9. Environ-ment
The stage your platform and how others see you.

12. The Clarifier
Only use if Outcome cards were not conclusive.

4. The Basis
Unconscious energy that wants to be made conscious.

8. The Self
This is your energy now. If a Major is here it is more significant.

Q: How long should the readings go for?

A: This is up to you.

You can use the simple three card spread and take up to an hour discussing the issues that arise, giving yourself and the client the time that is needed to discuss everything. Or just take five minutes to do a three card spread.

You can also take fifteen minutes to read a Celtic Cross spread or take this reading up to two hours. If you have the time and you are reading for a friend, two hours will seem like fifteen minutes.

Q: Is it important to stick to time limits?

If you are working in a shop and your readings are, for example, thirty minutes for $60, then you need to stick to your time limit because you have another client already waiting for their reading.

I always do my best to stick to the time limit even if I do readings for friends at home.

Q: Over what time period should you put on spreads?

A: Regarding timing on spreads, once again this is up to you. You can call how long the reading will last for.

For example, if it is the beginning of the new year, and I am doing a Celtic Spread, I would normally say the spread will last until the end of the year, because it will take all the year for the client to process everything that was discussed.

If I am doing the reading and it is only midyear, I would say the reading would last the whole year and half, take it right through to the end of the following year.

Q: If someone wants a relationship reading and all the wands cards show up in the spread (relating to work and career), do you answer them about their work or career?

A: Say that all the wands that have shown up are relating more towards the work and career life, you can also read these cards in reference to a relationship reading as well. For example, maybe they are working through a particular issue in their relationship, maybe this relationship is going to take much work. Maybe they met through the work place: many relationships do now-a-days, or maybe there is currently a lot of passion and energy between this couple.

Depending on the cards of course, and your interpretation of them, you should be able to tailor any tarot card in any spread for any question, in fact, you can use the one spread to either be a work and career reading, a relationship reading or even a personal growth reading. I teach my students to do this type of reading in my classes and without turning over any further cards.

Q: Can you do more than one spread for the client?

A: Of course you can. For example, you can start with a three card spread using only the Major Arcana to look at the bigger picture or the important theme that is currently going on in their life. Then follow this up with a Celtic Cross Spread using all the cards for the deeper insights.

I prefer not use a lot of cards or I stick to a couple of spreads when I do a reading for a client because I find the different spreads will show the same cards over again or they say the same story. If you do too many spreads, you can also confuse the client and/or contradict yourself.

Clients that want you to do many spreads have had an experience with a reader that uses many spreads in their readings and so the client thinks this is normal.

Q: Is it ok to design my own tarot deck or tarot spread?

A: Absolutely. What a wonderful and creative thing for you to do, especially if you are an artist. I would encourage you to create your own deck and to paint them in the colors that mean something to you.

There are also just plain black and white tarot cards already out there on the market place. This shows me that it does not even matter about the color, that it is the image that is archetypal and connects with your inner self.

There are also many books out there that are full of various spreads. Maybe get yourself some of these books to familiarize yourself and making yourself confident enough to then be able to create your own spread.

One of the items I get my students to do in my Tarot Advanced class is to create their own spread and then to practice it on each other in class.

Attachment 10

ACKNOWLEDGEMENTS and SOURCES

I have had a blessed life, and the reason is because I have had so many wonderful people in it. Here are some of them.

I loved all my Astrology education with Astro Synthesis, Brian Clark and Glenys Lawton at The Chiron Centre. This is where I also trained in becoming a tarotist with Anne Shotter. It was there that I also studied the Kabbalah with Evelyn Joffe and learned deeper esoteric studies. I felt like I finally became alive and now everyone was (finally) talking my language.

Then the Tarot Guild of Australia started thanks to Anne Shotter. I qualified to becoming a professional member of the Guild in 1995 and attended the monthly meetings for years. Finally, becoming a Tarot Guild Board Member with Linda Marson at the helm. I have wonderful memories resulting in traveling to Uluru and Alice Springs and meeting my favorite tarot masters; such as, Rachel Pollack and Mary K. Greer when we all organized the International Tarot Conference.

Here I now have to acknowledge the Rider Waite Tarot Cards by Arthur Edward Waite and Pamela Colman Smith. The wonderful insights and symbolism they have given me that I recognize and use in my life every day.

To Robert A. Johnson and his accomplice Jerry M. Ruhl PhD for their marvelous insights in capturing the works of Carl Jung and making it legible and understandable for the layman like me, I have read all his books!

To the Godfather of Mythology Joseph Campbell for his wonderful insights making sense out of all the religions and ancient stories, making it easy for us to see that it is all the same story. How I would have loved to be a student in their classrooms to hear these masters teach first hand.

Thanks to Danny Tiomkin for the title of the book. To Laureen and Robyn for the many years of tarot readings in the Fairy Shop in Niddrie, Francesca Sujevich and Kathryn Hendricksen for all the fun festivals and the Tarot T-shirts. Sue Caldwell and Marilyn Clymo for the love and trust in me for setting up the Kyneton Metaphysical Centre that has operated for over ten years. Together we created a community hub and spiritual meeting place in Kyneton. I am so grateful to have this wonderful experience and we remain good friends.

To the International Feng Shui Association and International Feng Shui Association – Australian Chapter. Where I had the privilege and honor to speak a couple of times at their International Conferences and have been invited to teach Tarot and Numerology every year since in Singapore.

The wonderful Merv Harvey from the Mind, Body and Spirit Festival is another special being in my life that has fashioned me into the Tarot reader I am today. Merv would give all the readers feedback every year to make sure we were all present in meeting a high standard in giving our clients the best readings ever.

In 1988, I did an EST program, followed by a workshop of the Landmark Forum. Then The Money & You program in 1990 with Jane and Stan Jordan where my love of Dr. R. Buckminster Fuller and Werner Erhart began, and the opportunity to meet Robert Kiyosaki. I enrolled myself to learn everything there was to learn about Bucky Fuller, also did Future by Design and Business by Design workshops and attended study groups with the knowledgeable physicist and drummer Jerry Speiser.

Since 1990 I have been the President and today, I am a Trustee of the GENI Foundation, an environmental organization fashioned from the works of Dr. R. Buckminster and along with Charles Kovess, Willem Oudyk, Danny Tiomkin and Alex Sprunt from Your Healthy Planet. It is here that I give voice to my love and commitment to making a difference to our beautiful planet. It is the biggest world game I know to play!

I have to also mention Anatole Kononewsky and Kalli Pulos – when I worked with them creating a systems folder for their organization *'Before It's Too Late'*. I will always remember the charity evening we organized with all the heads of various children's organizations, for example, Lighthouse Foundation, Alma Dople, Polly Woodside ship, Break the Cycle, Big Brother Big Sister, etc.

Anatole asked them all, "What do you need?" they all replied, "We need more money". Anatole then asked, "Yes, ok, but what do you need the money for?" This was revolutionary, not only for me but also for all the heads of these organizations. Then one said, "Well, we need blankets and a fridge". Another replied, "We have plenty of blankets we can give you". Another replied, "And we have a spare Fridge we can give you". He brought all these organizations together, it was a wonderful night. Together they can support each other and all the children far more than just being by themselves.

Now to another part of my life that I hold dear, which is Taekwondo martial arts. For me my martial arts training was still spiritual growth but in the physical form. To Danny Flint and the team at Dan's Martial Arts for all the years of fun and sweat, the physical training and all the hours of practice that has strengthened me into becoming that strong individual I am today. I will always remember my first gold medal!

To Andre Conate for her patience, love and support, with not only my martial arts training, but with support in setting up all that technical maintenance with my Tarot in Action website and also the creation of my Tarot videos. I have so much time for Andre and all her endeavors, there is just not enough time.

I have to mention another good friend in my life, Jay Garland. I have met another sole mate that loves Star Trek and Star Wars. Yep, I have to admit, I am a treky! We would often get together and watch all the series and movies then discuss their meanings and relevance to everyday life. We would also play Robert Kiyosaki's Cashflow game with various friends. From this we created a OneNote shared file called Generating Abundance, where we would share our knowledge with others also interested in creating wealth in our lives.

My love of alternative healings has been renewed since becoming a Reiki Master and sharing this beautiful gentle healing practice with clients and friends. And with becoming a Wellness Advocate in the doTerra Essential Oils organization, along with having the love and support of Rani So and Mark Sheppard who have been instrumental in helping me grow a doTERRA team, where I have been able to teach and share this new wealth of knowledge and healing with others once again.

There are heaps of my favorite quotes and stories that I have collected over the many years of teaching my *Tarot in Action* programs and I have included them in this book. When I do, I acknowledge the sources wherever possible.

Thank you so much to Pat Grayson from Heart Space Publications. Pat has spent hours editing my book and has shown me that my writing is not as bad as I thought it was — another revolutionary insight for me. I am so grateful to have met you and I really appreciate all the hours you have spent in making my book the wonderful teaching tool it has turned into.

I have to also mention here my gorgeous Book Club friends, we have been meeting since 2005, Phyllis Menos, Jane Litho, Janette Culbert, Josie Natoli, Helga Venohr, Jolanta Baldossa and Teresa La Rocca. Thank you for all the hours of reading awesome books, having awesome conversations and insights and sharing them with me.

Every time I presented a new *Tarot in Action* program, I would upgrade and include as much of the latest information as possible. I have all my students over the many years to thank for this, because every student opened up another insightful aspect or word to the tarot cards, therefore uncovering another level of understanding for us all.

Thank you to all the movies, courses, books, classes, work places, organizations I worked for and the people I have met since the beginning of my spiritual journey, you have made me the person I am today, forever grateful!

Thank you to all my students, my friends and those angelic guides that have challenged and inspired me to write this book.

Illustrations from the Rider-Waite Tarot Deck® reproduced by permission of U.S. Games Systems, Inc., Stamford, CT 06902 USA. Copyright ©1971 by U.S. Games Systems, Inc. Further reproduction prohibited. The Rider-Waite Tarot Deck® is a registered trademark of U.S. Games Systems, Inc.

** Printing of this book – Environment Responsibility https://www.lightningsource.com/ChainOfCustody/

Fractal Geometry for my Front Cover

Geometry is a mathematical assessment 'the way the different parts of something fit together in relation to each other'. The French mathematician Benoit Mandelbrot launched the field of fractal mathematics in 1975.

Fractals fascinate me the way twigs resemble the roots of the tree, or the way human lungs resemble the blood vessels branching throughout the body, same as small tributaries resemble the major rivers around the world.

This simply demonstrates that life keeps repeating itself, and we need only to look at the patterns to understand the answers we seek. Just like the Fool's journey, once you have completed one cycle, we commence again. This is why I especially wanted to use fractals for the cover of my book.

Why the color gold? Because gold represents all your hidden qualities. When you commence your shadow journey there is gold to be found.

Attachment 11

BIBLIOGRAPHY

A

Abo, Toru MD. & Hillyer, Kazuko Tatsumura PhD. *Your Immune Revolution.*
Adams, Douglas. *The Hitchhiker's Guide to the Galaxy.*
Alexander, Thea. *2150.*
Andersen, Uell S. *Three Magic Words.*
Andrews, Lynn V. *Medicine Woman.*
Anka, Darryl. *Bashar: Blueprint for Change.*

B

Bach, Richard. *Illusions.*
Baigent, Michael. Leigh, Richard. Lincoln, Henry. *Holy Blood and the Holy Grail.*
Boyd, Doug. *Rolling Thunder.*
Boissiere, Robert. *Meditations With the Hopi.*
Branson, Richard. *Losing My Virginity.*
Brown, Dan. *The Da Vinci Code.*
Buckminster Fuller, Dr. Robert. *Critical Path*
                              Cosmography
Buettner, Dan. *The Blue Zones.*
Burns, Lauren. *Fighting Spirit.*

C

Calson, George S. *The Richest Man in Babylon.*
Campbell, Joseph. *The Masks of God.*
Canfield, Jack. & Hansen, Mark Victor. *Chicken Soup for the Soul.*
Castaneda, Carlos. *The Wheels of Time.*
                 Tales of Power.
Cayce, Edgar. *Millennium Prophecies.*
Cialdini, Robert B. *Influence.*
Chapman, Gary. *5 Love Languages.*
Cheetham, Ericka. *The Prophecies of Nostradamus.*
Chilton Pearce, Joesph. *Magical Child.*
Clason. George Samuel. *The Richest Man in Babylon.*
Coello, Paolo. *The Alchemist.*
Connolly, Eileen. *Tarot Handbook for the Apprentice.*
                 The Handbook for the Journeyman.

Covey, Steven. Seven *Habits for Highly Effective People*
Cuhulain, Kerr. *Law Enforcement Guide to Wicca.*
Cunningham, Scott. *Wicca.*

D

De Martino. *Primitive Magic.*
Desmarquet, Michel. *Abduction to the 9th Planet.*
Deyo, Stan. *The Cosmic Conspiracy.*
Diamandis, Peter H. & Kotler, Steven. *Abundance.*
Diamant, Anita. *The Red Tent.*
Dispenza, Dr. Joe. *Breaking The Habit of Being Yourself.*
Doidge, Norman. *The Brain that Changes Itself.*
Donaldson, Evelynne & Terry. *Principles of Tarot.*
Donner, Florinda. *Being-In-Dreaming.*
Dyer, Wayne. *Real Magic.*

E

Estes, Clarissa Pinkola. *Women Who Run with the Wolves.*

F

Fast, Julius. *Body Politics.*
Fenton, Sasha. *Tarot in Action.*
    Fortune Telling by Tarot Cards.
Ferguson, Marilyn. *The Aquarian Conspiracy.*
Flynn, Mike. *Infinity in your Pocket.*

G

Garfield, Patricia. PhD. *Creative Dreaming.*
Gaskin, Ina May. *Spiritual Midwifery.*
Gerber. Michael. *The E Myth.*
Gilbert, Elizabeth. *Eat, Pray, Love.*
Glieick, James. *Chaos*
Goodard, Neville. *The Power of Awareness.*
Gray, Debra. How to be a Real Witch.
Gray, Dr. John. *Women are from Venus and Men are from Mars.*
    Venus and Mars in the Bedroom.
Greer, Mary. *Tarot for Yourself Workbook.*
    Tarot Mirrors.
    Tarot Constellations.
Guiley, Rosemary Ellen. *The Lunar Almanac.*

H

Hamilton, Clive. *Affluenza.*
Hand, Robert. *Planets in Transit.*
Hay, Louise. *You Can Heal Your Body.*
Hawking, Stephen. *A Brief History of Time.*
Hawkins, Dr. David. *Power Versus Force.*
                  Truth Versus Falsehood.
Hicks, Esther & Jerry. *The Law of Attraction.*
Hill, Napoleon. *Think & Grow Rich.*
Hitchens, Christopher. *God is Not Great.*
Hollingsworth, Elaine. *Take Control of Your Health.*
Homer. *The Illiad.*
Horne, Fiona. *Life's a Witch.*

I

Irwin, Terri. *My Steve.*

J

Jette, Christine. *Tarot Shadow Work.*
               Professional Tarot.
Johnson, Robert A. *Own Your Own Shadow.*
                  The Psychology of Romantic Love.
                  Balancing Heaven and Earth.
Johnson, Robert A. & Ruhl, Jerry M. *Living the Unlived life.*
Jung, Carl. *Man and His Symbols.*
             Memories, Dreams, Reflections.

K

Kahili King, Serge, *Urban Shaman.*
Kahneman, Daniel. *Thinking, Fast and Slow.*
Kaiser, Rudolf. *The Voice of Great Spirit.*
Kaku, Michio. *Visions.*
Kaplan, Stuart R. *The Encyclopedia of Tarot.*
King, Mary. *The Patriarchal Voice.*
              The Intuitive Voice.
Kiyosaki, Robert A. *Rich Dad Poor Dad.*
                    How To Be Rich and Happy and Not Go To School.
                    Second Chance.
Keyes Jnr, Ken. *The Hundredth Monkey.*
Konraad, Sandor. *Classic Tarot Spreads.*
Kovess, Charles. *Passionate People Produce.*
                Passionate Performance.
Kubler-Ross, Elisabeth. *On Death and Dying.*

L

Lennon, John. *The Penguin.*
Lenoir, Frederic. H*appiness*
Linn, Denise. *Sacred Space.*
        Quest.
Lipton, Dr. Bruce. *The Biology of Belief.*
Lundsted, Betty. *Astrological Insights into Personality.*

M

Marson, Linda. *Ticket, Passport and Tarot Cards.*
McCants, Glynis. *Love by the Numbers.*
McGraw, Dr Phil. *Life Code.*
Millman, Dan. *The Way of The Peaceful Warrior.*
        The Life You Were Born To Live.
Moorjani, Anita. *Dying To Be Me.*
Muchery, Georges. *The Astrological Tarot.*
Myss, Caroline. *Anatomy of The Spirit.*

N

Newton, Dr. Michael. *Life Between Lives.*
Ni, Hua-Ching. *I Ching.*
Nimoy, Leonard. *You & I.*

O

O'Connor, Peter. *Understanding Jung.*

P

Peck, Scott M. *The Road Less Travelled.*
       Further Along.
Peters, Thomas J. & Waterman Jr, Robert H. *In Search of Excellence.*
Pielmeier, Heidemarie. & Schirner, Marcus. *Illustrated Tarot Spreads.*
Pirsig, Robert M. *Zen and the Art of Motorcycle Maintenance.*
Plimer, Ian. *Telling Lies for God.*
Pollack, Rachel. *Seventy-Eight Degrees of Wisdom.*
    Seeker.
Prabhupada, Swami A. C. Bhaktivedanta. *Ramayana.*
                The Higher Taste.
Proctor, Bob. *You Were Born Rich.*

R

Redfield, James. *Celestine Prophecy.*
Reinhart, Melanie. *Chiron.*
Robbins, Tony. *Standing on the Shoulders of Giants.*
Ruiz, Don Miguel. *The Four Agreements.*
    Beyond Fear.
    The Voice of Knowledge.
Rumi. *Love's Ripening.*

S

Sark. *The Bodacious Book of Succulence.*
Succulent Wild Woman.
Semler, Ricardo. *Maverick.*
Sharman-Burke, Juliet. & Greene, Liz. *The Mythic Tarot.*
 The Complete Book of Tarot.
Shimon Halevi, Zev Ben, *Kabbalah.*
Sitchin, Zecharia. *The 12th Planet.*
Spiller & McCoy. *Spiritual Astrology.*
Starhawk. *Spiral Dance.*
Stewart, Mary. *The Mists of Avalon.*
Suzuki, David. *Time to Change.*
    Wisdom of the Elders.
Szandor La Vey, Anton. *The Satanic Witch.*

T

Taylor, Ariel Yvon. *Numerology Made Plain.*
Taylor, Eldon. *Mind Programming.*
Taylor, Sandra Anne. *Quantum Success.*
Tipping, Colin C. *Radical Forgiveness.*
Toen, Van. *The Astrologers Node Book.*
Tolle, Eckhart. *The Power of Now.*
    The New Earth.
Trump Donald J. & Kiyosaki, Robert A. *The Midas Touch.*
Trungpa, Chogyam. *Cutting Through Spiritual Materialism.*
    Shambhala.

W

Waite, Arthur Edward. *Rider Waite Tarot Deck.*
    The Key to the Tarot.
    Pictorial Key to the Tarot.
Wallace, Amy. *Sorcerer's Apprentice.*
Walsh, Peter. *It's All Too Much.*

Waterman Jnr, Peters. *In Search of Excellence.*
Weiss, Dr. Brian. *Many Lives Many Masters.*
Williamson, Marianne. *The Power of Love.*
                    A Woman's Worth.
White, Ruth. *Chakras.*
Whitehead, William. *The Magician's Way.*

Y

Yogananda, Paramhansa. *Autobiograpgy of a Yogi.*
Young, Robert O. & Young, Shelley Redford. *The PH Miracle.*

Z

Zimmer Bradley, Marion. *The Mists of Avalon.*
Zukav, Gary. *The Seat of the Soul.*

Attachment 12

INDEX

A

Adam 73, 75, 107, 179
Archetype 20-21, 26-27, 41, 80, 410, 412-413, 448-449
Archangel 41, 109, 170, 178-179, 193, 214, 216
Aliester Crowley 20, 125
Alchemy 58, 64, 168, 170, 173, 192
Angel 5, 139, 169-171, 175, 178-179
Anima 36, 43, 73, 80, 420
Animus 36, 42, 63, 80, 420
Anubis 140
Arthur Edward Waite 18, 122, 410, 444
Arcana 20-21, 26-27, 31, 38, 40-42, 52-53, 80, 146, 156, 187, 202, 224, 226, 229, 234, 242, 443, 448
Aries 14, 64, 90-91, 141, 230-231, 343, 356, 368, 381, 395, 414, 424
Athena 107, 147, 192, 224
Apollo 115, 209
Aquarius 14, 139, 184, 186, 191, 230-231, 236, 345, 362, 374, 387, 401, 415
Astrology 2-4, 6, 14, 27-28, 42, 54, 64, 74, 81, 90, 98-99, 107, 115, 123, 130, 138, 140, 147, 153, 162, 168, 175, 183, 191-192, 198, 203, 208, 215, 224, 231, 233, 236, 238, 342, 391, 410, 412, 414, 434, 444, 448, 449

B

Bast 383, 420
Bat 179
Bible 18, 123, 139
Black Friday 161

Body 8, 9, 40, 48, 90, 98-100, 178, 201, 209, 236, 239, 267, 292, 324, 338, 414, 425, 437, 445, 447

C

Caduceus 249
Cancer 14, 74, 115, 122, 198, 200, 204, 230-231, 238, 347, 365, 377, 390, 394, 405, 414, 424
Carl Jung 6, 14, 21, 27, 52, 131, 136, 223, 230, 410, 444
Capricorn 14, 90, 175, 177, 178, 230, 233, 344, 359, 371, 384-385, 387, 398, 415, 422
Chakra 11, 177, 226, 328, 455
Chariot 40-41, 45-46, 114-119, 127, 183, 187, 209-210
Chiron 98-99, 453
Christianity 17, 75
Colors 2, 6, 28, 57, 75, 149, 170, 192, 194, 217-218, 224-225, 248, 252, 265, 315, 325, 330, 357, 368, 403, 416, 448-449
Conscious 10, 16, 24, 27, 33, 36, 48, 50, 55, 57, 65, 68-69, 73, 77, 84, 101, 106, 108, 110, 132, 148, 178, 180, 183, 186, 192, 198, 204, 209, 236, 241, 249, 252, 281, 316, 329, 332, 336, 357-358, 360, 368, 373-374, 382, 389, 397, 407, 412, 425, 441
Crown 76, 84, 92, 100, 117, 147, 149, 163, 165, 172, 185, 265, 281, 317, 336-337, 383, 386, 389, 393, 397, 400, 403, 407, 417, 421

Cups 14, 27, 34, 65, 169-170, 172-173, 193-194, 231, 238-239, 241, 248, 251, 260-263, 269, 271, 278-280, 285, 288-289, 292, 299, 302, 309, 312, 319-322, 327, 329-332, 338, 340, 347, 349, 355, 360, 365, 367, 377, 379, 402, 448

D

Death 29, 39, 48, 100, 154, 161, 162-166, 170, 177, 198, 311, 415, 421, 426-427
Demeter 74, 82
Destiny 47, 65, 142, 144, 163, 218
Devil 41-42, 49, 107, 109, 173, 175-181, 202, 412, 439
Diana 115, 198, 394
Dionysus 54
Divination 17
Dreams 11, 14, 18, 21-22, 28, 31-32, 34, 43, 50-51, 60, 62, 73, 75, 79, 110, 194-195, 202-203, 205, 243, 255, 263, 320, 348, 360, 415, 448-449
Dr. R. Buckminster Fuller 11, 70, 186, 445

E

Eagle 139, 162, 176, 178, 379, 403, 422
Ego 10, 12, 16, 25-26, 32, 34, 36, 45-46, 49-50, 63, 70, 92, 114-120, 122, 127-128, 149, 155, 156, 158, 166, 178, 185, 189, 208-209, 225, 233, 265, 272, 300, 313, 328, 336-337, 343, 369, 383, 412, 421
Elements 14-15, 28, 43, 46, 68, 141, 169, 226, 230, 236, 342, 402, 410, 426, 448-449
Empress 21, 31, 39, 44, 81-86, 89, 91-94, 100-101, 108-109, 114, 124, 147, 149, 171, 223-224, 334, 351, 364, 367
Emperor 39, 44, 89-94, 100-102, 108-109, 117, 141, 149, 176, 353
Eve 22, 41, 43, 73, 107, 110, 179

F

Fate 47, 138, 142-143, 218, 415
Faith, Hope and Charity 260-261

Fool 39-60, 63, 73, 80-81, 97, 99, 106, 109, 114, 117-118, 122, 130, 137, 146, 149, 153, 161, 168, 183, 191, 197, 207, 210, 214, 217, 220, 223
Francis 131
Free Will 23-25, 34

G

Gabriel 41, 216
Gandalf 72, 131, 158
Garden of Eden 41, 110
Gemini 14, 64, 107, 109, 230-231, 236, 345, 362-363, 374-375, 387, 401, 403, 414
Goddess 16-17, 43, 74-75, 82, 140, 147, 169, 171, 192
Golden Dawn Group 18-20
Gypsies 16-17

H

Hades 64, 74, 162, 178, 215
Hanged Man 39, 48, 99, 153-158, 161, 164, 223-224, 337
Hermes 58, 64, 131, 140, 215, 332
Hermit 39, 42, 46-47, 58, 130-134, 137, 140-141, 143, 195, 197, 207, 210, 268, 309, 416, 419, 423
Hermetic 18, 57-58, 64
Hierophant 39, 44-45, 97-104, 106, 108, 111, 168
High Priestess 31, 39, 41, 43, 52, 73-75, 77-78, 80-83, 97, 100-102, 108, 114, 140, 146-147, 150, 153, 164, 171, 193-194, 214, 217-218, 223, 225, 239, 246, 289, 330-331, 392, 403, 407
Hindu 116, 200
Holy Grail 105, 309-310, 338, 393
Horus 116

I

Individuation 27, 52, 223, 225-226, 228
Infinity 66

Interpersonal 40, 230, 414-415
Ibis 193
Iris 169, 171, 423
Isis 82, 192

J

Jackal 140
Jester 60
Jesus 65, 77, 131, 154, 290, 310
Joan of Arc 155, 160
Joseph Campbell 18, 42, 174, 444
Joy Adams 125, 129
Judgement 6, 39, 41, 51, 214-216
Judas 154, 161
Jupiter 54, 138, 415
Justice 39, 47-48, 122, 137, 146-150, 153-154, 401, 425

K

Kabbalah 134, 192, 215, 434, 444, 448
Kabbalah Tree 325, 327
Kabbalists 20
Knights Templar 161, 218
Kundalini 125, 249

L

Lag 156, 159, 164, 253
Lemniscate 66-67, 126, 191, 210, 225, 244, 321, 423
Leo 14, 122-123, 125-126, 139, 149, 208-210, 230-231, 249, 343, 356-357, 368, 381-383, 395, 403, 414, 422-423
Leonardo Da Vinci 98
Libra 14, 82, 147, 230-231, 236, 285, 345, 362, 374, 387, 401, 415, 425
Lilith 75, 198
Lingam and Yoni 116
Lovers 39-41, 45, 106-108, 111-112, 175-176, 186-187, 414
Lucifer 41, 178

M

Maat 147, 150
Magician 39-40, 42-43, 52, 58, 63-69, 73, 78, 80-81, 90-91, 97, 100-103, 108, 114, 117, 124-125, 137, 148, 153, 165, 208, 210, 217, 223-225, 253, 289, 402
Mars 64-65, 90-91, 149, 183, 411, 414, 424
Masculine 14-15, 35-36, 42, 74, 76, 90, 100, 102, 108, 111, 115-118, 132, 148-149, 171, 210, 225-226, 231, 248-249, 255, 325, 418, 420-421, 434
Master Number 29-30, 146, 218, 419
Mercury 64, 107, 109, 141, 270, 387, 414-415
Metaphysical 4, 8-11, 36, 55, 66, 116, 186, 233, 254
Michael 41, 170, 193
Mind 10-11, 40, 63-65, 70, 72-73, 79, 100-101, 107, 111, 148, 157, 171, 236-237, 239, 247, 252, 257-258, 328, 336, 414, 416
Moon 36, 39, 50-51, 57, 74, 76, 78, 83, 102, 115, 117, 197-207, 209, 246, 310, 414, 424
Mountains 91-92, 110, 126, 131, 172, 217, 242, 247, 252, 269, 294, 309, 316, 334, 358, 361, 386, 422-423
Mythology 2, 18, 41-42, 54, 64, 74, 82, 90, 98, 107, 115, 123, 131, 138, 147, 154, 162, 169, 176, 185, 192, 198, 209, 215, 224, 444

N

Neptune 153-154, 156, 198, 415
Nirvana 225
Noble Truths 69
Numerology 2-4, 29, 31, 42, 53, 63, 73, 81, 89, 97, 106, 114, 122, 130, 137, 146, 153, 161, 168, 175, 183, 191, 197, 207, 214, 223, 342, 410, 418, 434, 444, 448-449

O

Odin 154
Ohm 53, 419
Oracle 17, 117
Ouroboros 66, 397, 424

P

Pagan 98, 138, 179, 352
Pamela Colman Smith 6, 18-20, 444
Pan 176
Pentacle 68-69, 98, 179, 244, 265, 294, 332, 334, 360, 373, 386, 399, 424
Pentagon 98
Pentagram 179
Persephone 74, 82, 85
Personal 2, 5, 8, 15-16, 20, 32-33, 40, 51, 58, 71, 95, 111, 113, 120, 122, 145, 155, 162, 175, 187, 193, 209, 212, 218, 230, 234, 250, 255, 265, 309, 314, 382, 402, 414, 443
Peter 154
Phoenix 116, 162, 168-169, 171, 187, 215, 358, 424
Physical 3, 8-11, 13-14, 26, 36, 45, 55, 66, 68, 81-82, 84, 88, 93, 106, 108, 112, 125, 166, 171, 184, 186-188, 194, 209, 233-235, 254-256, 277, 279, 287, 300, 303, 343, 345, 360, 364, 366, 372, 375, 399, 416, 421, 425, 445
Pied Piper 176
Pisces 14, 153-154, 198, 230-231, 238, 347, 365, 377, 390, 405, 415
Pillar 73, 77
Pluto 162, 175-176, 178, 201, 215, 415
Pomegranate 74, 110, 179, 424
Prometheus 154
Psychology 6, 27, 223, 391, 412, 436, 448-449

R

Raphael 41, 109
Responsibility 23, 26, 34, 40, 46-47, 90, 95, 126, 130, 134, 148, 150, 197, 211, 219, 222, 255, 305, 313, 353, 398, 416, 419, 438-439
River Styx 163-164, 166, 170, 203, 252, 287, 329
Roman Numerals 36
Roses 67, 69, 101, 165, 193-194, 242, 268, 318, 332, 334, 386-387, 417, 425

S

Salt 141
Saturn 90, 92, 162, 175-176, 224, 415
Sagittarius 14, 54, 168-169, 230-231, 343, 356, 368, 381-382, 395, 415
Scepter 84, 92, 400, 407
Scorpio 14, 58, 116, 139, 162, 176, 178, 201, 230-231, 238, 347, 365, 377, 390, 403, 405, 415
Scroll 76
Shadow 175
Shakespeare 19, 126, 176, 228
Shaman 60, 103
Silver Birch 83
Snake 21-22, 66, 107, 110, 140, 249, 300, 424, 426
Solomon's Temple 76
Sphinx 41, 118, 137, 139, 142, 146, 426
Spirit 5, 11-14, 19, 22, 33, 35-36, 39-42, 53, 56-59, 63, 80, 97, 100, 156, 180, 204, 208, 215, 225-226, 232, 267-268, 270, 334, 338, 357, 376, 382, 412-413, 416-417, 419-422, 425, 445
Star 30, 39, 50, 117, 132, 179, 191-196, 198, 424, 426
St Andrew's Cross 242, 289, 421
St Augustine 17
St George's Cross 41, 218

Strength 6, 10, 39-40, 46, 51, 91, 93, 116-117, 119, 122-129, 133, 149-150, 233, 239, 293, 307, 357, 382, 400-401, 404, 407, 418, 421, 424

Subconscious 21, 23-24, 48, 69, 77, 80, 83, 101, 405, 422

Sun 21-22, 30, 36, 39, 51, 53, 55-56, 91, 102, 115-116, 123, 141, 163-164, 170, 172, 184, 198, 203, 205, 207-212, 217, 235, 246, 249, 317, 383, 397, 414, 422-423, 426

Swords 14, 27, 150, 231, 236, 241, 246, 251, 257-258, 260, 263, 267, 271, 275-277, 280, 286-287, 290, 292, 296-297, 302, 307-308, 312, 317-318, 322, 328, 332, 336, 340, 345, 349, 352, 355, 362, 364, 374, 387, 389, 392, 401-402, 404, 406, 439, 448

Symbology 31-32, 55, 65, 75, 82, 91, 99, 108, 116, 124, 131, 139, 148, 157, 164, 170, 178, 186, 192, 201, 209, 216, 225, 297, 357, 360, 363, 366, 369, 372, 375, 379, 382, 386, 388, 392, 397, 399, 402, 406, 420, 428, 449

T

Taps 12-14, 24, 52, 184, 189, 222, 300, 360, 387

Taurus 14, 82, 98, 139, 230, 233, 344, 359, 371, 384-385, 387, 398, 400, 414

Temperance 39, 41, 48-49, 168-170, 173, 193, 202

Thoth 64

Tithing 283

Tora 41, 76, 101, 146, 425

Tower 39, 41, 49-50, 162, 183-188, 191, 194, 264, 325-326, 329, 426

Tower of Babel 41, 185, 190

Tudor Rose 165

Transformation 22, 29, 39, 48, 66, 110, 161, 164, 166-167, 211, 215, 311, 389, 420, 422, 426

Transpersonal 40, 217, 230, 415

Tree of Life 110, 154, 157, 179, 269, 274, 325, 426

Tree of Knowledge 110, 179

Trinity 76, 100, 171, 198, 260, 339, 426

T.S. Elliot 224

U

Unconscious 2, 10, 16, 21-24, 26-28, 32, 36, 47-50, 55-56, 58-59, 73, 75, 77-78, 99-100, 106, 109-110, 131-132, 143, 148, 171, 178, 180, 183, 188, 192-193, 197-198, 201-203, 207, 209-210, 217, 236, 239, 241, 252-253, 265, 282-284, 289, 299-300, 307, 315, 327, 348, 366, 389, 393, 399, 407, 412-413, 415-416, 420, 422-423, 425, 427, 435, 441

Universe 11-12, 15, 57-58, 67-68, 84, 90, 92, 98, 109, 115, 141, 150, 156, 180, 187, 189, 196, 200, 254, 282-283, 285, 299, 301, 306, 333-334, 337, 339, 427

Urim and Thummim 117

Uranus 184, 415, 423

V

Vatican Arms 101

Venus 81-83, 86, 92, 123, 147, 149, 215, 315, 414-415, 420, 426

Vipassana 133

Virgin Mary 75, 77, 216, 310

Virgo 14, 64, 130-132, 141, 230, 233, 304, 344, 359, 371, 384-385, 387, 398, 415

Vitruvian Man 98

W

Wands 14, 27, 226, 230-233, 241, 251-253, 263-264, 271-272, 280-281, 290, 292-293, 302-303, 312-313, 322-323, 332-333, 340, 343, 349, 351, 354, 356, 368, 381, 392, 395, 398, 442

Wheel of Fortune 29, 39, 41, 47, 137-139, 142, 146, 162, 207, 226, 283, 285, 335, 419

Wicca 98, 179, 352
Willpower 23, 42, 63, 69-71, 94, 114, 118-119, 128, 159, 208, 417, 423, 427
Witches 20, 147
World 2, 4, 6, 13, 16-19, 22, 24, 28, 30, 32, 34, 39, 42, 44-48, 50, 52, 55, 58-59, 62, 64, 68-70, 82, 84-85, 89, 91-93, 97-98, 100-102, 106-108, 110, 112, 114-115, 118, 121-122, 127, 133, 137, 146, 165, 171-172, 177, 184-186, 193-194, 201, 203, 205, 207, 209-210, 215-217, 219-220, 223-228, 232-234, 239, 241, 243, 246-247, 250-251, 253, 265, 268-269, 278, 323, 325-327, 334-335, 340-342, 352, 357, 360-361, 366-367, 391, 398, 407, 420-424, 426-427, 440, 447-448

Y
Yahweh 100, 339
Yods 141, 187, 200, 202, 333, 335, 337, 339

Z
Zarathustra 131, 136
Zeus 74, 90, 98, 107, 224
Zodiac 15, 28, 54, 57, 110, 123, 130, 132, 141, 153, 168, 191, 208, 230, 318, 394

Tarot Classes

Over the years throughout teaching my Tarot, Astrology and Numerology classes, I have met so many incredible people. The link for all of us coming together was our love of Tarot.

I have taught many people, all at different levels, some understood the Tarot cards intuitively, and they joined my class just to learn what the symbols mean. Others knew nothing about Tarot but their hunger to learn was simply overwhelming for them.

Many mothers and daughters do my program together. By using the Tarot, what a wonderful way for mother and daughter to open up, share and talk with each other.

Some people just want a change in career and/or are looking at earning extra income on the side.

I find people that those who are really searching for more in life are drawn to the Tarot. I have many people searching to fulfil a yearning within, answering questions and don't even know what questions to ask. Maybe their long-term relationship broke up, or they have lost their dream or direction, lost family and friends, there are so many reasons why are drawn to the Tarot.

My Tarot program details are:
- 2 hour class once a week
- 6 - 8 month Certificate Tarot program
- Approximately 2 terms of 10 weeks each
- I use the Rider Waite & Colman Tarot Deck throughout my classes, as I believe they use the best symbolism

The 1st term we look at:
- The Major Arcana, learning how to use them as milestones in your life today.
- Delving in to the Archetypes world and gaining understanding of how these energies work within ourselves.
- We will explore all the Greek, Roman, Egyptian Mythologies associated with each card.
- The Pythagorean Numerology associated with each card.
- Western Astrology and Eastern Astrology.
- The meaning of symbolism and their connection with Dreams.
- As well as all the Colors.
- And of course Psychology.
- We also look at the Kabbalah.
- Spreads only using the Major Arcana cards will be practiced gradually to build confidence.

The 2nd term we look at:
- The Minor Arcana cards, the everyday energies that we use to live out our lives in the area of work, our loves, our material world and our mental attitudes.
- The Four Elements of Fire, Earth, Air and Water and their association with the 4 Tarot suits of Wands, Pentacles, Swords and Cups, and how these Elements affect us.
- We continue with Colors, Psychology and Mythologies, etc...
- Gain further confidence when we practice spreads using all the Tarot cards.
- Learning so much more when we are in a class environment.
- Comparing all the different Tarot cards.
- We may also discuss Crystals, Essential Oil and other alternative healing modalities whatever else becomes available for us to use.

I hope you can join me, and together we travel down this wonderful journey of learning Tarot.

Tarot Video Classes

I now have made available my entire comprehensive beginners Tarot program on video. Yes, I have filmed comprising of an entire 6 month program.

The experience I wanted to convey in these videos is that you feel like you are part of this class. It is as if the students in the video are asking the questions like you were asking the questions yourself.

I find that after teaching Tarot since 1995 the questions today are pretty much the same as then. Having 22 videos and over 40 hours to work through you can imagine how many questions arise and we work through all of them.

Purchase the full set and save money! At the time of writing this, if you were to partake in my Tarot class the fee for a 6 month Tarot program is well over $1200. Plus, you will have to travel to my shop every week. By purchasing the whole set you can watch the classes when you want saving you time and money!

To watch a Sample of what my Tarot Video looks like so you can see what I mean about the class format style. Go to Tarot in Action on Youtube.

All this is available to you, so you can learn all about these extraordinary Tarot cards from the comfort of your home and all in your own sweet time!

We will cover in the video lessons:
- Archetypes, what are they? We will do exercises so you to understand how they apply in your everyday life. And how to interpret dreams.
- Astrology, every card is connected to either a planet or a zodiac sign.
- Numerology, every card is numbered, there are no mistakes the Death card is number 13.
- Symbology; understanding these symbols brings the cards to life, like cracking a code.
- Psychology, and understanding the being of human beings.
- Colors, the color grey means wisdom, the Hermit wears grey and has a grey beard, he is all about wisdom.
- The Elements of Fire, Earth, Air and Water.
- We also discuss relationships, career, spirituality, crystals and much much more...

All you need is the Rider Waite Tarot cards, pens and paper to write on. You have the capacity to wind and rewind through all the videos at your leisure to understand the lessons.

Learn a new skill and start your own Tarot business and start earning extra income!

All in the one purchase, you will receive:
- Well over 40 hours of tutoring.
- 22 Video Lessons in total.
- Includes all the Handouts.
- Includes a 1 Tb good quality Seagate Hard Drive.
- 5 Skype sessions with Ruanna to answer questions and learn Tarot Spreads
- There is a Certificate of Completion if you choose to do the 2 Tests.
- If you purchase from my Tarot in Action shop the price includes postage costs.

Go to my Tarot in Action Online Shop to purchase your copy of these Tarot Videos.